THE CRITICAL RECEPTION

OF ROBERT FROST

by

PETER VAN EGMOND

G. K. HALL & CO., 70 LINCOLN STREET, BOSTON, MASS. 1974

Library of Congress Cataloging in Publication Data

Van Egmond, Peter.
    The critical reception of Robert Frost.

    1. Frost, Robert, 1874-1963--Bibliography.
I. Title.
Z8317.78.V35   016.811'5'2   74-8210
ISBN 0-8161-1105-7

RESEARCH BIBLIOGRAPHIES IN AMERICAN LITERATURE: NO. 1

ISBN 0-8161-1105-7

This book is for Dot.

. . . strictly held by none, is loosely bound
By countless silken ties of love and thought

Lines quoted in the Dedication are:
From "The Silken Tent" from
THE POETRY OF ROBERT FROST
Edited by Edward Connery Lathem.

Foreword

If Walt Whitman is America's best poet, then certainly Robert Frost is America's best known. He was always a favorite of college audiences and of newspaper reporters, who found him eminently quotable. When, in 1961, he "said" his The Gift Outright at the inauguration of President John F. Kennedy, with radio and television coverage, his fame widened even further. Although he was considered a poet of New England, he was a success on his trips to South America, Israel, and the U.S.S.R. Whatever image or reputation Robert Frost did not establish by his own dint, the school teachers have done it for him. "The Road Not Taken" and "Stopping by Woods. . ." have provided many a subject-lesson for the day, along with plenty of what Frost called "sunset-raving."

His fame preceded him everywhere he went, and he went everywhere. The following compilation, therefore, is an attempt to provide an overview of the reception, both popular and critical, of Robert Frost, man and poet. My classifications are necessarily arbitrary, but hopefully they are clear and useful. The primary aim of this book has been to lay the groundwork for further biographical and critical studies. Of course, much work remains to be done and this is one step in that direction.

The material of this book falls into two parts. First, there are the things which seem closest to the man as poet--the views of his books, the interviews and talks, the letters, and news items about him. The second part of the book is devoted to those things associated with Robert Frost's work; that is, books and articles about him and his poetry, poems written to or about him, dissertations, and other similar things that reveal both the popular and the critical receptions that his poetry has found. The arrangement of the material, whether chronological or alphabetical, is designed as an attempt to provide a panoramic view of the man and his work. For example, interviews are listed chronologically; and articles, both critical and otherwise, are listed alphabetically by year.

Complete thoroughness in any bibliography is an obvious impossibility. Coupled with the fact that any bibliography, encyclopedia, or other compendium is obsolete the moment it is printed, one can only hope to be representative at least. Whatever degree of thoroughness this book has is due in large part to the generous assistance of countless people, in this country and

FOREWORD

abroad. My greatest debt is owed my colleague Jackson R. Bryer, who participated in the early stages of the book and who lent encouragement along the way. Others at the University of Maryland who helped significantly include Mrs. Joanne Giza, Mrs. Maria Otero Fletcher, and Mrs. Connie Hendrix and her magic typewriter. Librarians everywhere have been consistently helpful, including those at the McKeldin Library, University of Maryland; the Enoch Pratt Free Library, Baltimore; the Library of Congress; the University of Michigan libraries; the Robert Frost Library, Amherst College; the University of Massachusetts Library; and the University of North Carolina Library, Chapel Hill. Newspaper librarians and editors have assisted in locating fugitive pieces. Most of them are anonymous to me, but I can thank Edwin Gilcher, Cherry Plain, N.Y., and Leslie McShane of the Denver Post. Obviously I am also indebted to a multitude of Frost students and scholars, in particular the late Lawrence Thompson and Edward Connery Lathem. Finally, my daughter Katherine I thank for performing many a mundane chore at home and at the Library of Congress.

PETER VAN EGMOND

Contents

Introduction ix

Bibliography

   A. Reviews.. 1

   B. Interviews and Talks.................................... 41

   C. Published Letters....................................... 67

   D. News Items... 69

   E. Bibliographies and Checklists........................... 107

   F. Books and Pamphlets................................... 111

   G. Parts of Books... 121

   H. Articles... 147

   I. Anthologies.. 259

   J. Poems To or About 281

   K. Doctoral Dissertations................................. 287

   L. Foreign Criticism and Translation 295

Index of Critics 307

Introduction

When Robert Frost died in 1963, he had the satisfaction of knowing that he was the unofficial Poet Laureate of the United States. He had won every prize that the country offers its writers, yet the world had not conferred the Nobel. President John F. Kennedy led the mourners, and a horde of writers rushed into print with their eulogies or reminiscences. What the world did not know at the time was that Frost was a man of many strange paradoxes. He had constructed and maintained an image which projected him as gentle, kindly, and wise. His offhand manner was in fact carefully stage-managed. His apparent off-the-cuff wisdom was prepared and sharpened in advance. Lawrence Thompson, in his Robert Frost: The Early Years, 1874-1915, describes many of the fears, jealousies, and meannesses that those close to Frost had to endure. The reaction to Thompson's first two volumes as official biographer has been hostile, to say the least. The public response to Frost is exactly as he planned it, but the real Robert Frost, as presented by Thompson, is not what the world is willing to accept.

The duality of his nature and of his work is exemplified by the so-called "Trilling controversy," which arose after Frost's eighty-eighth birthday dinner in New York. Lionel Trilling delivered the main address (Item H342), concluding that Frost's greatness lay in his being "a terrifying poet." J. Donald Adams, of the New York Times, considered this an affront to Frost and wrote scathingly of Trilling's rudeness and his apparently Freudian view of literature. The camps divided quickly into a scholarly group and a popular group, each interpreting the poems in their own particular ways. This has been possible because the two possibilities are built into the poems and into the image the man made for himself.

Whether a synthesis of the two opposing views will ever be arrived at is impossible to prophesy. This book is offered in order to provide the material from which a synthesis conceivably could be extracted. In any case, the items listed and described here provide a record of the career of a great poet and a complex man.

The book is arranged in ten sections. A brief explanation of the way the material is arranged follows.

INTRODUCTION

A. REVIEWS

Early reviews of Frost's books show clearly the efforts of Ezra Pound, Edward Thomas, Amy Lowell, Lascelles Abercrombie, and others, to promote his work. As Lawrance Thompson's biography reveals, however, Frost did not completely appreciate their efforts. Nevertheless, for an American poet living in England, his American reception was made for him. And when he returned to the United States, he found himself virtually the American poet. There are surprisingly few reviews of A Boy's Will, but as Frost's reputation caught on, his books were reviewed more widely. As one can see, the reviewers of North of Boston saw their obligation to go back and examine A Boy's Will as well.

There is also obvious evidence that Frost's later reputation tempered the judgments of the reviewers, and in general their reviews were either favorable or noncommittal. The following list is not all-embracing, but it is an attempt to be representative--to present the development of Frost's critical reception and of his increasing fame as a spokesman for America and American life.

This section groups reviews under the titles of Frost's books, in the order in which the books were published. Each of those subsections is headed with the book's title and publication facts for the first English and American appearances of the book. Within each subsection the arrangement is chronological, in the order in which the reviews were published.

B. INTERVIEWS AND TALKS

Practically everything Robert Frost said was worth writing down, and he knew it. He was on stage to the world. In his private interviews and in his talks, he was always informal and almost offhand in what he said. This section might have been called "Interviews and Addresses," but Frost never really gave an "address" as such. He projected the image of a plain man, of a farmer who also happened to write poems. Beginning so late in his life to write poetry, he seemed older than other poets, and this appearance he used to his advantage. His remarks and ideas were readily accepted as the wisdom of a sage.

He won prizes and accolades from everywhere. Therefore, when he went to any place, the reporters and the literary hangers-on were ready for him. And he was equally ready for them. His mannerisms and his voice were thoroughly of New England, and his charm was undeniable. To his audiences, the fact that his poems had something genuine to say was secondary, frequently, to the man himself. But he seemed to know that, and his

INTRODUCTION

utterances were carefully aimed to lead eventually back to the poems themselves. An overview of the following list leads to that opinion. The man on
stage speaks for the man who preceded that stage, that appearance. The
poems are what count, ultimately. Even as early as his valedictory address
in high school in Lawrence, Massachusetts, Frost is trying, as he so often
said, to say something big, something that will be hard to get rid of.

The arrangement here is chronological, according to the date of publication of the interview, which naturally is not the precise date of the interview
itself.

C. LETTERS

Robert Frost's letters are not only important, but they are also interesting. Most of them are still unpublished, held in the libraries of Amherst
College, the University of Michigan, Dartmouth College, and other reposi-
tories. But those which have appeared provide a glimpse of a great man,
struggling against difficulties, some of them of his own making. He was
known for his streak of laziness in all things, and he was a hesitant letter-
writer. So true is this, in fact, that his "The Manumitted Student," originally a letter, is now considered a valuable prose piece, and consequently is
not included here.

The letters which have been published so far come very near the autobiography Frost refused to write. In a letter to Untermeyer, dated August 9,
1947, Frost wrote: "No friend has ever released me to such letter-writing."
We must be grateful to both men for the time and ink expended in such a devoted friendship. The letters of Robert Frost are comparable to those of
Mark Twain. Both write with the eyes and the minds of their correspondents
in clear view. Both men write with a sense of history and of the value of
their own work, but not for ego-building. They saw their responsibilities
and obligations as artists, particularly as artists in America, and tried to
fulfill what was to be expected of them.

The books of letters are arranged chronologically according to date of
appearance.

D. NEWS ITEMS

A thin line divides the newspaper accounts of Frost's travels or events in
his career from the interviews, however brief, that reporters found worth
recording. Another line, equally thin, separates the news items from the
more evaluative articles, many of them printed in newspapers. Basically,
therefore, these news items are non-evaluative, providing a record, albeit
incomplete, of Frost and his family. (Longer, evaluative newspaper articles
and editorials are included in Section H of this work.)

INTRODUCTION

A listing of every item, from every newspaper in this country and abroad, would be useful, but to make one would be impossible. The most representative things have been included in order to serve both the future biographer or critic for whom this material is essential and the reader for whom it is useful. The following list is enough to get a view of Frost's busy and ubiquitous life, remarkable in the light of Frost's own idea of himself as a very lazy person.

The arrangement of these items is chronological; when two or more items appeared on the same date, they are then listed alphabetically.

E. BIBLIOGRAPHIES AND CHECKLISTS

Bibliographies of Frost's work and checklists of works about Frost have been fragmentary and far from complete. For example, most of the critical books on Frost's poetry have brief checklists, listing the most outstanding or best-known works by such critics as Reginald Cook, Lawrance Thompson, Edward Connery Lathem, and others. But many studies have appeared in lesser-known journals and books. These have not been available to any but the most diligent scholar, poring over the quarterly checklists of American Literature or the PMLA Annual Bibliography. In addition, the scholar must search other sources such as the various general periodical indices and the indices of individual journals.

A full bibliography of Frost's own work has been undertaken by Professor Newton McKeon, Emeritus, Amherst College. That work, when published, combined with this one, will be an important contribution to the study of Robert Frost and his work.

The bibliographies and checklists are arranged alphabetically by author or compiler.

F. AND G. BOOKS, PAMPHLETS, CRITICISM OF BOOKS

Both these sections are arranged chronologically by date of publication. Multiple titles appearing in the same year are listed alphabetically.

H. ARTICLES

This section includes material published in journals, popular as well as scholarly, and newspapers. Therefore this part of the book includes a great variety of works, including reminiscences, "appreciations," critical studies, newspaper editorials, and review articles.

The arrangement is chronological, with an alphabetical arrangement of author for each year. Unsigned articles are listed by title, except when the author is known. In that case, the name or initial is indicated in brackets. A special effort has been made to find early material about Frost which will make succeeding editions of the book more thorough.

Cross-indexing here is deliberately limited. Whenever possible, the original item has been listed, rather than the reprinted version.

I. ANTHOLOGIES

The following list of anthologies demonstrates the development of Frost's acceptance by editors who, through their selections of poems from his books, set the pattern of their popular acceptance. For the most part, the editors have been inclined to choose the shorter poems over the longer dramatic poems. Thus, such poems as "Maple," "Paul's Wife," and even "Home Burial" seldom appear except in the larger anthologies. However, "Stopping by Woods. . .," "Fire and Ice," and "Design" have come to be known as the Frost poems.

This list is selective rather than exhaustive; it is an attempt to show how the popularity of certain of the poems developed, especially early in Frost's career. Perhaps it will also show what Frost meant when he said: "We read each other's books and we know what we're thinking about."

The arrangement of titles is chronological, then alphabetical, by editor, for multiple titles in the same year.

J. POEMS TO OR ABOUT FROST

The poems written to or about Frost range from the fatuous to the sublime, though they are all attempts to say something serious, using Frost's own medium. They show him as a man of wit, of sentiment, and of good conversation. Whether doggerel or tightly-controlled poetry, they all demonstrate a profound admiration and affection for Frost's accomplishment.

The arrangement here is chronological, and illustrates the development of his acceptance among poets, major and minor. Some of the poets are familiar to students of American literature--Amy Lowell, Robert Hillyer, Louis Untermeyer, Witter Bynner, Langston Hughes, and Carl Sandburg. And others may eventually be known.

K. DOCTORAL DISSERTATIONS

The proliferation of Doctoral dissertations and Master's theses, not included here, attests to the interest in Frost's work on college campuses. Several of the dissertations listed here have been made into significant book-length studies of Frost's poetry, or used as the basis for articles. (These

have not been cross-referenced, but can be found by using the index.)
These titles are arranged chronologically, then alphabetically.

L. FOREIGN CRITICISM

Although most of the items listed here have been verified, it has been
impossible to achieve total accuracy and completeness. Direct communication with the authors has helped, along with the aid of several language
specialists. The items are arranged alphabetically by country, and then
alphabetically by author, or title when the piece is unsigned.

BIBLIOGRAPHY

The Critical Reception of Robert Frost

A. REVIEWS

A BOY'S WILL, London: David Nutt, 1913; New York: Henry Holt, 1915

A1 B[RAITHWAITE], W. S. "A Poet of New England: Robert Frost A
New Exponent of Life," Boston Evening Transcript, April 28,
1915, Part 3, p. 4.
Frost has placed himself "with almost a single achievement in the very front rank of contemporary American poets."

A2 [DOUGLAS, NORMAN]. English Review, XIV (June 1913), 505.
Praises Frost for breaking away from the "outrageous
nonsense" that American poetry is.

A3 FLETCHER, JOHN GOULD. "Some Contemporary American
Poets," Chapbook, II (May 1920), 1-2.
"If Robinson's poetry clearly presents the mind of New
England, the poetry of Robert Frost no less clearly presents
its heart." Finds Frost a universal poet, however.

A4 F[LINT], F. S. Poetry and Drama, I (June 1913), 250.
". . . Mr. Frost has escaped from America, and . . . his
first book, A Boy's Will, has found an English publisher. So
much information, extrinsic to the poems, is necessary.
Their intrinsic merits are great, despite faults of diction here
and there, occasional inversions, and lapses, where he has
not been strong enough to bear his own simplicity of utterance."

A5 POUND, EZRA. Poetry, II (May 1913), 72-74.
"Mr. Frost's book is a little raw, and has in it a number
of infelicities; underneath them it has the tang of the New
Hampshire woods, and it has just this utter sincerity. It is
not post-Miltonic or post-Swinburnian or post-Kiplonian."

1

A. REVIEWS

A6   "Procession of the Muses," The Academy (London), Vol. 85, No.
      2159 (September 20, 1913), 359-60 [360].
          Roundup review including ABW. "We have read every
      line with that amazement and delight which are too seldom
      evoked by books of modern verse. Without need of qualifica-
      tion or a trimming of epithets, it is undoubtedly the work of a
      true poet."

NORTH OF BOSTON, London: David Nutt, 1914

A7   [ABERCROMBIE, LASCELLES]. "A New Voice," The Nation
      (London), XV (June 13, 1914), 423-24.
          On the simplicity of the poems. Compares Frost to
      Theocritus. ". . . the impulse of Mr. Frost's poetry is not an
      isolated phenomenon to-day-- therein is its significance; he is
      doing for New England life, in his own unique and entirely
      original way, what Mr. Wilfrid Gibson is so splendidly doing
      for the life of modern England."

A8   A[DAMS], F[RANKLIN] P[IERCE]. "The Conning Tower," New
      York Tribune, June 11, 1915, p. 9.
          "We confess to disappointment in Robert Frost's 'North of
      Boston.' Intellects broader and riper than ours have ac-
      claimed it as fine poetry. Mr. Frost begins his lines with
      capital letters, just the same as the poets we greatly admire.
      One test of poetry is to set it as prose."

A9   AKINS, ZOË. "In the Shadow of Parnassus," Reedy's Mirror,
      XXIV (May 7, 1915), 6-7.
          On Frost, Edgar Lee Masters, and Fannie Stearns Davis
      Gifford. Finds Spoon River Anthology superior to NB.

A10   BRAITHWAITE, WILLIAM STANLEY. "The Best Poetry of 1915,"
      in his Anthology of Magazine Verse for 1915 And Year Book of
      American Poetry. New York: Gomme and Marshall, 1915.
      Pp. 231-32.
          Compares Frost and Edgar Lee Masters. "Both have
      absolute genius, though I think Mr. Frost's art has consider-
      ably better possibilities for enlargements upon the material
      he works in."

2

THE CRITICAL RECEPTION OF ROBERT FROST

A11   "Current Poetry," Literary Digest, L (May 15, 1915), 1165.
　　　　Quotes from dust jacket of second American edition of NB.

A12   GARNETT, EDWARD. "A New American Poet," Atlantic Monthly,
　　　　CXVI (August 1915), 214-24.
　　　　On reading NB before it appeared in the U.S. "I read it,
　　　　and reread it. It seemed to me that this poet was destined to
　　　　take a permanent place in American literature."

A13   GIBSON, WILFRID WILSON. "Simplicity and Sophistication,"
　　　　Bookman (London), XLVI (July 1914), 183.
　　　　"In its quiet and unsensational way, Mr. Robert Frost's
　　　　'North of Boston' is the most challenging book of verse that
　　　　has been published for some time."

A14   HENDERSON, ALICE C[ORBIN]. "Recent Poetry," The Dial, LVII
　　　　(October 1, 1914), 253-54 [254].
　　　　"Doubtless there will be many readers who will find Mr.
　　　　Frost dull, and who will object to his verse structure. There
　　　　is no denying that his insistent monosyllabic monotony is ir-
　　　　ritating, but it may be questioned whether any less drab
　　　　monotony of rhythm would have been so successful in convey-
　　　　ing the particular aspect of life presented."

A15   HOWELLS, WILLIAM DEAN. "Editor's Easy Chair," Harper's,
　　　　CXXXI (September 1915), 634-37 [635].
　　　　NB and ABW "are very genuinely and unaffectedly expres-
　　　　sive of rustic New England, and of its deeps as well as its
　　　　shallows."

A16   LOWELL, AMY. "North of Boston," New Republic, II (February
　　　　20, 1915), 81-82.
　　　　". . . not only is his work New England in subject, it is so
　　　　in technique. No hint of European forms has crept into it. It
　　　　is certainly the most American volume of poetry which has ap-
　　　　peared for some time."

A17   POUND, EZRA. "Modern Georgics," Poetry, V (December 1914),
　　　　127-30.
　　　　"Mr. Frost's work is not 'accomplished,' but it is the
　　　　work of a man who will make neither concessions nor pre-
　　　　tences [sic]. He will perform no money-tricks. His stuff

A. REVIEWS

POUND, EZRA (cont.)
sticks in your head--not his words, nor his phrases, nor his
cadences, but his subject matter."

A18 RITTENHOUSE, JESSIE B. "North of Boston," New York Times
Book Review, May 16, 1915, p. 189.
"Just why a made-in-England reputation is so coveted by
the poets of this country, is difficult to fathom, particularly as
English poets look so anxiously to America for acceptance of
their work. . . . Mr. Frost and his medium are one. . . he has
struck bedrock, penetrated to the reality of life in the field he
interprets, and chosen the simplest and most human vehicle of
expression."

A19 "Some Recent Verse," Times Literary Supplement (London), July
2, 1914, p. 316.
Roundup review includes review of NB. "Poetry burns up
out of it--as when a faint wind breathes upon smouldering
embers."

A20 [THOMAS, EDWARD]. English Review, XVIII (August 1914), 142-
43.
Finds the poems "masterpieces of deep and mysterious
tenderness."

A21 "The Tragedy of Loneliness," Independent (New York), May 31,
1915, p. 368.
"The chief charm of these poems...is not in the pithy
verse, but in the psychological insight they reveal, in the
Browningesque quality of their drama."

A22 UNTERMEYER, LOUIS. "Robert Frost's 'North of Boston',"
Chicago Evening Post, April 23, 1915, p. 11.
A sympathetic review which helped to establish a lasting
friendship.

A23 [WHEELER, EDMUND J.] "Literature and Art," Current Opinion,
LVIII (June 1915), 426-28 [427-28].
This article remarks upon the irony of Frost's early
recognition in England rather than in New England.

THE CRITICAL RECEPTION OF ROBERT FROST

A. REVIEWS

MOUNTAIN INTERVAL, New York: Henry Holt, 1916

A24   BRADLEY, W. A. "Four American Poets," The Dial, LXI
       (December 14, 1916), 528-30.
           A roundup review of new books by Masters, Sandburg,
       Amy Lowell, and Frost's MI. "Mr. Frost is the one continu-
       ator at present of the 'tradition of magic' in American poetry."

A25   BRAITHWAITE, WILLIAM STANLEY. "Fifteen Important Volumes
       of Poems Published in 1916," in his Anthology of Magazine
       Verse for 1916 and Year Book of American Poetry. New York:
       Laurence J. Gomme, 1916. P. 247.
           "That indescribable magic which Mr. Frost evokes from
       the plain and severe quality of New England life and character
       glows again in these pages."

A26   COLUM, PADRAIC. "The Poetry of Robert Frost," New Republic,
       IX (December 23, 1916), 219-22.
           ". . . Mountain Interval has more of the personal, less of
       the communal life" than North of Boston --"Mr. Frost is a
       poet because he knows and because he can show us a spiritual
       history."

A27   COX, SIDNEY. "The Sincerity of Robert Frost," New Republic,
       XII (August 25, 1917), 109-11.
           "Mountain Interval . . . manifests as its fundamental and
       embracing quality, sincerity -- sincerity in perception, sinceri-
       ty in thought, sincerity in feeling and sincerity in expression."
       Reprinted as Robert Frost, Original "Ordinary" Man. New
       York: Holt, 1929. 1000 copies.

A28   M[ONROE], H[ARRIET]. "Frost and Masters," Poetry, IX (January
       1917), 202.
           ". . . it is important that two rich districts of this country,
       each an individual and powerful personality, are finding modern
       interpreters. Who will speak, as well for the South, and for
       the Far West between sea and mountains?"

A29   "A New England Poet," Spectator, CXXVI (January 22, 1921), 114.
           Finds Frost "pleasantly reflective" and "competent."

A. REVIEWS

NEW HAMPSHIRE. A POEM WITH NOTES AND GRACE NOTES, New York: Henry Holt, MCMXXIII

A30 FARRAR, JOHN. "The Poet of New England's Hill-men," Literary Digest International Book Review, I (November 1923), 25-26.
"Perhaps this is the perfection of Frost's singing. Perhaps this is the fruit of his ripest powers. It is a book of which America may well be proud, which is quite above cavil and prejudice."

A31 LITTELL, ROBERT. "Stone Walls and Precious Stones," New Republic, XXXVII, Part II (December 5, 1923), 24-26.
"Maybe this is not poetry. But does that matter? Or does it matter very much that so many of Mr. Frost's lines sound as if they had been overheard in a telephone booth...?"

A32 MORTON, DAVID. "Poet of the New Hampshire Hills," Outlook, CXXXV (December 19, 1923), 688-89.
Frost is limited to his locale, but that makes his work significant.

A33 "New Hampshire--Robert Frost's New Volume," Michigan Alumnus, XXX (January 17, 1924), 429.
Brief noncommital review.

A34 UNTERMEYER, LOUIS. "Robert Frost's New Hampshire," in "The Book of the Month" section, Bookman (New York), LVIII (January 1924), 578-80.
The poetry is "full of heat and humor." It belongs "not only to the America of our own day but to the richest records of English verse."

SELECTED POEMS, New York: Henry Holt, 1923; New York: Heinemann, 1923

A35 "Frost, Robert," Booklist, XXV (March 1929), 256.
Two non-evaluative sentences.

A. REVIEWS

A36   "Prose and Poetry," Times Literary Supplement (London), March
         29, 1923, p. 213.
              Compares Frost's narrative poems with Wordsworth's
         The Prelude. Says of Frost ". . . we are perplexed that one
         capable of enshrining a vision so simply and richly should
         write so much prose in iambic decasyllabics."

A37   "Selected Poems, by Robert Frost," The Dial, LXXXVI (May 1929),
         436.
              One-paragraph review. "He has created a blank-verse
         form of his own through which he is able to give us something
         of the secret life of the earth, the secret life of men and
         women."

WEST-RUNNING BROOK, New York: Henry Holt, 1928

A38   B., M. K. Catholic World, CXXIX (June 1929), 377.
              One-paragraph review of WRB included with reviews of
         books by Hardy and Masefield. Frost's book ". . . is stamped
         with that New England asceticism which has so little of the
         mystical about it."

A39   BRICKELL, HERSCHEL. "Four Books of Poetry," in "The
         Literary Landscape" section, North American Review,
         CCXXVI (December 1928), [n. p.].
              Brief review. Says WRB offers variety and ". . . the
         quality. . . is unquestionably high."

A40   CLEGHORN, SARAH N. "West-Running Brook," World Tomorrow,
         XII (March 1929), 135.
              Considers WRB the interpreter for Frost's other work.
         It is "an interpreter of life."

A41   CRAWFORD, JOHN. "Frost's Poems Do Not Waste Away in
         Pathos," New York Evening Post, November 24, 1929, p. 9.
              Review of WRB which emphasizes Frost's satire and use of
         contrast. "Out of. . . a brook that runs west when all the
         others run east, he makes his simple, unassuming statements
         somehow shake all the known securities."

THE CRITICAL RECEPTION OF ROBERT FROST

A. REVIEWS

A42   DEUTSCH, BABETTE. "Inner Weather," New York Herald Tribune
       Books, November 18, 1928, p. 1.
             Critical analysis of WRB. "Where he was formerly con-
       tent to . . . give the texture of a patch of countryside, or a
       rural character, and by the way suggest an atmosphere, a
       mood, a point of view, here the emphasis is primarily on the
       poet's emotion, with which the external scene is in key."

A43   DEUTSCH, BABETTE. "Poets and Poetasters," The Bookman
       (New York) LXVIII (December 1928), 471-73 [471-72].
           Says WRB has several pieces which are unworthy of inclu-
       sion, but ". . . the book as a whole has the seriousness and
       acuteness which marks all of Frost's work."

A44   The Dial, LXXXVI (May 1929), 436.
           One-paragraph review of WRB. The poems are "gnomic
       verses that read as if the poet had entered a world where
       words and movement do not matter so much. . . . "

A45   "Frost, Robert." Booklist, XXV (February 1929), 201.
           "Mr. Frost is, unlike so many modern poets, undisturbed
       by the encroachments of a hard, unyielding machine civilization
       upon his New England quietude."

A46   HALL, EDWARD B. "Robert Frost as a Significant Poet," Boston
       Evening Transcript, December 15, 1928, Book Section, p. 5.
           "Whatever dissension there may be regarding the merits
       of this poet's versification and technique, there can be no
       question of his masterly management of language."

A47   HUTCHISON, PERCY. "New Poems by Robert Frost in 'West-
       Running Brook'," New York Times Book Review, November 18,
       1928, p. 2.
           Adds WRB to the list of excellent verse published in recent
       months. "Frost's style is that of chiseled marble, of cut
       diamonds. . . . "

A48   PIERCE, FREDERICK E. "Three Poets Against Philistis," Yale
       Review, XVIII (December 1928), 364-66 [365-66].
           Combined review of books by MacLeish, Millay, and
       Frost. "His present book arouses mingled admiration and disap-

A. REVIEWS

PIERCE, FREDERICK E. (cont.)
pointment. Our admiration is for the sincerity and delicate
insight with which the theme is handled. Our disappointment
is because of the smallness, limitation, almost barrenness of
the theme itself."

A49 REELY, MARY KATHERINE, ed. "A Selected List of Current
Books," Wisconsin Library Bulletin, XXV (February 1929), 71.
Selected Poems contains the best of Frost's poetry while
the poems of WRB are ". . . charming but of slighter value."

A50 "Robert Frost's Poems and Outlook on Life," Springfield Union-
Republican, December 30, 1928, p. 7E.
The book "shows no advance over his earlier works."

A51 ROOT, E. MERRILL. "Encore for the Morning Stars!" Christian
Century, XLVI (January 3, 1929), 18-20 [19-20].
Combined review of books by Sandburg, Robinson, Millay,
and Frost's WRB. Says of Frost's book, "Here are poems
where the poet has dipped his pen in magic -- till we truly see
'The colors run', all sorts of wonder follow."

A52 UNTERMEYER, LOUIS. "Still Robert Frost," Saturday Review of
Literature, V (December 22, 1928), 533, 536.
The poems are the ". . . fruit of intuition rather than ex-
perience."

A53 WHIPPLE, LEON. "Poets Americano," Survey, XLI (November 1,
1928), 168-70 [169].
Most of the article is devoted to brief reviews of twelve
other American poets, but Whipple implies with reference to
WRB that Frost is ". . . amused, skeptic, not impassioned or
bent on reform."

SELECTED POEMS, New York: Henry Holt, 1928

A54 M[ONROE], H[ARRIET]. "A Frugal Master," Poetry, XXXIII
(March 1929), 333-36.
Combined review of WRB and Selected Poems. Of WRB
". . . these poems are Frost's own, all right, but none of them

A. REVIEWS

M[ONROE], H[ARRIET] (cont.)
may be ranked among Frost's best." Of Selected Poems, "It
is a good selection . . . . One finds most of one's favorite
poems, and misses but few."

A55 SPENCER, THEODORE. "West-running Brook," New Republic,
LVIII (February 20, 1929), 24-25.
Review of WRB and Selected Poems. "One feels that
[Frost] has lost or abandoned a view of life which was, in its
implications, tragic, and adopted instead an allegorizing meth-
od which is far less important."

A56 VAN DOREN, MARK. "North of Eden," The Nation, CXXVIII
(January 23, 1929), 110.
Review of WRB and Selected Poems. The poems in the
volumes are those in which Frost is ". . . in the act of standing and looking at some very definite thing . . . standing and
looking at it and talking about it in such a way that it suddenly
weirdly becomes a world."

A WAY OUT. A ONE ACT PLAY, New York: Harbor Press, 1929

A57 B., C. "Frost's Poetry Shows Lyricism," Denver Post, January 13,
1929, Sec. 2, p. 8.
Compares Frost with Browning in brief review.

A58 B[RAITHWAITE], W. S. "A Way Out: Robert Frost Writes a Fine
Play of New England," Boston Evening Transcript, July 13, 1929,
Book Section, p. 1.
"The action is very simple, but it is the dialogue with its
rich idiomatic, country speech, its undercurrent of ironic
humor, that is most effective and appealing."

A59 EATON, WALTER P. "A Frost Drama," New York Herald Tribune
Books, October 6, 1929, p. 25.
The play ". . . makes one regret that Frost has not written more in the dramatic form. He has the evident capacity
greatly to enrich the repertoire of our little theatres...."

THE CRITICAL RECEPTION OF ROBERT FROST

A60   HUTCHISON, PERCY. "Some Novelists and Poets Troop into the
       Theatre, " New York Times Book Review, July 28, 1929, p. 8.
            The play as a whole lacks the clarity necessary for drama-
       tic impact, ". . . although there is dramatic intensity to
       every line. "

COLLECTED POEMS, New York: Random House, 1930; New York: Henry
    Holt, 1930; London, New York, Toronto: Longmans, Green, 1930

A61   B., F. "Robert Frost, A Collected Edition of the Work of an
       American Poet, " Boston Evening Transcript, January 10, 1931,
       Book section, p. 3.
            ". . . the sense of his personality is so strong that it
       seems at times as if one could hear his voice telling the story
       to us individually...."

A62   BASCOM, ELVA L., ed. Among Our Books [Carnegie Library of
       Pittsburgh], XXXVI (February 1931), 13.
            "A welcome volume, which gathers together the contents
       of the five volumes beginning with A Boy's Will. "

A63   CARPENTER, FREDERIC I. New England Quarterly, V (January
       1932), 159-60.
            "Although Mr. Frost disclaims the title of merely 'the
       poet of New England, ' he is not, and can never become, 'the
       poet of America. ' He lacks power. "

A64   CHURCH, RICHARD. "Seven From the Forest, " The Spectator
       (London), CXLVI (February 21, 1931), 277-78.
            Review of seven poetry collections, including CP (Long-
       mans). Frost's vision ". . . is quite unliterary, and his poet-
       ry is the result of infinite literary consciousness...."

A65   "Collected Poems, " in "Books in Brief" section. Christian Century,
       XLVIII (February 18, 1931), 242.
            One-paragraph review. "It is wonderful how a man can
       hold a mood through all seasons for twenty years or more...."

A66   "Frost, Robert." Booklist, XXVII (January 1931), 197.
            One sentence listing contents of CP and "attractive format."

A. REVIEWS

A67 GRIGSON, GEOFFREY. "Still Waters," Saturday Review (London)
 CLI (April 4, 1931), 505.
 "Behind the charm of . . . poem after poem there is an
 emotional depth which does not always give itself to a first or
 second reading."

A68 HICKS, GRANVILLE. "The World of Robert Frost," New Republic, LXV (December 3, 1930), 77-78.
 Frost rejects the theories of Freud and of modern psycho-
 analysis.

A69 MOORE, VIRGINIA. "Robert Frost of New Hampshire," Yale Review, XX (March 1931), 627-29.
 "Never a false note; never a breach of taste; never a cheap
 effect. There are moods beyond which he cannot go. But the
 man, so far as he goes, goes true."

A70 NICHOLL, LOUISE TOWNSEND. "From the New Poetry," Outlook
 and Independent, CLVI (December 10, 1930), 590.
 One-paragraph sympathetic review.

A71 "Preferences," Canadian Forum, XI (June 1931), 336-37.
 ". . . if you wanted to get the better of Wordsworth or
 Browning in an argument as to the true way for poetry to
 philosophize you couldn't do better than throw Robert Frost's
 'armful' at them and ask them to stack it out for you."

A72 REELY, MARY KATHERINE, ed. "A Selected List of Current
 Books," Wisconsin Library Bulletin, XXVI (December 1930),
 347.
 Too expensive for small libraries which already have the
 separate editions.

A73 "Robert Frost," New Statesman, XXXVI (December 27, 1930), 365.
 Review of CP (Longmans). Praises Frost's ability to make
 the "common neglected spots become magical." Frost's
 ". . . humour is superb; a dignified, subtle force, probing its
 ways into life and finding a form of self-expression that has to
 be known to be believed."

A74 "Robert Frost," Times Literary Supplement (London), January 29,
 1931, p. 75.

"Robert Frost" (cont.)
Review of CP (Longmans). Frost has been unable to escape the dangers of using ordinary speech in his longer poems but his "subdued utterance" has "an inward warmth and radiance that are rare enough in poetry today."

A75   SCHNEIDER, ISDOR. "Robert Frost," The Nation, CXXXII (January 28, 1931), 101-02.
Review praises Frost's descriptive power and individual style, but Frost is ". . . singularly out of touch with his own time. . . . Mr. Frost's work is weakest in ideas."

A76   STRONG, L. A. G. "A Fine Poet," Nation and Athenaeum, XLVIII (January 10, 1931), 486.
Review of CP (Longmans). Compares Frost to Wordsworth. "Robert Frost is a notable figure in a great tradition. His work is original. He is like a host, who slowly, kindly, and humorously shows you the places where he lives."

A77   TAGGARD, GENEVIEVE. "Robert Frost, Poet," New York Herald Tribune Books, December 21, 1930, pp. 1, 6.
"Here is a mind that grows but never changes, that understands with each poem accomplished more and more about the mastery of form, storing much observation and illustration from experience, handling actualities with assurance, but a mind, nevertheless, that does not change, because it gives to experience something more spiritual, more creative than the things it takes away."

A78   UNTERMEYER, LOUIS. "One Singing Faith," Saturday Review of Literature, VII (January 17, 1931), 529-30.
". . . while it represents the author through five books, it gives rise to no premature finalities; it is inclusive, but not conclusive."

A79   WARREN, C. HENRY. "An American Poet," Fortnightly Review, [n. s.], CXXIX (February 2, 1931), 282.
Favorable review of CP (Longmans). "Frost's poetry is as direct and unmoral as the song of a bird."

A80   WARREN, C. HENRY. " 'An Original, Ordinary Man,' Robert Frost and His Vision of Nature," The Bookman (London),

A. REVIEWS

WARREN, C. HENRY (cont.)
LXXIX (January 1931), 242-44.
On Frost's appeal to the English reader.

A81   WILSON, JAMES SOUTHALL. "Robert Frost: American Poet,"
Virginia Quarterly Review, VII (April 1931), 316-20.
". . . if passion is depth and intensity of feeling, Robert
Frost is the most passionate poet America has ever produced."

FROM SNOW TO SNOW, New York: Henry Holt, 1936

A82   NEWDICK, ROBERT S. "The Book Table" section, Amherst Graduates' Quarterly, XXV (May 1936), 287-88.
Brief review and bibliographical description of a twenty-
page booklet of poems called "From Snow to Snow," distributed
as compliments of Holt.

SELECTED POEMS, Chosen by the Author. With Introductory Essays by
W. H. Auden, C. Day Lewis, Paul Engle, and Edwin Muir. London:
Jonathan Cape, 1936

A83   HOLMES, JOHN. "Robert Frost Conquers the Poetic Realm,"
Boston Evening Transcript, February 13, 1937, Sec. 6, pp. 1-2.
Emphasizes the essays.

A84   MAC CARTHY, DESMOND. "A Country Poet: Mr. Robert Frost's
Verse," London Sunday Times, May 16, 1937, p. 6.
". . . Mr. Frost is a 'Peter Bell' among country poets, to
whom a primrose is a primrose, a plough a plough."

A FURTHER RANGE, New York: Henry Holt, 1936; London: Jonathan Cape,
1937

A85   ARVIN, NEWTON. "A Minor Strain," Partisan Review, III (June
1936), 27-28.
Frost's "place has always been and still is on the sandy

A. REVIEWS

ARVIN, NEWTON (cont.)
and melancholy fringes of our actual life, and his poetry derives its special, its estimable cachet, as well as its limitations, from that very fact."

A86   BENÉT, WILLIAM ROSE. "Wise Old Woodchuck," Saturday Review of Literature, XIV (May 30, 1936), 6.
"And if anybody should ask me why I still believe in my land, I have only to put this book in his hand and answer, 'Well - here is a man of my country.'"

A87   BLACKMUR, R. P. "The Instincts of a Bard," The Nation, CXLII (June 24, 1936), 817-19.
"Mr. Frost does not resort to the complete act of craft. His instincts as a bard do not drive him to the right labor, the complete labor, except by accident and fragmentarily, in a line here and a passage there."

A88   "Books to be published in the Spring," New York Times Book Review, March 15, 1936, p. 24.
Advertisement of AFR, with a photograph of Frost.

A89   BRAGDON, ELSPETH. "Robert Frost Again Sings New England," Springfield Sunday Republican, June 21, 1936, p. 7E.
"To his familiars, and, if there are any, to new acquaintances, 'A Further Range' will prove a satisfying and heart-warming delight."

A90   BRICKELL, HERSCHEL. "The Literary Landscape," Review of Reviews, XCIV (July 1936), 12.
Brief review of AFR, "which is a clear call to the restoration of the individual to his place as the most important thing in the universe. . . ."

A91   BRICKELL, HERSCHEL. "Robert Frost's Book of Poems, 'A Further Range,' Filled With Expected Wisdom and Beauty," New York Post, May 29, 1936, p. 7.
Subheading: "Poet Submits His Own Five-Year Plan for Saving the Country in 'Build Soil' and Touches, as Usual, on Many Contemporary Problems."

A. REVIEWS

A92 BROOKS, PHILIP. "Notes on Rare Books," New York Times Book
     Review, June 14, 1936, p. 20.
          Review of AFR and Thompson's Robert Frost: A Chrono-
     logical Survey. Points out limitations and virtues of the Survey.

A93 DABBS, JAMES MCBRIDE. "The Uses of Ambiguity," Yale Review,
     XXV (June 1936), 826-27.
          Review of AFR, a poetic game of hide-and-seek.

A94 DE SELINCOURT, BASIL. "Poets and Pessimism: Idealism in the
     Storm," The Observer (London), April 4, 1937, p. 5.
          "Frost is a poet of delicatest degrees, but universal in
     this sense that he sees in these degrees the very secret of
     truth." Also reviews Stephen Vincent Benét's "Burning City."

A95 DOUGHTY, LEGARDE S. "More Good Poems," Commonweal,
     XXIV (September 4, 1936), 450.
          Comments comparing Frost's iambus and Coffin's trochee,
     both Pulitzer Prize winners writing about New England.

A96 EMERSON, DOROTHY. "Poetry Corner," Scholastic XXIX (Sep-
     tember 19, 1936), 6-7.
          Includes a brief biography and reprints "The Figure in The
     Doorway," "Departmental," "A Leaf Treader."

A97 FEENEY, LEONARD. "Coolidge with a Lyre," America, LV (July
     4, 1936), 309.
          Praises the poet's style but raising doubts as to the quality
     of his epigrams and his economic philosophy.

A98 FITTS, DUDLEY. New England Quarterly, IX (September 1936),
     519.
          "It is as a lyrist in a special field that Frost is supreme,
     and A Further Range is a book of the greatest distinction in so
     far as it is a reaffirmation of a standard already established."

A99 "Frost: He is Sometimes a Poet and Sometimes a Stump-Speaker,"
     News-Week, VII (May 30, 1936), 40.
          Finds the book "disappointing."

A100 "A Further Range," Booklist, XXXII (July 1936), 315.
          Three-line review.

The Critical Reception of Robert Frost

A. REVIEWS

A101   GANNETT, LEWIS. "Books and Things, " <u>New York Herald Trib-</u>
<u>une,</u> May 30, 1936, p. 9.
     "Bard he is, with a steadfastness maintained by no other
of the present generation of poets. "

A102   GREGORY, HORACE. "Robert Frost's New Poems, " <u>New Republic,</u>
LXXXVII (June 24, 1936), 214.
     Gregory would not compare Frost to either Emerson or
Whittier, but praises the use of everyday speech.

A103   HALL, JAMES NORMAN. "<u>A Further Range</u> by Robert Frost, " in
"The Bookshelf" column, <u>Atlantic Monthly</u>, CLVIII (September
1936), [n. p.].
     Favorable review pointing out Frost's "force in under-
statement. "

A104.   HOLMES, JOHN. "In 'A Further Range, ' Robert Frost Advances, "
<u>Boston Evening Transcript,</u> May 29, 1936, Book Section, p. 3.
     "His lines are surer than ever before, if one can speak of
degrees in the matter. "

A105   HOLMES, JOHN. "Up the Sleeve, " in "Poetry Now" column, <u>Boston</u>
<u>Evening Transcript,</u> July 11, 1936, Book Section, pp. 6, 8.
     A review of the reviews of <u>AFR</u>. ". . . I am getting a
good deal of amusement these days laughing up my sleeve at
certain of the critics who put themselves on record as placing
Frost as a minor and belated Georgian, a Yankee-talker, a
Calvin Coolidge with his head in a woodchuck hole. "

A106   HUMPHRIES, ROLFE. "A Further Shrinking, " <u>New Masses</u>, XX
(August 11, 1936), 41-42.
     "The further range to which Frost has invited himself is
an excursion into the field of the political didactic, and his ad-
dress is unbecoming . . . . <u>A Further Range</u>? A further
shrinking. "

A107   KNOWLTON, EDGAR C. "Poems by Robert Frost, " <u>South Atlantic</u>
<u>Quarterly</u>, XXXV (October 1936), 460-62.
     There are, in Frost's work, some subtle references to
modern industrial society, to Freudian theories, and some
advice for farmers.

THE CRITICAL RECEPTION OF ROBERT FROST

A. REVIEWS

A108 "Literary Horizon," in "The World in Books" section, <u>Current History</u>, XLIV (July 1936), 6-7.
AFR "deserves and will receive a large circulation; it will undoubtedly please the author's many admirers, though not as thoroughly, perhaps, as his <u>North of Boston</u>, or <u>Mountain Interval</u>."

A109 M., T. <u>Catholic World</u>, CXLIII (September 1936), 756.
A "political pastoral," one of Frost's masterpieces.

A110 MOORE, MERRILL. "Poetic Agrarianism: Old Style," <u>Sewanee Review</u>, XLV (October - December 1937), 507-09.
Frost's "most cheerful book."

A111 MORLEY, CHRISTOPHER. "<u>A Further Range</u>, by Robert Frost," <u>Book-of-the-Month Club News</u> (May 1936), pp. 2, 3.
Praises simplicity and fluidity of Frost's verse.

A112 NETHERCOT, ARTHUR H. "Professor Nethercot, Reviewing Robert Frost's New Book, Finds That the Poet Still is a Non-Intellectual," <u>Evanston Daily News-Index</u>, June 4, 1936, p. 5.
Frost "is the poet of the heart, and not of the brain." He is not as great as Robinson.

A113 NEWDICK, ROBERT S. "Frost's Latest Poems - <u>A Further Range</u>," <u>Columbus Sunday Dispatch</u>, June 14, 1936, "Passing Show" section, p. 6.
"...it is unquestionably a book for the years."

A114 NEWDICK, ROBERT S. "Robert Frost Speaks Out," <u>Sewanee Review</u>, XLV (April - June 1937), 239-41.
"As Frost grows older his emphasis naturally shifts perceptibly from the lyric left to the more meditative right, yet the familiar Frost remains to cheer and delight the pattern-squirrels...."

A115 NEWDICK, ROBERT S. "Uncollected Poems of Robert Frost," <u>Book Collector's Journal</u>, II (February 1937), 1-2.
Describes and analyzes the book on the basis of the new poems and old ones not included.

The Critical Reception of Robert Frost

A116   PAYNE, L. W., Jr. "Robert Frost's New Book Has Characteristic
        Tone, " Dallas News, May 31, 1936, section 3, p. 10.
           "This new book...is altogether made up of authentic
        Frostian verse, but naturally not all of it is of equal value as
        poetry. "

A117   R., E. "Best Selling Books, " Delineator, CXXIX (September 1936),
        55.
           Five-line review. "Latest poems of the quiet Yankee poet
        --freer with humor than are his former works. "

A118   R., J. "Mr. Frost Ranges Further, " Christian Science Monitor
        Weekly Magazine Section, June 17, 1936, p. 14.
           Discerns political and social overtones behind the placid
        appearance of the work.

A119   REELY, MARY KATHERINE, ed. "A Selected List of Current
        Books, " Wisconsin Library Bulletin, XXXII (July 1936), 84.
           A sympathetic five-line review.

A120   ROOT, E. MERRILL. "Here is Victory?" Christian Century, LIII
        (October 7, 1936), 1329-30.
           "This, Frost's finest book, indicates no end, but magnifi-
        cent growth toward a final word that he may take two books to
        reach. "

A121   SNOW, WILBERT. "Cheerful New England Poems, " New York
        Herald Tribune Books, June 7, 1936, p. 4.
           "There is a sheaf of good poems here--enough to
        make this book a priceless addition to the Frost saga. And it
        is unquestionably the most cheerful book he has written. "

A122   STEPHENS, JAMES. "Mr. Frost's New Poems, " London Sunday
        Times, April 4, 1937, p. 9.
           "It may be said of him--Howe'er it be) and tho' it shines
        or snows, upon a man, upon a tree, and each one dies, or
        grows), his muse, his musings go with him, howso, and where
        he goes. "

A123   STROBEL, MARION. "Robert Frost Charms Again With Volume of
        Singing Poems, " Chicago Daily Tribune, June 6, 1936, p. 10.
           Frost's "poems exist for the best of all reasons: their own

A. REVIEWS

STROBEL, MARION (cont.)
singing. They have humor, sympathy, kindliness, and self-respect. "

A124   THOMPSON, RALPH. "Books of the Times, " New York Times,
May 5, 1937, p. 23.
"Any honor that may come to Robert Frost must please all his readers, for he is surely one of our great poets. Honest, modest and peculiarly American. "

A125   UNTERMEYER, LOUIS. "Robert Frost: Revisionist, " American
Mercury, XXXIX (September 1936), 123-25.
Favorable review. In this volume Frost "solidifies his position . . . as the most rewarding and likewise the most richly integrated poet of his generation. " The article attempts to classify Frost and decides on the term "revisionist" because Frost has the "power not only to restate but to revise too easily accepted statements. " The article concludes with a brief discussion of style.

A126   WALTON, EDA LOU. "New Poems by Robert Frost, " New York
Times Book Review, May 31, 1936, pp. 1, 14.
Somehow Frost in his poetry reconciles life's contradictions.

A127   WHICHER, HARRIETT F. "The Book Table" section, Amherst
Graduates' Quarterly, XXV (August 1936), 407-09.
The poems seem much like Frost's conversation. "There can be no better way to face the future than his--with a sense of the shape of things, the power of laughter, a warm heart, and a free mind. "

A128   "Yankee Poet, " Time, XXVII (June 8, 1936), 83.
"Without laboring analogies Poet Frost yet manages to convey in his homespun terms a philosophy that has both personal and political implications. "

A129   ZABEL, MORTON D. "Poets of Five Decades, " Southern Review,
II (1936-37), 160-86 [171-73].
Frost sometimes carries too far his indulgence for "the rather complacent mock-innocence" found in former works.

The Critical Reception of Robert Frost

COLLECTED POEMS OF ROBERT FROST 1939, New York: Henry Holt, 1939; New York: Halcyon House, 1939.

A130   BARRETT, ALFRED. America, LXI (April 29, 1939), 70.
        Rather negative evaluation, some praise for "Death of the Hired Man."

A131   BOGAN, LOUISE. "Verse," New Yorker, XV (March 4, 1939), 76-78.
        Praises Frost's natural tone and his pastoral subjects.

A132   "Bookwright," New York Herald Tribune Books, May 14, 1939, p. 17.
        Analyzes Frost's new "Preface."

A133   BRÉGY, KATHERINE. Commonweal, XXXI (October 27, 1939), 19.
        "The further one reads through Frost's pages the more one is impressed by the honesty and reverence of his emotion and the artistic integrity, of his purposely simple style."

A134   CLEMENS, CYRIL. "The Quarterly Recommends" section, Mark Twain Quarterly, III (Spring 1940), 19-20.
        Quotes freely from Frost's "Preface," with little added comment.

A135   "Harvest of Poetry: Studies in To-day's Contrasts," Times Literary Supplement (London), November 18, 1939, p. vi.
        Review of CP and W. J. Turner's Selected Poems, 1916-1936. "Mr. Frost's qualities as a poet are now fully recognized."

A136   LEACH, HENRY G. "Poetry of Permanence," Forum and Century, CI (April 1939), 240.
        Four-line review comparing Frost's soil to Einstein's space.

A137   "The Muse; Collected Poems of Robert Frost," Time, XXXIII (May 15, 1939), 83-85, 87.
        "As they wear onward, Frost's Collected Poems show an increasing self-complacence of poetic purpose: from the initial effort to write true things acceptable to his muse to writing good things acceptable to himself. . . ." This article is mostly biographical.

The Critical Reception of Robert Frost

A. REVIEWS

A138   ORTON, VREST. [Review of Collected Poems, 1939.] <u>New England Quarterly</u>, XII (September 1939), 563-67.
        "Moving from complexity to simplicity, as all real artists must, Frost has gained an audience for poetry while other writers have been losing it."

A139   RITCHEY, JOHN. "The Figure a Poet Makes," <u>Christian Science Monitor Weekly Magazine Section</u>, July 22, 1939, p. 10.
        "What Frost is surest of and what the reader is surest to get is the theme of freshness, a fresh way of looking at an old world so as to make it seem new."

A140   RUKEYSER, MURIEL. "In a Speaking Voice," <u>Poetry</u>, LIV (July 1939), 218-24.
        Frost "wants his poem to have 'the wonder of unexpected supply'."

A141   TINKER, EDWARD L. "New Editions, Fine and Otherwise," <u>New York Times Book Review</u>, April 2, 1939, p. 24.
        "In this quintessential of his life's work is the perfect portrait of Robert Frost as well as his philosophy --an inevitable measure of the impregnable integrity he has achieved-- an integrity without which there can be no true genius."

A142   WILSON, JAMES SOUTHALL. "The Figure a Poet Makes," <u>Virginia Quarterly Review</u>, XV (Spring 1939), 303-05.
        Frost is neither pure idealist nor pure realist.

A WITNESS TREE, New York: Henry Holt, 1942

A143   BENÉT, STEPHEN VINCENT. "Frost at Sixty-Seven," <u>Saturday Review of Literature</u>, XXV (April 25, 1942), 7.
        AWT "is a book to read, a book to remember, and a book that will be part of our inheritance."

A144   <u>Booklist</u>, XXXVIII (May 15, 1942), 344.
        "Characteristically quiet poems with little emotional stress. Some have nature topics, others touch on history and the present time; many have a sly humor." (Quoted in its entirety.)

A145 Bookmark [of New York State Public Library], III (May - August 1942), 9.
". . . this sheaf of some 40 lyrics is distinguished by the philosophic, reflective mood, the occasional glint of incisive wit, the sharp etching of the little story."

A146 B[RÉGY], K[ATHERINE]. Catholic World, CLV (August 1942), 625-26 [626].
"Here again are honestly beautiful nature poems, true to nature and to himself, with the kind of originality that is part of personal integrity."

A147 COLUM, MARY M. "The New Books of Poetry," New York Times Book Review, May 3, 1942, p. 5.
"These lyrics of Frost's have that wisdom, that power of revelation that is time's last gift to the mature and powerful mind."

A148 DONAGHY, WILLIAM A. "Three Contemporary Poets," America, LXVII (September 5, 1942), 607-08.
Review of AWT; John Malcolm Brinnin, The Garden is Political; Mary Fabyan Windeatt, Sing Joyfully. "It is Frost at his best." Laments Frost's agnosticism.

A149 HILLYER, ROBERT. Atlantic Monthly, CLXIX (June 1942), "Atlantic Bookshelf" section, [n. p.].
"When Frost names things and tells facts, they are what he means. He lacks the contemporary fad for duplicity. . . . A Witness Tree represents Robert Frost at his best."

A150 "Life and Nature," Times Literary Supplement (London), July 3, 1943, p. 322.
The qualities of Frost's earlier poetry are also found in this collection, "but there is more in it of mental discovery than of rural incident."

A151 MARGOSHES, ADAMS. "Robert Frost, Semi-Poet," Current History, II (June 1942), 302-03.
The book contains some of Frost's best poetry; Frost is one of the best American poets, yet Frost is not essentially a poet at all. "Frost himself is certainly nothing better than a semi-good poet--or a semi-poet."

The Critical Reception of Robert Frost

A. REVIEWS

A152   MERTINS, LOUIS. "Silver-Fish," Southern Literary Messenger,
         IV (July 1942), 327.
            Primarily an affectionate reminiscence of Frost at Derry.

A153   New Yorker, "Briefly Noted" section, XVIII (May 9, 1942), 79-80.
            "Two memorable poems--'Come In' and 'A Considerable
         Speck'--in his best manner, together with the gnomic epigrams
         and rather arch philosophizing characteristic of his later
         phase."

A154   Open Shelf [of the Cleveland Public Library], May - June 1942, p. 12.
            Merely quotes "The Secret Sits."

A155   PORTER, KENNETH. New England Quarterly, XV (September
         1942), 547-49.
            Reviewed along with Robert P. Tristram Coffin's There
         Will Be Bread and Love. "Whereas Mr. Coffin aims at the
         pictorial, Mr. Frost, working in essentially the same material,
         is philosophical. . . ."

A156   Pratt Institute Library Quarterly Booklist, Series VI, No. 10
         (December 1942), p. 16.
            "Distinguished verse by a favorite American poet."
         (Quoted in its entirety.)

A157   REELY, MARY KATHERINE, ed. "A Selected List of Current
         Books," Wisconsin Library Bulletin, XXXVIII (June 1942), 95.
            "Poems to read once and then to read over, and many
         times. All of the earlier qualities are here: the sense of one-
         ness with the earth (The wind and the rain); the quizzical humor
         (A considerable speck); the restrained emotion (Never again
         would bird song be the same); the lyric gift, and with the
         deepened wisdom of later life." (Quoted in its entirety.)

A158   SCOTT, W. T. "Frost's Seventh Book," Poetry, LX (June 1942),
         146-49.
            Frost's real triumph "comes in the surprising number of
         lyrics in which that weight of implication and that ease of
         words combine to indisputable and lasting poetry."

A159   SNOW, WILBERT. "Robert Frost, Dean of American Poetry," New
         York Herald Tribune Books, May 10, 1942, p. 5.

A. REVIEWS

SNOW, WILBERT (cont.)
"'A Witness Tree' . . . contains a half dozen poems which. . . stand with the best things he has written."

A160   Time, XXXIX (May 18, 1942), 91-92.
"A Witness Tree is a testimony and a revelation of what Frost has managed to keep, through the happy and tragic years of his life."

A161   WHICHER, GEORGE F. "Frost's Seventh," Yale Review, XXXI (June 1942), 808-10.
"Offhand I cannot think of any kind of thing that he has previously done that is not equalled or surpassed in the present volume, and all the kinds are here."

COME IN AND OTHER POEMS, New York: Henry Holt, 1943; London, Jonathan Cape, 1944
Selection, biographical introduction, and commentary by Louis Untermeyer.

A162   BISHOP, F. J. "New Volume By and About Dean of American Poets," Chicago Sun Book Week, I (April 18, 1943), 8.
Bishop calls Untermeyer Frost's Boswell.

A163   Booklist, XXXIX (May 1, 1943), 351.
"The most popular poems chosen from several volumes, with appreciative introductions and pleasing drawings of rural scenes." (Quoted in its entirety.)

A164   Bookmark [of New York State Library], IV (March 1943), 10.
"Unusually attractive in format. . . ."

A165   COLLINS, THOMAS LYLE. "Meet Robert Frost," New York Times Book Review, April 11, 1943, p. 12.
Reviewer does not understand the purpose of this volume since all but ten of the poems are gathered in Collected Poems. Finds Untermeyer's introduction and interpretive criticism poor.

A166   DONAGHY, WILLIAM A. America, LXIX (June 5, 1943), 246.
"The book is a valuable record of a soul, rich, warm, vexed

A. REVIEWS

DONAGHY, WILLIAM A. (cont.)
with eternal wistfulness but still tenaciously keeping faith."

A167 JAKEMAN, ADELBERT M. "Frost, Late and Early," Springfield
Sunday Union and Republican, April 4, 1943, Sec. E, p. 7.
". . . one of the most distinguished volumes of poetry to
appear in a long while."

A168 JORDAN, ALICE M. Horn Book, XIX (May 1943), 172.
"The book is perhaps designed as an introduction to Robert
Frost for young people, and with the drawings, which are happy reminders of Robert Frost's New England, it will make a
lovely gift."

A169 M[AYNARD], T[HEODORE]. Catholic World, CLVII (August 1943),
552-54 [552-53].
Considers Untermeyer's commentary pleasant though not
brilliant and says that the illustrations catch Frost's spirit and
are superior to the J.J. Lankes woodcuts in previous volumes.

A170 REELY, MARY KATHERINE, ed. "A Selected List of Current
Books," Wisconsin Library Bulletin, XXXIX (May 1943), 71.
"To his selection of some 80 of Robert Frost's poems, Mr.
Untermeyer has added a biographical introduction and appre-
ciative commentary which invites continuous reading. With the
beautifully interpretative illustrations by John O'Hara Cosgrove,
it is a volume to give distinction to any poetry collection."
(Quoted in its entirety.)

A171 SLOAN, FLORENCE BETHUNE. "Come and Read" section,
Christian Science Monitor, August 26, 1943, p. 4.
"This is a charming introduction to Robert Frost, the man,
and to his poetry-- a choice book for your own library."

A172 STRACHAN, PEARL. "The World of Poetry," Christian Science
Monitor Weekly Magazine, May 1, 1943, p. 10.
Untermeyer's comments about the poems are considered
"done with taste and sympathy."

A173 SWALLOW, ALAN. "A Review of Some Current Poetry," New
Mexico Quarterly Review, XIII (Summer 1943), 215-18 [218].
Swallow considers Untermeyer's selection of poems as no

THE CRITICAL RECEPTION OF ROBERT FROST

SWALLOW, ALAN (cont.)
more than adequate because he leaves out some of Frost's best
poems. The commentary is worthless except to total novices
in reading poetry.

A174   "Untermeyer on Frost," Time, XLI (April 12, 1943), 100.
Untermeyer has made a sound selection from Frost's previously published works, but his commentary tends to obscure
rather than illuminate the poems.

A175   WHICHER, GEORGE F. "Robert Frost's Best," New York Herald
Tribune Weekly Book Review, April 4, 1943, p. 4.
"Both editor and artist have worked at this production as at
a labor of love. The result has been an unusually happy col-
laboration of their talents with the spirit of the poet."

A MASQUE OF REASON, New York: Henry Holt, 1945

A176   ADAMS, J. DONALD. "Speaking of Books," New York Times Book
Review, April 8, 1945, p. 2.
It is beneficial that Frost sometimes approaches "the
gravest themes in a playful spirit."

A177   AIKEN, CONRAD. "Whole Meaning or Doodle" section, New Republic, CXII (April 16, 1945), 512-14 [514].
"It's all great fun, of course, and not too dangerously
orthodox; but there are times when the cracker-barrel wise-
crack grates a little, and when the texture and text alike become too thin."

A178   BACON, LEONARD. "Robert Frost and the Man of Uz," Saturday
Review of Literature, XXVIII (March 24, 1945), 24.
"For all its brevity and beauty this is a difficult book."

A179   BOGAN, LOUISE. New Yorker, XXI (April 7, 1945), 83-85.
"It is interesting to trace the line of middle-class reasonable conformity in Frost's little jeu d'esprit and to recognize
how difficult it is, even in an era of the utmost tragedy, for a
poet who has chosen the middle road to be serious in tone and
searching in intent."

A. REVIEWS

A180   Booklist, XLI (April 1, 1945), 221.
"In an interlude in the desert, eons after his biblical trials, Job asks God for an adequate explanation of why God put him to the test. Job's wife and the Devil are also involved as comic relief. Blank verse. Different from the poet's more familiar work." (Quoted in its entirety.)

A181   "Book Window," Christian Science Monitor Weekly Magazine, April 21, 1945, p. 12.
"Mr. Frost has added little to the great discussion of the problem of good and evil, with which the world has been concerned for so long."

A182   BOYLE, FRANCES ALTER. Library Journal, LXX (March 1, 1945), 219.
Does not consider the Masque successful and does not recommend purchase by small public libraries.

A183   BRÉGY, KATHERINE. Catholic World, CLXI (September 1945), 522.
The reviewer contends that Frost is almost trivial in his interpretation of Job, Job's wife, God, and Satan.

A184   DUPEE, F. W. "Frost and Tate," in "Verse Chronicle" section, The Nation, CLX (April 21, 1945), 464-66.
"The trouble with such humor in Frost is that it is too often not a laugh but a smirk--the reflex of an incorrigible complacency."

A185   FORGOTSON, E. S. "A Shift of Scenery and a Change of Cast," Poetry, LXVI (June 1945), 156-59.
"Since Frost's religious view of the world places the responsibility for human evil in supernatural hands, he can only be 'discontented' with that evil, he cannot take any action potent to reduce it."

A186   FREMANTLE, ANNE. Commonweal, XLI (March 30, 1945), 592-93.
"It does not seem that Mr. Frost's forte is thought, or the use of reason."

A187   "Jehovah, Satan, and the Jobs," Newsweek, XXV (April 2, 1945), 100-02.

A. REVIEWS

"Jehovah, Satan, and the Jobs" (cont.)
"Robert Frost's 43rd Chapter of the Book of Job is delightful and, probably, meaningful reading."

A188   KENNEDY, LEO. "Now Robert Frost Essays the Full-Dress Biblical Poem," Chicago Sun Book Week, III (March 25, 1945), 3.
Frost ". . . has written a delightful trifle which is full of tolerance and sly humor."

A189   KILMER, KENTON. Best Sellers, V (April 1, 1945), 3.
The total import of the book "is a blank abyss of nothingness." Recommended only for those who want complete knowledge of Frost.

A190   "New England Questions," Time, XLV (May 7, 1945), 99-100.
"The 23 pages are good latter-day Frost: the ruminative philosophic wit whose pentameters are salted with gentle satire and unobtrusive learning."

A191   Open Shelf [of the Cleveland Public Library], May - June 1945, p. 11.
"A brief mask [sic] in blank verse. The principal characters are God and Job-- the theme, Job's request for an explanation from God of the troubles which befell him." (Quoted in its entirety.)

A192   OPIE, THOMAS F. Churchman, CLIX (July 1945), 19.
This is "a literary event of major importance. . . . It makes thrilling reading--and inspired."

A193   PRESCOTT, ORVILLE. "Books of the Times" section, New York Times, March 26, 1945, Sec. I, p. 17.
People who consider Frost more intellectual than poetical will find further support for their view "for this slim trifle is slight indeed."

A194   REELY, MARY KATHERINE, ed. "A Selected List of Current Books," Wisconsin Library Bulletin, XLI (May 1945), 53.
"Brief verse drama in which the dialog is carried by three characters: Job, Job's wife, and God. Satan appears also, but reduced to a mere shadow of his former self. Witty, ironic, perhaps irreverent; a rather special item for larger collections." (Quoted in its entirety.)

A. REVIEWS

A195   SCHORER, MARK. <u>Atlantic Monthly,</u> CLXXV (March 1945), 133.
Frost has produced "a kind of ballet in verse," an extension of the dramatic element in his lyrics. Expresses surprise at the tone of the book, "The tone of ancient wisdom, which carries with it the full weight and weariness of that skepticism to which intelligence is doomed."

A196   <u>Springfield Sunday Union and Republican,</u> March 25, 1945, p. 4D.
"Surely this poem of two dozen pages is bubbling with mischievous wit and salty wisdom which have nothing to do with youth or age. . . ."

A197   <u>Theatre Arts,</u> XXIX (October 1945), 607.
More a <u>précis</u> than a review.

A198   THOMPSON, LAWRANCE. "Robert Frost Rediscovers Job," <u>New York Times Book Review,</u> March 25, 1945, p. 3.
". . . the ideas expressed in 'A Masque of Reason' are but satirical variations on themes already hidden away in his poems. . . ."

A199   <u>United States Quarterly Book List,</u> I (June 1945), 7.
"<u>A Masque of Reason</u> is in the middle ground in treatment of its subject. It lacks the 'high seriousness' of some derogatory attacks on the idea of Divine Wisdom. . . yet . . . is not one of those which treat the unknown with light humor and nothing more."

A200   UNTERMEYER, LOUIS. "Submission to Unreason," <u>Virginia Quarterly Review,</u> XXI (Spring 1945), 286-89.
This is a bold book in its mingling of profundity and playfulness, daring in "its philosophical banter and metaphysical fancy."

A201   VAN DOREN, MARK. "Why Robert Frost is Ageless at Seventy," <u>New York Herald Tribune Weekly Book Review,</u> March 25, 1945, pp. 1-2.
"The humor of Robert Frost is so serious that it regularly takes the form of reminding us how hard the world is."

A202   "We Recommend," <u>Boston Daily Globe,</u> March 28, 1945, evening edition, p. 17.

A. REVIEWS

"We Recommend, " (cont.)
". . . this poem. . . is different than [sic] anything he has done before, but has all Mr. Frost's impishness and profundity. Because anything the poet writes is important. "

A203   WHICHER, GEORGE F. "Chapter Forty-Three of Job, " Yale Review, XXXIV (Spring 1945), 549-51.
There is no pretense in the Masque. "It is the ripe product of a writer who is both philosopher and poet. " The great triumph of the work is Thyatira, Job's wife.

STEEPLE BUSH, New York: Henry Holt, 1947

A204   BACON, LEONARD. "Robert Frost's 'Intricate Simplicity', " Saturday Review of Literature, XXX (May 31, 1947), 15.
Frost "is the most careful of workmen, but he always has something worth his while to work on. Any one of his poems is the incarnation or symbol of something completed in the mind. "

A205   BATES, ESTHER WILLARD. "For Humbly Proud Thinkers, " Christian Science Monitor, June 16, 1947, p. 16.
"As happens with older poets, the music and a certain loveliness go, but the wisdom increases. So is it here. This is poetry such as Hardy might have written, had Hardy possessed Frost's hope and courage. "

A206   Booklist, XLIII (June 15, 1947), 328.
"America's popular lyric poet in his latest volume ranges from lyrics of nature and personal feeling to shrewd, wry comment on today's world and its catchwords. " (Quoted in its entirety.)

A207   BRÉGY, KATHERINE. Catholic World, CLXVI (December 1947), 279.
A combined review with Collected Poems of Sister M. Madeleva. The reviewer considers Frost's achievement slight when compared with the poems by Sister M. Madeleva.

A208   "Briefly Noted" section, New Yorker, XXIII (June 7, 1947), 112.
"The old ability to catch at the reader's heart is a little

A. REVIEWS

"Briefly Noted" (cont.)
less apparent and the 'homespun' philosophy is as conservative
as ever, but there is plenty here to please."

A209 CAMPBELL, GLADYS. "'A World Torn Loose Went By Me',"
Poetry, LXXI (December 1947), 145-49.
The book "has its by-paths that seem insignificant, its
plateaus that stretch too far, but the mountains rise, and the
total landscape is worthy of its author."

A210 "Hardy Perennial," Time, XLIX (June 16, 1947), 102-04.
"The 43 poems of Steeple Bush do nothing to enlarge his
greatness and no one of them could begin to displace the best
of his Collected Poems."

A211 JARRELL, RANDALL. "'Tenderness and Passive Sadness'," New
York Times Book Review, June 1, 1947, p. 4.
". . . most of the poems merely remind you, by their persistence in the mannerisms of what was genius, that they are
productions of somebody who once, and somewhere else, was a
great poet." Considers Frost's "Directive" unequalled by
other poems in the book.

A212 MCDONALD, GERALD. "Poetry" section, Library Journal, LXXII
(June 1, 1947), 889.
Frost "is aware of the crisis of our time and offers
shrewd comment on it, but he has not lost his composure."

A213 ROSS, MALCOLM. Canadian Forum, XXVII (November 1947), 191.
"The volume is technically uneven, often lapsing into ama-
teurish doggerel," obviously a product of Frost's old age.

A214 SNELL, GEORGE. San Francisco Chronicle, July 13, 1947, "This
World" section, p. 20.
Review of SB and books by Lawrence P. Sprigarn, J.V.
Cunningham, and Weldon Kees. Frost's book shows "no dimi-
nution" of poetic power.

A215 STAUFFER, DONALD A. "The New Lyrics of Robert Frost,"
Atlantic Monthly, CLXXX (October 1947), 115-16.
Frost's achievement is the reduction of complex ideas to
common speech without the loss of subtlety.

THE CRITICAL RECEPTION OF ROBERT FROST

A. REVIEWS

A216   United States Quarterly Book List, III (September 1947), 242.
". . . if he has not made a contribution to the history of ideas, he has certainly advanced the history of American poetry in its main tradition, which is rural in the broadest sense, and regional as well."

A217   UNTERMEYER, LOUIS. "Still Further Range," Yale Review, XXXVII (September 1947), 138-39.
Although this is a small book, it has a very wide range. It is ". . . neither Frost's most commanding nor his most coordinated volume."

A218   WHICHER, GEORGE F. "Ripeness of a Poet's Wisdom," New York Herald Tribune Weekly Book Review, July 6, 1947, p. 2.
"The present gathering of poems. . .is more topical, more sharply intellectual, and more given to teasing than any of its predecessors."

A MASQUE OF MERCY, New York: Henry Holt, 1947

A219   ADAMS, WALTER WOOD. "Drama and Ballad," Voices, CXXXII (Winter 1948), 49-52.
". . . in foregoing the persuasive personal charm of lyricism, Frost has achieved an accomplishment of a high order, possible and proper for him, and possible for few other poets of his time."

A220   COX, SIDNEY. "Mr. Frost's Blank Verse Dialogue," New York Times Book Review, November 9, 1947, p. 6.
"The humor of the masque is proportional to its seriousness. Reading it is difficult delight. It is worth many readings."

A221   MCMILLIN, LAWRENCE. "A Modern Allegory," Hudson Review, I (Spring 1948), 105-07.
Considers the masque to be more successful than A Masque of Reason, but it has more technical defects. Questions Frost's ability to write prophetic poetry.

THE CRITICAL RECEPTION OF ROBERT FROST

A. REVIEWS

A222   OLSON, LAWRENCE. Furioso, III (Spring 1948), 47-51 [50-51].
        Review of MM, and Howard Griffin, Cry Cadence; Selden
        Rodman, The Amazing Year; Rolfe Humphries, Forbid Thy
        Ravens. ". . . a distinct advance over the other masque be-
        cause the dilemma it explores comes closer to our daily lives,
        and so is more interesting. But it is not likely to add anything
        to the reputation of its author."

A223   WILLIAMS, WILLIAM CARLOS. "The Steeple's Eye," Poetry,
        LXXII (April 1948), 38-41.
        "My own taste would call . . . for a richer verse than Mr.
        Frost prefers, richer in verbal resources and metric than I
        find in this Masque. But if the plainness of the speech is once
        accepted the effectiveness and beauty of the lines rise, at times,
        as spires above the countryside, with references far removed
        from their immediate limitations."

COMPLETE POEMS OF ROBERT FROST 1949, New York: Henry Holt, 1949;
    London: Jonathan Cape, 1951

A224   Booklist, XLV (July 15, 1949), 396.
        "The first collection of Frost's poems published since 1937
        has the contents of 10 separate volumes, and a few poems that
        have not appeared in books." (Quoted in its entirety.)

A225   Bookmark [of New York State Library], IX (October 1949), 4.
        "Adds A Witness Tree, Steeple Bush, A Masque of Reason,
        A Masque of Mercy, and several new poems to the earlier
        work of the leading American poet. Photograph frontispiece."
        (Quoted in its entirety.)

A226   "Briefly Noted" section, New Yorker, XXV (October 15, 1949), 127.
        "The lyric vein runs pure and unchallengeable throughout,
        but the thought, especially when it becomes thoroughly middle-
        class, as it often does, can be challenged at many points."

A227   DAICHES, DAVID. "Enduring Wisdom From A Poet-Sage," New
        York Times Book Review, May 29, 1949, pp. 1, 13.
        "Frost likes to see men in elemental postures and, having

34

DAICHES, DAVID (cont.)
so arranged them, to draw conclusions either explicitly or with
an affected shyness."

A228 FITZGERALD, ROBERT. "Patter, Distraction, and Poetry," New
Republic, CXXI (August 8, 1949), 17-19 [18-19].
"Frost is a master within his range, and a reading of his
lifework makes it clear that his range is wider than people
often suppose."

A229 HOLMES, JOHN. "Designs of Self-Discovery," Saturday Review of
Literature, XXXII (July 16, 1949), 9-10.
Attention is given to Frost's manner of large-scale organ-
ization and his carefulness in arranging poems within a volume.

A230 HUMPHRIES, ROLFE. "Verse Chronicle" section, The Nation,
CLXIX (July 23, 1949), 92-93.
Frost's accomplishment lies in three areas: his lyric poetry, his dramatic monologues, and his observation of nature or
occupation. Frost should explore more fully the problem of
evil in man.

A231 "The Intolerable Touch," Time, LIII (June 27, 1949), 94, 96, 98,
100.
Of the poems in CP "almost every one of them is complete
as a work of art."

A232 JOHNSTON, J. H. Commonweal, L (July 8, 1949), 324-25.
Frost's poetry is very uneven in quality. His lyrical poetry is a considerable accomplishment, but if his poems are
pressed "they often reveal a disturbing indetermination and
shallowness."

A233 KENNEDY, LEO. "He Looks Like Poet--he is a poet," "Book Day"
column, Chicago Sun, June 20, 1949, p. 44.
"This book bulges with richness. It contains all the poems
that Robert Frost wishes to keep. It retains several that his
most earnest admirers could wish he would throw away."

A234 MC DONALD, GERALD. "Poetry" section, Library Journal,
LXXIV (September 15, 1949), 1326-27 [1327].
Considers CP to be the most obvious choice of the year's
poetry for library purchase, and in multiple copies.

The Critical Reception of Robert Frost

A. REVIEWS

A235 Open Shelf [of the Cleveland Public Library], July-August-September 1949, p. 15.
"It is good to have in one attractive volume the complete poetry of this most widely acclaimed American poet. His poetry is a favorite with many readers." (Quoted in its entirety.)

A236 POORE, CHARLES. "Books of the Times" section, New York Times, June 2, 1949, Sec. I, p. 25.
Quotes from poems with little comment.

A237 VAN DOREN, MARK. "Our Great Poet, Whom We Read and Love," New York Herald Tribune Weekly Book Review, May 29, 1949, pp. 1, 11.
"No other living poet has so much art, or so much subject matter."

A238 VIERECK, PETER. "Parnassus Divided," Atlantic Monthly, CLXXXIV (October 1949), 67-70 [67-68].
Review of CP, Edith Sitwell's Song of the Cold, and Ezra Pound's Pisan Cantoes, and others. Considers CP to be the most important book of 1949. Frost is more complex than he may appear upon first reading. Frost's cheerfulness is compared with that of ancient Greeks who "looked so deeply into life's tragic meaning that they had to protect themselves by cultivating a deliberately superficial jolliness in order to bear the unbearable."

IN THE CLEARING, New York: Henry Holt, 1962

A239 BOGAN, LOUISE. "Briefly Noted" section, New Yorker, XXXVIII (November 17, 1962), 242, 244.
"Very formal, very direct; very dry, very nice."

A240 Booklist and Subscription Books Bulletin, LVIII (May 1, 1962), 599.
One-paragraph noncommittal review.

A241 Bookmark [of the New York State Library], XXI (June 1962), 256.
"A collection of new poems including the one written for 'John F. Kennedy His Inauguration'."

The Critical Reception of Robert Frost

A. REVIEWS

A242   BOOTH, PHILIP. "Journey Out Of a Dark Forest," New York
Times Book Review, March 25, 1962, pp. 1, 44.
"What unknown conflicts a poet must survive, in order to
find his own terms of survival, no one knows better than Robert
Frost. Lost as he once was in the dark woods, he has by his
own 'Directive' fully found himself 'In the Clearing,' and has
earned every right to 'wait to watch the water clear'."

A243   CIARDI, JOHN. "Robert Frost: American Bard," Saturday Review,
XLV (March 24, 1962), 15-17, 52-54.
"Let the School System make a whited saint of Mr. Frost
if it must; and as, alas, it will. The man himself remains an
hombre." Ciardi suggests that Frost should receive the Nobel
Prize.

A244   DAVISON, PETER. "Robert Frost: His Own Tradition," Atlantic
Monthly, CCIX (May 1962), 100-01.
"Robert Frost has taken the privilege of age in this volume;
he has turned his back, for the most part, on the soft lyrical
manner of many of his earlier poems and has set aside the
details of nature in favor of nature in the large, in favor of
political and philosophical speculation."

A245   DEEN, ROSEMARY F. "Frost's New Power," Commonweal,
LXXVI (May 4, 1962), 155.
"In a way the most remarkable thing about this book is its
evidence that Frost's lyric gift remains perfectly fresh and
alive."

A246   ENRIGHT, D. J. New Statesman, LXIV (October 19, 1962), 530-32
[530].
Review of IC and five other poets. In Frost's book
"originalities rub shoulders with trivialities on practically
every page."

A247   H., W. "From the Sierra to Outer Space," in "This World" section,
San Francisco Chronicle, March 25, 1962, p. 30.
"Mostly Mr. Frost writes about the woods, man, nature
--from the Sierra to Outer Space."

A248   HARDING, WALTER. "At 88 His Poems Still Show the Master's
Touch," Chicago Sunday Tribune Magazine of Books, March 25,

A. REVIEWS

HARDING, WALTER (cont.)
1962, p. 1.
". . . age has not narrowed Robert Frost's range. If anything, it has enlarge it." Frost is "the eternal Romanticist."

A249   HOLMES, JOHN. "All the Robert Frosts Are in His New Book, 'In
the Clearing'. 'He Has Told Us the Best He Knows About
Life'." Christian Science Monitor, March 29, 1962, p. 11.
"The great poem in Robert Frost's new book is 'Kitty
Hawk,' perhaps the profoundest statement he has ever simpli-
fied into his kind of language. . . ."

A250   KELL, RICHARD. "Veteran Verse," [Manchester, Eng.]
Guardian, October 19, 1962, p. 6.
Roundup review says Frost's book has wide range and is
skilful in light verse.

A251   KIMBROUGH, ROBERT. Wisconsin Studies in Contemporary Literature, III (Spring - Summer 1962), 104-07.
". . . the variety of content, style, and mood in all the
poems prove that Frost is neither philosophically deductive nor
a regional literalist; rather he has the kind of comic detach-
ment that leads to emblematic projections of life."

A252   KUNITZ, STANLEY. "Frost, Williams, & Company," Harper's,
CCXXV (October 1962), 100-03, 108 [100].
Reviewed along with Williams' Pictures from Brueghel and
Other Poems, Jack Gilbert's Views of Jeopardy, Robert Cree-
ley's For Love: Poems 1950-60, and Kenneth Koch's Thank You
and Other Poems. "The new image of Frost as official bard of
the administrative establishment and fireside poet to the
American people has certain comic overtones, for he is anything but 'progressive' (in the liberal Democratic tradition)...."

A253   MEREDITH, WILLIAM. "Robert Frost in Book Reviews and Under
the Aspect of Eternity," Poetry, CI (December 1962), 200-03.
Frost's work is "a single work. It has grown like a tree
of a new species: the layer of live wood is a perennial miracle
of new life, but the tree itself is what is altogether astonishing
-- a new tree -- even before it was the giant it stands today."

The Critical Reception of Robert Frost

A. REVIEWS

A254 MILLER, VINCENT. "The Home of Robert Frost," National Review, XII (June 5, 1962), 411-12.
The book "may well become an international best seller." Frost has become the "ideal manifestation of American character, as well as of American poetic genius." Discusses Frost's poetry in general. He "was engaged in his lifetime effort to find familiar old ways to confront an unfamiliar world. . . ."

A255 O'DONNELL, WILLIAM G. "Robert Frost at Eighty-eight," Massachusetts Review, IV (Autumn 1962), 213-18.
The book "may have no supremely accomplished poems, . . . but when it is added to the Complete Poems, it will take an honored place in the Frost canon . . . ."

A256 POORE, CHARLES. "Books of the Times" section, New York Times, March 27, 1962, p. 35.
"It is our duty to read many other illustrious poets; it is our pleasure to read Robert Frost."

A257 ROBIE, BURTON A. Library Journal, LXXXVII (April 15, 1962), 1616.
"If ever there should be a Poet Laureateship in this country (and why not) [Frost's] would be the certain honor."

A258 ROSENTHAL, M. L. "The Two Frosts," The Reporter, XXVI (April 12, 1962), 50-52.
There is a "real" Frost and an "official" one.

A259 S., R. Wisconsin Library Bulletin, LVIII (July - August 1962), 240.
Frost's work is "closer to jingles than to the memorable poetry we associate with his name."

A260 STEVENSON, ADLAI E. "The American People Find Their Poet," New Republic, CXLVI (April 9, 1962), 20-21.
"In Robert Frost, the American people have found their poet, their singer, their seer-- in short, their bard."
Reprints Frost's essay, "Nothing More Gentle Than Strength."

A261 "The Old Masters," Times Literary Supplement (London), December 21, 1962, p. 987.
Review of IC and of Robert Graves's New Poems 1962.

A. REVIEWS

"The Old Masters" (cont.)
"Mr. Frost is nearly ninety and the poems in In the Clear-ing have the odd, chirpy grasshopper lightness, the strange lack of gravitas which is sometimes a mark of genius in ex-treme old age."

A262   WILBUR, RICHARD. "Poems That Soar and Sing and Charm," New York Herald Tribune Books, March 25, 1962, p. 3.
"This is a high-spirited, high-minded book. Despite its Frostian skepticisms and paradoxes, it is sweepingly assertive, and ought to satisfy the sort of critic who values poetry for the philosophy which may be shaken out of it--as some children eat the Cracker Jack for the sake of the prize."

B. INTERVIEWS AND TALKS

1892

B1   Valedictory address: "A Monument to Afterthought Unveiled, " Lawrence [Mass.] High School Bulletin, Vol. XIII, No. 10 (June 1892), p. 10.

        "Not in the strife of action, is the leader made, nor in the face of crisis, but when all is over, when the mind is swift with keen regret, in the long after-thought. "

1915

B2   BRAITHWAITE, WILLIAM STANLEY. "Robert Frost, New American Poet: His Opinions and Practice-- An Important Analysis of the Modern Bard, " Boston Evening Transcript, May 8, 1915, Part 3, pp. 4, 10.

        "No American poet of today has come into so sudden a recognition as Robert Frost. "

1916

B3   WILMORE, CARL. "Finds Famous American Poet in White Mountain Village, " Boston Post, February 14, 1916, p. 16.

        "I always go to farming when I can. I always make a failure and then I have to go to teaching. I'm a good teacher, but it doesn't allow me time to write. "

B4   "Poetry of Axe Handles Urged by Robert Frost: Sentiments True to Nature's Grain Are Advocated by Yankee Versifier Who 'Recently Arrived', " Philadelphia Public Ledger, April 4, 1916, p. 11.

        " 'Art should follow lines in Nature like the grain of an axe-handle. False art puts curves on things that haven't any curves. '"

B. INTERVIEWS AND TALKS

1918

B5   TILLEY, M. P. "Notes from Conversations with Robert Frost,"
      The Inlander, XX (February 1918), 3-8.
          Frost comments on his friends, his mother, and some
      English poets.

1920

B6   ANTHONY, JOSEPH. "Robert Frost, Realist and Symbolist," New
      York Times Book Review and Magazine, July 4, 1920, p. 19.
          Article-interview, including an anecdote of Frost's frank
      criticism of a student writer. He told an Amherst student that
      he would not be a poet. "Because you don't know how to get in
      trouble unselfconsciously."

1921

B7   WAITT, PAUL. "America's Great Poet Revels in Beauties of Old
      Vermont," Boston Traveler, April 11, 1921, p. 6.

B8   CLARK, DELBERT. "Dauntless Spirit and High Ideals Explain Suc-
      cess of Frost's Career." Michigan Daily, October 9, 1921,
      pp. 1, 10.
          Frost: "I never write in the afternoon. My time then is
      always free. Sometimes I do not write a thing for six months,
      and sometimes I write steadily for six months."

B9   "Robert Frost: Michigan's Guest," Michigan Alumnus, XXVIII
      (October 20, 1921), 43-45.
          On Frost's going to the University of Michigan for a year
      as poet-in-residence.

B10   "Robert Frost Outlines Artistic Aims before Audience at Union Re-
      ception," Michigan Daily, November 16, 1921, p. 1.
          Frost: "When we have in our colleges an intellectual enter-
      prise rightly directed and of ever increasing force, America
      may hope to attain a position in philosophy and the arts equal
      to that now held in science."

B11   BOWEN, STIRLING. "A Poet on the Campus of the University of
      Michigan," Detroit News, Part Seven, November 27, 1921, p. 1.

B. INTERVIEWS AND TALKS

BOWEN, STIRLING (cont.)
"I am not like Louis Untermeyer . . . . Untermeyer could be run down by an automobile and then write a poem about it as the ambulance bore him off. He writes with his coattails flying."

B12   "Some Observations by Robert Frost," Michigan Alumnus, XXVIII (December 1, 1921), 234.
A brief account of Frost's talk before the A. A. U. W. group on October 29. Frost recalled his student days and said: ". . . I walked out of Harvard hilariously and feeling glad that my serious friends could not understand me."

1922

B13   STEWART, BERNICE. "Reviewing Robert Frost's Year at Ann Arbor," Detroit Free Press, Magazine Section, June 25, 1922, pp. 3, 7.
"In summing up, one is justified in concluding that beyond all question the fellowship has benefited the campus and the community, that it has imposed a little on the poet. . . ."

B14   SMITH, KATHERINE G. "Robert Frost and the Ann Arbor Fellowship in Creative Art," The Lyric West, II (September 1922), 28-29.
Frost comments briefly on his appointment at Michigan.

B15   "Robert Frost, Returning, Gives Views On Life, Art, Education," Michigan Daily, October 13, 1922, p. 2.
"The only artists worth patronizing are the ones who would do their work whether they were paid for it or not."

1923

B16   RASCOE, BURTON. "A Bookman's Day Book," New York Tribune Book News and Reviews, January 14, 1923, p. 23.
After reading several of Frost's poems, Rascoe finds "The Road Not Taken" is the only one "that awakened anything in me."

B17   COWLES, JASON. "An Au Revoir to Robert Frost," Michigan Daily, Sunday Magazine, May 20, 1923, pp. 1, 3.

B. INTERVIEWS AND TALKS

COWLES, JASON (cont.)
An overview of Frost's influence at the University of
Michigan.

B18   FELD, ROSE C. "Robert Frost Relieves His Mind," New York
Times Book Review, October 21, 1923, pp. 2, 23.
"America means certain things to people who come here.
It means the Declaration of Independence, it means Washington,
it means Lincoln, it means Emerson -- never forget Emerson
...."

1924

B19   MABIE, MURCHISON. "Robert Frost Gives Mr. Mabie A Few
Pointers On This And That," Michigan Daily, April 1, 1924,
p. 1.
Very brief, very superficial account of a visit with Frost.

B20   JACKSON, GARDNER. " 'I Will Teach Only When I Have Something to Tell'," Boston Sunday Globe, November 23, 1924,
Editorial Section, p. 3.
"His informality, his candor and his humor combine to
make him a highly attractive person, but one must have a ro-
bust disregard for the conventional views of life if a conversation with him is not to prove upsetting."

1925

B21   BATAL, JAMES A. "Poet Robert Frost Tells of His High School
Days in Lawrence," Lawrence Telegram, March 28, 1925, p. 14.

B22   "A Literary Dialogue," Amherst Writing, XXXIX (May 1925), 4-6.
Frost talks informally with students on the literary magazine staff.

B23   S., A. G. "Brilliant Opening of Bowdoin Institute," Lewiston
[Maine] Evening Journal, May 5, 1925, p. 3.
An account of Frost's address opening the series of lec-
tures.

B24   "In Memoriam: Marion LeRoy Burton," Christian Science Monitor,
May 29, 1925, p. 11.
Reports Frost's eulogy.

B. INTERVIEWS AND TALKS

B25   "Tribute Is Paid to Dr. Burton," Christian Science Monitor, May 29, 1925, p. 5.

In a eulogy for Marion L. Burton, President of the University of Michigan, Frost said that "Dr. Burton's ideal teacher was 'one who would insist on turning the teacher's claim on the student into the student's claim on the teacher.'"

B26   "Robert Frost Speaks in Memory of Dr. Burton," Michigan Alumnus, XXXI (June 6, 1925), 703-04.

"Mr. Frost did not attempt a formal tribute. He knew and loved President Burton and he knew that he was addressing an audience which shared his feelings. What he had to say was intimate and personal."

B27   M., J. "Robert Frost on Poetic Drama," Christian Science Monitor, July 14, 1925, p. 5.

Frost: "The height of poetry is in dramatic give and take. Drama is the capstone of poetry."

B28   SCHOENFIELD, ALLEN. "Science Can't Dishearten Poets, Says Robert Frost." Detroit News, October 11, 1925, p. 6.

Replying to the notion that scientific advancement and standardization in American society have squelched individuality, Frost says, ". . . I am not fearful of uniformity, even though it led to external monotony. For this monotony cannot go beyond externals. The ultimate things are too spiritual for that."

B29   ABBOT, WALDO. "Robert Frost -- Professor of English," Michigan Alumnus, XXXII (December 12, 1925), 208-09.

After a year as Fellow in Creative Arts, Frost becomes Professor of English at Michigan.

B30   MABIE, JANET. "Robert Frost Interprets His Teaching Method," Christian Science Monitor, December 24, 1925, p. 11.

Frost suggests "education by presence" of great scholars on a school campus.

B. INTERVIEWS AND TALKS

1926

B31   "Robert Frost Talks on Metaphors, " <u>Bryn Mawr College News</u>,
        February 10, 1926, p. 1.
           "All the philosophers had metaphors, but a philosopher is
        a person with one metaphor who lives all his life studying and
        amplifying it. A poet dashes off a new one every hour, and
        leaves it for the next. "

1927

B32   "Frost Claims Poems Often Lose Their Real Meaning When Back-
        ground Is Overdeveloped, " <u>Michigan Daily</u>, March 31, 1927,
        p. 1.
           " 'The danger, ' concluded the poet, 'is in one's becoming
        lost in detail; one must be unbogged, extricated, the spirit
        must be kept ever fresh.'"

B33   "New England Poet Applies Verse to Farm Occupations, " <u>Buffalo</u>
        [N.Y.] <u>Evening News</u>, November 11, 1927, p. 27.
           On a reading at University of Buffalo Grosvenor Library
        the previous day.

B34   "Robert Frost on Education" in Gorham B. Munson, <u>Robert Frost:</u>
        <u>A Study in Sensibility and Good Sense</u>. New York: George H.
        Doran Company, 1927. Appendix C. Pp. 127-29.
           Extracts from a talk given at Wesleyan University Decem-
        ber 1926.

1928

B35   MELCHER, DANIEL. "' English Classes Should Not Analyze Books,'
        Says Poet, " <u>The Mountaineer</u>, January 13, 1928, pp. 1, 3.
           Interview in the Montclair, New Jersey, high school paper.

B36   " 'Colleges Are Like Individuals, ' Says Robert Frost In Interview, "
        <u>Michigan Daily</u>, March 27, 1928, p. 1.
           " 'Colleges are like individuals; they think the important
        thing is to be "advanced, " whereas the really important thing
        with colleges as well as individuals is to be original.'"

B. INTERVIEWS AND TALKS

B37   "Fear Of All Kinds Is A Motivating Influence, Says Robert Frost, "
       Michigan Daily, March 31, 1928, p. 5.
             "We are afraid lest we will not be taken by some compel-
       ling ideal. "

B38   "Frost Here, " in "The Week on the Campus" section, Michigan
       Alumnus, XXXIV (March 31, 1928), 529.
             Frost gives readings in Mimes Theater. Frost says "the
       really important thing with colleges as well as individuals is to
       be original. "

                              1930

B39   "Address at the Dedication of the Davison Memorial Library, 1930,"
       in Bread Loaf Folder, No. 8. Middlebury: Bread Loaf School
       of English, 1930. Pp. 7-8.
             Frost says he would like for Wilfred Davison to be remem-
       bered personally for as long as possible. "The way I should
       like to see his memory prolonged would be by keeping the bent
       he gave the school. . . ."

B40   "Noted Poet Talks On Sound Function, " Michigan Daily, April 9,
       1930, p. 1.
             " 'The ultimate thing . . . is the sound, not of vowel and
       consonant or of music, but the sound of the meaning in relation
       to a meter and the deeper the meaning, the richer is the
       sound.'"

B41   BARC, HELEN. "Robert Frost Gives Discussion Of Tourism, Po-
       ets, And Writing, " Michigan Daily, April 10, 1930, p. 5.
       Frost describes superficiality as "tourism. "

B42   "Frost Lectures On 'Pure Poetry', " Michigan Daily, April 10, 1930,
       p. 1.
             " 'Pure poetry . . . does not choose its subject and the
       writer.'" It begins with mood.

                              1931

B43   "Education by Poetry: A Meditative Monologue, " Amherst Gradu-
       ates' Quarterly, XX (February 1931), 75-85.
             A rambling discourse on metaphor and its relation to both

                                47

B. INTERVIEWS AND TALKS
    "Education by Poetry. . ." (cont.)
    science and poetry. Part of the text was later published as
    The Four Beliefs.

B44   "The Poet of Today," in "They Say--" column, New York Times,
       March 22, 1931, Sec. IX, p. 2.
           Excerpt from speech to Yale students on "the trouble with
       undergraduate poetry . . . . The difference between good po-
       etry and free verse . . . is that the good poet reveals his idea
       at the very last line. And when the last word has been said,
       every reader should wish that he had been able to sense that
       very idea before the poet expressed it."

B45   LANDIS, BENSON Y. "Poetry and Rural Life: An Interview with
       Robert Frost," Rural America, IX (June 1931), 5-6.
           Frost talks about the value of country life. ". . . the race
       lives best to itself--first to itself-- storing strength in the
       more individual life of the country-- of the farm-- then going to
       market and socializing in the industrial city."

B46   "Frost Lectures at Bread Loaf," New York Times, July 12, 1931,
       Sec. II, p. 18.
           One paragraph on Frost's return to Bread Loaf. He says,
       "Education . . . is a kind of insurance against being made a
       fool of by failure and being made a fool of by success."

B47   BARRY, MARY RUTH. "Robert Frost, on Lecture Trip Here,
       Raps Moderns," [Denver] Rocky Mountain News, July 17, 1931,
       p. 5.
           Of extreme modern artists Frost says, "They do not care
       whether their communication is intelligible to others."

B48   CHAPIN, L. A. "Poet Visits Denver To Warn Students Not To Write
       Verse," Denver Post, July 17, 1931, p. 4.
           "People should take advantage of their natural laziness.
       The idea that humans are born full of natural ambition is all
       wrong. As a matter of fact, everyone is born lazy."

1932

B49   M[UNSON], G[ORHAM] I., "Readers and Writers" section, New
       English Weekly, July 21, 1932, pp. 330-31.
           Numerous quotations from Frost's six lectures at the New
       School for Social Research in New York City.

B. INTERVIEWS AND TALKS

B50   SHIPPEY, LEE. "Frost at Occidental College, " in his column,
"The Lee Side of L. A., " <u>Los Angeles Times,</u> September 29,
1932, p. 4.
   "Poetry is not an easy road to riches. But probably it is
the only thing in which I could have found even moderate success, or peace of mind. "

B51   WAYNE, FRANCIS. "Robert Frost, Famous Poet, Praises Farm
Strike Idea, " <u>Denver Post</u>, October 11, 1932, p. 14.
   Frost says: "It is the duty of presidents and kings to promote farming. The French nation rests on a wide agricultural
base. We Americans are doing everything to narrow, industri-
alize and mechanize this base. "

B52   "Robert Frost Calls Writing of Poem Performance in Belief, "
<u>Michigan Daily</u>, October 18, 1932, p. 1.
   "Writing a great poem is largely a 'performance in belief.'
. . . 'Poems are not worried into shape, ' Mr. Frost said, 'but
believed in. A poem, like a game, is played when it is played
and should not be definite until the last word is written. That
is what you judge by. The writing of a poem depends on the
performer's condition. Everything must be just right.'"

B53   " 'Writing Has to Be Casual' Is Frost's Advice to Young Poets, "
<u>Michigan Daily</u>, October 23, 1932, p. 1.
   "As a writer, I have only one regularity, and that is that I
never write in the afternoon, often in the morning and often in
the evening, but I can remember no time in my life when I have
written poetry during the hours from noon until dinner time. "

1935

B54   "Robert Frost on Sixtieth Birthday Talks of Joys of Living, Says
He'd Like to be Older, " <u>Amherst Student</u>, LXVIII (March 25,
1935), 1, 2.
   ". . . sixty is only a pretty good age. It is not advanced
enough. The great thing is to be advanced. Now ninety would
be really well along and something to be given credit for. "

B55   "Robert Frost. Remarks at Senior Chapel, " <u>Amherst Alumni Coun-
cil News</u>, VIII (July 1935), 83-85.

B. INTERVIEWS AND TALKS

"Robert Frost. Remarks. . ." (cont.)
Frost's remarks are summarized. They are primarily about individualism and politics.

B56   SMITH, MARY GILBERT. "Robert Frost, " Boston Globe, September 5, 1935, p. 16.
Brief account of a talk with Frost at South Shaftsbury.

1936

B57   "Latest Poem By Robert Frost Versifies New Deal is Lost: New England Poet Strums His Lyre, And Says The Nation's Plight is Dire As Projects Swerve 'Twixt Pan And Fire, " Baltimore Sun, February 26, 1936, pp. 25, 5.
On "To a Thinker in Office, " published in Saturday Review of Literature, January 11, p. 11. Hopes for Henry Wallace are lost.

B58   "Poems Read by Robert Frost, " Services of the University of New Hampshire in Memory of Edward Morgan Lewis . . . May 25, 1936 (Durham, N.H., 1936). Pp. 17-19.
Includes opening remarks of Frost.

B59   "Poet Would Give Young Folks More Time to Find Themselves, " Burlington [Vt.] Free Press and Times, August 19, 1936, p. 2.
Subheading: "Robert Frost Advocates Extension of General Education, Postponing Specialization Until Later. "

1938

B60   "The Poet's Next of Kin in a College, " Biblia, IX (February 1938), 16-18.
Talk given at Princeton University on October 26, 1937.

B61   "Poverty and Poetry, " Biblia, IX (February 1938), 9-15.
A talk given at Haverford College, October 25, 1937.

B62   "What Became of New England?" Oberlin Alumni Magazine, XXXIV (May 1938), 5-6.
Commencement address at Oberlin College that year, in which Frost makes one of his most outspoken comments on his own religious belief.

B. INTERVIEWS AND TALKS

1939

B63   "Frost Regrets the Arts Lack 'Prize Ring' Fight, " New York Times,
          April 30, 1939, p. 20.
                At an arts conference in Colorado Springs Frost says: " 'I
          wish we had something like the prize ring, where we could
          fight to a finish, where work went down on the mat and had its
          arm lifted by the judges at the end.' "

B64   CAREY, FRANCIS E. "Robert Frost at 'Factory' For Making
          'Self-Starters', " Springfield [Mass.] Sunday Union and Repub-
          lican, November 12, 1939, p. 8A.
                Frost, as teacher at Harvard, hopes his students will
          show signs of intelligence.

1940

B65   CLEMENS, CYRIL. "A Chat with Robert Frost, " Mark Twain
          Quarterly, III (Spring 1940), 14-16, 18.
                On a chat with Frost in St. Louis in March 1937 when Frost
          received the Mark Twain medal.

1941

B66   LEE, HENRY. "Frost Owes Success to Not Swallowing Nails, "
          New York World-Telegram, February 4, 1941, p. 3.
                Frost recalls his days as a cobbler's apprentice. He sug-
          gests that he might run for Congress. "'You'd better not say I
          will run from Vermont, ' he said reflectively. 'Vermont hasn't
          heard about it yet.' "

1942

B67   VAN GELDER, ROBERT. "An Interview with Mr. Robert Frost, "
          New York Times Book Review, May 24, 1942, pp. 2, 17.
                Frost provides a scattered account of his life and work.

1946

B68   "Frost Raps War Poets, " New York Times, September 4, 1946,
          Sec. I, p. 21.

B. INTERVIEWS AND TALKS

> "Frost Raps War Poets" (cont.)
> In an interview at Bread Loaf Conference, Frost said that current war poetry is "too crude to be good."

B69   HUTCHENS, JOHN K. "Oracle, Visitor," in "People Who Read and Write," New York Times Book Review, September 15, 1946, p. 12.
> On an interview with Frost at Bread Loaf Conference. Frost commented that he had just read The Great Gatsby and was disappointed by it, saying that, "we are ever so much nastier now than even Fitzgerald was then." Hutchens considers this "the most astonishing literary judgement of the season."

1947

B70   ROY, RUTH. " 'Dean of American Poets,' University's Guest on Charter Day, Maintains That Form in Poetry Comes Naturally in Writing," Daily Californian [Berkeley], March 26, 1947, p. 6.
> " 'The forms, either loose or strict iambic style, are right there,' he explained."

B71   SCHOTT, FRED. "Students, Poet Both Pleased With Talks," Michigan Daily, April 4, 1947, pp. 1, 2.
> Frost's real interest is "Americana." He also says he wrote "Spring Pools" in Ann Arbor.

1949

B72   BREIT, HARVEY. "Talk With Robert Frost," New York Times Book Review, November 27, 1949, p. 20.
> "I am not a regionalist: I am a realist. I write about realms of democracy and realms of spirit. The land is always in my bones."

B73   HUTCHENS, JOHN K. "Vermonter" in "On the Books -- On An Author" section, New York Herald Tribune Book Review, XXVI, December 4, 1949, p. 2.
> Frost: "I write [poems] to see if I can make them sound different from each other."

B. INTERVIEWS AND TALKS

1950

B74   "Poet Frost Sees Solution To World Ills in 20 Acres, " New York
         Times, March 25, 1950, p. 19.
               Sees solution to world problems in 20 acres "for every
         man"; Senate votes birthday greetings.

1952

B75   POTTER, JOHN MASON. "Robert Frost Lives on Poetry, " Boston
         Post Magazine, April 27, 1952, p. 7.
               An interview at Frost's home in Cambridge. Some of
         Frost's comments:
               Without prosperity the arts suffer.
               I have never learned to typewrite.
               I don't like a too technical interest in verse, even though
               I am a versifier. It is the tune that I am interested in.

B76   MC KENNA, PATSY, AND ALAN GUSSOW. [Untitled], Middlebury
         Campus, XLIII (May 15, 1952), 9.
               A tour of Frost's summer house at Ripton, Vermont.
         Frost comments on subjects from Eliot to fraternities.

B77   HAMBURGER, PHILIP. "Men of Faith" in "Television" section
         New Yorker, XXVIII (December 13, 1952), 167-69.
               Interview with Frost at seventy-seven at Ripton. "He had
         a great many things to say. " Frost comments on courage,
         farming, teaching, and newspapers.

1953

B78   COON, HENRY. "Robert Frost: Opinions On Education, Thought, "
         Amherst Student, LXIV (October 19, 1953), 1, 2.
               Frost is "a curious admixture of farmer and intellectual. "
         Points out the poet's knowledge of Latin and Greek even though
         he avoids classical allusions in his poetry. Quotes Frost: "I'm
         a lazy writer. . . . I've lived a lot more than I've written. "
         Frost claims that writers have no need of literature courses;
         they are for readers. He feels writers should read history,
         science, and philosophy.

B. INTERVIEWS AND TALKS

1954

B79   FREEMAN, IRA HENRY. "Frost at 80 Tells World To Relax,"
        New York Times, March 26, 1954, p. 23.
            Frost says men "must learn by 'craft and courage' to keep
        the world from hurrying and crowding him too much."

B80   HORNADAY, MARY. "Frost Scorns Hydrogen-Bomb Tremors,"
        Christian Science Monitor, March 26, 1954, p. 1.
            Frost comments on the "wildness" of poetry. "Poetry is
        the place where wildness lives. . . . It's where wild things
        live."

B81   "A Poet Reflects," Newsweek, XLIII (April 5, 1954), 46.
            Interview the day before Frost was eighty. Frost com-
        ments on McCarthyism, life, freedom, and poetry; says he is
        one-half teacher, one-half farmer, and one-half poet.

B82   BREIT, HARVEY. "In and Out of Books" column, New York Times
        Book Review, April 11, 1954, p. 8.
            On Frost's 80th birthday. Frost says "I am not quite a
        liberal -- because I find I can never take my own side of the
        argument."

B83   "Robert Frost, 80, Gives A Recipe for Diplomats," New York
        Times, August 11, 1954, p. 27.
            Gives views on international relations; interview, Rio de
        Janeiro. " 'Decency, honor, and not too much deceit . . . are
        about the best one can aspire to in international relations.'"

B84   COOK, REGINALD. "Deeds That Count Are Liberties Taken with
        the Conventions," The Listener, LII (August 26, 1954), 319-20.
            Interview at Middlebury College when Thoreau's Walden
        was honored. Frost's comment was that the book was "every-
        thing from a tale of adventure. . . to a declaration of inde-
        pendence and a gospel of wisdom."

B85   BALL, MARKHAM. "Robert Frost -- Farmer, Poet, Speaker --
        Reminisces On His Life," Amherst Student, LXV (November 1,
        1954), 3.
            Frost "does not take himself seriously" though "there are
        others eager to do so."

1955

B86   SHERRILL, JOHN. "Robert Frost: A Strange Kind of Laziness, "
       Guideposts, X (August 1955), 1-5.
           An interview aimed at "what God meant to him [Frost] in
       his poetry. " Frost refuses to be pinned down. A poem's
       meaning is as each reader sees it. "It must be personal with
       you. "

B87   COOK, REGINALD L. "A Walk with Frost, " Yankee, XIX (Novem-
       ber 1955), 18-26.
           Describes walks with Frost in and around Ripton, Vermont.

B88   HANDY, MARY. "Something Brave to Do, " Christian Science
       Monitor, December 21, 1955, p. 9.
           Quotes Frost: "Nearly everybody is looking for something
       brave to do. I don't see why people shouldn't write poetry.
       That's brave. " Frost feels there aren't enough poets. Too
       many people who have poetry in them become English teachers
       and spend all their time reading papers. Also reveals that he
       "has never written a thing in the afternoon. "

B89   "Frost Suggests Career In Arts as Bravery Test, " New York Times,
       December 26, 1955, p. 17.
           Frost on hardship of poetry as career in NBC TV interview.

1956

B90   "American Poetry from 1912 to the Present, " American Academy of
       Arts and Letters and The National Institute of Arts and Letters
       Proceedings. Second Series. Number Six. New York, 1956.
       Pp. 61-70.
           "Mr. Frost interspersed his reading with a running com-
       mentary, selections from which follow . . . . "

B91   GROSS, LEONARD. "Wise Man, " Collier's, CXXXVII (April 27,
       1956), 42.
           Interview done on educational TV. "In four days of ram-
       bling discourse, Frost provided a sampling of the wit and wis-
       dom that stamp a man as wise. " At 82 Frost says "Ultimately
       this is what you go before God for: You've had bad luck and
       good luck and all you really want in the end is mercy. "

B. INTERVIEWS AND TALKS

B92   "A Talk for Students," The Fund for the Republic, June 7, 1956,
        pp. 1-16.
            An extemporaneous talk at the 28th annual commencement
        of Sarah Lawrence College, Bronxville, New York, June 7, 1956.

B93   "Frost Finds U. S. 'Freest of Free'," New York Times, December
        24, 1956, p. 15.
            Discusses freedom in U. S.; interview on Meet the Press
        TV program; is first poet who is program's guest on "live"
        show.

B94   BRINKLEY, DAVID, AND LAWRENCE SPIVAK. " 'I Like My
        Freedom Best; It's Like Old Clothes, Mine Fits Me' Robert
        Frost," Boston Sunday Globe, December 30, 1956, Sec. A, p. 5.
            Interview on "Meet the Press." Frost recites a poem on
        freedom, "The Gift Outright." ... both poetry and freedom
        have their own discipline.

1957

B95   "Frost Disclaims A 'Literary Life'," New York Times, May 19,
        1957, p. 87.
            Comments on his upcoming trip to England; discusses his
        career.

B96   "Robert Frost Still 'Goes On And On For Our Delight,'" Manchester
        Guardian, May 31, 1957, p. 16.
            Interview when Frost was on English tour. Frost com-
        ments on Edward Thomas, liberals, and poetry. Article says,
        "He merely had the appearance of a great man."

1958

B97   NELSON, JAMES, ed. Wisdom: Conversation With the Elder Wise
        Men of Our Day. New York: Norton, 1958. Pp. 13-23.
            Frost speaks of courage, poetry, his childhood, politics,
        and philosophy.
            Interview with Bela Kornitzer. Frost claims he wrote
        "Stopping by Woods" in 20 minutes. Denies that the poem is
        "a suicide poem." Frost describes his father. Concludes:
        "Freedom lies in being bold."

B. INTERVIEWS AND TALKS

B98   LEWIS, C. DAY. "It Takes a Hero to Make a Poem," Claremont
        Quarterly, V (Spring 1958), 27-34.
                A conversation broadcast over the B.B.C. September 13,
        1957. Frost: "A poet never takes notes. You never take notes
        in a love affair."

B99   BARBER, CARTER. "A Poet Speaks of Poets," Los Angeles Times,
        May 22, 1958, Part 3, p. 5.
                Frost comments on Ezra Pound and his part in securing
        Pound's release from St. Elizabeth's Hospital.

B100   BARRON, JOHN. "Frost Knows How to Lobby for the Arts,"
        Washington Evening Star, May 22, 1958, p. A-25.
                After his work in helping to get Ezra Pound released,
        Frost says he feels more like a lawyer than a poet.

B101   FURMAN, BESS. " 'Poet in Waiting' Turns to Artists," New York
        Times, October 16, 1958, p. 39.
                Frost tells a news conference at Library of Congress that
        he wants to borrow four famous paintings to hang in his office
        to help him "get out of the small potatoes class."

B102   BRACKER, MILTON. "The 'Quietly Overwhelming' Robert Frost,"
        New York Times Magazine, November 30, 1958, pp. 15, 57,
        58-59, 62.
                "At 84 the new poetry consultant to the Library of Congress
        looks like the symbol of a poet. And he can move his hearers
        to an 'admiration bordering on awe'."

B103   "Frost Complains Of Lack of Work," New York Times, December
        10, 1958, p. 21.
                Poetry Consultant Frost calls news conference in jest to
        complain he is not being consulted enough; cites few requests
        by Supreme Court and White House.

B104   MC GRORY, MARY. "Poet Frost Aspires To Be A Senator, So He
        Can Give Advice on Anything," Washington Evening Star,
        December 10, 1958, p. 29.
                At a Library of Congress press conference, Frost, as
        Poetry Consultant, complains at not being consulted.

B. INTERVIEWS AND TALKS

1959

B105   SKOGSTAD, KATHERINE. "Frost Battles Here For Individualism,"
       Atlanta Journal, January 31, 1959, p. 6.
              Remarks at Agnes Scott College, Decatur, Georgia, on the
       previous day.
              "Too long we have adhered to this doctrine of original sin
       which says, 'I'm to blame because Adam fell out of an apple
       tree' or 'We must share our table with the humble and stupid
       because it is our fault they're stupid.' ... It is simply not true."

B106   LATHEM, EDWARD CONNERY. "Freshman Days," Dartmouth
       Alumni Magazine, LI (March 1959), 16-22.
              Cover photographs and excerpts from New Yorker, (De-
       cember 13, 1952), 167-69.
              Frost recalls his term as freshman at Dartmouth. He
       left Dartmouth because "I sort of lost my interest."

B107   CIARDI, JOHN. "Robert Frost: Master Conversationalist at Work,"
       Saturday Review of Literature, XLII (March 21, 1959), 17-20,
       54.
              Frost talks of his age, his forthcoming book, The Great
       Misgiving, and poetry. Says the poet believes that poetry is
       the "singing of our race." Calls a poem an "arrest of disor-
       der." Also quotes Frost: "I want to write two or three hard
       poems that will be hard to get rid of."

B108   PETERSEN, ANNA. "Robert Frost, on 85th Birthday, Romps
       Through Interview Here," New York Times, March 27, 1959,
       p. 21.
              Interview; sees Senator John F. Kennedy as next President;
       caricature by Oscar Berger.

B109   MORRISON, CHESTER. "A visit with Robert L. Frost," Look,
       XXIII (March 31, 1959), 76-78, [80-81].
              "His voice and his hands are not as firm as they once were.
       But his opinions get firmer all the time . . . . His rambling,
       yet organized, talk is not something a sensible listener wants
       to interrupt. . . ."

B110   DOLBIER, MAURICE. "Press Conference: Robert Frost at 85,"
       New York Herald Tribune Book Review, April 5, 1959, p. 2.

B. INTERVIEWS AND TALKS

DOLBIER, MAURICE (cont.)
"Science cannot be scientific about poetry, but poetry can be poetical about science. It's bigger, more inclusive."

B111 LORENZ, CHARLES J. "A Visit with Robert Frost," Dubuque [Iowa] Telegraph-Herald, April 14, 1959, p. 6.
Frost shines at Loras College, but is hounded by reporters. " 'You can't do this to me', he remarked. 'This is inhuman.'"

B112 LORENZ, CHARLES J. "We Called on Robert Frost," The Spokesman (Loras College, Dubuque, Iowa), LVI (Summer 1959), 18-24.
An account of Frost's visit in April. He comments on "poetic duplicity" and his refusal to explicate.

B113 "On Emerson," Daedalus: Journal of the American Academy of Arts and Sciences, LXXXVIII (Fall 1959), 712-718.
Upon receiving the first Emerson-Thoreau medal given by the Academy.

1960

B113a POIRIER, RICHARD. "The Art of Poetry: Robert Frost," Paris Review, Vol. VI, No. 24 (1960), pp. 88-120.

B113b Reprinted in Writers at Work: The Paris Review Interviews (Second Series), New York: Viking Press, 1963. Pp. 7-34.
Frost comments on his stay in England, his reading, and Ezra Pound. Frost: "I look at a poem as a performance. I look on the poet as a man of prowess, just like an athlete. He's a performer. And the things you can do in a poem are various."

B114 ROGERS, W. G. "Of Books and Men" column, Denver Post, April 7, 1960, p. 32.
During National Library Week, Frost talks on the importance of books and libraries.

B115 "Statement of Robert Frost, Honorary Consultant in the Humanities, Library of Congress," Congressional Record, Vol. 218 [1960], pp. 9-19.
Testimony before U.S. Senate Subcommittee on Education,

B. INTERVIEWS AND TALKS

"Statement of Robert Frost, . . ." (cont.)
May 5, 1960, in behalf of the establishment of a National
Academy of Culture.

B116   "I Want Poets Declared Equal To . . . ," New York Times Magazine,
May 15, 1960, pp. 23, 105-06.
Excerpts from Frost's testimony in support of creating a
National Academy of Culture.

B117   JUNKINS, DONALD. "Mountain Interval: A Visit with Robert Frost
in Ripton, Vermont," Indian Literature (New Delhi), III (April
- September 1960), 30-37.
Frost comments on a variety of things including pornogra-
phy and Ezra Pound.

B118   KAHN, ROGER. "A Visit With Robert Frost," Saturday Evening
Post, LLXXXIII (November 19, 1960), 26-27, 93-94, 97-98.
Frost, at home in Ripton, gives his views on democracy,
Fidel Castro, sports, and poetry.

1961

B119   "A New England Tribute," Official Program. Inaugural Ceremonies
of John F. Kennedy . . . and Lyndon Johnson . . . Washington,
D. C.: Kennedy-Johnson Inaugural Committee, January 20, 1961,
p. 43.
An early version of Frost's introduction, with an incomplete version of "The Gift Outright."

B120   UBELL, EARL. "Robert Frost to 'Rumple' Israeli Students," New
York Herald Tribune, March 10, 1961, p. 19.
At a press conference, Frost said: "I'll simply rumple
their brains fondly. . . you have to put in the word fondly. . . ."

B121   DOLBIER, MAURICE. "More From Robert Frost," New York
Herald Tribune, March 14, 1961, p. 27.
At his press conference Frost said he would be in Israel
only ten days. "I've got America to tend to."

B122   STONE, EDWARD. "The Middle Name is Lee," Ohio Alumnus, XL
(April 1961), 12, 26.
A recollection of Frost's visit and talk at Ohio University
the previous year.

B. INTERVIEWS AND TALKS

B123   WOLFE, THOMAS. "Poet Frost's Coffee Hour Gives Press Strong Taste of His Ideas," Washington Post, May 2, 1961, p. Bl.
    "I like anything that penetrates the mysteries. And if it penetrates straight to hell, then that's all right, too."

B124   "Poet Frost's 'Kaffeeklatsch' A Frost as Coffee Gets Cold," Denver Post, May 2, 1961, p. 5.
    The reporters' coffee got cold as they scribbled quotable quotes. Frost covers several topics, including the burden of literary manuscripts.

B125   "The Poet as Performer" and "No Tears in the Writer," in "Treasure Chest" column, New York Times Book Review, June 11, 1961, p. 2.
    Excerpts from interview with Frost published in Paris Review.

B126   "Remarks on the Occasion of the Tagore Centenary," Poetry, XCIX (November 1961), 106-19.
    Frost reads Tagore's poetry and his own.
    "From the tape-recording of a talk given on April 19, 1961, at Town Hall, New York, under the sponsorship of the Asia Society." Frost finds Tagore a statesman and an artist for art's sake.

B127   HARRIS, MARK. "Old Enough to Know, Young Enough to Care," Life, LI (December 1, 1961), [101], [103] - 04, 106, 108, 110, 113, 116, 119, 120, 122. [113, 116, 119].
    Interview at Ripton deals with Frost and Sandburg. "I'm always saying something that's just the edge of something more. Symbols are what fly off everything."

1962

B128   "Introduction" to Frederic Fox, 14 Africans vs. One American. New York: Macmillan, 1962. Pp. xi-xix.
    From a Boston address taped by radio station WGBH December 3, 1961.

B129   "Between Prose and Verse," Atlantic Monthly, CCIX (January 1962), 51-54.
    Frost speaks at Breadloaf on the importance of meter and

G. PARTS OF BOOKS

WHICHER, GEORGE (cont.)
A discussion of American writers as to whether or not they are academic. Says Frost "may be loosely associated with the scholarly group. Though he has been a loyal friend of many professors, . . . his interest in education has been like the fearful fascination felt by monkeys for a basket with a snake in it. He has made free with colleges, loving the intercourse with young minds, but distrustful of all kinds of all forms of institutionalism."

G73   BROOKS, CLEANTH. An Approach to Literature. Third edition. New York: Appleton-Century-Crofts, 1952. Pp. 305-07, 346-47.
A discussion of "The Wood Pile" and "The Need of Being Versed in Country Things."

G74   DEUTSCH, BABETTE. "Glove of a Neighborhood." In her Poetry in Our Time. New York: Henry Holt, 1952. Pp. 55-78[61-78] and passim.
Discusses the rural New England aspects of Frost's poetry and gives special attention to "Acquainted With the Night" and "Come In."

G75   RAIZISS, SONA. The Metaphysical Passion: Seven Modern American Poets and The Seventeenth-Century Tradition. Philadelphia: University of Pennsylvania Press, 1952. P. 14.
Frost is "not technically metaphysical."

G76   SCHERMAN, DAVID E., AND ROSEMARIE REDLICH. Literary America. New York: Dodd, Mead, 1952. Pp. 116-17.
Frost "has brought a freshness into American poetry which until then had been staggering under the load of romantic sentimentality."

G77   WEST, HERBERT FAULKNER. John Sloan's Last Summer. Iowa City, Iowa: Prairie Press, 1952. Pp. 30-32.
Anecdote concerning Frost's hospitalization in 1951.

G78   WILSON, EDMUND. The Shores of Light: A Literary Chronicle of the Twenties and Thirties. New York: Farrar, Straus, and Young, 1952. P. 111.
"Robert Frost has a thin but authentic vein of poetic sensi-

B. INTERVIEWS AND TALKS

"The Poet Laureate" (cont.)
poetry at public readings.

B138   "Nothing More Gentle Than Strength, " New Republic, CXLVI (April
9, 1962), 21-22.
On how it feels to be an American.

B139   "Poet's Reflections on America and the World, " U.S. News and
World Report, LII (April 9, 1962), 55.
Quotations from an interview on Frost's eighty-eighth
birthday, after receiving a medal from President Kennedy,
authorized by Congress.

B140   TALESE, GAY. "Y.M.H.A. Here Shares 88th Birthday With Frost,
New York Times, April 16, 1962, p. 34.
Frost receives a citation from Y.M.H.A. Frost says:
"There's more poetry outside of verse than in; more religion
outside of church than in; more love outside of marriage than
in. "

B141   "Campus Revisited, " Michigan Alumnus, LXVIII (May 1962), 261.
Frost returns to the University of Michigan and says that
there "is a right and a wrong way to read poetry: 'The right
way is like catchy songs. The right way is to like it before
you've studied your way into it.'"

B142   "Robert Frost Farmer Teacher, " Wooster Alumni Bulletin, LXXVI
(June 1962), 12.
Quotations from a talk by Frost at the dedication of the
library building at Wooster College [Ohio], May 19, 1962.
"One time I was asked, 'Is New England in a state of decay?'
My answer was, 'If it is, it's the richest compost heap in the
nation.'"

B143   TOPPING, SEYMOUR. "Robert Frost Talks and Jokes With Moscow
Pupils and Poets, " New York Times, September 2, 1962, pp.
1, 7.
Frost finds an "uncommon enthusiasm" in Moscow for the
arts. Adds that he intends to tease the Russians a little.

B144   MILLER, DAVID. "A 'Tramp Poet' Chats With A 'Ruffian', " New
York Herald Tribune, September 9, 1962, pp. 1, 24.

G. PARTS OF BOOKS

COFFIN, ROBERT TRISTRAM (cont.)
Tenn.: George Peabody College, 1954. Pp. 31-36.
Reprint of lecture delivered on July 12, 1951, on the revolution in poetic diction. Language is becoming "the sharp words, the exact words, the words on people's lips in times of excitement and depression." Frost is a pioneer in this language revolution.

G86   KUNITZ, STANLEY, AND HOWARD HAYCRAFT, eds. Twentieth Century Authors: A Biographical Dictionary of Modern Literature. New York: Wilson, 1955. Pp. 345-46.
Biographical sketch.

G87   MEARS, LOUISE W. They Come and Go: Short Biographies. Boston: Christopher, 1955. Pp. 94-95.
Describes a Frost reading. "When Frost finished. . . there was . . . a silent tribute to the poem and the author."

G88   MEDINA, HAROLD R. "Birthday Dinner, Robert Frost." In Maxine B. Virtue, ed., Judge Medina Speaks: A Group of Addresses by Harold R. Medina. New York: Bender, 1954. Pp. 295-98.
Remarks at the celebration of the 80th birthday of Frost, March 25, 1954. "I have no license to discuss poetry and I shall not do so except by indirection. . . . Robert Frost is a creative artist of the first rank; his humanism has a touch of the universal in it. . . . Can one doubt that Robert Frost is the greatest living interpreter of the spirit of America and perhaps the greatest of all time?"

G89   TATE, ALLEN. Sixty American Poets 1896-1944. Washington: Library of Congress, 1954. Pp. 53-58.
Frost "has produced a body of poetry which is as impressive as any of our time." Gives checklist by Frances Cheney of early works, collections, and criticism, and a checklist of recordings.

G90   RICHARDS, ROBERT F., ed. Concise Dictionary of American Literature. New York: Philosophical Library 1955. Pp. 89-90.
Biographical sketch of Frost.

B. INTERVIEWS AND TALKS

B151 LATHEM, EDWARD CONNERY, ed. "Robert Frost on 'Extrava-
gance'," Dartmouth Alumni Magazine, LVI (March 1963), 21-24.
Frost, in his last college lecture, comments on extrava-
gance in nature, politics, and good literature.

POSTHUMOUSLY PUBLISHED

B152 DREW, FRASER B. "A Teacher Visits Robert Frost," New York
State Education, LI (December 1963), 20-21.
A reminiscence of a brief visit with Frost in Ripton "not
too many years ago."

B153 "Before The Beginning and After The End of A Poem," The Carrell:
Journal of the Friends of the University of Miami Library, VI
(December 1965), 6-8.
Extemporaneous remarks at the Winter Institute in 1931.
Frost recalls a conversation with Wallace Stevens.

B154 BREIT, HARVEY, ed. "Robert Frost Speaks Prose," Esquire,
LXIV (December 1965), 230, 308.
Subtitle: "In herky-jerky sentences, a verbatim talk with
the poet about art, freedom and the gift of hate."

B155 LAING, DILYS (ed. by Alexander Laing). "Interview With a Poet,"
Southern Review, n.s. (Autumn 1966), 850-54.
Frost: "It is well known that the poet cannot attain the
proper poetic frenzy unless he starves. Can you imagine Cas-
sandra understanding the oracle after steak and onions?"

B156 LATHEM, EDWARD C., ed. Interviews with Robert Frost. New
York: Holt, Rinehart and Winston, 1966.
Reprints B2, B3, B4, B5, B7, B15, B17, B19, B26, B27, B29,
B44, B46, B47, B55, B57, B63, B69, B70, B71, B73, B74, B76,
B77, B78, B82, B83, B84, B86, B92, B93, B94, B96, B98, B99,
B100, B102, B108, B111, B112, B113, B116, B118, B119, B121, B125,
B128, B129, B131, B132, B133, B134, B141, B144.

B157 HUDSON, ARTHUR PALMER, ed. "A Trip to Currituck, Elizabeth
City, and Kitty Hawk (1894)," North Carolina Folklore, XVI
(May 1968), 3-8.
Transcription of a tape-recorded conversation, March 31,

B. INTERVIEWS AND TALKS

HUDSON, ARTHUR PALMER (cont.)
1961, in Chapel Hill, North Carolina.

B158   QUINAN, DOROTHY C. " 'Poet is a Praise Word,'" Yankee,
        XXXIII (September 1969), 91, 120, 123, 124, 125.
            A reminiscence of Frost at Ripton.
            " 'Poet is a praise word. I never call myself a poet. It's
        like a girl telling you how beautiful she is. Let it come from
        another source,' he growled."

B159   "A Tribute to Wordsworth," Cornell Library Journal, No. 11
        (Spring 1970), 77-99.
            An address given at Cornell University April 20, 1950,
        recorded on tape.

C. PUBLISHED LETTERS

C1   "Frost, Robert," Autograph Album, I (December 1933), 56.
          Brief description of autograph letter signed by Frost. In-
      cludes a paragraph on Pound. "I think him the real poet of all
      this modernismus."

C2   UNTERMEYER, LOUIS, ed. The Letters of Robert Frost to Louis
      Untermeyer. New York: Holt, Rinehart and Winston, 1963.
      388 pp.
          Includes an introduction and a running account of the two
      poets' friendship.

C3   THOMPSON, LAWRANCE, ed. Selected Letters of Robert Frost.
      With Introduction. New York: Holt, Rinehart and Winston,
      1964. 645 pp.
          Letters, from first notes in high school until before his
      death in 1963.

C4   GRADE, ARNOLD, ed. Family Letters of Robert and Elinor Frost.
      Foreword by Lesley Frost. Albany: State University of New
      York Press, 1972. 293 pp.
          Contains 183 previously unpublished letters, 133 written by
      Robert Frost and 50 by Elinor Frost.

D. NEWS ITEMS

D1   B[ARTLETT], J[OHN] T. "Formerly at Pinkerton: Robert Frost Gaining a Reputation As a Writer of Choice Poems," Derry News [N.H.], November 7, 1913, p. 8.

D2   DOLE, NATHAN HASKELL. "A Migration of Poets," Bellman, XVIII (April 24, 1915), 532-33.
      A note on Frost's stay with the Dole family in March 1915, describing Frost's activities in and around Boston. He was beginning to meet certain influential American writers such as Amy Lowell.

D3   "Tufts College: Phi Beta Kappa Initiates New Members and Elects Officers," Boston Evening Transcript, May 6, 1915, p. 16.
      Frost read "The Sound of Trees," "The Road Not Taken," and "Birches."

D4   "Short Stories in Verse," New York Evening Post, June 11, 1915, p. 14.
      Editorial. "Disguised as poetry, the very short story is finding a market."

D5   "Abbot Academy Notes," Andover Townsman, January 14, 1916, p. 4.
      On Frost's reading at the Academy on January 13, 1916.
"He read as if he loved to do it, and at once gained the sympathy of his audience by his humor, frankness and very interesting personality. . . ."

D6   "Boston Association," Dartmouth Alumni Magazine, VIII (March 1916), 231.
      Brief mention of Frost's reading before the Dartmouth Alumni Association in Boston.

D7   "Lawrence Born Poet Lectures: Robert Frost Talks on 'The Sound of Poetry' in White Fund Course," Lawrence Telegram, Janu-

D. NEWS ITEMS

"Lawrence Born Poet. . ." (cont.)
   ary 20, 1916, p. 1.
      A report of Frost's reading and talk the previous day.
   The headline is in error; Frost was born in San Francisco.

D8   Exeter [N. H.] News-letter, January 21, 1916, p. 1.
         Announcement of Frost's upcoming reading on January 26.
      A brief report appeared on January 28, p. 1.

D9   "Well Known Poet Gives Reading of His Verses," Amherst Student,
         April 10, 1916, p. 1.
            On Frost's reading and talk on April 8.

D10   "Noted American Poet To Succeed Prof. Churchill," Amherst Stu-
         dent, December 18, 1916, p. 1.
            "Mr. Frost will take over two courses already begun by
         Professor Churchill, a special Senior seminar on the theory of
         poetry and an elective for Juniors on the rise and development
         of the English drama. He will also work with a Freshman
         section in composition."

D11   "Briefs," Amherst Student, March 26, 1917, p. 6.
            "An innovation has been introduced into Prof. Robert
         Frost's course in pre-Shakespearean drama. Several plays
         have been abridged by members of the class for dramatic use,
         and will be presented in College Hall."

D12   "Professor Frost at C[hristian] A[ssociation]," Amherst Student,
         November 5, 1917, pp. 1, 3.
            "Professor Frost's entire talk was given in an interesting
         manner and explained the attitude of the poet to his listeners.
         He concluded his readings with a serious poem ending in 'The
         glory of God is all in all.'"

D13   "Masquers To Present Play By Prof. Frost," Amherst Student,
         February 3, 1919, p. 1.
            Frost will also choose the actors for "The One Way"[sic].

D14   "Robert Frost's Play 'A Way Out' To Be Produced," Amherst Stu-
         dent, February 17, 1919, p. 1.

D. NEWS ITEMS

D15   "The Masquers, " <u>Amherst Student,</u> February 27, 1919, p. 1.
       "A Way Out" was well received and drew "appreciative applause. "

D16   "Robert Frost Reads Poems, " <u>Bennington</u> [Vt.] <u>Banner,</u> September 26, 1919, p. 3.
       On Frost's reading before the Poetry Society of Southern Vermont. "To the large and breathlessly attentive audience . . . , he read poem after poem as though he were that moment composing them; as though they were as new to him as to anyone. "

D17   "Literature and the Colleges, " <u>Christian Science Monitor,</u> October 18, 1920, p. 3.
       Quotation from Frost's letter to the Reeling and Writhing Club of Bryn Mawr College.

D18   "News and Views, " <u>Harvard Alumni Bulletin,</u> XXIII (March 3, 1921), 497-98.
       Comments favorably on new Fellowships in Creative Art.

D19   <u>Regents Proceedings</u> (University of Michigan), June 1921, p. 224.
       President Burton reports a gift of $5, 000 to provide a fellowship for Frost. The gift is from the Hon. Chase S. Osborne.

D20   "Robert Frost, the Poet, To Come to the University, " <u>Michigan Alumnus,</u> XXVII (August 1921), 600-01.
       "Mr. Frost will do no teaching in the University, nor will he be expected to accomplish anything definite, unless he has something authentic to say. "

D21   "Frost Goes West of Boston, " <u>Christian Science Monitor,</u> October 4, 1921, p. 4.
       On Frost's going to the University of Michigan to become Poet-in-Residence.

D22   STEWART, BERNICE. "Robert Frost Comes to Ann Arbor, " <u>Detroit Free Press,</u> October 16, 1921, Magazine Section, p. 5.
       "May this country keep him! And more especially may Ann Arbor keep him, not for a year but for years, for his whimsical humor, his honesty and his very flawless art add

D. NEWS ITEMS

STEWART (cont.)
markedly to the beauty of the world."

D23   "Robert Frost--Michigan's Guest," Michigan Alumnus, XXVIII
(October 20, 1921), 43-45.
The writer suspects the academic atmosphere at Michigan
will more likely be changed than Frost's poetry will. Frost is
"absolutely authentic."

D24   MEISS, EDWIN R. "Robert Frost and the Career of a Poet,"
Michigan Chimes, III (November 1921), 7.
Not verified.

D25   "Coach Yost Vs. Robert Frost," Michigan Daily, April 21, 1922,
p. 2.
Frost is becoming as popular as the University football
coach, which suggests that the "students reverence intellectual
as well as physical prowess."

D26   "Our Fellowship In Creative Art," Michigan Alumnus, XXVIII (May
11, 1922), 837.
"We know of no single influence that has been more pro-
ductive of good results than the influence of Mr. Frost upon
Faculty and students, or contributed more to public regard for
the University."

D27   "The Fellowship in Creative Art," Michigan Alumnus, XXVIII (May
25, 1922), 918-19.
Board of Regents votes to continue the fellowship "provided
funds from a private source shall make it possible."

D28   Regents Proceedings (University of Michigan), June 1922, p. 542.
Honorary Master of Arts degree approved. Frost is "wise,
gracious, and stimulating."

D29   "Did Vermont Have No Candidate?," Editorial, New York Times,
June 9, 1922, p. 14.
On Frost, a resident of New Hampshire, being named
Poet Laureate of Vermont.

D30   GILCHRIST, HALLEY PHILLIPS. "Mr. Frost of Vermont," New
York Times, June 18, 1922, Section 7, p. 8.

D. NEWS ITEMS

GILCHRIST, HALLEY PHILLIPS (cont.)
A letter to the editor correcting errors in the editorial of
June 9.

D31 "Degrees of High Distinction Given to Eleven Today," Michigan
Daily, June 19, 1922, p. 1.
Frost received an honorary Master of Arts degree from
the University of Michigan.

D32 CLEGHORN, SARAH N. "Mr. Frost, Vermont and Free Verse,"
New York Times, June 24, 1922, p. 12.
Letter to the editor in defense of Frost's selection as Poet
Laureate of Vermont.

D33 "The Fellowship in Creative Art," Michigan Alumnus, XXVIII
(August 10, 1922), 1032-33.
Board of Regents will seek a permanent endowment for the
Fellowship.

D34 [FROST, LESLEY]. "LONG TRAIL, 225 MILES, YIELDS TO
YOUTH AND VIGOR. Entire Length Traversed in One Continu-
ous Hike. The First Time on Record. Three Bennington
County Girls and One Boy are the Conquerors." Bennington
[Vt.] Banner, September 13, 1922, p. 1.
On a hike which Frost began but failed to complete.

D35 Regents Proceedings (University of Michigan), October 1922, p. 634.
The Board accepts an anonymous donation of $5,000 to
continue Frost's fellowship.

D36 "Frost Will Again Hold Fellowship in Creative Art," Michigan
Daily, October 10, 1922, p. 1.

D37 Wellesley News, November 2, 1922, p. 2.
On Frost's reading at Wellesley College on October 24.
"As a preface to the usual program of readings, Mr. Robert
Frost, at his recital . . . gave a brief talk to young writers on
the importance of tone in sentences . . . ."

D38 "Robert Frost, New England Poet, Here Thursday, Nov. 16,"
Baylor Lariat, November 11, 1922, p. 1.
"Frost is a great New England poet. He is much like the

D. NEWS ITEMS

"Robert Frost, . . ." (cont.)
great English poet, Browning. He stands well in England,
where he has been most cordially received."

D39   "Robert Frost Reappointed," Michigan Alumnus, XXIX (November
16, 1922), 185.
An anonymous gift of $5,000 enables Regents to reappoint
Frost to the Fellowship in Creative Art.

D40   " 'Second to No U.S. Poet of Today' A Waco Guest," Waco [Texas]
News-Tribune, November 16, 1922, p. 1.
Not verified.

D41   RENICK, DOROTHY. "Frost Reads Own Poems at Baylor," Waco
[Texas] Times-Herald, November 17, 1922, p. 4.
Not verified.

D42   WECTER, DIXON. "Robert Frost Gives Reading . . . Proves That
Some Poets Do Possess a Delightful Sense of Humor," Baylor
Lariat, November 18, 1922, p. 3.
Frost proves Amy Lowell was wrong when she said he was
"utterly devoid of any humorous nature . . . ."

D43   "Turned Away from Big Boston Hotel, Says Robert Frost, Poet,"
Boston Herald, October 18, 1923, p. 6.
"Robert Frost, one of the most distinguished of living
American poets, is telling women's clubs a joke on Boston so
utterly unfair that for the city's good name he must be exposed
before he immortalizes his experience in imperishable verse."

D44   "Frost, Broom and Bat Fight Bizarre Battle," Allegheny College
[Pa.] Campus, XLII (March 25, 1924), 1.
On Frost's killing a bat in the Allegheny College Chapel
during a reading.

D45   "Robert Frost To Arrive Here For Short Stay," Michigan Daily,
March 27, 1924, p. 1.
"Robert Frost . . . will arrive in Ann Arbor Sunday
morning with Mrs. Frost. While in the city, Mr. and Mrs.
Frost will be the guests of Dean Joseph A. Bursley."

D46   Michigan Daily, April 2, 1924, p. 4.
"The Ann Arbor Playmakers are presenting an invitation

Michigan Daily (cont.)
> performance of Robert Frost's one-act tragedy, 'A Way Out,'
> in honor of the author's visit, this evening, in the Dodo Play-
> shop. The audience will be composed of the members of
> Whimsies and the Writers' Club as well as several other
> guests."

D47   C., D. "Frost Reads His Own Poems To Enthusiastic Audience,"
Michigan Daily, April 3, 1924, p. 1.
> Frost "concluded reading poems selected by the audience
> with 'The Star in a Stoneboat'--'and I defy you to understand
> it,' he said."

D48   "Bridges Arrives To Assume Chair," Michigan Daily, April 5,
1924, p. 1.
> On Robert Bridges' arrival to begin a two-month stay as
> poet-in-residence. "Last night, Dr. Bridges and Mrs. Bridges
> were in attendance at the special performance of 'Captain Ap-
> plejack' given by the Comedy Club in honor of the visiting
> schoolmasters. Mr. Robert Frost and Mrs. Frost and Prof.
> Stuart P. Sherman were also present as guests of the Burtons."

D49   "College Notes: The Faculty," Amherst Graduates' Quarterly, XIII
(August 1924), 311.
> Mentions Frost's winning the Pulitzer Prize.

D50   Regents Proceedings (University of Michigan), September 1924,
p. 416.
> "On motion of Regent Sawyer, the Board voted that the post
> of Fellow in Creative Arts on a permanent basis, with stipend
> of $6,000 per year out of University funds, should be tendered
> to Robert Frost beginning with the University year 1925-1926."

D51   "Poet to Return," Michigan Daily, October 10, 1924, p. 1.
> Photograph of a bust of Frost by Aroldo Du Chene announ-
> cing Frost's Fellowship.

D52   "Robert Frost of Ann Arbor," Michigan Daily, October 12, 1924,
p. 4.
> Endorses Frost's Fellowship.

D. NEWS ITEMS

D53   "Whole Campus Rejoices at News of Frost's Return, " in "The Week on the Campus" section, Michigan Alumnus, XXXI (October 16, 1924), 40.
        Short paragraph on Frost's return to Ann Arbor.

D54   "Frost Will Speak At Memorial For President Burton, " Michigan Daily, April 25, 1925, p. 1.
        Frost is chosen by the Board of Regents.

D55   "Frost Will Speak at Burton Memorial Convocation, " in "The Week on the Campus" section, Michigan Alumnus, XXXI (May 9, 1925), 629.
        Announces memorial arrangements for President Burton.

D56   HURD, JOHN, JR. "Poets and Writers Flock to Bowdoin for the Round Table of Literature, " Boston Sunday Globe, May 10, 1925, Editorial and News Feature Section, p. 12.
        Frost at a writer's roundtable at Bowdoin along with Hatcher Hughes, Irving Babbitt, and Edna St. Vincent Millay.

D57   "Frost Arrives To Take Up Residence, " Michigan Daily, October 4, 1925, p. 3.
        The Frosts will be temporary guests of Dean Joseph A. Bursley and Mrs. Bursley.

D58   "We Have With Us This Year, " Michigan Alumnus, XXXII (October 10, 1925), 18.
        Mentions Frost's appointment as Fellow in Letters.

D59   "Robert Frost Reads Verses At Law Club, " Michigan Daily, November 19, 1925, p. 1.
        Frost describes "The Star-Splitter" as "partly legal, partly agricultural, and very immoral!"

D60   ABBOT, WALDO. "Robert Frost -- Professor of English, " Michigan Alumnus, XXXII (December 12, 1925), 208-09.
        On Frost's return as Professor of English.

D61   "Robert Frost Returns to Amherst, " Amherst Graduates' Quarterly, XV (August 1926), 271-73.
        "In his two previous associations with Amherst College Robert Frost created for himself a unique place as a pioneer

"Robert Frost Returns. . ." (cont.)
in what he calls 'detached education,' meaning thereby education conducted by the teacher and undertaken by the student in
the spirit of adventure."

D62   "Amherst College Opens," New York Times, September 24, 1926,
p. 22.
Frost returns to Amherst faculty after his year at Michigan.

D63   "Frost Sponsors Poet Lecturing in Chapel," Amherst Student,
February 3, 1927, p. 1.
"Edward Davison, one of the outstanding young Englishmen
produced by the war, will lecture in Johnson chapel next Monday at 8:30 P.M."

D64   "Davison Discusses Tendencies in Verse," Amherst Student,
February 11, 1927, p. 1.
A report on Edward Davison's lecture, "An Approach to
Poetry," arranged for by Frost.

D65   "Frost To Attend Gridiron Dinner," Michigan Daily, March 25,
1927, p. 1.
"Mr. Frost will arrive in Ann Arbor for a short stay previous to the annual affair and will be the guest of J.A. Bursley,
dean of students."

D66   "Frost Talks To Picked Students," Michigan Daily, March 29, 1927,
p. 1.
Frost talks to "advanced students in composition and
literature . . . ."

D67   "Public Reading Given By Frost," Michigan Daily, April 1, 1927,
p. 1.
On Frost's reading the previous day.

D68   "Frost To Give Two Readings At Mimes," Michigan Daily, March
28, 1928, p. 1.
Frost announces "he will read by request not 'his newer
and better poems but some of the old favorites.'"

D. NEWS ITEMS

D69   "Robert Frost Gives Second Reading Here, " Michigan Daily, March
       31, 1928, p. 8.
              Brief notice of Frost's second and last reading before re-
       turning to his farm.

D70   H., G. "Robert Frost's Poems and Outlook on Life, " Springfield
       [Mass.] Sunday Union and Republican, December 30, 1928,
       p. 7E.
              Uses poems from West-Running Brook to show that Frost
       is "a poet of ideas. "

D71   "Untermeyer Gives Robert Frost First Place Among Modern Poets, "
       Michigan Daily, February 19, 1929, p. 1.
              Close behind, Untermeyer says in an interview, "would
       come Edward [sic] Arlington Robinson, Edna St. Vincent Mil-
       lay, and Robinson Jeffers. "

D72   "Robert Frost Will Give Reading Thursday Night, " Amherst Student,
       March 11, 1929, p. 1.
              Frost will read the works of "an Amherst poet, " but will
       not reveal his identity.

D73   "Frost Interprets J. M. March's Poem, " Amherst Student, March
       18, 1929, p. 1.
              "Professor Robert Frost's reading, previously announced
       as from the works of 'an Amherst poet, ' drew to a close the
       annual series of faculty readings in Williston Hall, at 7:30
       Thursday evening, March 14. The largest group which has
       turned out for any of this year's series was in attendance. "
       Frost reads and discusses March's "The Set Up. "

D74   "Inlander Plans Poetry Contest, " Michigan Daily, April 4, 1929, p. 1.
              Michigan literary magazine to sponsor a contest with
       Frost proposed as judge.

D75   "Frost To Revisit Campus And Town, " Michigan Daily, November
       17, 1929, p. 3.
              Frost will give lectures on April 8 and 9.

D76   "Frost Will Read Poetic Selections At League, Mimes, " Michigan
       Daily, April 4, 1930, p. 1.
              Includes a biographical sketch.

The Critical Reception of Robert Frost

D77   "Robert Frost, Noted Author, Will Read Poetry Selections Today And Tomorrow, " Michigan Daily, April 8, 1930, p. 1.
       "This time, I think I shall speak about 'What Sound a Poem Makes.'"

D78   "Exhibit To Show Faculty Pictures, " Michigan Daily, January 23, 1931, p. 2.
       Portraits by Leon A. Makielski, including one of Frost, will be displayed in Detroit.

D79   "Two Pulitzer Prizes are Won by Women, " New York Times, May 5, 1931, pp. 1, 16.
       Announces Frost's Pulitzer Prize award for The Collected Poems.

D80   "Frost Receives Pulitzer Award, " Michigan Daily, May 6, 1931, p. 1.
       Brief mention of Frost's receiving the Pulitzer Prize.

D81   "Give Medal to Frost to Open Poetry Week, " New York Times, May 25, 1931, p. 16.
       Description of ceremony in which Frost received gold medal for his appointment as national honor poet of Poetry Week.

D82   "Owen D. Young Urges Broader Education, " New York Times, October 13, 1931, p. 5.
       Frost receives honorary degree of Doctor of Humane Letters from Wesleyan University.

D83   "Robert Frost Wins Loines Poetry Prize, " in "The Week on the Campus" section, Michigan Alumnus, XXXVIII (January 30, 1932), 314.
       Frost selected by the National Institute of Arts and Letters to receive the $1, 000 prize.

D84   "Robert Frost to Arrive in City Monday, " Michigan Daily, October 14, 1932, p. 1.
       "Mr. Frost will arrive in Ann Arbor Monday. He will speak before a meeting of graduate students in English and members of the English department at 8 p.m. in the Union.

D. NEWS ITEMS

"Robert Frost. . . " (cont.)
Tuesday Mr. Frost will give readings of his poetry at 4:15 p.m. in Lydia Mendelssohn Theatre."

D85   "Robert Frost Visits In Ann Arbor," in "The Week on the Campus" section, Michigan Alumnus, XXXIX (October 29, 1932), 79.
Frost attends a faculty dinner and the following day gives a reading.

D86   DYER, WALTER A. "Overlooking the Common" column, Amherst Record, March 20, 1935, p. 2.
Laments no celebration for Frost's upcoming sixtieth birthday.

D87   "Milestones In The Life of Robert Frost," Amherst Record, March 20, 1935, p. 6.
A chronology, listing important events in Frost's career.

D88   "A Poet's Word to Youth," New York Times, April 6, 1935, p. 14.
On Frost's optimistic outlook on life.

D89   WICKENDEN, L. D. "Robert Frost Speaks to Large Crowd Here," Amherst Student, May 23, 1935, p. 1.
Frost reads and talks on "how poetry thinks."

D90   WICKENDEN, L. D. "Frost's Second Talk Stresses Originality," Amherst Student, May 27, 1935, p. 1.
Frost talks on "good originality" and "bad originality."

D91   CRAIG, DONALD W. "Professor Frost Delivers Lectures on Poetry," Amherst Record, May 29, 1935, p. 8.

D92   "Crowd Overflows C. U. Theater for Frost's Lecture," Boulder [Colo.] Daily Camera, July 31, 1935, pp. 1, 2.
A crowd of 650 hear Frost say: "A poet has the right to be 'cruelly happy' to hunt for what happiness he can find in life and leave the reform of economic ills of the world to politicians."

D93   KERR, DAVID. "House Packed For First Frost Lecture; Over 150 Attend Dinner Tuesday," Silver and Gold (Univ. of Colorado), August 1, 1935, p. 1.
"One hundred and fifty writers and would-be writers at-

D. NEWS ITEMS

KERR, DAVID (cont.)
tended the writers conference dinner, given in connection with the 6th annual Writers' conference at Blanchard's ranch in Boulder canyon . . . ." Frost is called "America's greatest living poet."

D94 "Well-known Amherst Poet Appears in First Social Union of Season," Massachusetts Collegian, XLVI (November 14, 1935), 1, 6.

D95 "Robert Frost Reads Well-Known Works at Social Union, " Massachusetts Collegian, XLVI (November 21, 1935), 1, 6.

D96 "Pulitzer Prize Poet Gets Harvard Post, " Boston Herald, January 21, 1936, p. 5.
On Frost's appointment as Charles Eliot Norton Professor.

D97 "American Poet to Lecture in Institute of Literature, " Miami Herald, January 27, 1936, p. 5a.
Not verified.

D98 HOLMES, JOHN. "Robert Frost Wins His Fight to Be an Ordinary Man, " Boston Evening Transcript, February 8, 1936, Magazine Section, p. 4.
Subheading: "Next Charles Eliot Norton Lecturer at Harvard, He Comes from a Wooden House in Amherst; Talks Poetry, But Not His Own; and Believes in a University Where Students Are Considered Last."

D99 "Recruit Legislator, " Baltimore Sun, February 27, 1936, p. 10.
Editorial comments on interview published in the Sun on February 26. Deals with Frost's "To a Thinker."

D100 "Poets in Politics, " New York Times, February 28, 1936, p. 20.
On "To a Thinker." On the jabs at Franklin D. Roosevelt and his policies.

D101 DAME, LAWRENCE C. "1000 Hear Robert Frost, Poet, Give Views on Life in Harvard Lecture, " Boston Herald, March 19, 1936, p. 29.
"I must have life around me--violence. You know, we can stand lots of violence before we begin to talk like babies about security."

D. NEWS ITEMS

D102   "The Norton Lectures," Harvard <u>Alumni Bulletin</u>, XXXVIII (March
20, 1936), 777.
      On the enthusiastic reception of Frost's lectures.

D103   HOLMES, JOHN. "Robert Frost as He Talks to Multitudes,"
<u>Boston Evening Transcript</u>, March 21, 1936, Book Section, p. 1.
      Revised and reprinted in <u>Recognition of Robert Frost</u>, as
"Harvard: Robert Frost and the Charles Eliot Norton Lectures
on Poetry."
      "Much of the time he is talking to poets. Surely no one
can get from what he says all that working poets can get."

D104   "Robert Frost's Book Chosen by Book-of-the-Month Club," <u>Am-
herst Record</u>, March 25, 1936, p. 3.
      <u>A Further Range</u> selected.

D105   NEWDICK, ROBERT S. "How a Columbus Mother Helped Her Son
to Become the Dean of America's Living Poets,"
[Ohio] <u>Sunday Dispatch</u>, May 17, 1936, Graphic Section, p. 5.
      Biographical sketch of Isabelle Moodie Frost and then of
Robert Frost.

D106   "The Pulitzer Prizes," <u>New York Times</u>, May 5, 1937, p. 24.
      Mentions Frost in passing.

D107   "Wells Bemoans 'Big-Book' World," <u>New York Times</u>, November 17,
1937, p. 24.
      H.G. Wells, Robert Hillyer, Mark Van Doren, and Frost
participate in the <u>New York Times</u> National Book Fair in
Rockefeller Center.

D108   RITCHEY, JOHN. "Poetry, the Rediscovery of Words," <u>Christian
Science Monitor Weekly Magazine Section</u>, May 4, 1938, pp.
5, 13.
      An overview of several poets. Two paragraphs on Frost.

D109   "Robert Frost Will Lecture In Denver," <u>Denver Post</u>, April 21,
1939, p. 14.
      "Robert Frost, one of America's top-ranking poets, will
give a lecture-recital in Denver on April 26, in Central
Christian Church, sponsored by the Colorado Poetry Fellowship and Theodore Fisher."

D110 "Robert Frost Has Operation," <u>New York Times</u>, January 13, 1940, Sec. I, p. 30.
> Very brief item in which no details of the operation are given, though Frost is reported in satisfactory condition.

D111 "Frost Honorary Head of Poets," <u>New York Times</u>, November 22, 1940, Sec. I, p. 18.
> "The Poetry Society of America announced yesterday that Robert Frost has accepted its honorary presidency, succeeding the late Edwin Markham." (Quoted in its entirety.)

D112 "Frost Receives Medal," <u>New York Times</u>, February 1, 1941, Sec. I, p. 18.
> "Robert Frost received the annual medal presented by the Poetry Society of America at its annual dinner held at the Hotel Biltmore last night."

D113 "Frost Sets Up Poet's Scholarship," <u>New York Times</u>, March 20, 1941, Sec. I, p. 19.
> "Robert Frost has established a scholarship in memory of his late wife, Elinor Frost, at Middlebury College's Bread Loaf School of English."

D114 "War Pledges Given in Princeton Talks," <u>New York Times</u>, June 18, 1941, Sec. I, p. 17.
> Frost receives honorary doctorate. "Robert Frost, recognized by English-speaking peoples everywhere as the most distinguished poet of the generation which brought new life to poetry in America . . . ."

D115 FISCHER, C. M. "Neighbors: Walls No Help," in "Mail-Bag Excerpts" column, <u>New York Times</u>, June 29, 1941, Sec. IV, p. 9.
> Mention of a blunder made by Professor Luther P. Eisenhart in presenting Frost with the Princeton honorary degree. Eisenhart spoke of Frost as believing that good fences make good neighbors.

D116 "Notes on Poets," <u>New York Times</u>, September 6, 1941, Sec. I, p. 14.
> Editorial on Frost's statement that he would as soon play tennis with the net down as write free verse.

D. NEWS ITEMS

D117   "Award to Wilder Is Second For Play," New York Times, May 4,
1943, Sec. I, p. 4.
> Brief biographical notes and photographs of Frost and the
other Pulitzer winners.

D118   CHAMBERLAIN, JOHN. "Books of the Times" column, New York
Times, May 4, 1943, Sec. I, p. 4.
> "As for Robert Frost, whose 'A Witness Tree' has just
made him a four-time Pulitzer winner, the fact that lightning
has struck again in a very familiar spot may argue a shortage
of good poets. But it does not deny Mr. Frost's quality."
(Quoted in its entirety.)

D119   "Pulitzer Prizes," New York Times, May 4, 1943, Sec. I, p. 22.
> "Robert Frost's 'The Witness Tree' is proclaimed the
peak of the year's American poetry. Some poets write themselves out and keep at it after they have ceased to have anything to say. Mr. Frost continues to be fresh and strong."

D120   FISHER, DOROTHY CANFIELD. "Gallery of American Leaders,"
New York Times Magazine, September 24, 1944, pp. 20-21,
46 [20].
> On the coming exhibition of works by Enit Kaufman at
National Museum in Washington, D.C. Includes Kaufman
sketch of Frost.

D121   "Observes 79th Year/University of California Honors Robert Lee
Frost," New York Times, March 23, 1947, Sec. I, p. 63.
> University of California confers honorary degree on Frost
during exercises honoring its seventy-ninth anniversary.

D122   "Frost Recites Poems In Thanks for Award," New York Times,
November 17, 1949, Sec. I, p. 26.
> Mark Van Doren presents medal to Frost at a breakfast at
the Waldorf-Astoria.

D123   HOLMES, JOHN. "Close-up of an American Poet at 75," New York
Times Magazine, March 26, 1950, pp. 12, 72-73, 75-77.
> Describes Frost as both radical and conservative. "He
has deep roots that keep his tree of life nourished and will keep
his memory green."

D. NEWS ITEMS

D124   DAVIDSON, JOHN F. "Radicals, " Letter to the Editor, <u>New York</u>
        <u>Times Magazine</u>, April 9, 1950, p. 4.
           A semantic quibble on "radical. "

D125   PURCELL, W. H. "Poet As Teacher, " Letter to the Editor, <u>New</u>
        <u>York Times Magazine</u>, April 23, 1950, p. 4.
           The writer is "pleased to note that Frost lists himself as
        a teacher" when the profession is so badly thought of.

D126   "Arts Group Hears Key To Wise Rule, " <u>New York Times</u>, May 26,
        1950, p. 21.
           Speaks at annual ceremonial of American Academy and
        National Institute of Arts and Letters. " 'Enslave yourself to
        the right leader's truth', he admonished. "

D127   ADAMS, J. DONALD. "Speaking of Books" column, <u>New York</u>
        <u>Times Book Review</u>, October 22, 1950, p. 2.
           An account of Frost at Kenyon College, Gambier, Ohio,
        for a conference on "The Poet and Reality. "

D128   ADAMS, J. DONALD. "Speaking of Books" column, <u>New York</u>
        <u>Times Book Review</u>, November 12, 1950, p. 40.
           J. D. Adams on mathematics and the arts; cites Prof.
        Marston Morse and Frost views.

D129   "Copy of Frost Book Is Sold for $3,500, " <u>New York Times</u>, Decem-
        ber 13, 1950, p. 32.
           Copy of "Twilight" auctioned for $3,500; that, 230 other
        Frost items bring $14,699.

D130   "Frost's Works On View, " <u>New York Times</u>, March 22, 1951, p. 29.
           Unpublished play, "The Guardeen, " other works shown,
        Morgan Library, New York City.

D131   <u>Michigan Alumnus</u>, LVIII (October 27, 1951), 89.
           Frost, Honorary A.M. ('22), mentioned in "News By
        Classes" as being on the cover of the <u>Atlantic Monthly</u>.

D132   GOULD, JACK. "Radio and Television" column, <u>New York Times</u>,
        November 24, 1952, p. 30.
           Review of Bela Kornitzer's interview on television the
        previous day.

D. NEWS ITEMS

D133 "Pulitzer Prize Poet Wins $5, 000 Academy Award, " New York
Times, March 3, 1953, p. 12.
   Awarded American Poets Academy fellowship.

D134 "North Carolina Honors 5", New York Times, June 9, 1953, p. 16.
   Frost receives honorary degree at the University of
North Carolina at Chapel Hill.

D135 "Robert Frost At Eighty, " New York Times, March 26, 1954, p. 20.
   Editorial describes Frost as an "intensely American
poet. "

D136 POORE, CHARLES. "Books of the Times" column, New York
Times, April 3, 1954, p. 13.
   "Aforesaid" quoted in a review of Gene Fowler, Minutes
of the Last Meeting.

D137 "Book Group Is Honored, " New York Times, May 12, 1954, p. 37.
   Limited Editions Club awards medals to 25 American
authors, illustrators, book designers and printers for
"classics of our time. "

D138 "Writers' Parley On in Brazil, " New York Times, August 10, 1954,
p. 17.
   Brief mention of Frost at International Writers' Congress,
Sao Paulo.

D139 "University to Confer Doctorate Upon Poet, " New York Times,
October 24, 1954, p. 84.
   To get honorary degree, Cincinnati University.

D140 "Theodore Roosevelt 'Radical' Too, Bunche Notes in Receiving
Award, " New York Times, October 28, 1954, p. 37.
   Gets Theodore Roosevelt Association award, along with
Ralph Bunche and others.

D141 "Robert Frost Honored, " New York Times, November 16, 1954,
p. 31.
   Honorary degree, Cincinnati University; lectures under
Elliston Foundation auspices.

D. NEWS ITEMS

D142   "Peak Named For Robert Frost," New York Times, May 20, 1955,
p. 7.
>Vermont House approves naming mountain near Ripton
home for him.

D143   "Dartmouth Gives Frost New Honor," New York Times, June 13,
1955, p. 46.
>Speech, Dartmouth commencement; gets second honorary
degree.

D144   BRACKER, MILTON. "Business Tactics To Save 'Poetry'," New
York Times, November 13, 1955, p. 130.
>Industrial leaders, other prominent figures, to honor
Frost and aid magazine Poetry at Chicago Arts Club fete;
Frost to make public appearance.

D145   "Frost to Get New N.Y.U. Medal," New York Times, March 23,
1956, p. 5.
>Awarded new New York University medal with Latin motto
meaning "to persist and to excel." Photographs of both sides
of the medal.

D146   "Sarah Lawrence Gains," New York Times, June 8, 1956, p. 26.
>Commencement, speeches; Sarah Lawrence College.
"Robert Frost, the poet, urged the graduates to retain all the
cultural hobbies they had pursued in college."

D147   "213 Graduated at Colby," New York Times, June 12, 1956, p. 31.
>At Colby College; gets honorary degree.

D148   "Fifteen Americans Who Made Literary History," New York Times
Book Review, October 7, 1956, pp. 8-9.
>Two pages of photographs of the fifteen, from Stephen
Crane to Faulkner and T.S. Eliot.

D149   "Dartmouth Adds Books," New York Times, January 31, 1957, p. 13.
>Dartmouth College Baker Library gets addition to Frost
collection given by Harold Goddard Rugg.

D150   "Frost to Visit England," New York Times, April 25, 1957, p. 36.
>Frost to visit England on lecture and reading tour spon-
sored by State Department.

D. NEWS ITEMS

D151 "Poet Emplanes for London," New York Times, May 20, 1957,
      p. 17.
          Mentions Frost's departure for England.

D152 "Oxford Honors Frost," Denver Post, June 4, 1957, p. 6.
          Associated Press squib.

D153 "Oxford Honors Robert Frost," New York Times, June 5, 1957,
      p. 37.
          Brief mention that Frost receives honorary degree.

D154 "Robert Frost Honored Again," New York Times, June 14, 1957,
      p. 3.
          Brief mention that Frost receives honorary degree,
      Cambridge.

D155 "Frost Honored in Ireland," New York Times, June 20, 1957, p. 30.
          Gets honorary degree, National Institute of Ireland.

D156 "Robert Frost Honored," New York Times, November 16, 1957,
      p. 16.
          Frosts gets Holland Society medal. Frost describes self
      as an "obstinate nationalist."

D157 "Poetry Is His Purpose," New York Times, January 17, 1958, p. 27.
          Gets American Poetry Society medal; honored at dinner;
      President Eisenhower tribute.

D158 "Poetry Society Again Honors Robert Frost," Denver Post, January
      17, 1958, p. 23.
          Associated Press squib.

D159 "M. Robin Fraser Engaged To Wed," New York Times, January 20,
      1958, p. 17.
          Granddaughter Marjorie Robin Fraser to wed David B.
      Hudnut.

D160 "Frost Dines At White House," New York Times, February 28,
      1958, p. 23.
          Brief mention that Frost is luncheon guest of Presidential
      Assistant Adams and Attorney General Rogers at White House.

D. NEWS ITEMS

D161 "Harvard Radios A Plea For Funds, " New York Times, March 29,
1958, p. 19.
    CBS carries radio program to promote drive for College;
Pusey asks higher pay for faculty; show produced by W. F.
Suchmann aided by group including A. MacLeish; Sen. Kennedy,
others, speak: NYC mayor Wagner proclaims Harvard Day;
fund receives cash or pledges totalling $35 million. Frost
participates.

D162 "Marjorie Fraser Wed in Princeton, " New York Times, April 13,
1958, p. 89.

D163 "U.S. Asked To End Pound Indictment, " New York Times, April 15,
1958, p. 19.
    Frost, backed by other notable poets and writers, asks
Pound's release.

D164 "Poets Carry Day For Ezra Pound, " New York Times, April 20,
1958, Sec. IV, p. E7.
    Comment on role of Frost, Eliot, other poets, in helping
secure Pound's dismissal.

D165 "Names in the News, " Denver Post, May 21, 1958, p. 10.
    Mentions Frost's appointment as Poetry Consultant at the
Library of Congress.

D166 "Frost in Library of Congress Post, " New York Times, May 22,
1958, p. 16.
    On Frost's appointment to Library of Congress as Poetry
Consultant.

D167 SAMPSON, PAUL. "Robert Frost Pays Visit As New 'Poet Laureate', " Washington Post, May 22, 1958, p. C18.
    News conference at the Library of Congress to announce
formally Frost's becoming Poetry Consultant. Frost defines
his duties as "making the politicians and statesmen more a-
ware of their responsibility to the arts. "

D168 "Academy Honors Frost, " New York Times, October 9, 1958, p. 29.
    American Academy of Arts and Sciences medal to Frost.

D. NEWS ITEMS

D169   EDSON, ARTHUR. "America's Dean of Poets Meets the Press,"
        Denver Post, October 16, 1958, p. 6.
            Associated Press account of Frost speaking as Poetry
        Consultant on a variety of subjects.

D170   FURMAN, BESS. " 'Poet in Waiting' Turns To Artists," New York
        Times, October 16, 1958, p. 39.
            Frost takes office; comments on his work and paintings
        he would have in his office; gives first lecture.

D171   "Poem 'Saying' by Frost Packs Auditorium Here," New York Times,
        November 13, 1958, p. 35.
            Frost's "saying" of his poems draws capacity crowd, New
        School for Social Research, New York City; Frost insists he
        "says" poems, does not read them.

D172   "Gathering of Eight Major U.S. Poets 'Pretty Conventional' to Big
        Audience," New York Times, November 16, 1958, p. 137.
            Report of a poetry festival at Johns Hopkins University.
        Frost attends, along with Marianne Moore, E.E. Cummings,
        Archibald MacLeish, John Crowe Ransom, Yvor Winters,
        R.P. Blackmur, and Mark Van Doren.

D173   "Names in the News," Denver Post, November 17, 1958, p. 11.
            Mentions Frost's receiving the Huntington Hartford Award
        for 1958.

D174   "Hartford Foundation Honors Robert Frost," New York Times,
        November 18, 1958, p. 31.
            Huntington Hartford Foundation $5,000 award to Frost.

D175   "Poet Frost Wants To Advise Congress," Denver Post, December
        10, 1958, p. 8.
            " 'I want to be consulted on everything . . . . I don't
        want to run for office,' he said, 'but I want to be a statesman'."

D176   "Poet Named to Succeed Frost as a U.S. Adviser," New York
        Times, March 11, 1959, p. 25.
            Richard Eberhart to succeed Frost as Poetry Consultant.

D177   SALZMAN, ERIC. "1-Act Opera Based On Poem By Frost," New
        York Times, March 24, 1959, p. 47.

SALZMAN, ERIC (cont.)
The Hired Hand by Robert L. Milano produced in Carl
Fischer Hall; based on Frost's Death of the Hired Man.
Milano's work is "slow and inclined toward the sentimental."

D178   "Senate Marks Frost's Birth," New York Times, March 26, 1959,
p. 14.
"The Senate today congratulated Robert Frost, Vermont
poet, on his eighty-fifth birthday tomorrow." (Quoted in its
entirety.)

D179   " 'Rubber Stamp' Opinions Not To Poet Frost's Liking," Denver
Post, March 27, 1959, p. 7.
A.P. quotes Frost as saying, "In theatres what we want
is what is new and different. I want to meet people who have
seen what I have not seen."

D180   ADAMS, J. DONALD. "Speaking of Books" column, New York
Times Book Review, April 12, 1959, p. 2.
Adams disputes remarks made by Professor Trilling at
birthday dinner.

D181   NICHOLS, LEWIS. "In And Out Of Books" section, New York
Times Book Review, April 12, 1959, p. 8.
On Frost's remarks after Lionel Trilling's comments at
Frost's birthday dinner. Describes Frost as "obviously
shaken."

D182   "Conquest of Space Bores Robert Frost," Denver Post, April 22,
1959, p. 6.
"I'd rather go to the Adirondacks . . ." than take a trip in
space, Frost says in A.P. story.

D183   "Dickinson to Honor Frost," New York Times, May 3, 1959, p. 48.
Frost to get Dickinson College first annual arts award of
Wedgewood ceramic medallion and $1,000.

D184   "Letters to the Editor," New York Times Book Review, May 3,
1959, p. 24.
The Trilling controversy continues in eleven letters from
various people.

D. NEWS ITEMS

D185   "Frost Asks Aid to Arts, With Touch of the Poet," New York
Times, May 20, 1959, p. 8.
         Frost suggests government arts department, headed by a
poet; would have post of Cabinet rank, "because poets are
spokesmen while other arts are silent."

D186   "Recent Letters to the Editor," New York Times Book Review,
May 24, 1959, p. 42.
         Letters on the Trilling controversy from William Van
O'Connor and John Gassner in defense of Trilling.

D187   "Tufts Graduates 841," New York Times, June 8, 1959, p. 22.
         Gets honorary degree, Tufts University.

D188   "Frost at Dartmouth," New York Times, June 21, 1959, p. 56.
         Frost receives alumni award, says he "fell in love with
poetry" while a student at Dartmouth.

D189   "Panelists Announced For UNESCO Parley," Denver Post, August
19, 1959, p. 49.
         A.P. squib announces Frost will be on a panel in Denver
to examine "distinctly Western Hemisphere accents in the
fields of literature, music, theater, arts, architecture and
the plastic arts."

D190   "Robert Frost Gets Honorary Post," New York Times, August 29,
1959, p. 15.
         Appointed Library of Congress Consultant in the Humani-
ties; text of acceptance letter to Library of Congress Librarian
Mumford.

D191   TRILLING, LIONEL. "Text," in "Letters To The Editor," New
York Times Book Review, September 20, 1959, p. 32.
         Trilling letter comments on Adams' remarks on Trilling's
speech; urges full text be read in current Partisan Review,
summer issue.

D192   CALLAHAN, JOHN P. "Values Stressed For Nuclear Age," New
York Times, September 30, 1959, p. 39.
         Symposium on future of man held, New York City, by Dis-
tillers Corp.-Seagrams; Frost, Sir Julian Huxley, Lord Russell, D.C. Josephus, Drs. Montagu, Muller, M.S. Eisenhower

D. NEWS ITEMS

CALLAHAN, JOHN P. (cont.)
participate; questioned by W. L. Laurence, Douglas Edwards, Inez Robb.

D193   "TV: A Poetic Discussion," New York Times, October 12, 1959, p. 41.
     Small World program in its seasonal premiere. Frost, A. P. Herbert, Consul General Vasconcellos participate.

D194   "Almost Born in Lewistown / Robert Frost Says / Father Taught Here," Lewistown [Pa.] Sentinel, November 6, 1959, p. 1.

D195   STROUP, J. MARTIN. "Lewistown Academy: Setting for Romance," Lewistown [Pa.] Sentinel, November 13, 1959, pp. 14, 16.
     On Frost's courtship of Elinor White.

D196   "2 Verse Plays By MacLeish And Frost In ANTA Matinee Series," New York Times, November 25, 1959, p. 19.
     A Masque of Reason and Archibald MacLeish's "This Music Crept by Me Upon the Waters." Produced by the American National Theatre and Academy. The masque "received a negligible production."

D197   "Poets Get Salute From Eisenhower," New York Times, January 22, 1960, p. 19.
     Henry Holt and Company first Robert Frost award and various other poetry awards given at American Poetry Society 50th anniversary dinner.

D198   "Book Drive Again," New York Times, January 24, 1960, p. 75.
     Bookshelf Committee formed for Freedom House; Archibald MacLeish heads it.

D199   "Robert Frost Predicts Bostonian President," Denver Post, March 26, 1969, p. 2.
     A. P. story reports Frost's comments on his 85th birthday.

D200   "Poet Is 85," New York Times, March 27, 1960, p. 6.
     Photograph with short cutline. Frost says, "New England sounds awfully alive."

D. NEWS ITEMS

D201   "Hebrew Union Degree Will Honor Poet Today," New York Times,
          April 2, 1960, p. 15.
                  Frost to get honorary degree from Hebrew Union College-
          Jewish Institute of Religion.

D202   "Frost Asks New Status For Poets," Denver Post, May 6, 1960, p. 8.
                  A.P. story quotes Frost as saying "poets are the equal of
          big businessmen."

D203   "Poet Pleads For Bill," New York Times, May 6, 1960, p. 16.
                  Frost backs bill for National Culture Academy, Senate
          Subcommittee.

D204   "'I Want Poets Declared Equal To--,'" New York Times, May 15,
          1960, Sec. VI, p. 23.
                  Some highlights of Subcommittee hearing.

D205   "Robert Frost Chair Set Up At School," New York Times, May 17,
          1960, p. 24.
                  Amherst, Mass., Regional High School sets up teaching
          chair honoring Frost.

D206   "House Favors Frost Medal," New York Times, August 31, 1960,
          p. 10.
                  House of Representatives passes bill authorizing award of
          gold medal for his poetry.

D207   "House Votes Medal For Robert Frost," Denver Post, August 31,
          1960, p. 5.
                  Associated Press squib.

D208   "Robert Frost Honored," New York Times, September 14, 1960,
          p. 16.
                  Bill signed by President Eisenhower to award $2,500 gold
          medal to Frost.

D209   "Poem For Inauguration," New York Times, December 18, 1960,
          p. 36.
                  Frost to read poem at Kennedy's request at Capitol cere-
          monies.

D210   "Inaugural Book A Literary Event," <u>New York Times</u>, December 26, 1960, p. 14.
        Inaugural Committee Program Chairman Milton Kronheim details plans; Kennedy, other contributors, noted.

D211   "Memory Aids Eyes; Poet Outshines Sun," <u>Denver Post</u>, January 21, 1961, p. 2.
        The Associated Press account.

D212   "Robert Frost Adds Poet's Touch," <u>New York Times</u>, January 21, 1961, p. 9.
        Recites his poem, "The Gift Outright," at President Kennedy's inauguration; unable to read verses written as preface because of glare and wind. Includes "The Preface" and "The Gift Outright."

D213   "Sunday Caller," <u>New York Times</u>, January 23, 1961, p. 12.
        Photograph of Frost being taken on White House tour by President Kennedy.

D214   RESTON, JAMES. "Poetry and Power Is the Formula," <u>New York Times</u>, January 25, 1961, p. 32.
        Reston on Frost's advice to Kennedy not to fear power.

D215   "3 Poets to Write U.S. Center Creed," <u>New York Times</u>, February 8, 1961, p. 27.
        Frost, Carl Sandburg, and Archibald MacLeish asked to write special creed for National Cultural Center, Washington, D.C., to open in 1964.

D216   "Window of the World," <u>Denver Post</u>, February 21, 1961, p. 5.
        Announces President Kennedy to appear on television to talk about Frost's poetry.

D217   GOULD, JACK. "TV: Soaring Poetry, Drama and Opera," <u>New York Times</u>, February 27, 1961, p. 49.
        The TV program "was one of fragile mood superbly sustained, a quiet oasis of contemplative serenity and private thought amid all the noisiness of the modern world."

D218   PHILLIPS, MC CANDLISH. "President Hails Bond With Frost," <u>New York Times</u>, February 27, 1961, p. 14.

D. NEWS ITEMS

        PHILLIPS, MC CANDLISH (cont.)
              Honored by TV program; President Kennedy appears; extols him, explains why he invited him to speak at inauguration; Frost calls New Frontier "age of poetry and power."

D219   SPIEGEL, IRVING. "Frost Takes Off for Jerusalem," New York Times, March 10, 1961, p. 10.
              Frost to lecture on U.S. culture, first lecturer in chair established by Samuel Paley; interview; honored by American Friends of the University; first edition of his North of Boston presented to Frost Collection at University library by Charles E. Feinberg.

D220   "Robert Frost Reaches Israel," New York Times, March 11, 1961, p. 13.
              Frost welcomed by English department heads.

D221   "Frost Opens Israeli Lectures," New York Times, March 14, 1961, p. 6.
              A thousand people attend.

D222   "Frost Pays Tribute To Tagore's Work," New York Times, April 20, 1961, p. 20.
              Birth centenary of Rabindranath Tagore marked by Asia Society; Frost and J.D. Rockefeller, 3rd, speak; tributes by Prime Minister Nehru and President Kennedy.

D223   "Correction," New York Times Book Review, April 30, 1961, p. 36.
              Corrects April 23 quotation from "The Gift Outright."

D224   HALBERSTAM, DAVID. "Udall, the Democrats Art Lover, Is 'Hatchet Man' to Republicans," New York Times, May 2, 1961, p. 25.
              Frost honored by Cabinet-sponsored program, initiated by Stewart Udall; Mrs. John F. Kennedy attends.

D225   HALBERSTAM, DAVID. "Udall Accused of Seeking Party Aid From Oil Man," New York Times, May 3, 1961, p. 1.
              Frost is Udall's luncheon guest.

D226   "Robert Frost Has Operation," New York Times, June 17, 1961, p. 50.

D. NEWS ITEMS

"Robert Frost . . ." (cont.)
>One-paragraph item. Frost has minor surgery, is re-
ported in very good condition.

D227 "Poet Frost on the Mend," Denver Post, June 18, 1961, p. 6A.
>Photograph, with cutline describing Frost after minor
surgery.

D228 "Vermont Honors Poet Frost, Gets Thanks in Verse," Denver Post,
July 22, 1961, p. 2.
>The Associated Press account.

D229 "Robert Frost Inducted As Vermont's Laureate," New York Times,
July 23, 1961, p. 42.
>Frost named official poet laureate of Vermont.

D230 "Robert Frost Park Urged," New York Times, October 8, 1961,
p. 60.
>Udall urges creation of national park in Frost's honor.

D231 "His 'Greatest Honor'," Denver Post, January 8, 1962, p. 8.
>Photograph, with cutline describing the naming of a
Lawrence, Mass., elementary school for him.

D232 "Robert Frost School Dedicated," New York Times, January 8,
1962, p. 19.
>Frost attends dedication of grade school named for him
the previous day.

D233 TERTE, ROBERT H. "Cherne's Bust of Frost Unveiled At Poetry
Awards Dinner Here," New York Times, January 19, 1962,
p. 29.
>Annual dinner of Poetry Society of America; accepts Leo
Cherne bust of Frost for Society.

D234 GELB, ARTHUR, AND BARBARA GELB. "Culture Makes A Hit At
the White House," New York Times Magazine, January 28,
1962, pp. 9, 64-66.
>On President John F. Kennedy's efforts to make official
acknowledgement of American poets and other artists.

D. NEWS ITEMS

D235   "Robert Frost Leaves Hospital," New York Times, February 17, 1962, p. 20.
> Leaves Baptist Hospital in Miami after virus illness.

D236   WHITE, JEAN. "Robert Frost's First Book to be Shown," Washington Post, March 25, 1962, p. A6.
> Announces celebration of Frost's 88th birthday. Copy of "Twilight," along with manuscripts, first editions, and photographs to be shown at the Library of Congress.

D237   "America's 'Bard'-- That's Frost," Ann Arbor News, March 27, 1962, p. 1.
> Associated Press report of Frost's birthday dinner.

D238   "Culture is an Overworked Word," Washington Post, March 27, 1962, p. B5.
> Reception and dinner held at the Hall of the Americas of the Pan-American Union. Speakers included Felix Frankfurter, Adlai Stevenson, Secretary of the Interior Stewart Udall, and publisher Alfred Edwards.

D239   "Robert Frost Honored on 88th Birthday," Washington Post, March 27, 1962, p. A1.
> Photograph with President John F. Kennedy and explanatory cutline.

D240   Regents Proceedings (University of Michigan), April 1962, p. 683.
> Recorded that Frost will receive honorary degree in June.

D241   "Group Fetes Frost as 'Leading Poet,'" Denver Post, April 16, 1962, p. 1.
> Associated Press account of Frost's remarks at a dinner for him in New York.

D242   "Gift By Robert Frost," New York Times, April 20, 1962, p. 24.
> Frost gives manuscript of In the Clearing to Dartmouth College at dedication of Robert Frost Room in Baker Library.

D243   "4 Plays By Frost Staged In Boston," New York Times, May 31, 1962, p. 23.
> Masque of Reason, The Bonfire, Masque of Mercy and The Generations of Men; The Poet's Theatre, Cambridge, Mass.,

"4 Plays By Frost. . ."(cont.)
in the Kresge Little Theatre. Frost did not attend.

D244   "Honorary Degrees, June 1962," Regents Proceedings (University
of Michigan), June 1962, p. 751.
Frost is, "among poets distinctively American easily
chief, and . . . our nation's laureate."

D245   "Honorary Degrees Given," New York Times, June 17, 1962, p. 27.
Frost receives honorary degree from University of Michigan along with several others.

D246   "The '62 Commencement," Michigan Alumnus, LXVIII (July 1962),
338-40 [339].
Frost receives honorary degree with several others, including Theodore Roethke.

D247   "Frost Will Visit Soviet In a Cultural Exchange," New York Times,
August 17, 1962, p. 5.
Frost to visit U.S.S.R. on White House initiative;
U.S.S.R. poet Aleksandr Tvardovsky to visit U.S. in exchange.

D248   "Robert Frost Argues Marx With Russian," Denver Post, September 2, 1962, p. 4.
The Associated Press account.

D249   "Muscovites Hear Reading by Frost; The Topic: a Wall," New York
Times, September 6, 1962, p. 3.
Frost recites "Mending Wall" in Moscow; some in audience
see obvious reference to Berlin Wall.

D250   "Robert Frost's 'Needle' Charms Russ," Denver Post, September
6, 1962, p. 1.
The Associated Press account of Frost's reading "Mending
Wall" in Moscow.

D251   "Nikita Has 'Hearty Talk' With Visiting Robert Frost," Denver
Post, September 7, 1962, p. 12.
The Associated Press account.

D252   SHABAD, THEODORE. "Russians Ask Udall For an 'Energy Race,'"
New York Times, September 8, 1962, pp. 1, 3.

D. NEWS ITEMS

SHABAD, THEODORE (cont.)
Frost has "a warm talk" with Premier Nikita Khrushchev, according to Tass, the Soviet press agency.

D253   "Frost Urges Nikita To Try Horse Trade," Denver Post, September 9, 1962, p. 1A.
The United Press International account.

D254   "Frost Recites at Embassy," New York Times, September 9, 1962, p. 4.
"His first words to the group were: 'Hello, you damn Yankees.'"

D255   "Frost Says Khrushchev Thinks U.S. Won't Fight," Denver Post, September 10, 1962, p. 8.
The Associated Press account.

D256   "Soviet Poet Pays Tribute to the Ideals of Frost," New York Times, September 11, 1962, p. 4.
Pravda published Aleksei A. Surkov's tribute to Frost; Frost gave Khrushchev copy of his book, In the Clearing. Also adds that President Kennedy "had not yet received a message that Robert Frost had said he was to deliver to the President from [Khrushchev]."

D257   "Transcript of the President's News Conference on Foreign and Domestic Matters," New York Times, September 14, 1962, p. 12.
President Kennedy says he has not read any message from Khrushchev through Frost.

D258   "Amherst Gets 3.5 Million To Build a New Library," New York Times, September 29, 1962, p. 48.
Amherst College gets $3,500,000 from an anonymous alumnus for new library to be named for Frost.

D259   "Random Notes in Washington: Long Session a Boon to Kennedy," New York Times, October 15, 1962, p. 18.
Mentions that a U.S. Embassy film of Frost's visit was borrowed for a Russian television showing with lines 35 and 36 of "Mending Wall" deleted in the translation.

THE CRITICAL RECEPTION OF ROBERT FROST

D. NEWS ITEMS

D260   "Frost Gives Poet's View Of Mental Age in College," New York
        Times, October 29, 1962, p. 24.
            Chalmers Memorial Library dedicated at Kenyon College.
        The mental age of college students should be between "liking
        to be told and wanting to do the telling."

D261   "MacDowell Medal Is Given To Frost," New York Times, Novem-
        ber 9, 1962, p. 12.
            Academy of American Poets MacDowell Colony Medal to
        Frost; gets congratulations from White House. Frost says:
        "Thank you for my medal. ... Now I have to deserve it!"

D262   "Surgery on Poet," Denver Post, December 24, 1962, p. 10.
            Photograph, with cutline describing Frost's condition as
        hopeful.

D263   "Robert Frost Suffered Heart Attack in Hospital," Denver Post,
        December 27, 1962, p. 12.
            The United Press International account.

D264   "Frost Had Heart Attack, But Upturn Is Reported," New York
        Times, Western edition, December 28, 1962, p. 7.
            Frost has mild heart attack while recovering from urinary
        operation.

D265   "Frost Has a Comfortable Night," Denver Post, January 3, 1963,
        p. 4.
            The Associated Press account.

D266   "Clot in Lung Slows Recovery of Frost," New York Times, January
        9, 1963, p. 5.
            Frost undergoes minor surgery after suffering a small
        pulmonary embolism.

D267   "Frost Able To Leave Bed," New York Times, January 12, 1963,
        p. 5.
            Yevgeni Yevtushenko sends message: "Today I read your
        poems again and again. I am happy that you live on the earth."

D268   "Frost House Is Up for Sale," Denver Post, January 15, 1963, p. 40.
            U.P.I. story says Frost's South Shaftsbury house is for
        sale for $27,500.

The Critical Reception of Robert Frost

D. NEWS ITEMS

D269   "Robert Frost Progresses," New York Times, January 15, 1963,
p. 5.
Frost is described as "making good progress." He "sat
up in bed and read the morning newspapers."

D270   "Poet Robert Frost Reported Improving," Denver Post, January 20,
1963, p. 11A.
Associated Press squib.

D271   "Frost's Condition Worsens Boston Hospital Announces," New York
Times, Western edition, January 29, 1963, p. 5.

D272   CHAPIN, DARLENE. "Death of Poet Robert Frost Stirs Eulogies
Here," Ann Arbor News, January 29, 1963, p. 15.
Local reaction to Frost's death by colleagues and neigh-
bors.

D273   "Death Takes Robert Frost 88, Beloved Dean of America's Poets, "
Ann Arbor News, January 29, 1963, pp. 1, 8, 21.
Associated Press report.

D274   "Renowned Poet Frost Dies at 88, " Denver Post, January 29, 1963,
p. 1.
The Associated Press acount.

D275   "Robert Frost Dies at 88; Kennedy Leads in Tribute, " New York
Times, January 30, 1963, pp. 1, 5.
"Robert Frost, dean of American poets, died today at the
age of 88. He was pronounced dead at Peter Bent Brigham
Hospital at 1:50 A.M." A long eulogistic obituary follows.

D276   "Frost Is Cremated, Private Rites Today, " New York Times,
January 31, 1963, p. 7.
Ashes to be interred in Old Bennington, Vermont, in the
Spring. Private service to be held at Memorial Chapel, Har-
vard, on January 31. A public memorial service is to be held
at Amherst College on February 17.

D277   "Robert Frost's Will is Filed, " New York Times, February 5,
1963, p. 5.
Frost "left his estate to his family and his secretary, Mrs.
Kathleen Morrison of Cambridge, Mass."

THE CRITICAL RECEPTION OF ROBERT FROST

D278   NICHOLS, LEWIS. "Stockholder, " in "In and Out of Books" column, New York Times Book Review, May 5, 1963, p. 8.
   In 1928 Henry Holt and Company gave Frost 18 shares of stock now worth $28,000.

D279   "School Here Named for Frost, " New York Times, August 22, 1963, p. 24.
   New York City junior high-school in the Bronx named for Frost.

D280   "Frost Poetry Award, " in "Books and Authors" section, New York Times, August 30, 1963, p. 19.
   American Poetry Society sets up Robert Frost Poetry Award of $1,000 under Holt, Rinehart, and Winston grant.

D281   "Kennedy, Honoring Frost, Bids U.S. Heed Its Artists, " New York Times, October 27, 1963, pp. 1, 87.
   Library honoring Frost dedicated at Amherst College; President Kennedy and Archibald MacLeish speak.

D282   "President Dedicates Poet Frost Library." Denver Post, October 27, 1963, p. 11A.
   New York Times News Service account.

D283   "Text of President's Address at Amherst, " New York Times, October 27, 1963, p. 87.
   "Because of Mr. Frost's life and work, because of the life and work of this college, our hold on this planet has increased."

D284   "Volume of Poetry By Robert Frost Sold Out in Soviet, " New York Times, December 1, 1963, p. 32.
   First publication of Frost's From Nine Books quickly sold out. More than 10,000 copies.

D285   BENJAMIN, PHILIP. "Frost's Library Is Given To N.Y.U., " New York Times. January 10, 1964, p. 41.
   Daughter Mrs. Ballantine gives 3,000-volume library to New York University, because "I think it's more important to let the world see it than to keep it for myself. "

D286   PHILLIPS, MC CANDLISH. "Friends of Frost Score N.Y.U. Gift, " New York Times, January 11, 1964, p. 21.

D. NEWS ITEMS

PHILLIPS, MC CANDLISH (cont.)
Some friends of Frost hold he wanted gift to go to Amherst College's Frost Library; cite his close ties with the college; Mrs. Ballantine replies that she gave the collection to N.Y.U. because she lives near the N.Y.U. campus and wanted always to be near her father's books.

D287   "Robert Frost Portrait," Michigan Alumnus, LXX (January 1964), p. 113.
Portrait by Leon A. Makielski to hang in Alumni Memorial Hall.

D288   "Colleague Of Frost Recalls His Poetry," New York Times, March 24, 1964, p. 32.
Louis Untermeyer lectures on Frost under the Whittal Poetry Fund auspices at the Library of Congress.

D289   "Loretto Plans Production on Frost's Poetry," Denver Post, October 22, 1964, p. 60.
" 'The Seasons of Robert Frost', a readers' theater production by the Loretto Heights College speech and drama department, will be presented . . . on October 25 . . . ."

D290   "27 Robert Frost Letters Bring $11,500 at Auction," New York Times, May 21, 1965, p. 7.
Letters auctioned for $11,500 to El Dieff, a dealer who also bought fifty letters of E.E. Cummings for $2,600.

D291   GILROY, HARRY. "Theater: Robert Frost," New York Times, October 12, 1965, p. 56.
An Evening's Frost, by Donald Hall, enthusiastically reviewed.

D292   "Frost Library To Be Dedicated," New York Times, October 24, 1965, p. 52.
Amherst College set to dedicate library named for him on October 26.

D293   "New Frost Library," Denver Post, October 26, 1965, p. 40.
Associated Press squib.

D294   "Special 'Frost' Performances Set," Michigan Alumnus, LXXII
           (January 1966), p. 15.
                  An Evening's Frost, currently playing in New York, will
           also be presented in Washington, D.C., at the Library of
           Congress.

D295   " 'Evening's Frost' to End Run," New York Times, January 29,
           1966, p. 13.
                  Donald Hall's An Evening's Frost to close; tour set, in-
           cluding two performances in Washington at the Library of Con-
           gress.

D296   "Proposed Highway Threatens Poet's Home," Denver Post, July 29,
           1966, p. 36.
                  Associated Press account.   Secretary of the Interior Udall
           proposes an alternate route.

D297   "Farm To Become Frost Memorial," New York Times, December
           30, 1966, p. 23.
                  Ripton, Vt., farm home bought by Middlebury College;
           150 acres to be operated as memorial.

D298   GILROY, HARRY. "Demand Growing For Frost's Works," New
           York Times. April 29, 1967, p. 35.
                  Estate executor A.C. Edwards reports Frost's literary
           properties have grown since his death; Federal tax authorities
           had agreed to treat future income on assumption that it would
           decline in 8 years after his death.

D299   "A Little Journey to the Home of a Donor," Bulletin of the Society
           For the Libraries of New York University. Special Supplement.
           No. 72 [1967]. [3 pp. unnumbered.]
                  About Lesley Frost Ballantine and her New York apartment.

D300   "Robert Frost Bust Given To Smithsonian Gallery," New York
           Times, December 19, 1968, p. 55.
                  Jose Buscaglia's bronze bust of Frost, last portrait done
           from life, unveiled at National Portrait Gallery, Washington,
           D.C.

D301   "Frost in Painting and Sculpture," Bulletin of the Society for the
           for the Libraries of New York University. Special Supplement.

D. NEWS ITEMS

"Frost in Painting. . ." (cont.)
No. 75 [1969]. [5 pp. unnumbered.]
Includes a checklist of paintings and sculpture of Frost.

D302   GILROY, HARRY. "Ex-Farm Hand of Frost Winner of Poet's
Award," New York Times, April 11, 1969, p. 38.
American Poetry Society Awards; Wade Van Dore among
winners, was once farm hand for Frost; ceremony is a tribute
to Walt Whitman; Sen. Eugene J. McCarthy participates; winners listed.

D303   "Robert Frost," "Letters" section, New York Times Book Review,
September 27, 1970, p. 40.
Lesley Ballantine corrects Helen Vendler's statement that
the Frost family life was "disastrous." Frost's daughter
describes it as "splendid" but "struck too often by tragedy...."

D304   MADDRY, LAWRENCE. "Some Fond Memories of a Man Who
Went Soaring," [Norfolk] Virginian-Pilot, December 5, 1971,
p. C2.
On Frost at Kitty Hawk, North Carolina.

D305   MADDRY, LAWRENCE. "A Touch Of Frost On the Outer Banks,"
[Norfolk] Virginian-Pilot, December 5, 1971, pp. C1, C2.
On Frost's sojourn in the Dismal Swamp.
Reprinted as "Lovelorn Poet Wandered About The Dismal
Swamp," Chapel Hill [N.C.] Weekly, December 8, 1971, Third
Section, pp. 1, 2.

D306   "Frost program will dedicate highway in honor of poet," Bennington
[Vt.] Banner, August 24, 1972, p. 9.
On the dedication ceremonies for the Frost Wayside Area
between Ripton and Bread Loaf.

D307   LEANING, JOHN. "A Robert Frost poem inaugurates college year,"
Bennington [Vt.] Banner, September 8, 1972, pp. 1, 14.
"Two Tramps in Mud Time" read at the inauguration of Dr.
Gail T. Parker as President of Bennington College.

D308   " 'Frostiana' performed before capacity audience at Dorset," Man-
chester [Vt.] Journal, September 21, 1972, p. 3.
A presentation at the United Church of Dorset of several
Frost poems set to music.

E. BIBLIOGRAPHIES AND CHECKLISTS

E1   BOUTELL, H. S. "A Bibliography of Robert Frost, " Colophon, old series, Vol. I, Part II [May 1930]. [3 pp. unnumbered.] Lists works from Twilight to The Cow's in the Corn.

E2   BYERS, EDNA HANLEY, comp. Robert Frost at Agnes Scott College. Decatur, Ga.: McCain Library, Agnes Scott College, 1963. 75 pp.
      A handsome checklist of primary and secondary materials collected since Frost's first visit in 1935.

E3   CLYMER, W. B. SHUBRICK, AND CHARLES R. GREEN. Robert Frost: A Bibliography. Foreword by David Lambuth. Amherst, Mass.: The Jones Library Inc., 1937. 158 pp.
      Includes collation with number of each edition given; first appearance of poems in periodicals; first appearance of poems in books other than Frost's; readings of poetry (or record); separate printings; prose; translations and appreciations in foreign languages; chronology; parodies; books dedicated to Frost; selected list of essays and reviews in newspapers and periodicals.

E4   COOK, REGINALD L. "Robert Frost." In Jackson R. Bryer, ed. Fifteen Modern American Authors: A Survey of Research and Criticism. Durham, N.C.: Duke University Press, 1969. Pp. 239-73.
      An essay describing Frost's publishing career and the critical studies concomitant with it.

E5   An Exhibition of the Work of Robert Frost In connection with the Opening of The John Scott Craig Reading Room in the Reis Library and the delivery of Mr. John C. Sturtevant Lecture. Meadville, Pa.: Allegheny College, 1938. [8 pp. unnumbered.]
      Includes a bibliography and "Introduction" by Martin K. Howes.

107

E. BIBLIOGRAPHIES AND CHECKLISTS

E6 GREINER, DONALD J. Checklist of Robert Frost. (Merrill Checklists.) Columbus, Ohio: Charles E. Merrill, 1969. 42 pp.
  A checklist of primary and secondary material with occasional annotations.

E7 MELCHER, FREDERIC. "Robert Frost and His Books," Colophon,
Vol. I, Part II [May 1930]. [7 pp. unnumbered.]
  Describes Frost's books through 1929.

E8 MERTINS, LOUIS AND ESTHER. The Intervals of Robert Frost: A
Critical Bibliography. Introduction by Fulmer Mood. Berkeley: University of California Press, 1947. 91 pp.
  On the various places Frost lived, and what he wrote
there.

E9 NASH, RAY, ed. Fifty Years of Robert Frost A Catalogue of the
Exhibition held in Baker Library in the Autumn of 1943.
Hanover, N.H.: Dartmouth College Library, 1944. 14 pp.

E10 NEWDICK, ROBERT S. "Foreign Responses to Robert Frost,"
Colophon, n.s., II (Winter 1937), 289-90.
  Presents Newdick's bibliography of foreign works on Frost.

E11 NEWDICK, ROBERT S. "Robert Frost, Teacher and Educator: An
Annotated Bibliography," Journal of Higher Education, VII
(June 1936), 342-44.
  A short checklist of secondary material, with annotations.

E12 PARAMESWARAN, UMA. "Robert Frost, a Bibliography of Arti-
cles and Books, 1958-1964," Bulletin of Bibliography, XXV
(January - April 1967), 46-48.
  A checklist of secondary material, without annotations.

E13 PARAMESWARAN, UMA. "Robert Frost, 1958-1964 - Part 2,"
Bulletin of Bibliography, XXV (May - August 1967), 58, 69, 72.

E14 "Plymouth State College Library Given Early Robert Frost Documents, Photos and Poetry," Conning Tower Gleanings (Plymouth State College Alumni Association), XIX (Winter 1969),
4-8.
  Description of the Frost material in the papers of George
H. Browne.

E. BIBLIOGRAPHIES AND CHECKLISTS

E15 TEMPLETON, RICHARD H. Robert Frost: His Poems, Portraits
and Printers, 1913-1963; a Comprehensive Exhibit. (Catalogue
of an exhibit held on March 24, 25, and 26, 1963, at Lake
Forest Academy, Lake Forest, Ill., 1963.) [12 pp. unnumbered.]
Templeton's collection of Frostiana, begun at Amherst in
1928, is shown.

E16 [THOMPSON, LAWRANCE, comp.] Robert Frost: A Chronological
Survey. (An exhibit of works at Olin Memorial Library, Wes-
leyan University.) Middletown, Conn.: The Library, 1936.
58 pp.
Illustrated with woodcuts by J.J. Lankes. Different
bindings, issues, and editions are indicated. Organization
roughly chronological, compilation unsystematic.

F. BOOKS AND PAMPHLETS

F1   MUNSON, GORHAM B. Robert Frost: A Study in Sensibility and
Good Sense. New York: George H. Doran, 1927, 135 pp.
More than half the book is devoted to biographical information, and the remainder deals with Frost's techniques. Of
Frost's style, Munson writes, "It is this simplicity and co-
herence of imagery that created the concreteness of Frost's
vision. At the same time, grandiose though the theme is, the
language is utterly like talk . . . ." Reprinted, N.Y.: Haskell
House Publishers, 1967.

F2   COX, SIDNEY. Robert Frost, Original "Ordinary Man." New
York: Henry Holt, 1929. 43 pp.
A first-hand account of Frost's personality and tempera-
ment. "Robert Frost makes it hard, just as life itself does,
to say a summarizing word." Rewritten as A Swinger of
Birches: A Portrait of Robert Frost. New York: New York
University Press, 1957. With an introduction by Robert Frost.

F3   FORD, CAROLINE. The Less Travelled Road-- A Study of Robert
Frost. Cambridge, Mass.: Harvard University Press, 1935.
Reprinted, London: Humphrey Milford, 1936. (Radcliffe
Honors Theses in English, No. 4.) 59 pp.
Miss Ford examines Frost's sensitivity to nature, to the
peasants who live close to nature, and to God who is the over-
riding principle in everything.

F4   THORNTON, RICHARD, ed. Recognition of Robert Frost: Twenty-
fifth Anniversary. New York: Henry Holt, 1937. 312 pp.
Reprinted criticism by a host of writers from the beginning of Frost's career to 1937.

F5   COFFIN, ROBERT P. TRISTRAM. New Poetry of New England:
Frost and Robinson. Baltimore: Johns Hopkins Press, 1938.
148 pp.

F. BOOKS AND PAMPHLETS

COFFIN, ROBERT P. TRISTRAM (cont.)
Six lectures originally delivered at Johns Hopkins: "The World That Is Gone," "The Artist in the Wrong World," "The Poet in a New World," "A New Language For Poetry," "A Wider Pattern of Sympathy," "A New Kind of Salvation."

F6   THOMPSON, LAWRANCE. Emerson and Frost: Critics of Their Times. An essay read before a meeting of the Philobiblon Club at Philadelphia on 24 October 1940, and now privately printed for the Members of the Club. Philadelphia: The Philobiblon Club, 1940. 250 copies. 43 pp.
A comparison of Emerson and Frost as poets. "The similarity between these two poets . . . is the more striking when we discover their independence from each other."

F7   THOMPSON, LAWRANCE. Fire and Ice: The Art and Thought of Robert Frost. New York: Henry Holt, 1942. 241 pp.
Analyzes Frost's "Poetry in Theory," "Poetry in Practice," and "Attitude Toward Life."

F8   Middlebury College. Middlebury: Middlebury College Press, 1954. [14 pp. unnumbered.]
The college "wishes to honor [Frost] on the occasion of his eightieth birthday with this booklet of photographs."

F9   COOK, REGINALD L. The Dimensions of Robert Frost. New York: Rinehart, 1958. 241 pp.
Reprinted, N.Y.: Barnes and Noble, 1968. With chapters on "Local and Personal Dimensions," "Ars Poetica," "The Organic," "The Parablist," "Dimension in Art," "Dimensions in Nature, Society, Science and Religion," "Dimension in Time and Space."

F10   BASLER, ROY P. "All the Difference: A Talk on the Occasion of the Dedication of the Robert Frost Room in the Jones Library, Amherst, Massachusetts, October 21, 1959." [n.p., 1959] 7 pp.
An informal talk on Frost's "wizardry," his humanism, his debt to Emerson.

F11   THOMPSON, LAWRANCE. Robert Frost. University of Minnesota Pamphlets on American Writers, No. 2. Minneapolis: Uni-

F. BOOKS AND PAMPHLETS

THOMPSON, LAWRANCE   (cont.)
   versity of Minnesota Press, 1959. 43 pp.
      An overview of Frost's career and of the ideas in the
   poems.

F12   LYNEN, JOHN F. The Pastoral Art of Robert Frost. New Haven:
   Yale University Press, 1960. 210 pp.
      On the various sorts of pastoralism in the poems.

F13   NITCHIE, GEORGE W. Human Values in the Poetry of Robert
   Frost: A Study of Poetic Convictions. Durham, N.C.: Duke
   University Press, 1960. 242 pp.
      A biographical study of Frost, working through the poems.

F14   SERGEANT, ELIZABETH SHEPLEY. Robert Frost: The Trial by
   Existence. New York: Holt, Rinehart and Winston, 1960.
   451 pp.
      A biography, though "necessarily unfinished and imperfect
   . . . . The book will not tell all that the reader wants to know
   about one of the most beloved poets and sages of our midtwenti-
   eth century."

F15   GREENBERG, ROBERT A., AND JAMES G. HEPBURN, eds.
   Robert Frost: An Introduction. New York: Holt, Rinehart and
   Winston, 1961. 177 pp.
      A "controlled research text" for students, with poems and
   reprinted criticism.

F16   COX, JAMES M., ed. Robert Frost: A Collection of Critical Es-
   says. Twentieth Century Views. Englewood Cliffs, N.J.:
   Prentice-Hall, 1962. 205 pp.
      Reprinted criticism by Lawrance Thompson, Malcolm
   Cowley, W.G. O'Donnell, Yvor Winters, Randall Jarrell,
   Harold H. Watts, John T. Napier, Marion Montgomery, Lionel
   Trilling, George W. Nitchie, and John F. Lynen. Contains an
   "Introduction" which describes the main themes in the poems.

F17   DOYLE, JOHN ROBERT, Jr. The Poetry of Robert Frost: An
   Analysis. Johannesburg: Witwatersrand University Press; New
   York: Hafner, 1962. 303 pp.
      Analysis of specific poems "for the general reader."

F. BOOKS AND PAMPHLETS

F18   ISAACS, ELIZABETH. An Introduction to Robert Frost. Denver:
         Alan Swallow, 1962. 172 pp.
              "It is the purpose of this book to provide a synthesis of the
         current basic information that may bring a better understand-
         ing of Frost's work."

F19   MUNSON, GORHAM. Making Poems for America: Robert Frost.
         Chicago: Encyclopaedia Britannica Press, 1962. 190 pp.
              Britannica Bookshelf--Great Lives for Young Americans
         series.

F20   ADAMS, FREDERICK B., Jr. To Russia With Frost. Boston:
         Club of Odd Volumes, 1963. 41 pp.
              A reminiscence of Frost's visit to Russia. Adams at
         Frost's request, went along to help "look out for" the poet.

F21   ANDERSON, MARGARET BARTLETT. Robert Frost and John
         Bartlett: The Record of a Friendship. New York: Holt, Rine-
         hart and Winston, 1963. 224 pp.
              An account of the long and intimate friendship of the Bart-
         lett and Frost families.

F22   BLUMENTHAL, JOSEPH. Robert Frost and the Spiral Press. New
         York: Spiral Press, 1963. 9 pp. 450 copies.
              Issued as holiday greetings, December 1964, by Ann and
         Joseph Blumenthal. Blumenthal printed almost all of Frost's
         Christmas-greeting poems.

F23   BROWER, REUBEN A. The Poetry of Robert Frost: Constellations
         of Intention. New York: Oxford University Press, 1963.
         246 pp.
              "The object of the chapters that follow is 'circulation' in
         Frost's sense, 'getting among the poems' in order to read
         each one with success and with finer awareness of its position
         in the Frostian and the larger universes of poetry. With these
         aims in mind I have tried also to bring out some 'constellations
         of intention' in both form and meaning in Frost's work as a
         whole."

F24   KENNEDY, JOHN FITZGERALD. The Amherst Address Delivered
         by President Kennedy, October 26, 1963. New York, 1963.
         [11 pp. unnumbered.]

F. BOOKS AND PAMPHLETS

KENNEDY, JOHN FITZGERALD (cont.)
"If Robert Frost was much honored during his lifetime, it was because a good many preferred to ignore his darker truths."

F25   LATHEM, EDWARD CONNERY, AND LAWRANCE THOMPSON, eds. Robert Frost: Farm-Poultryman. With Introduction. Hanover, N.H.: Dartmouth Publications, 1963. 116 pp.
The story of Robert Frost's career as a breeder and fancier of hens and the texts of eleven long-forgotten prose contributions by the poet, which appeared in two New England poultry journals in 1903-05, during his years of farming at Derry, New Hampshire.

F26   LYONS, LOUIS MARTIN. Robert Frost: Memorial Service. Amherst, February 17, 1963. New York: Spiral Press, 1963. [6 pp. unnumbered.]
Boston news analyst and commentator eulogizes Frost. "Great poet of our land. More than poet. Taken as sage and seer by Presidents and people."

F27   SQUIRES, RADCLIFFE. The Major Themes of Robert Frost. Ann Arbor: University of Michigan Press, 1963. 119 pp.
"The whole form of Frost's knowledge is different from that of the typical contemporary. If one were to delineate the typical modern poet who has been writing and publishing since, say, 1930, he would be obliged to devote much of the portrait not to the materials of the poet, for these vary greatly, but to the attitude toward the materials."

F28   FABER, DORIS. Robert Frost: America's Poet. Englewood Cliffs, N.J.: Prentice-Hall, 1964. 79 pp.
A biography for young people. Illustrated by Paul Frame.

F29   GOULD, JEAN. Robert Frost: The Aim Was Song. New York: Dodd, Mead, 1964. 302 pp.
An interpretive study of Frost's life and poetry, not unflawed.

F30   JENNINGS, ELIZABETH. Frost. Edinburgh and London: Oliver and Boyd, 1964. 119 pp.

F. BOOKS AND PAMPHLETS

JENNINGS, ELIZABETH (cont.)
A general overview of Frost's career and his critical reception.

F31 KENNEDY, JOHN FITZGERALD. "The Place of the Artist in Society."
Spoken at the dedication of the Robert Frost Library, Amherst College, Mass. New York: Spiral Press, 1964. [6 pp. unnumbered.]
Six hundred copies issued as holiday greetings, December 1964, by Ann and Joseph Blumenthal. The "especial significance" of Frost is that he "brought an unsparing instinct for reality on the platitudes and pieties of society."

F32 REEVE, F. D. Robert Frost in Russia. Boston: Little, Brown, 1964. 135 pp.
A day-by-day account of Frost's visit to Russia in 1962.

F33 SMYTHE, DANIEL. Robert Frost Speaks. New York: Twayne Publishers, 1964. 158 pp.
An account of several of Frost's lectures and readings between 1939 and 1962.

F34 UNTERMEYER, LOUIS. Robert Frost: A Backward Look. Washington, D.C.: Library of Congress, 1964. 40 pp.
"A lecture presented under the auspices of the Gertrude Clarke Whittall Poetry and Literature Fund, with a selective bibliography of Frost manuscripts, separately published works, recordings, and motion pictures in the collections of the Library of Congress."

F35 GRANT, DOUGLAS. Robert Frost and His Reputation. [Parkville, Victoria:] Melbourne University Press, 1965. 13 pp.
Reprint of a lecture providing a general overview of Frost's popularity, especially in England.

F36 MERTINS, LOUIS. Robert Frost: Life and Talks-Walking. Norman: University of Oklahoma Press, 1965. 450 pp.
Thirty years of walks and talks recorded in Mertins' diary.

F37 GERBER, PHILIP L. Robert Frost. Twayne United States Authors Series, 107. New York: Twayne, 1966. 192 pp.
An overview of Frost's life, career, craftsmanship,

GERBER, PHILIP L. (cont.)
theories, and themes.

F38   THOMPSON, LAWRANCE. Robert Frost, the Early Years, 1874-
      1915. New York: Holt, Rinehart and Winston, 1966. 641 pp.
          The first volume of an authoritative account of Frost's
      life and personality-- through the publication of NB. Reprinted,
      London: Cape, 1967.

F39   WILSON, ELLEN. Robert Frost: Boy With Promises to Keep.
      Indianapolis: Bobbs-Merrill, 1967. 200 pp.
          Illustrated by Al Fiorentino "Childhood of Famous Ameri-
      cans" series.

F40   RICHARDS, NORMAN. People of Destiny: Robert Frost. Chicago:
      Children's Press, 1968. 94 pp.
          Biography, read in manuscript by Lawrance Thompson,
      for young people.

F41   FROST, LESLEY. New Hampshire's Child: The Derry Journals of
      Lesley Frost. With Notes and Index by Lawrance Thompson
      and Arnold Grade. Albany: State University of New York, 1969.
      [Unpaginated.]
          Journals kept by Frost's daughter between 1905 and 1909.
      Facsimile reproduction.

F42   GREINER, DONALD J. Guide to Robert Frost. (Merrill Guides.)
      Columbus, Ohio: Charles E. Merrill, 1969. 42 pp.
          A general overview of the ideas in Frost's poetry.

F43   REICHERT, VICTOR EMANUEL. Out for Stars: An Appreciation
      of Robert Frost. Cincinnati: Literary Club, 1969. 22 pp.
          "A paper read before the Literary Club on Monday, Novem-
      ber 11, 1957 . . . Cincinnati, Ohio, " by Rabbi Emeritus of
      Rockdale Temple, Cincinnati. An affectionate reminiscence
      with many quotations from Frost's poems and sayings.

F44   SOHN, DAVID A., AND RICHARD H. TYRE, eds. Frost: The Poet
      and His Poetry. Revised edition. New York: Bantam Books,
      1969. 134 pp.
          Reprinted poems, prose, excerpts from interviews, with
      running commentary and questions for students.

F. BOOKS AND PAMPHLETS

F45 TATHAM, DAVID. A Poet Recognized, Notes About Robert Frost's
First Trip to England and Where He Lived. [Syracuse, N.Y.:
Syracuse University Press], 1969. [8 pp. unnumbered.]
Describes the Frosts' sojourn in England, and their many
friends there. Reprinted, with a three-page letter by Lesley
Frost, 1970.

F46 THOMPSON, LAWRANCE. Robert Frost: The Years of Triumph,
1915-1938. New York: Holt, Rinehart and Winston, 1970.
744 pp.
Frost's official biographer surprises and even shocks
readers with paradoxical revelations only slightly veiled in the
poems and the appearances of Frost.

F47 LATHEM, EDWARD CONNERY, ed. A Concordance to The Poetry
of Robert Frost [1969]. New York: Holt Information Systems, a
division of Holt, Rinehart and Winston, 1971. 640 pp.
Computer-concordance, omitting "high-frequency, non-
significant words . . . ."

F48 SIMPSON, LEWIS P., comp. Profile of Robert Frost. With Intro-
duction. Charles E. Merrill Profiles. Columbus, O.: Charles
E. Merrill, 1971. 118 pp.
Reprinted criticism by Lloyd N. Dendinger, James M.
Cox, Isadore Traschen, Alvan S. Ryan, Robert Penn Warren,
Nina Baym, William H. Pritchard, and Alfred Kazin.

F49 FRANCIS, ROBERT, ed. Frost: A Time to Talk. Conversations &
Indiscretions Recorded By Robert Francis. Amherst: University of Massachusetts Press, 1972. 100 pp.
Francis' written record of conversations with Frost in the
periods 1933-35 and 1950-59.

F50 GRADE, ARNOLD, ed. Family Letters of Robert and Elinor Frost.
Foreword by Lesley Frost. Albany: State University of New
York Press, 1972. 293 pp.
Lesley Frost writes: "These letters speak for themselves.
As source material, they provide an unusual opportunity to
trace the love-coherence of a family, both parental and grand-
parental. And it must be remembered that it was a family
fraught with and tempered by the powerful complexities of my
father's genius."

F. BOOKS AND PAMPHLETS

F51   BARRY, ELAINE. Robert Frost on Writing. New Brunswick,
         N. J. : Rutgers University Press, 1973. 188 pp.
              Reprints letters, prefaces, reviews, etc. Introduction
         analyzes Frost as a critic, both theoretical and practical.

G. PARTS OF BOOKS

G1 LOWELL, AMY. Tendencies in Modern American Poetry. New
    York: Macmillan, 1921. Pp. 79-136.
        "Mr. Frost is as New England as Burns is Scotch, Synge
    Irish, or Mistral Provençal, and it is perhaps not too much to
    say that he is the equal of these poets, and will so rank to
    future generations."

G2 MAYNARD, THEODORE. "Robert Frost: His Frostiness." In his
    Our Best Poets, English and American. New York: Henry Holt,
    1922. Pp. 169-80.
        "If I had to sum Frost up with a word I would use the word
    'frost.' Winter lies over all his landscapes; his brooks are
    sealed with ice and his hills covered with snow."

G3 UNTERMEYER, LOUIS. "Robert Frost." In his American Poetry
    Since 1900. New York: Henry Holt, 1923. Pp. 15-41.
        Chronological survey of Frost's poetry starting with A
    Boy's Will — "a subjective volume which the author, not so
    frankly, has tried to unify by a table of contents." In North of
    Boston "what really unifies the volume is nothing more binding
    than the spirit of youth and a groping towards an original ex-
    pression." It is the book in which "Frost found his own full
    utterance and himself." There are in-depth discussions of
    specific poems such as "Mowing," "Mending Wall" and
    "Birches" among others. Mountain Interval is described as
    like North of Boston. "[It] is rich in the blend of fact and fancy,
    in the intermingling of scenic loveliness and a psychological
    liveliness. . . . New Hampshire synthesizes Frost's con-
    flicting qualities; it combines the stark unity of North of Bos-
    ton and the geniality of Mountain Interval."

G4 BOYNTON, PERCY HOLMES. "Robert Frost." In his "The Per-
    sonal Equation in Literature," Some Contemporary Americans.
    Chicago: University of Chicago Press, 1924. Pp. 33-49.

G. PARTS OF BOOKS

BOYNTON, PERCY HOLMES (cont.)
Discusses Frost's use of rhythm and his theory of versification, Frost's poetry as lyrics or sketches. Brief biographical note.

G5 FARRAR, JOHN, ed. The Literary Spotlight. New York: George H. Doran, 1924. Pp. 213-21.
"Some of his best pictures [in the poems] are of grim and terrible events, and the whole body of his writing indubitably shows a decaying and degenerating New England."

G6 VAN DOREN, CARL. "The Soil of the Puritans: Robert Frost." In his Many Minds. New York: Alfred A. Knopf, 1924. Pp. 50-66.
Compares Frost with Robert Burns. Discusses Frost's ". . . Yankee rhythm and Yankee attitude." Of all New Englanders Frost most resembles Thoreau. (See H23.)

G7 GREEN, PAUL, AND ELIZABETH LAY GREEN. "Robert Frost." In their Contemporary American Literature, A Study of Fourteen Outstanding American Writers. Vol. VII, No. 5, Revised Edition. Chapel Hill: University of North Carolina Press, 1925. Pp. 41-44.
An outline study guide to Robert Frost, including a biographical outline of points to consider in Frost's work before 1920, and an outline of important considerations in a study of "New Hampshire." References listed at end of article.

G8 HOLLIDAY, ROBERT CORTES. "Small Hours With Robert Frost." In his Literary Lanes and Other Byways. New York: George H. Doran, 1925. Pp. 27-32.
Describes a talk with Robert Frost, how he talked on everything from horse-trading to his striving to achieve "speech rhythm" in his poetry. "He talked. . . not at all to sound clever, but in an amiable way groping-- like a man with his hands out-- toward his thought."

G9 JONES, LLEWELLYN. "Robert Frost." In his First Impressions. New York: Alfred A. Knopf, 1925. Pp. 37-52.
After arguing that "art does not need a big subject matter in order to be great," Jones writes, "the most general characteristic of the poetry of Robert Frost is just this ability to dis-

G. PARTS OF BOOKS

JONES, LLEWELLYN (cont.)

> pense with sensational subject matter and yet achieve un-
> doubtedly poetic effects by the simple ability to come close
> enough to daily living to get under its skin of accustomedness,
> brush from its aspect the artificialities of practical life . . .
> and exhibit it in its original movement."

G10 KREYMBORG, ALFRED. Troubadour: An Autobiography. New
York: Boni and Liveright, 1925. Pp. 335-37.

> Frost: "I wonder do you feel as badly as I do when some
> other fellow does a good piece of work?"

G11 WOOD, CLEMENT. "Robert Frost: The Twilight of New England."
In his Poets of America. New York: E.P. Dutton, 1925.
Pp. 142-62.

> Includes biographical data and discussion of poems in A
> Boy's Will, North of Boston, and New Hampshire. "Whitman
> labored diligently to elide the accustomed poeticisms . . .
> from his verse. . . . Robinson followed him in all but the
> exotic eccentricity. Robert Frost, with no fanfare of trumpets
> but with arduous application, has discovered and brought to
> poetry another speech--a less artificial one, a more living
> one--the speech that falls from the lips of a living man."

G12 MONROE, HARRIET. "Robert Frost." In her Poets and Their Art.
New York: Macmillan, 1926. Pp. 56-62.

> Discusses Frost as a New England poet, but ". . . this
> poet, however loyally local, is bigger than his environment;
> and his art, plunging beneath surfaces and accidents, seizes
> upon the essential, the typical, in the relations of men and wo-
> men with each other and with the earth, the sky, and all that
> lives and moves between them."

G13 MUNSON, GORHAM B. "Robert Frost." In Lewis W. Smith, Current Reviews. New York: Henry Holt, 1926. Pp. 319-28.

> "Frost . . . miraculously takes his place beside the an-
> tique Greeks and against the modern world. He proves that a
> classicism resting on personal discovery is still possible."

G14 RITTENHOUSE, JESSIE B. "Poetry of New England." In William
Stanley Braithwaite, ed., Anthology of Magazine Verse For
1926 and Yearbook of American Poetry. Boston: B.J. Brimmer,

G. PARTS OF BOOKS

RITTENHOUSE, JESSIE B. (cont.)
1926. Pp. 1-27 [16-20].
"Frost has humor and whimsicality and mellowness; not the polished, ironical humor of Robinson in 'Miniver Cheevy' . . . ."

G15 BURNSHAW, STANLEY A. "New Hampshire." In C. A. Cockayne, ed., Modern Essays of Various Types. New York: Charles E. Merrill, 1927. Pp. 291-92.
New Hampshire merits praise because "its particular excellence is revealed in the intensification of the Frostian idiom; and this is true of both the lyrics and the blank verse."

G16 COHEN, HELEN LOUISE. "A Way Out by Robert Frost." In her More One-Act Plays By Modern Authors. New York: Harcourt, Brace, 1927. Pp. 353-70.
Includes a reprinting of the play, a bibliography, and an introduction in which the editor writes that "A Way Out . . . exhibits most of the outstanding characteristics of Robert Frost's brief poetic dialogues and monologues."

G17 LOWDEN, SAMUEL MARION. "Mending Wall." In his Understanding Great Poems. Harrisburg: Handy Book Corporation, 1927. Pp. 91-100.
Includes an interpretation of the poem and instructions for teaching it. "This poem is packed with subtle suggestions and double meanings. It is intensely dramatic while being calmly objective."

G18 FREEMAN, JOHN. "Robert Frost." In J. C. Squire, ed., Contemporary American Authors. New York: Henry Holt, 1928. Pp. 15-42.
Discusses A Boy's Will, North of Boston, and New Hampshire. Says of Frost, "No poet of our time is so little sensuous, none clamours so little, none sings or whistles so naturally, none makes, of piercing sorrow, and of tragedy deeply realised, a music more tranquil."

G19 WHIPPLE, T. K. "Robert Frost." In his Spokesmen: Modern Writers and American Life. Foreword by Mark Schorer. New York: D. Appleton, 1928. Pp. 94-114.

G. PARTS OF BOOKS

WHIPPLE, T. K. (cont.)
> On Frost as a realist poet. His "is preeminently a farmer's poetry."

G20 KREYMBORG, ALFRED. "The Fire and Ice of Robert Frost." In his Our Singing Strength: An Outline of American Poetry (1620-1930). New York: Coward-McCann, 1929. Pp. 316-32.
> Discusses in detail poems from North of Boston, with some comments on A Boy's Will in which Frost ". . . had discovered his own idiom, but not yet perfected it," and West-Running Brook, which is a disappointment ". . . due to the book's slender outlines." Frost is ". . . a blend of the direct power and subtle sophistication essential to the deepest folk poetry."

G21 BRENNER, RICA. "Robert Frost." In her Ten Modern Poets. New York: Harcourt, Brace, 1930. Pp. 3-28.
> A general overview of Frost's life and work. The proper material and method for literature, according to Frost, is "Common in experience--Uncommon in writing."

G22 UNTERMEYER, LOUIS. "Robert Frost." In John O. Beaty, Ernest E. Leisy, and Mary Lamar, eds., Facts and Ideas For Students of English Composition. New York: F.S. Crofts, 1930. Pp. 207-09.
> Reprinted from Untermeyer, Modern American Poetry. Brief comments on A Boy's Will, North of Boston, and Mountain Interval. New Hampshire ". . . synthesizes Frost's qualities: it combines the stark unity of North of Boston and the diffused geniality of Mountain Interval. If any one thing predominates, it is a feeling of quiet classicism, the poet has lowered his voice but not the strength of his convictions."

G23 BLANKENSHIP, RUSSELL. "Robert Frost." In his American Literature. New York: Henry Holt, 1931. Pp. 588-94.
> Discusses "Frost and the New England Character," "Frost as a Realist," "Frost and Society," and Frost's career.

G24 KUNITZ, STANLEY JASSPON. "Robert Frost." In his Living Authors: A Book of Biographies. New York: H.W. Wilson, 1931. Pp. 135-36.
> Biographical sketch and portrait of Frost.

G. PARTS OF BOOKS

G25　AUSTIN, MARY. Earth Horizon. Boston and New York: Houghton
　　　　Mifflin, 1932. P. 334.
　　　　　　"I remember a talk I had with Robert Frost I
　　　　thought he would catch what I was driving at in the rhythms of
　　　　the local speech. And after we had finished, he went away,
　　　　and Madame Bianchi asked me what I thought of him, and I told
　　　　her that he came nearer getting the local rhythm than anybody
　　　　else. She was quite vexed with me. She said nobody in his own
　　　　country thought much of him; they thought him merely a clod-
　　　　hopper. Madame Bianchi had no consenting for any other New
　　　　England poet. Not even for Edwin Arlington Robinson."

G26　GROVER, EDWIN OSGOOD, ed. Annals of an Era: Percy MacKaye
　　　　and the MacKaye Family 1826-1932. Introduction by Edwin
　　　　Osgood Grover. Prefatory Note by Gamaliel Bradford.
　　　　Washington, D.C.: Pioneer Press, 1932. Passim.
　　　　　　Includes (p. 53) text of 1921 Frost letter to Percy MacKaye
　　　　and scattered Frost references throughout.

G27　LEWISOHN, LUDWIG. Expression in America. New York and
　　　　London: Harper and Brothers, 1932. Pp. 497-501.
　　　　　　In discussing the naturalist revolt in American literature,
　　　　Lewisohn says that Frost's revolt is classical in that he
　　　　". . . cleaves straight to permanent essentials in his delinea-
　　　　tions of both man and nature."

G28　WARD, A. C. American Literature, 1880-1930. New York: Lin-
　　　　coln MacVeagh, Dial Press, 1932. Pp. 162-66.
　　　　　　Discusses Frost under chapter subtitle "Tradition Ex-
　　　　panded." Frost is ". . . entirely original and entirely tradi-
　　　　tional. . . . "

G29　HICKS, GRANVILLE. "The Poets: Amy Lowell, Lindsay, Sandburg,
　　　　Robinson, Frost." In his The Great Tradition: An Interpreta-
　　　　tion of American Literature Since the Civil War. New York:
　　　　Macmillan, 1933. Pp. 237-47 [245-46].
　　　　　　Discusses Frost in relation to new forces in American
　　　　literature that emerged from 1912 to the end of the war. In the
　　　　several paragraphs devoted to Frost, Hicks comments that
　　　　though he has a world of his own, ". . . it cannot be denied that
　　　　Frost has achieved unity by a definite process of exclusion."

G. PARTS OF BOOKS

G30   SESSIONS, INA B. "The Dramatic Monologue as used by Frost, Robinson, and others." In her A Study of the Dramatic Monologue in American and Continental Literature. San Antonio: Alamo Printing Company, 1933. Pp. 93-116.
        Three pages devoted to Frost's use of the dramatic monologue in "A Servant to Servants," prefaced by comment on Frost's style.

G31   HALLECK, REUBEN POST. The Romance of American Literature. New York: American Book Company, 1934. Pp. 275-80.
        Contains biographical sketch and a brief discussion of Frost's poetry. ". . . because his comparatively lean harvest has such a fruity flavor of originality, of sane joy in the beauty of field, wood, and sky, such moving sympathy for the dramas of lowly lives, he ranks among the foremost living American poets."

G32   WEYGANDT, CORNELIUS. "Frost in New Hampshire." In his The White Hills: Mountain New Hampshire Winnepesaukee to Washington. New York: Henry Holt, 1934. Pp. 231-54.
        "Robert Frost is of the very essence of New Hampshire, with the full flavor of its folks, cidery, wind-bitten, rugged, flesh of their flesh, granite of their granite."

G33   DEUTSCH, BABETTE. This Modern Poetry. New York: W. W. Norton, 1935. Pp. 40-45.
        Portrait of an "honest, homely poet." Frost's favorite subjects are New England, rural people, the smells and sounds of the countryside.

G34   HICKS, GRANVILLE. "Two Roads." In his The Great Tradition: An Interpretation of American Literature Since the Civil War. Revised edition. New York: Macmillan, 1935. Pp. 245-46 and passim.
        Frost "has chosen to identify himself with a moribund tradition."

G35   SULLIVAN, MARK, ed. National Floodmarks: Week by Week Observations on American Life As Seen by Collier's. New York: George H. Doran, 1935. P. 92.
        "Poets like Masefield and Gibson, and, among Americans, Robert Frost and Edgar Masters are really short-story writers

G. PARTS OF BOOKS

SULLIVAN, MARK (cont.)
who use verse to tell their stories: generally rather grim ones."

G36 BEACH, JOSEPH WARREN. "Vanishing Point." In his Concept of
Nature in Nineteenth Century English Poetry. New York: Mac-
millan, 1936. Pp. 551-53.
In English and American poetry, the philosophical concept
of nature has virtually disappeared. Yet a few men, such as
Frost, have retained a sense of nature. Quotes from West-
Running Brook.

G37 CANBY, HENRY S. "Homespun Philosophers." In his Seven Years'
Harvest: Notes on Contemporary Literature. New York:
Farrar and Rinehart, 1936. P. 52.
"Robert Frost, the Yankee poet, whose simple language
of New Hampshire farmers is so racy and so deceptive in its
homely provincialism. It took the English to see that here was
another of the well-known American breed. We laughed at him
in the beginning as a vain fellow who tried to make hired men
pathetic and stone walls a subject for wit."

G38 CANBY, HENRY S. "Homespun Philosophers." In 1936 Essay Annual. New York: Scott, Foresman, 1936. Pp. 93-96.
Mention of Frost as poet of New Hampshire and the simple
people.

G39 GILLIS, ADOLPH, AND ROLAND KETCHUM. "Robert Frost: New
England Seer." In Our America: A Survey of Contemporary
America as Exemplified in the Lives and Achievements of
Twenty-Four Men and Women Drawn from Representative
Fields. Boston: Little, Brown, 1936. Pp. 83-98.
Finds Frost's poetry and his life unconventional. Gives a
brief biographical sketch and quotes freely from the poems.

G40 HICKS, GRANVILLE. "The World of Robert Frost." In Groff
Conklin, ed., New Republic Anthology: 1915-1935. New York:
Dodge Publishing, 1936. Pp. 361-64.
Limiting himself to a few experiences in life, Frost has
created a little "world of his own."

G41 SCHREIBER, GEORGES, ed. Portraits and Self-portraits. Boston:
Houghton Mifflin, 1936. Pp. 47-50.

G. PARTS OF BOOKS

SCHREIBER, GEORGES (cont.)
>Includes a thumbnail sketch, a drawing of Frost, and "The Lost Follower."

G42   FLETCHER, JOHN GOULD. Life Is My Song. New York: Farrar and Rinehart, 1937. P. 204.
>On the differences between Amy Lowell's and Frost's responses to New England. "I understood the causes for this praise [of Frost] better in her case than in the case of Ezra Pound. . . . It was because Frost stood in her mind for unfamiliar New England, not the New England of the cultivated and the affluent, among whom she had always lived, but the remote, shy, hermitlike New England of Thoreau and the backwoods farmer. . . ."

G43   LOGGINS, VERNON. "Regional Variations." In his I Hear America. . .: Literature in the United States Since 1900. New York: Thomas Y. Crowell, 1937. Pp. 198-207.
>Compares Frost with Wordsworth. Concludes: "He is not a Wordsworth, nor an imitator of Wordsworth."

G44   BROOKS, CLEANTH. "Frost, MacLeish, and Auden." In his Modern Poetry and the Tradition. Chapel Hill: University of North Carolina Press, 1939. Pp. 110-16.
>Discussion of Frost's poetry as exhibiting "the structure of symbolist-metaphysical poetry."

G45   CLEMENS, CYRIL. My Cousin Mark Twain. Introduction by Booth Tarkington. Emmaus, Pa.: Rodale Press, 1939. Pp. 210-11.
>Contains text of a 1937 letter from Frost to Cyril Clemens regarding awarding of Mark Twain Medal to Frost.

G46   MOORE, JOHN. The Life and Letters of Edward Thomas. London: William Heinemann Ltd., 1939. Passim.
>Recounts episodes in Frost's friendship with Thomas.

G47   UNTERMEYER, LOUIS. From Another World. New York: Harcourt, Brace, 1939. Pp. 206-28 and passim.
>Untermeyer relates his first encounter with Frost and the development of their friendship. Also describes some aspects of the similarities between Frost and E. A. Robinson.

G. PARTS OF BOOKS

G48   VAN DOREN, MARK. "The Permanence of Robert Frost." In his
       The Private Reader: Selected Articles and Reviews. New York:
       Henry Holt, 1942. Pp. 87-96.
           The clearest sign of Frost's durability as a poet is that he
       is admired both by the professionals and by untrained readers.
       The conversational tone of Frost's verse is his strength rather
       than his weakness.

G49   WELLEK, RENÉ, AND AUSTIN WARREN. Theory of Literature.
       New York: Harcourt, Brace and World, 1942. Revised edition,
       1956. Pp. 179, 292.
           Frost is a "natural" symbolist.

G50   UNTERMEYER, LOUIS. "Robert Frost: The Man and the Poet."
       Introduction to Come In and Other Poems by Robert Frost. Il-
       lustrated by John O'Hara Cosgrave. New York: Henry Holt,
       1943. Pp. 3-16.
           "The truth has been Frost's central passion." Reprinted
       as Introduction to A Pocketbook of Robert Frost's Poems. New
       York: Washington Square Press, 1946.

G51   WELLS, HENRY W. The American Way of Poetry. Columbia
       Studies in American Culture, No. 13. New York: Columbia
       University Press, 1943. Pp. 106-21 and passim.
           Discusses the degrees to which Frost was cosmopolitan or
       a representative of New England provincialism.

G52   COOPER, CHARLES W., in consultation with John Holmes. "Indi-
       vidual Poets--John Keats and Robert Frost." Preface to Poetry.
       New York: Harcourt, Brace, 1946. Pp. 580-608 and passim.
           Compares the two poets as writing biographically.
       Includes Frost's discussion with Holmes on the composition of
       "Stopping by Woods. . . ."

G53   GREGORY, HORACE, AND MARYA ZATURENSKA, eds. "The
       Horatian Serenity of Robert Frost." A History of American
       Poetry: 1900-1940. New York: Harcourt, Brace, 1946. Pp. 150-
       62.
           "If he may be justly considered the Horace of our day, he
       is one who has lived with admirable independence, well out-
       side the shadow of a Maecenas." Discusses the influence of

G. PARTS OF BOOKS

GREGORY, HORACE. . . (cont.)
Edward Rowland Sill. Describes Frost's "masks" including his "Horatian" one.

G54 DUNBAR, OLIVIA HOWARD. "Robert Frost--W. W. Gibson." In her A House in Chicago. Chicago: University of Chicago Press, 1947. Pp. 135-49 and passim.
Brief mention (pp. 135-38) of Frost's trip to Chicago in 1917 and his friendship with Harriet Moody. Includes texts of two 1917 Frost letters to Mrs. Moody.

G55 WEST, HERBERT F. "My Robert Frost Collection." In his The Mind on the Wing: A Book for Readers and Collectors. New York: Coward-McCann, 1947. Pp. 51-72 and passim.
Personal reminiscences and discussion of some problems in collecting editions of Frost's work. Reprints Frost's "The Four Beliefs," originally published by Ray Nash, 1943.

G56 THORP, WILLARD. "The 'New' Poetry." In Robert E. Spiller, et al., Literary History of the United States. Vol. II. New York: Macmillan, 1948. Pp. 1189-96.
Frost is a modern poet who works well with traditional meters.

G57 WELLS, HENRY W. Where Poetry Stands Now. Toronto: Ryerson Press, 1948. Pp. 45-46.
Frost's achievement is compared with that of Hart Crane, Sandburg, and Stevens.

G58 BENÉT, LAURA. Famous American Poets. Famous Biographies For Young People series. New York: Dodd, Mead, 1950. Pp. 128-32.

G59 BROOKS, CLEANTH, AND ROBERT PENN WARREN. Understanding Poetry. Revised edition. New York: Henry Holt, 1950. Pp. 388-97.
Contains a discussion of "After Apple-Picking" and "Birches."

G60 SOUTHWORTH, JAMES G. "Robert Frost." In his Some Modern American Poets. New York: Macmillan, 1950. Pp. 42-87.
Sees Frost as a poet of love, a critic of life, and a poet of nature. Frost "never for a moment compromises with his

G. PARTS OF BOOKS

SOUTHWORTH, JAMES G. (cont.)
most deeply-based beliefs and convictions as a thinker and as
an artist. . . . He does not write of the subject as an observer, but as one who has experienced its innermost mysteries
and is richer for the experience."

G61 UNTERMEYER, LOUIS. "Robert Frost: An Appreciation." In
Robert Frost, Complete Poems. Volume One. New York:
Limited Editions Club, 1950. Pp. v-xxvi.
Frost's "is a poetry which contemplates and sometimes
criticizes the world, but regards everything about it with love
and tolerant pity."

G62 WAGGONER, HYATT HOWE. "Robert Frost: The Strategic Retreat." In his The Heel of Elohim: Science and Values in Modern American Poetry. Norman: University of Oklahoma Press,
1950. Pp. 41-60.
Compares Frost to Robinson; calls Frost "a satisfied,
perhaps a complacent, realist. . . . The symbols most characteristic of his poetry. . . are symbols of diminution, of depri-
vation, of retreat and acceptance."

G63 WHICHER, GEORGE F. Mornings at 8:50: Brief Evocations of the
Past for a College Audience. Northampton, Mass.: Hampshire
Bookshop, 1950. Pp. 34-38.
A brief reminiscence of Frost at Amherst.

G64 BOGAN, LOUISE. Achievement in American Poetry: 1900-1950.
Chicago: Henry Regnery, 1951. Pp. 47-51.
Contends that Frost never realized the tragic power that
North of Boston promised in 1914.

G65 BROWER, REUBEN ARTHUR. The Fields of Light: An Experiment
in Critical Reading. New York: Oxford University Press, 1951.
Pp. 19, 21-23, 32, 33, 42, 74, 133.
Compares Shelley's "Ode to the West Wind" to Frost's
"Once by the Pacific" in a discussion of "who" speaks in a
poem and "how."

G66 COFFMAN, STANLEY K., Jr. Imagism: A Chapter for the History
of Modern Poetry. Norman: University of Oklahoma Press,
1951. P. 17.

G. PARTS OF BOOKS

COFFMAN, STANLEY K., Jr. (cont.)
Brief reference to Frost's and Pound's competing for Amy Lowell's attention.

G67   DOUGLAS, LOIS SMITH. Through Heaven's Back Door: A Biography of A. Joseph Armstrong. Waco, Texas: Baylor University Press, 1951. Pp. 134-39, 140, 208.
Armstrong was Professor of English at Baylor and corresponded with Frost asking him to visit Baylor in 1922.

G68   EASTMAN, MAX. Enjoyment of Poetry: With Anthology For Enjoyment of Poetry. Two volumes in one. New York: Charles Scribner's Sons, 1951. Vol. I, pp. 185-86; Vol. II, pp. 57-58.
Takes issue with Frost's statement that "metaphor . . . is the whole of thinking." Eastman asks, "if metaphor is all there is, and it is best taught in poetry--why did science ever appear upon the scene at all?" Concludes by calling Frost's philosophy an "almost uneducated simplicity."

G69   HARCOURT, ALFRED. Some Experiences. Riverside, Conn.: [No publisher], 1951. Pp. 18-23 and passim.
Harcourt recalls his days as editor at Holt and Frost's first two published books.

G70   MATTHIESSEN, F. O., ed. The Oxford Book of American Verse. With Introduction. Oxford University Press, 1950. Pp. 538-85.
In the Introduction Matthiessen calls Frost "a major figure of our times." Frost has "a naturalistic faith which has not always escaped complacence."

G71   MILES, JOSEPHINE. The Primary Language of Poetry in the 1940's. U. of California Publications in English. Vol. 19, No. 3. Berkeley: University of California Press, 1951. Passim, pp. 383-542.
On the grammatical emphasis in the language of most of the great poets of 1900-1940. Frost's poetry emphasizes the verb.

G72   WHICHER, GEORGE. "In the American Grain." In Arthur Hobson Quinn, ed. Literature of the American People. New York: Appleton-Century-Crofts, 1951. Pp. 900-13 [903-07].

G. PARTS OF BOOKS

WHICHER, GEORGE (cont.)

A discussion of American writers as to whether or not they are academic. Says Frost "may be loosely associated with the scholarly group. Though he has been a loyal friend of many professors, . . . his interest in education has been like the fearful fascination felt by monkeys for a basket with a snake in it. He has made free with colleges, loving the inter-course with young minds, but distrustful of all kinds of all forms of institutionalism."

G73 BROOKS, CLEANTH. An Approach to Literature. Third edition. New York: Appleton-Century-Crofts, 1952. Pp. 305-07, 346-47.

A discussion of "The Wood Pile" and "The Need of Being Versed in Country Things."

G74 DEUTSCH, BABETTE. "Glove of a Neighborhood." In her Poetry in Our Time. New York: Henry Holt, 1952. Pp. 55-78[61-78] and passim.

Discusses the rural New England aspects of Frost's poet-ry and gives special attention to "Acquainted With the Night" and "Come In."

G75 RAIZISS, SONA. The Metaphysical Passion: Seven Modern Ameri-can Poets and The Seventeenth-Century Tradition. Philadelphia: University of Pennsylvania Press, 1952. P. 14.

Frost is "not technically metaphysical."

G76 SCHERMAN, DAVID E., AND ROSEMARIE REDLICH. Literary America. New York: Dodd, Mead, 1952. Pp. 116-17.

Frost "has brought a freshness into American poetry which until then had been staggering under the load of romantic senti-mentality."

G77 WEST, HERBERT FAULKNER. John Sloan's Last Summer. Iowa City, Iowa: Prairie Press, 1952. Pp. 30-32.

Anecdote concerning Frost's hospitalization in 1951.

G78 WILSON, EDMUND. The Shores of Light: A Literary Chronicle of the Twenties and Thirties. New York: Farrar, Straus, and Young, 1952. P. 111.

"Robert Frost has a thin but authentic vein of poetic sensi-

G. PARTS OF BOOKS

WILSON, EDMUND (cont.)
bility; but I find him excessively dull, and he certainly writes very poor verse. He is, in my opinion, the most generally overrated of all [the current] group of poets. "

G79 FISHER, DOROTHY CANFIELD. "Robert Frost." In her Vermont Tradition: The Biography of an Outlook on Life. New York: Little, Brown, 1953. Pp. 383-90.
Frost "knows how to speak of the depth within human beings, to speak luminously and yet without losing the ineffable loveliness of silence. " Includes discussion of "Spring Pools, " "Stopping by Woods. . . , " and "The Pasture. "

G80 MORRIS, RICHARD B. , ed. Encyclopedia of American History. New York: Harper, 1953. P. 662.
A brief biographical sketch with incorrect birthdate 1875.

G81 UNGER, LEONARD, AND WILLIAM VAN O'CONNOR, eds. Poems for Study. New York: Holt, Rinehart, 1953. Pp. 592-603.
Frost "shows no marked departure from the poetic practices of the nineteenth century. " Includes a discussion of "Stopping By Woods. . . . "

G82 WHALLEY, GEORGE. Poetic Process. London: Routledge and Kegan Paul, 1953. Pp. 40, 92, 111.
Quotes "The Figure a Poem Makes" in a chapter on "symbolic extrication. "

G83 AGNEW, J. KENNER, AND AGNES L. MC CARTHY, eds. Prose and Poetry of the World. Syracuse, N.Y.: L.W. Singer, 1954. Pp. 207-10, 758.
Short biographical sketch and an explication of and study questions for "Two Tramps in Mud Time. "

G84 CARTER, EVERETT. Howells and the Age of Realism. Philadelphia: J.B. Lippincott, 1954. Pp. 266-67 and passim.
Comparison of Frost with Howells based on "The Egg and the Machine" and "Mending Wall. "

G85 COFFIN, ROBERT TRISTRAM. "The Revolutions of Modern Poetry. " In Literature in the Modern World: Lectures Delivered at George Peabody College for Teachers 1951-1954. Nashville,

G. PARTS OF BOOKS

COFFIN, ROBERT TRISTRAM (cont.)
Tenn.: George Peabody College, 1954. Pp. 31-36.
Reprint of lecture delivered on July 12, 1951, on the revolution in poetic diction. Language is becoming "the sharp words, the exact words, the words on people's lips in times of excitement and depression." Frost is a pioneer in this language revolution.

G86 KUNITZ, STANLEY, AND HOWARD HAYCRAFT, eds. Twentieth Century Authors: A Biographical Dictionary of Modern Literature. New York: Wilson, 1955. Pp. 345-46.
Biographical sketch.

G87 MEARS, LOUISE W. They Come and Go: Short Biographies. Boston: Christopher, 1955. Pp. 94-95.
Describes a Frost reading. "When Frost finished. . . there was . . . a silent tribute to the poem and the author."

G88 MEDINA, HAROLD R. "Birthday Dinner, Robert Frost." In Maxine B. Virtue, ed., Judge Medina Speaks: A Group of Addresses by Harold R. Medina. New York: Bender, 1954. Pp. 295-98.
Remarks at the celebration of the 80th birthday of Frost, March 25, 1954. "I have no license to discuss poetry and I shall not do so except by indirection. . . . Robert Frost is a creative artist of the first rank; his humanism has a touch of the universal in it. . . . Can one doubt that Robert Frost is the greatest living interpreter of the spirit of America and perhaps the greatest of all time?"

G89 TATE, ALLEN. Sixty American Poets 1896-1944. Washington: Library of Congress, 1954. Pp. 53-58.
Frost "has produced a body of poetry which is as impressive as any of our time." Gives checklist by Frances Cheney of early works, collections, and criticism, and a checklist of recordings.

G90 RICHARDS, ROBERT F., ed. Concise Dictionary of American Literature. New York: Philosophical Library 1955. Pp. 89-90.
Biographical sketch of Frost.

G. PARTS OF BOOKS

G91   SPILLER, ROBERT E. "Second Renaissance: Dreiser, Frost." In
his The Cycle of American Literature: An Essay in Historical
Criticism. New York: Macmillan, 1955. Pp. 211-42 [238-42].
      "Frost. . . was a conservative as well as an experiment-
or."

G92   UNTERMEYER, LOUIS. "Robert Frost." In Makers of the Modern
World: The Lives of Ninety-two Writers, Artists, Scientists,
Statesmen, Inventors, Philosophers, Composers, and Other
Creators Who Formed The Pattern of Our Century. New York:
Simon and Schuster, 1955. Pp. 468-77.
      A biographical sketch of Frost's life and publishing career,
with a description of each of Frost's books. Frost's readers
"have been charmed and, at the same time, challenged. . . .
Never has poetry accomplished a more complete act of shar-
ing."

G93   WHICHER, GEORGE R. "Out for Stars: A Meditation on Robert
Frost." In his Poetry and Civilization. Collected and edited
by Harriet F. Whicher. Ithaca: Cornell University Press,
1955. Pp. 19-30.
      Whicher attacks the idea that "a poem should not mean
but be." Discusses Frost's "Come In" to show that meaning
does not lessen the impact of the poetry. Sees "many levels of
implication beneath the innocent-looking surfaces of Robert
Frost's poems. . . ."
      Reprinted from Atlantic Monthly CLXXI (May 1943), 64-67.

G94   BREIT, HARVEY. "Robert Frost." In his The Writer Observed.
Cleveland: World, 1956. Pp. 95-97.
      Reprinted interviews and articles on American writers.
Quotes Frost as saying "Too many poets delude themselves by
thinking the mind is dangerous and must be left out. Well, the
mind is dangerous and must be left in."

G95   CADY, EDWIN HARRISON, FREDERICK J. HOFFMAN, AND ROY
HARVEY PEARCE. The Growth of American Literature. Vol.
II. New York: American Book Company, 1956. Pp. 378-90.
      Frost is a traditionalist because of his use of accepted
verse forms. Frost's most useful form is the "blank verse
dramatic poem." Points out his reliance upon the relation of
an area and its people and his "scorn of the new arts and fads."

G. PARTS OF BOOKS

CADY, EDWIN HARRISON, et al. (cont.)
Frost's poems are "hard of texture, compounded of wit and
tightly phrased metaphors, and charged with irony. . . ."

G96   COWIE, ALEXANDER. American Writers Today. Stockholm:
Radiotjänst, 1956. Pp. 7-9.
     Brief remarks on Frost's life, publications, and general
aspects of the poetry.

G97   SCHERMAN, DAVID E., AND ROSEMARIE E. REDLICH. America: The Land and Its Writers. New York: Dodd, Mead, 1956.
Pp. 66-67.
     Emphasizes Frost's love for New England and includes a
photograph of Frost's first farm in Derry, New Hampshire.

G98   SCHLAUCH, MARGARET. Modern English and American Poetry:
Techniques and Ideologies. London: Watts, 1956. Pp. 157, 190.
     "Twentieth Century poets have been experimenting with
rhythm. . . ." Frost's "Once by the Pacific" is an example of
"monotonously regular feet."

G99   TAYLOR, WALTER FULLER. The Story of American Letters.
Chicago: Henry Regnery, 1956. Pp. 313-19.
     Discusses Frost as lyrical poet, dramatic and narrative
poet, and philosophical poet. Frost's underlying theory is of
"enthusiasm tamed by metaphor."

G100   COOK, LUELLA B., and others, eds. People in Literature. New
York: Harcourt, Brace, 1957. Pp. 175-81, 600-01, 669.
     Explication of "The Death of the Hired Man" and comments
on "Once By the Pacific." Includes brief biographical sketch.

G101   FARJEON, ELEANOR. Edward Thomas: The Last Four Years,
Book One of the Memoirs of Eleanor Farjeon. New York: Oxford University Press, 1958. Pp. 113-21 and passim.
     On Thomas' meeting Frost in 1914 and the effect of Frost
in undamming the stream of poetry in Thomas.

G102   HAVIGHURST, WALTER. The Miami Years: 1809-1959. New York:
G.P. Putnam's Sons, 1958. Pp. 195-97.
     Mentions Frost's correspondence with Percy MacKaye in
1921.

G. PARTS OF BOOKS

G103   SCHWARTZ, DELMORE. "The Present State of Poetry." In John
        Crowe Ransom, Delmore Schwartz, and John Hall Wheelock,
        American Poetry at Mid-Century. Washington: Library of
        Congress, 1958. Pp. 15-31.
            Quotes Frost as saying "a number of poets have become
        teachers" and have "the best audiences poetry ever had in this
        world." Also uses "Stopping By Woods. . . " to contrast first
        part of the century with the middle.

G104   THOMPSON, LAWRANCE. "Robert Frost." In Frank Magill, ed.
        Cyclopedia of World Authors. New York: Harper and Row,
        1958. Pp. 391-95.
            "The qualities of Robert Frost's seemingly simple poetic
        idiom are actually complicated, subtle, elusive. . . . His
        imagery is developed in such a way as to endow even the most
        prosaically represented object with implied symbolic exten-
        sions of meaning."

G105   COX, HYDE. "Foreword." In Robert Frost, You Come Too:
        Favorite Poems For Young Readers. New York: Holt, 1959.
        Pp. 6-10.
            "All young people who read this selection of poems (and
        some may be as old in years as the poet himself) will find, I
        think, what I have found . . . that he is ageless; and as a poet,
        for the ages."

G106   DODD, LORING H. "North of Boston and Robert Frost." Celebri-
        ties at Our Hearthside. Boston: Dresser, Chapman and Grimes,
        1959. Pp. 39-46, 234-35.
            A reminiscence of Frost's visit to Clark University in
        1922.

G107   DREW, ELIZABETH. Poetry: A Modern Guide to Its Understanding
        and Enjoyment. New York: W. W. Norton, 1959. Passim.
            "His subject may seem to be nature, but his theme is man."

G108   KARSH, YOUSUF. Portraits of Greatness. New York: Thomas
        Nelson and Sons, 1959. P. 84.
            A collection of photographs of great men and women and a
        discussion of each. Photograph of Frost at his Cambridge
        home in 1958. Karsh describes his conversation with Frost as
        he photographed the poet.

G. PARTS OF BOOKS

G109   PHELPS, ROBERT H., ed. "Robert Frost." In his Men in the
        News--1958: Personality Sketches from the New York Times.
        Philadelphia: Lippincott, 1959. P. 95.
            Frost "is the kind of man who likes to carry an axe, to
        pitch rocks into a tin can, to talk deep into the night. . . .
        He will say that he is half farmer, half teacher, and half poet,"
        and he smiles at having three halves.

G110   UNTERMEYER, LOUIS. "New Trends in America," Lives of the
        Poets: The Story of One Thousand Years of English and Ameri-
        can Poetry. New York: Simon and Schuster, 1959. Pp. 629-36.
            "Often falsely classified as a 'nature poet,' Robert Frost
        . . . was more concerned with people than with places."
        Concludes that Frost had "a lover's quarrel with the world"
        that "characterizes the spirit of the man and his poetry."

G111   ROSENTHAL, M. L. "Rival Idioms: The Great Generation,
        Robinson and Frost." In his The Modern Poets: A Critical
        Introduction. Oxford: Oxford University Press, 1960. Pp.
        104-12 [109-12].
            Concludes that Frost's thought and form are "weaker . . .
        than they might be."

G112   PEARCE, ROY HARVEY. "Frost." In his The Continuity of Ameri-
        can Poetry. Princeton, N.J.: Princeton University Press, 1961.
        Pp. 271-83 and passim.
            Frost lacks the variety of Emily Dickinson, "the product
        of a mind which dares to be more capacious than his. That is
        what is lost, the expense of Frost's greatness: variety and
        capaciousness. Frost manages in his poems to create nothing
        less than an orthodoxy-- as against Emerson's heterodoxy-- of
        the self."

G113   AUDEN, W. H. "Robert Frost." In his The Dyer's Hand and
        Other Essays. New York: Random House, 1962. Pp. 337-53.
            "His poetic style is what I think Professor C.S. Lewis
        would call Good Drab. . . . I cannot think of any other modern
        poet. . . who uses language more simply."

G114   FAIRCHILD, HOXIE NEALE. "Realists." In his Religious Trends
        in Poetry, Vol. V, 1880-1920. New York: Columbia University
        Press, 1962. Pp. 222-53 [234-38].

G. PARTS OF BOOKS

FAIRCHILD, HOXIE NEALE (cont.)
Finds an influence from Emerson, though Frost has "cast aside" trancendentalism.

G115   JARRELL, RANDALL. "Robert Frost's 'Home Burial.'" In Don Cameron Allen, ed., The Moment of Poetry. The Percy Graeme Turnbull Memorial Lectures on Poetry. Baltimore: Johns Hopkins University Press, 1962. Pp. 99-132.
" 'Home Burial' and 'The Witch of Coös' seem to me the best of all Frost's dramatic poems --though 'A Servant to Servants' is nearly as good." A thorough analysis of "Home Burial."

G116   O'CONNOR, WILLIAM VAN. "Robert Frost: Profane Optimist." In his The Grotesque: An American Genre and Other Essays. Preface by Harry T. Moore. Crosscurrents/Modern Critiques. Carbondale: Southern Illinois University Press, 1962. Pp. 137-54.
"There is comedy in Frost. . ., but it seems to have its source in whimsy, an ironic playfulness, rather than in a deep joie de vivre. He has contemplated the world in all its variety and decided that, all things considered, it is better to be an optimist."

G117   SIMPSON, CLAUDE. "Robert Frost and Man's 'Royal Role'." In Richard M. Ludwig, ed., Aspects of American Poetry: Essays Presented to Howard Mumford Jones. Columbus: Ohio State University Press, 1962. Pp. 121-47.
Favorable overview of published poems later to be collected in In The Clearing.

G118   GRAVES, ROBERT. "Introduction" to Selected Poems of Robert Frost. New York: Holt, Rinehart and Winston. Rinehart and Winston. Rinehart Editions, 1963. Pp. ix-xxiv. Includes biographical note and bibliography.
Poems selected by Frost. Graves describes some of Frost's attitudes toward poetry. Frost's "chief preoccupation is freedom: freedom to be himself, to make discoveries, to work, to love, and not to be limited by any power except personal conscience or commonsense."

G. PARTS OF BOOKS

G119   HOWE, IRVING. "Robert Frost: A Momentary Stay." In his A
       World More Attractive: A View of Modern Literature and
       Politics. New York: Horizon Press, 1963. Pp. 144-57.
              "The best of Robert Frost, like the best of most writers,
       is small in quantity, narrow in scope and seldom the object of
       popular acclaim." Frost's lyrics "speak of the hardness and
       recalcitrance of the natural world. . . ."

G120   REED, MEREDITH. Our Year Began in April. New York: Lothrop,
       Lee and Shepard, 1963. Pp. 83-110.
              Some side glimpses of Frost by a former student at
       Pinkerton Academy.

G121   BENÉT, LAURA. Famous Poets For Young People. Famous Biog-
       raphies For Young People. New York: Dodd, Mead, 1964.
       Pp. 145-47.
              Brief biographical sketch gives incorrect birthdate as
       1875.

G122   COOK, REGINALD L. "A Parallel of Parablists: Thoreau and
       Frost." In Walter Harding's The Thoreau Centennial: Papers
       Marking the Observance in New York City of the One Hundreth
       [sic] Anniversary of the Death of Henry David Thoreau.
       [Albany]: State University of New York Press, 1964. Pp. 65-79.
              "Each has dramatized the terms of man's appeal from
       cosmic insignificance: Thoreau in terms of his intense moral
       perfectionism, and Frost in terms of his 'passionate prefer-
       ences'."

G123   ELMEN, PAUL. "Robert Frost: The Design of Darkness." In
       Nathan A. Scott, Jr., ed. Four Ways of Modern Poetry.
       Richmond, Va.: John Knox Press, 1965. Pp. 33-50.
              In his poetry Frost asks: "Is there a universal principle, a
       controlling metaphor by which the intolerable fullness of the
       world may be ordered and loved without fear?"

G124   ROBBINS, J. ALBERT. "America and the Poet: Whitman, Hart
       Crane and Frost." Brown, John Russell, Irvin Ehrenpreis,
       and Bernard Harris, eds. American Poetry. Stratford-upon-
       Avon Studies, No. 7. London: Edward Arnold, 1965. Pp. 45-
       67 [60-64].

G. PARTS OF BOOKS

ROBBINS, J. ALBERT (cont.)
Finds the influence of Emerson, though different, in all three poets.

G125   SMITH, CHARD POWERS. Where the Light Falls: A Portrait of Edwin Arlington Robinson. New York: Macmillan, 1965. Pp. x, xiv, 3, 4, 221, 361, 382.
Robinson, late in life, says "I'm afraid Frost is a jealous man."

G126   DAMON, SAMUEL FOSTER. Amy Lowell--A Chronicle With Extracts From Her Correspondence. Hamden, Conn. : [No Publisher], 1966. Pp. 174, 234, 272, 284, 289, 291, 300, 303, 305, 307, 316, 334, 339, 342, 344, 351, 365, 381, 386; classified as evolutionist by Miss Lowell, 427, 430, 433-35, 443, 556, 566; mishaps in introducing Miss Lowell to an Ann Arbor audience, 602; 604, 618, 635; learns truth of authorship of A Critical Table in English Who's Who Sketch of Miss Lowell, 652, 657, 687, 710, 712.

G127   MADISON, CHARLES A. The Owl Among the Colophons: Henry Holt as Publisher and Editor. New York: Holt, Rinehart and and Winston, 1966. Pp. 124, 165-85.
Describes Frost's relationship with Mr. and Mrs. Holt and the Holt firm. Gives a book-by-book account of Holt's publishing of Frost's poems.

G128   MARTIN, WALLACE. " 'The Forgotten School of 1909' and the Origins of Imagism." In A Catalogue of the Imagist Poets. New York: J. Howard Woolmer, 1966. Pp. 7-38.
Mentions Frost on page 36.

G129   HARD, MARGARET. A Memory of Vermont--Gun Life in the Johnny Appleseed Bookshop--1930-1965. New York: Harcourt, Brace and World, 1967. Pp. 46, 120, 159-67, 212-17.
On Frost's friendship with Vermont poet Walter Hard and his family.

G130   SNOW, C. P. Variety of Men. New York: Charles Scribner's; London: Macmillan, 1967. Pp. 130-50.
On Frost in old age and his "fantastication" and his acquaintance with Snow.

G. PARTS OF BOOKS

G131   KJØRVEN, JOHANNES. "Two Studies in Robert Frost: I. 'The Road
        Not Taken', and II. The American Poet in England: Robert
        Frost and His English Critics 1913-ca. 1950." In Sigmund
        Skard, ed. Americana-Norvegica: Norwegian Contributions to
        American Studies. Vol. II. Philadelphia: University of Penn-
        sylvania Press, 1968. Pp. 191-218.

G132   WAGGONER, HYATT H. "The Strategic Retreat." In his Ameri-
        can Poets: From the Puritans to the Present. Boston: Houghton
        Mifflin, 1968. Pp. 293-327.
            Frost's "retreats" are "strategic," in order for both man
        and artist to survive.

G133   ANDERSON, GEORGE K. Bread Loaf School of English: The First
        Fifty Years. Middlebury: Middlebury College Press, 1969.
        Pp. 30-34, 87, 90, 121, 142, 164.
            "Frost never offered a course at the School of English.
        He would give a reading in the evening, spend the remainder of
        the night--almost, but never quite--in conversation. . . ."

G134   BROWN, TERENCE. "Robert Frost's In the Clearing: An Attempt
        to Reestablish the Persona of the 'Kindly Grey Poet'." In
        Robert Partlow, ed. Studies in American Literature in Honor
        of Robert Dunn Faner, 1906-1967. Papers on Language and
        Literature (Supplement), V (Summer 1969), 110-18.
            ". . . the Frost of In the Clearing is the 'kindly grey poet'
        and not the Frost who wrote of the terror and the tragedy in the
        human dilemma."

G135   DABNEY, LEWIS M. "Mortality and Nature: A Cycle of Frost's
        Lyrics." In David J. Burrows, Lewis M. Dabney, Milne
        Holton, and Grosvenor E. Powell, eds. Private Dealings:
        Eight Modern American Writers. Stockholm: Almqvist &
        Wiksell, 1969. Pp. 11-31.
            "Frost rides upon poetic tradition and, in his metaphors,
        renews it through the special characteristics of the New
        England scene."

G136   GORDON, JAN B. "Robert Frost's Circle of Enchantment." In
        Jerome Mazzaro, ed. Modern American Poetry: Essays in
        Criticism. New York: David McKay, 1970. Pp. 60-92.
            Since "the mind and nature are partners in alienation,"

G. PARTS OF BOOKS

GORDON, JAN B. (cont.)
Frost weaves protective "circles of enchantment" in his poems.

G137 PRITCHARD, WILLIAM H. "Wildness of Logic in Modern Lyric."
In Reuben A. Brower, ed. Forms of Lyric: Selected Papers
from the English Institute. New York: Columbia University
Press, 1970. Pp. 127-50.
Taking his cue from Frost, Pritchard describes "the
lyric impulse to soar in contention and cooperation with a wry-
ly satiric and earth-bound one; dream and fact engaging in
their endless argument."

H. ARTICLES

1915

H1 BAXTER, SYLVESTER. "Talk of the Town, " <u>Boston Herald</u>, March
    9, 1915, p. 12.
        Frost "is a most agreeable personality. . . 'one of the most
    loveable men in the world'-- declared one of his new literary
    friends, prominent in New England letters. He is still in his
    thirties, but remains youthful in face and figure; dark brown
    hair, handsome gray blue eyes, a well-modelled head and
    mobile features. "
        Revised and enlarged as "New England's New Poet, "
    <u>American Review of Reviews</u>, LI (April 1915), 432-34.

H2 "Discovered in England --A Real American Poet, " <u>Current Opinion</u>,
    LVIII (June 1915), 427-28.
        "All the authoritative English critics acclaimed the work
    of Mr. Frost as 'much finer, much more near the ground, and
    much more national, in the true sense, than anything that
    Whitman gave the world. '"

H3 "Irving's Mexico, " <u>New York Times Book Review</u>, August 8, 1915,
    p. 284.
        Frost is quoted as saying "he 'never offered a book to an
    American publisher, and didn't cross the water seeking a
    British publisher. ' The thing 'just happened. ' And so, there
    is not 'another case of American inappreciation' to record. "

1916

H4 "The Adventurers in Poetry, " <u>Harvard Alumni Bulletin</u>, XVIII
    (June 21, 1916), 707.
        On the impetus of recent poetry in the United States.
    Finds Frost a worthy model for emulation.

H. ARTICLES

H5   BROWNE, GEORGE H. "Robert Frost, a Poet of Speech," The
Independent (New York), LXXXVI (May 22, 1916), 283-84.
"Mr. Frost is not a Socialist nor a profound moralist, but
he is sane and simple and moral. He is a philosopher, even
if he doesn't preach and interpret. He is above all a dramatist,
for all poetry is to him dramatic."

H6   CHILDS, FRANCIS LANE. "Robert Frost," Dartmouth Alumni
Magazine, VIII (January 1916), 105-07.
On Frost as a student at Dartmouth.

1917

H7   ERSKINE, JOHN. "The New Poetry," Yale Review, n.s., VI
(January 1917), 379-95, [389-90].
"Mending Wall" "gives assurance of powers not yet developed in [Frost]." Compares the new poetic freedoms with
nineteenth-century English poetry.

1918

H8   HEDGES, M.H. "Creative Teaching," School and Society, VII
(January 26, 1918), 117-18.
Questions Frost's appointment as lecturer at Amherst.
". . . one wonders if Amherst has not made a happy blunder
that will be quickly repaired."

H9   JEPSON, EDGAR. "Recent United States Poetry," English Review,
XXVI (May 1918), 419-28.
Lindsay, Masters, and Frost represent a "new school of
poetry--United States poetry."

H10   PHELPS, WILLIAM L. "Advance of English Poetry in the Twentieth
Century," The Bookman (New York), XLVII (April 1918), 125-
38.
"The difference between Vachel Lindsay and Robert Frost
is the difference between a drum-major and a botanist." Also,
Frost lacks range.

H11   WILKINSON, MARGUERITE. "Poets of the People No. V: Robert
Frost," Touchstone (Amherst), III (April 1918), 70-74.
Frost "is a new personal force. . . . Mr. Frost has been

WILKINSON, MARGUERITE (cont.)
called a realist. But if that description be true, he is a realist with vision, a realist who uses his imagination constantly."

1919

H12   ELLIOTT, GEORGE R. "The Neighborliness of Robert Frost,"
The Nation, CIX (December 6, 1919), 713-15.
Revised and enlarged as "The Neighborly Humor of Robert Frost" in his The Cycle of Modern Poetry, Princeton: Princeton University Press, 1929, 112-34.
Discusses Frost's humanitarianism and sense of humor.

1920

H13   BENJAMIN, P. L. "Robert Frost, A Poet of Neighborliness," Survey, XLV (November 27, 1920), 318-19.
". . . I think of Robert Frost as a rare comrade, a poet of neighborliness and good-humor, one who loves the soil and the folk of the countryside, a friend who reads with infinite understanding the tragedies, the impulses, the blitheness, and the defeats of the human spirit."

H14   "The 'Poet of Frost'," Literary Digest, LXVI (July 17, 1920), 32-33.
Quotes at length a recent article by Theodore Maynard in the New York Tribune. "Mr. Maynard, being English, may be calculated to become Frost's English champion."

H15   RIDGE, LOLA. "Covered Roads," New Republic, XXIII (June 23, 1920), 131-32.
"Frost stands just to one side of life, not above as on a high hill, but simply to one side."

1921

H16   SAYLER, OLIVER M. "Return of the Pilgrim," New Republic, XXVII (August 10, 1921), 302-03.
On the production of George Pierce Baker's "The Pilgrim Spirit" for which Frost wrote the finale, "The Return of the Pilgrims."

H. ARTICLES

1922

H17   "America's Literary Stars, " Literary Digest, LXXIV (July 22,
1922), 28-29.
"Chosen by their contemporaries, " Joseph Hergesheimer
was first with 22 votes, followed by Eugene O'Neill, 14; Sher-
wood Anderson, 13; Willa Cather, 12; with Frost and James
Branch Cabell tied for fifth with 8 votes.

H18   BOYNTON, PERCY H. "American Authors of Today II. Robert
Frost," English Journal, XI (October 1922), 455-62.
"As a so-called modern poet Mr. Frost is both old-
fashioned and new-fashioned in his manner of writing. "
Boynton finds "reticent optimism" in the poems.

H19   "An Editorial Word Or Two, " Whimsies (University of Michigan),
III (November 1922), 3.
"To the unknown person we give thanks; to our good friend
Robert Frost we extend, with admiration, a warm, quiet
welcome. "

1923

H20   "An Appreciation of Robert Frost, " Michigan Alumnus, XXIX
(March 8, 1923), 641.
Quotes from H23.

H21   "The Literary Spotlight XIX: Robert Frost, " The Bookman (New
York), LVII (May 1923), 304-08.
Finds Frost's humor "clumsy" and "If Mr. Frost starts
out to think a deep thought, the house may burn about his ears,
but he will think his thought to the conclusion that satisfies Mr.
Frost. "

H22   "A Poet Among the Hills, " Literary Digest, LXXIX (October 6,
1923), 31-32.
Reports that Frost has taken over Will Carleton's position
as "poet of the country people. "

H23   VAN DOREN, CARL. "The Soil of the Puritans. Robert Frost:
Quintessence and Subsoil, " Century Magazine, CV (February
1923), 629-36.

VAN DOREN, CARL (cont.)
"If Robert Frost talks as becomes a Yankee poet, so does he think as becomes one. In particular there is his close attention to the objects he sees in his chosen world. He seems never to mention anything that he has merely glanced at."
(See G6.)

1924

H24   "Fleas and Mores Close Kin Avers Local Poet," Amherst Student, January 7, 1924, p. 2.
     A parody-article on Frost as poet and teacher.

H25   JONES, LLEWELLYN. "Robert Frost," American Review, II (March - April 1924), 165-71.
     Finds NB shows "Frost at his greatest. . . ." Frost's poems "are never merely decorative," but are filled with "penetrating observations of nature."

H26   MC CORD, DAVID. "Robert Frost," Harvard Alumni Bulletin, XXVI (May 29, 1924), 985-87.
     Frost is a New Englander out of the "endlessly rocking cradle" which produced Emerson, Lowell, and Whittier.

H27   M[ONROE], H[ARRIETT]. "Comment: Robert Frost," Poetry, XXV (December 1924), 146-53.
     Frost, "however loyally local, is bigger than his environment; and his art, plunging beneath surfaces and accidents, seizes upon the essential, the typical, in the relations of men and women with each other and with the relations of men and women with each other and with the earth, the sky, and all that lives and moves between them."

1925

H28   BOWLES, ELLA SHANNON. "Robert Frost--A Belated Appreciation," Granite Monthly, LVII (July 1925), 267-70.
     "Have you noticed the masterly hand with which he brings out the emotions of his characters and, at the same time, plays upon the reader's emotions?"

H. ARTICLES

H29   ELLIOTT, G[EORGE] R. "An Undiscovered America in Frost's
        Poetry," Virginia Quarterly Review, I (July 1925), 205-15.
           "The Frostian humour is peculiarly important for America.
        No other of our poets has shown a mood at once so individual
        and so neighborly. . . . His poetic humour is on the highway
        toward the richer American poetry of the future, if that is to
        be."

H30   MUNSON, GORHAM B. "Robert Frost," Saturday Review of Litera-
        ture, I (March 28, 1925), 625-26.
           Discusses Frost as a classicist. Frost ". . . takes his
        place beside the antique Greeks and against the modern world.
        He proves that a classicism resting on personal discovery is
        still possible."
           Reprinted in Lewis Worthington Smith, Current Reviews.
        New York: Henry Holt, 1926. Pp. 319-28.
           Collected in Munson's Robert Frost: A Study in Sensibility
        and Good Sense (F1).

H31   FREEMAN, JOHN. "Contemporary American Authors II: Robert
        Frost," London Mercury, XIII (December 1925), 176-87.
           Frost ". . . is an exception . . . among modern American
        poets in his evidence of the traditional, and is naturally in our
        eyes none the worse for it."

H32   SCHERER, RUTH VON BACK. "A Welcome Back to Robert Frost,"
        Michigan Chimes, VII (October 25, 1925), 1, 3, 7.
           Not verified.

H33   SERGEANT, ELIZABETH SHEPLEY. "Robert Frost: A Good Greek
        Out of New England," New Republic, Fall Literary Section,
        XLIV (September 30, 1925), 144-48.
           Discusses the classical simplicity of Frost's poetry.
        "The language of his poetry, though so markedly that of New
        England speech, is symbolic; his subject-matter, for all its
        clear geographical limits, is universal."
           Reprinted in her Fire Under the Andes: A Group of North
        American Portraits. New York: Alfred A. Knopf, 1927. Pp.
        285-303.

H34   SWAIN, FRANCES. "The Robert Frost of the Whimsies Evenings,"
        The Inlander, V (April 1925), 24-28.
           Not verified.

H35   CESTRE, CHARLES. "Amy Lowell, Robert Frost, and Edwin
       Arlington Robinson," Johns Hopkins Alumni Magazine, XIV
       (March 1926), 363-88 [369-75].
           Six and a half pages devoted to Robert Frost. "Skill in
       composition, with Frost, is only a means to impart the truth
       of the situations and of the characters. In this he is verily the
       great poet. His outlook. . . is restricted to the life of New
       England farmers; but, within this field, he reaches the uni-
       versally human."

H36   FISHER, DOROTHY CANFIELD. "Robert Frost's Hilltop," The
       Bookman (New York), LXIV (December 1926), 403-05.
           Description of Robert Frost's house with woodcuts by
       J.J. Lankes. ". . . once the old stone house on the hill was
       thought of, there could be no doubt that it had been built for no
       other purpose than for the Frosts to live in."

H37   "Robert Frost," in "The Week On The Campus" section, Michigan
       Alumnus, XXXII (March 6, 1926), 408-09.
           Quotes Professor Bruce Weirick, of the University of Il-
       linois, as saying: "Robert Frost is one of the greatest modern
       poets. . . ."

H38   "Robert Frost Returns to Amherst," Amherst Graduates' Quarterly,
       XV (August 1926), 271-73.
           "Robert Frost returns to a secure place in the affections
       of Amherst men. It is hoped and expected that the arrangement
       commenced next year will prove lasting."

H39   THAL, NORMAN R. "The 'Chair of Culture' At the University of
       Michigan," Intercollegiate World (University of Michigan), I
       (April 1926), 19-24.
           Describes the procedures involved in arranging the first
       poet-in-residence in an American university.

                                  1927

H40   FARRAR, JOHN. "Robert Frost and Other Green Mountain Writ-
       ers," English Journal, XVI (October 1927), 581-87 [582-83].

H. ARTICLES

FARRAR, JOHN (cont.)
Frost could not have written any place but New England.
"He is a Puritan, courting rebellion but never achieving it, and
being almightily shocked by it when it crosses his doorstep."

1928

H41 "Can You Name These Modern Poets?" Ladies' Home Journal, XLV
(March 1928), 22.
Includes a portrait of Frost with the first lines of "Mending
Wall" printed below. Ten other poets and similar clues.

H42 LOWE, ORTON. "Robert Frost," Scholastic, XIII (September 22,
1928), 13.
Gives a brief account of Frost's background and general
description of his poetry. "His poetry comes out of his life
as philosopher, dreamer, and worker with his hands."
Includes "The Need of Being Versed in Country Things" and
"The Runaway."

1929

H43 AYKROYD, GEORGE O. "The Classical in Robert Frost," Poet
Lore, XL (Winter 1929), 610-14.
"He has demonstrated that poetry can be just as intelligi-
ble to the layman as to the initiate. His poems possess ir-
resistible appeal for even the most Victorian of us despite the
fact that in his published works there are only five classical
allusions."

H44 "Robert Frost, Author of West-Running Brook," Wilson Bulletin,
IV (November 1929), 100.
Brief biographical sketch and photograph.

H45 ULMANN, DORIS. "Portrait Photographs of Fifteen American
Authors," The Bookman (New York), LXX (December 1929), 418.
Full-page photograph of Frost, the first of fifteen contem-
porary American writers.

H46 UNTERMEYER, LOUIS. "New Poetry," Saturday Review of Literature, V (July 13, 1929), 1174.
Review of The Poetry Quartos. Twelve brochures, each

H. ARTICLES

UNTERMEYER, LOUIS (cont.)
containing a new poem by an American poet. Designed,
printed and made by Paul Johnston and published by Random
House. Ranks "The Lovely Shall be Choosers" as one of two
outstanding poems in the collection. It is ". . . a particularly
intense communication, keyed higher than most of his work...."

1930

H47 MUNSON, GORHAM B. "Robert Frost and the Humanistic Temper,"
The Bookman (New York), LXXI (July 1930), 419-22.
Examination of some of poems in WRB in attempt to show
that Frost is "a humorous lover of distinctions" and "an up-
holder of the dignity of man" whose "sense of contraries is not
far from the humanist's declaration that in man there is a
duality of consciousness, a struggle between his impulse to
unify himself and his impulse to drift with the stream of life."

H48 WALPOLE, HUGH. "London Letter November, " New York Herald
Tribune Books, November 30, 1930, 9.
Frost's Collected Poems "is for me more sure of immor-
tality than any other book of the last five years, whether in
England or America."

1931

H49 FAIR, JESSIE FRANCES. "Robert Frost Visits the Demonstration
Class, " English Journal, XX (February 1931), 124-28.
On Frost's visit in 1930 to the Colonel White Junior High
School in Dayton, Ohio.

H50 "The Pulitzer Awards, 1931, " Publisher's Weekly, CXIC (May 9,
1931), 2312-13.
Announces Frost's award of $1000 for Collected Poems as
"the best volume of verse published during the year by an
American author."

H51 WILSON, JAMES SOUTHALL. "Robert Frost: American Poet. "
Virginia Quarterly Review, VII (April 1931), 316-20.
Discusses Frost as a passionate, mystical, and philosophic
poet. "Frost is typical of the whole of America and of the
traditions of America."

H. ARTICLES

H52   "Conning the Campus" column, Michigan Alumnus, XXXVIII (January 30, 1932), 303.
        Comments on Frost's winning the Loines Prize for Poetry.

1932

H53   HILLYER, ROBERT. "Robert Frost 'Lacks Power'," New England Quarterly, V (April 1932), 402-04.
        In rebuttal to Frederic I. Carpenter, Hillyer claims that Frost has the two-fold power that exists in any art: "impulse and restraint." (See A69.)

H54   O'HAGAN, THOMAS. "Looking Over the Field Again," Canadian Bookman, XIV (February 1932), 21.
        Discusses the degeneracy of American poetry. "If you strip a poem of all ecstasy and divine beauty you make it poor indeed, in the simplicity of its nakedness." Cites Frost's "The Pasture" as an example of a poor poem.

H55   SMITH, FRED. "The Sound of a Yankee Voice," Commonweal, XV (January 13, 1932), 297-98.
        Discusses Frost's readings of his own poetry. "Poetry, as [Frost] writes it, is something to be heard rather than read on a printed page."

1933

H56   HALL, JAMES NORMAN. "The Spirit of Place," Atlantic Monthly, CLII (October 1933), 478-83.
        "I can recall no more beautiful tribute paid to the influence of a spirit of place than that to be found in 'My November Guest'." Includes reprint of the poem.

H57   KREYMBORG, ALFRED. "American Poetry After the War. I," English Journal, XXII (March 1933), 175-84.
        Links Frost with Robinson as being the Yankee poets in the romantic movement that arose before the war. A general, undetailed overview.

H58   KREYMBORG, ALFRED. "American Poetry After the War. II," English Journal, XXII (April 1933), 263-73.

The Critical Reception of Robert Frost

1934

H59 COX, SIDNEY HAYES. "New England and Robert Frost, " <u>New Mexico Quarterly</u>, IV (May 1934), 89-94.
The New Englander is a product of a shrewd and tempered environment, and similarly Robert Frost is a New Englander who "doesn't tell all he knows. He uses it. . . . If we look we find every poem of his is a specimen, a sample. Like a generalization it stands for many experiences, but it has not lost, in the process of abstraction, reality. "

H60 DABBS, J. MC BRIDE. "Robert Frost and the Dark Woods, " <u>Yale Review</u>, XXIII (Spring 1934), 514-20.
In discussing romantic qualities in Frost's poetry, Dabbs writes that "though his poetry is immediately notable for its fresh, living quality, its realism, it is memorable for its rich after-images, and its deeply based idealism. "

H61 EISENHARD, JOHN. "Robert Frost, Peasant Poet, " <u>Scholastic</u>, XIV (April 28, 1934), 28-29.
On Frost's sense of tragedy and humor, and his imagery.

1935

H65 CARROLL, GLADYS HASTY. "New England Sees it Through, " <u>Saturday Review of Literature</u>, XIII (November 9, 1935), 3-4, 14, 17.
Describes Frost as the first New England poet, since Sarah Orne Jewett "lacked only fire to be New England's fair claim to an actual literary genius. "

H63 CLYMER, SHUBRICK. "Robert Frost, the Realist, " <u>Yankee</u>, I (October 1935), 22-25.
"Whether posterity as a whole will be kinder to him than his own generation has been remains to be seen. "

H64 LOVEMAN, AMY. "Clearing House, " <u>Saturday Review of Literature</u>, XIII (December 28, 1935), 20.
"S. S. " of Bryn Mawr writes in for help in finding materials for his book on Frost.

H. ARTICLES

H65 "Mr. Frost at 60, " Daily New Hampshire Gazette, March 29, 1935,
   p. 10.
     Editorial. Not verified.

H66 NEWDICK, ROBERT S. "The Early Verse of Robert Frost and
   Some of His Revisions, " American Literature, VII (May 1935),
   181-87.
     On 14 poems published before 1913 and their subsequent
   revisions. They "reveal the poet, who has always been slow
   to publish, as capable of rethinking, rephrasing, and even re-
   hearsing, his already most carefully wrought verses. "

H67 NEWDICK, ROBERT S. "Three Poems by Robert Frost, " American Literature, VII (November 1935), 329.
     On "The Quest of the Orchis, " "Warning, " "Caesar's
   Lost Transport Ships. " First appeared in The Independent
   (August 20, 1896, January 14, 1897, September 9, 1897, re-
   spectively).

H68 POUND, LOUISE. "Miscellany: Phonograph Records of Robert
   Frost, " American Speech, X (December 1935), 314.
     Short paragraph announcing four new recordings by Frost.

1936

H69 COLUM, PADRAIC. "Robert Frost, " Book-of-the-Month Club News,
   May 1936, p. 5.
     On the importance of scholarship in Frost's poetry and
   Frost's sojourn in England.

H70 DABBS, JAMES MC BRIDE. "Robert Frost, Poet of Action, " English
   Journal, XXV (June 1936), 443-51.
     ". . . he is the poet of action (and so of life as action),
   the interpreter of typical rural activities. He has done certain
   things until his body knows them: mended wall, built bonfires,
   fought snowstorms, and sat on the steps at evening to watch
   the moon down early. "

H71 "Dividends from a Poet, " Saturday Review of Literature, XIII
   (February 15, 1936), 8.
     Notes merits of a poet becoming a teacher, as Frost is
   appointed Charles Eliot Norton Lecturer at Harvard.

H72   HOLMES, JOHN. "A Fine Study of Robert Frost's Verse," Boston
      Evening Transcript, February 8, 1936, Book Section, p. 2.
            Review of Caroline Ford's The Less Travelled Road.
      ". . . readers who make claim to anything like a full collection,
      will wish to own this attractive pamphlet."

H73   NEWDICK, ROBERT S. "Bibliographies and Exhibits of the Work of
      Robert Frost," Amherst Graduates' Quarterly, XXVI (Novem-
      ber 1936), 79-80.
            Review of Lawrance Thompson's Robert Frost: A Chrono-
      logical Survey.

H74   NEWDICK, ROBERT S. "Robert Frost and the American College:
      Facts, Fundamental Principles, and Procedures of Frost's
      Educational Philosophy," Journal of Higher Education, VII
      (May 1936), 237-43.
            Frost believed that teaching could work only through per-
      sonal contact, according to the needs and abilities of the
      individual student.

H75   NEWDICK, ROBERT S. "Robert Frost as Teacher of Literature
      and Composition," English Journal, XXV (October 1936), 632-
      37.
            "Robert Frost's insistence, whatever be the position of
      academic authorities with reference to credits, is on reading
      poetry as poetry."

H76   NEWDICK, ROBERT S. "Robert Frost: Impressions and Observa-
      tions," Ohio Stater, II (May 1936), 3, 18-19.
            "Robert Frost talks like a man, dresses like a man, and
      acts like a man, because, while essentially an extra-ordinary
      man, by fixed purpose he has persisted in being an ordinary
      man."

H77   "Phonograph Records of Robert Frost," English Journal, XXV (May
      1936), 417.
            Announcement of four phonograph records of Frost reading
      his poetry in a series sponsored by the National Council of
      Teachers of English, American Speech, and Erpi Picture
      Consultants.

H. ARTICLES

H78   POUND, LOUISE. "Miscellany: Phonograph Records of Robert
Frost," American Speech, XI (February 1936), 98.
        Brief announcement of recordings of Frost reading his own
poetry.

H79   ROOT, EDWARD TALLMADGE. "New England Honors Her Leading Poet," Christian Century, LIII (April 15, 1936), 581.
        This brief article provides a biographical account of
Frost and a description of his reception at Harvard for his
lectures as the Charles Eliot Norton Professor of Poetry.

H80   VAN DOREN, MARK. "The Permanence of Robert Frost," American Scholar, V (Spring 1936), 190-98.
        "Mr. Frost is as skilful a Symbolist as anyone, and his
critics acknowledge that this is so; but the mystery in his poems is never of the sort which makes so many contemporary
poems sound like puzzles."

H81   WHEELWRIGHT, JOHN. "Back to the Old Farm," Poetry, XLIX
(October 1936), 45-48.
        Frost's merits and deficiencies; comparison of Frost and
Robinson. Frost "holds his own because he is distinct among
all his rivals and because a teeming welter of talent, finer in
prosody and firmer in philosophy, is so indistinct by reason
of keen rivalry that no critic has picked any one poet to match
against Robert Frost."

H82   W[INTERICH], J. T. "The New Books: Belles Lettres," Saturday
Review of Literature, XIV (August 8, 1936), 21.
        Review of Lawrance Thompson's Robert Frost: A Chrono-
logical Survey.

1937

H83   ADAMS, FREDERICK B., Jr. "The Crow's Nest," Colophon, n.s.
II (Summer 1937), 465-79 [470-77].
        Collation of revisions in A Boy's Will, North of Boston,
Mountain Interval, New Hampshire, West-Running Brook.

H84   BENÉT, WILLIAM ROSE. "Phoenix Nest: Contemporary Poetry,"
Saturday Review of Literature, XV (April 10, 1937), 16.
        Reviews meeting of the Poetry Society of America honoring
Frost.

H85   DE VOTO, BERNARD. "The Pulitzer Prize Winners: The Poetry
Award," Saturday Review of Literature, XVI (May 8, 1937), 4.
Brief report on A Further Range.

H86   WHICHER, GEORGE F. "Poetry in Amherst," Amherst Record,
July 14, 1937, p. 2.
      A long article on poetry in general, concluding with a
comparison of Frost and Emily Dickinson.

H87   HICKS, GRANVILLE. "A Letter to Robert Hillyer," New Republic,
XCII (October 20, 1937), 308.
      Review, in verse, of Hillyer's A Letter to Robert Frost
and Others (J9).

H88   NEWDICK, ROBERT S. "Children in the Poems of Robert Frost,"
Ohio Schools, XV (September 1937), 286-87, 313.
      Describes the "children real and imagined who run
through [the poems] like threads of silver and black and gold."

H89   NEWDICK, ROBERT S. "Design in the Books of Robert Frost,"
Reading and Collecting, I (September 1937), 5-6, 15.
      A description of the illustrations and type-faces in Frost's
books; a bibliographical checklist on page 15.

H90   NEWDICK, ROBERT S. "Robert Frost and the Dramatic," New
England Quarterly, X (June 1937), 262-69.
      Some comments on the dramatic qualities of A Way Out.

H91   NEWDICK, ROBERT S. "Robert Frost and the Sound of Sense,"
American Literature, IX (November 1937), 289-300.
      Frost "values ear-images over eye-images; and, however
masterfully he evokes the latter in his poetry, he purposefully
exalts the former."

H92   NEWDICK, ROBERT S. "Some Notes on Robert Frost and Shak-
spere," Shakespeare Association Bulletin, XII (July 1937), 187-
89.
      "... at the very heart of Frost's credo and practice as an
artist lies his conviction of the complete supremacy of the
dramatic and Shaksperian."

H. ARTICLES

H93 WINTERICH, JOHN T. "The Compleat Collector: Rare Books;
      Frostana," Saturday Review of Literature, XVI (May 29, 1937),
      20.
          On errors in Clymer-Green bibliography (E3).

                              1938

H94 COLLAMORE, H. B. "Some Notes on Modern First Editions,"
      Colophon, n.s. III (Summer 1938), 354-56.
          On the bindings of first issue editions of A Boy's Will and
      North of Boston.

H95 DE VOTO, BERNARD. "The Critics and Robert Frost," Saturday
      Review of Literature, XVII (January 1, 1938), 3-4, 14-15.
          Review of Thornton, Recognition of Robert Frost. A
      critique of the critics. Approves of Untermeyer, Lewisohn,
      Kreymborg; dismisses the rest.

H96 MATTHIESSEN, F. O. "Letter to the Editor," Saturday Review of
      Literature, XVII (February 5, 1938), 9.
          Defends R.P. Blackmur's criticism of Frost. (See H95.)

H97 S., P. P. "What Critics Have Written in Praise of Robert Frost,"
      Christian Science Monitor Weekly Magazine Section, February
      16, 1938, p. 11.
          Review of Thornton, Recognition of Robert Frost. "If it
      serves no other purpose, the book will at least bring comfort
      to those who, 25 years ago, on the publication of that first
      slender volume, 'A Boy's Will,' said, in substance, 'Here's a
      poet, a real poet, an American poet, an honest poet.'"

H98 UNTERMEYER, LOUIS. "Play in Poetry," Saturday Review of
      Literature, XVII (February 26, 1938), 3-4, 14, 16.
          A condensation of two chapters from Untermeyer's Play in
      Poetry (Harcourt, Brace, 1938). Contains first printing of
      Frost's "Willful Homing."

                              1939

H99 AGARD, WALTER R. "Frost: A Sketch," Touchstone (Amherst),
      IV (Spring 1939), 9.

AGARD, WALTER R. (cont.)
   A former student recalls Frost's "disciplined energy and sober power."

H100   BRACE, GERALD. "An Unimportant Recollection of Robert Frost," Touchstone (Amherst), IV (February 1939), 21.
   Some students did not realize at the time what Frost was trying to do at Amherst. "We spoke of him as Bobby with more condescension than affection. . . ."

H101   CHALMERS, GORDON K. "The Poet as Nonconformist," Touchstone (Amherst), IV (February 1939), 22.
   Describes a few of Frost's practical jokes.

H102   DICKINSON, PORTER. "Robert Frost And His New England," Touchstone (Amherst), IV (February 1939), 10.
   Frost participates in, yet sees the wholeness, of northern New England.

H103   ENGLE, PAUL. "About Robert Frost," American Prefaces, IV (April 1939), 100.
   This article is a welcome to Frost from Iowa City prior to his visit there. It praises Frost especially because "He has made the art of poetry as native to Vermont as maple sugar." It hopes that he will teach them "to make poetry at home in Iowa."

H104   FOSTER, CHARLES H. "America's One-Man Revolution," American Prefaces, IV (April 1939), 101.
   Written in a casual personal tone, this article praises Frost as "man thinking, ... an original, a one-man revolution."

H105   "Frosty Beer," Time, XXXIV (November 27, 1939), 38.
   On Frost's pedagogical methods at Harvard.

H106   "Gold Medal Poet," Scholastic, XXXIV (February 4, 1939), 25E.
   One paragraph on Frost's winning the gold medal of the National Institute of Arts and Letters.

H107   LADD, HENRY A. "Memories of Robert Frost," Touchstone (Amherst), IV (February 1939), 13, 32.

H. ARTICLES

LADD, HENRY A. (cont.)
A former student recalls Frost's "acceptance of life and people," but also his "violent prejudice."

H108   MAY, STACY. "Robert Frost: A Reminiscence," Touchstone (Amherst), IV (February 1939), 19, 32.
Recalls a dinner and conversation where Frost's watch fails, making him late to a party.

H109   MCNEILL, LOUISE. "The Sick Mind," American Prefaces, IV (April 1939), 102, 103.
Troubled people may find comfort in reading Frost's work. (Frost is mentioned only incidentally in one sentence.)

H110   MORSE, RICHARD ELY. "An Impression of Frost," Touchstone (Amherst), IV (February 1939), 23.
A brief recollection of Frost talking "earnestly and brilliantly, with wit and with wisdom."

H111   NEWDICK, ROBERT S. "Robert Frost Looks at War," South Atlantic Quarterly, XXXVIII (January 1939), 52-59.
"It cannot be disputed that, though it has not submerged [Frost's] faith in some kind of survival of human will, war has led him to ever harder and sharper thinking, and to conclusions that, however they may disappoint wishful pacifists, must satisfy even hard bitten political realists."

H112   RICHARDS, E. A. "A Reality Among Ghosts," Touchstone (Amherst), IV (February 1939), 20.
A general account of impressions of Frost at Amherst.

H113   RODMAN, TOM. "Robert Frost at Amherst," Touchstone (Amherst), IV (February 1939), 7-8.
A biographical introduction to the "Robert Frost Symposium" issue.

H114   ROOT, E. MERRILL. "Robert Frost At Amherst: 1917," Touchstone (Amherst), IV (February 1939), 11-12.
An affectionate reminiscence, bordering on idolatry.

H115   VAN DORE, WADE. "Poet of the Trees," Christian Science Monitor Weekly Magazine, December 23, 1939, pp. 3, 14.
This is a personal reminiscence of Frost as literally a

VAN DORE, WADE (cont.)
    planter of trees. Written by a man who worked together with
    Frost as 'hired man' on his farm. Frost "will leave many
    famous poems behind him, but he will leave a greater number
    of trees. "

H116   WHITE, OWEN S. "What The Lizard Learned, " Touchstone (Am-
        herst), IV (February 1939), 14, 31, 32.
            A recollection of Frost's innovative handling of his drama
        course in 1916.

H117   YOUNG, STARK. "A Letter From Stark Young, " Touchstone (Am-
        herst), IV (February 1939), 9.
            With tongue in cheek Young concludes his noncommittal
        letter: "The thought that I had a share in the effort to bring
        Frost to Amherst College has always seemed to me part pay-
        ment on [Young's debt to Amherst]. I can only hope that such
        a statement will carry with it the full meaning it has for me. "

1940

H118   BENÉT, WILLIAM ROSE. "Poetry Today in America, " Saturday
        Review of Literature, XXII (August 10, 1940), 3-4, 17.
            Frost is mentioned in passing in regard to his having had
        to go to England to get his first books published.

H119   CHURCH, RICHARD. "Robert Frost -- A Prophet in his own Coun-
        try, " Fortnightly, CLIII (May 1940), 539-46.
            Discusses Frost's decade-long residence in England and
        its influence on him. Calls him a major poet --"one who
        brings into a language and its poetry a new element of thought
        and experience, and a new twist of phraseology. " Of Frost's
        simplicity he writes: "That is his philosophy. Reject nothing;
        but minimize it, in order to see it more roundly, and to locate
        it in its place in the chain of endless eventuality. "

H120   COLUM, PADRAIC. "Frost in Dublin, " Mark Twain Quarterly,
        III (Spring 1940), 11.
            Recalls his experience of a visit to Dublin Castle with
        Frost who, upon inquiring about his coat of arms, found out
        that they were "a grey squirrel and a pine tree. "

H. ARTICLES

H121   HEYWOOD, TERENCE. "Homage to Frost," Poetry Review,
           XXXI (March - April 1940), 129-35.
               Heywood pays tribute to Frost for being a "sane, natural
           and very human person" in his poetry.

H122   HOWE, M. A. DE WOLFE. "You Used to Read It, Too," Saturday
           Review of Literature, XXI (March 23, 1940), 3-4, 17-18.
               Howe discusses his experience as corresponding editor of
           the Youth's Companion in which Frost published some of his
           early poems.

H123   NEWDICK, ROBERT S. "Robert Frost and the Classics," Classi-
           cal Journal, XXXV (April 1940), 403-16.
               Frost read widely in the classics, but in his own poetry
           he is most nearly akin to Vergil.

H124   NEWDICK, ROBERT S. "Robert Frost's Other Harmony," Sewanee
           Review, XLVIII (July - September 1940), 409-18.
               On Frost's prose style which, like that of his poetry, is
           "marked by simplicity in vocabulary and diction, by numerous
           short packed sentences, and by homely talking images and il-
           lustrations."

H125   DU BOIS, ARTHUR E. "Nobody Fears Robert Frost," Mark Twain
           Quarterly, III (Spring 1940), 9-11.
               A discussion of the "tentative" and quiet tone of Frost's
           poetry.

H126   ECKERT, ROBERT P., Jr. "Robert Frost in England," Mark
           Twain Quarterly, III (Spring 1940), 5-8, 23.
               On Frost's career in England and his relationship with
           Edward Thomas.

H127   FLETCHER, JOHN GOULD. "Robert Frost the Outlander," Mark
           Twain Quarterly, III (Spring 1940), 3-4, 23.
               Discussion of Frost as a poet who has maintained his
           individuality in an age of "movements."

H128   GARLAND, HAMLIN. "Quiet Acceptance," Mark Twain Quarterly,
           III (Spring 1940), 11.
               "I take pleasure in his friendship which I hope he will
           continue to hold even if he does not put it into words."

H129   HERRICK, DAPHNE. "Robert Frost Reads at a Vermont Inn,"
       Mark Twain Quarterly, III (Spring 1940), 12-13.
           Recalls her reactions to Frost reading his own work.
       Speaks of Frost's "great capacity to recognize the essence of
       life in whatever form he encountered it, and to express that
       experience in words that make it more real to other people."

H130   [Introduction] to An Anniversary - Robert Frost. Phi Beta Kappa,
       Delta Chapter, Tufts College, May 7, 1915 - May 22, 1940.
       Unpaginated [1 p.].
           Brief biographical note which gives account of Frost's
       reading at Tufts on May 7, 1915, his first public appearance in
       the United States.

H131   "John Masefield Pays Tribute," Mark Twain Quarterly, III (Spring
       1940), 13.
           Cites Masefield's tribute to Frost on his 65th birthday in
       which he calls Frost "one of the truest and best of living poets,
       who has sought his inspiration in the enduring things of life...."

H132   MAC VEAGH, LINCOLN. "Sees Life Steadily and Whole," Mark
       Twain Quarterly, III (Spring 1940), 13.
           A tribute to Frost for his "classic pre-occupation with the
       universal seen through the particular, and his majestic range."

H133   "Robert Frost the American Horace," Mark Twain Quarterly, III
       (Spring 1940), 1-2.
           Introduces special Frost 65th birthday number. Gives
       brief biographical sketch and praises Frost for sincerity in
       his poetry.

H134   WOLFE, CARMIE S. "Robert Frost," Scholastic, XXXVI (April 1,
       1940), 20.
           A brief discussion of the life, career, and literary achieve-
       ment of Frost.

1941

H135   WAGGONER, HYATT HOWE. "Humanistic Idealism of Robert
       Frost," American Literature, XIII (November 1941), 207-23.
           Examines influence of Emerson upon Frost, particularly
       that of Emerson's essay "Fate." Frost "finds support for his

H. ARTICLES

WAGGONER, HYATT HOWE (cont.)
idealism neither in the scholastic theologians nor in the Greek classics but in Emerson and James and his own experience."

1942

H136   BERKELMAN, ROBERT G. "Robert Frost and the Middle Way," College English, III (January 1942), 347-53.
On Frost's sense of moderation as expressed in his personal life and in his poetry. Frost is "Aristotle's golden mean dressed in American overalls."

H137   NASH, RAY. "Meeting of Mounted Men," Print, III (Spring 1942), [Unpaginated].
"Two men on their two winged horses riding together, riding high, riding easy: Robert Frost and J.J. Lankes."

H138   SAUL, GEORGE BRANDON. "Brief Observations on Frost and [James] Stephens," News Letter of the College English Association, IV (October 1942), 5.
Finds a parallel in Stephens' "Rhymes and Rhythms" and Frost's "The Wind and the Rain."

H139   Survey Graphic, XXXI (May 1942), 256. Reproduction of an etching of Frost by Theodore Brenson to announce publication of A Witness Tree.

1943

H140   BOLTÉ, CHARLES G. "Robert Frost Returns: Poet Welcomed Back to Dartmouth as Ticknor Fellow," Dartmouth Alumni Magazine, XXXVI (November 1943), 13-15, 26.

H141   BRÉGY, KATHERINE. "Frost, Perennial Pulitzer Winner," America, LXIX (September 11, 1943), 633-34.
Brief history of Frost's life and career and praise for his "sanity and simplicity."

H142   COFFIN, ROBERT P. TRISTRAM. [Review of Fire and Ice], American Literature, XIV (January 1943), 435-40.
Review of Lawrance Thompson's Fire and Ice: The Art and Thought of Robert Frost (F7). Criticizes Thompson for failing

COFFIN, ROBERT P. TRISTRAM (cont.)
to capture Frost in his critical net and for representing Frost "as more systematic in his thought than he really is." Praises Thompson's analysis of Frost as a man. Concludes that "This is decidedly a good book on one side of Robert Frost. The side of the mind. Unfortunately, the heart comes out a poor second."

H143   CORBIN, HAROLD H., Jr. "Frost's 'Neither Out Far Nor In Deep'," Explicator, I (May 1943), Item 58.
The poem "is an incompleted and therefore typically more realistic version of a traditional theme: the futile, world-wide quest for perfection (here certainty) which is resolved only upon the return to the hearth, the beggar at the moat, etc."

H144   HENDRICKS, CECILIA HENNEL. [Frost's "Neither Out Far Nor In Deep"], Explicator, I (May 1943), Query 26.
"Stanzas three and four of 'Neither Out Far Nor In Deep' are. . . not experience but implication or suggestion of the way human beings, 'the people along the sand,' look at life and truth, or as line ten, look for truth."

H145   E., J. "Frost's 'Neither Out Far Nor In Deep'," Explicator, I (April 1943), Query 26.
Request for an explanation of stanzas three and four.

H146   MORSE, STEARNS. "The Wholeness of Robert Frost," Virginia Quarterly Review, XIX (Summer 1943), 412-16.
Defends Frost against the charge that he is not concerned with the fate of the country because he is not turning out war poetry to order. Says that the kind of patriotism expressed by Frost is more subtle and enduring than that which bids people to jump on band wagons.

H147   "Some Woodcuts of J. J. Lankes & Some Talk of Robert Frost," Month at Goodspeed's, XIV (January 1943), 86-89.
Record of a discussion with Lankes about his woodcuts of Frost country.

H148   WHICHER, GEORGE F. "Out for Stars: A Meditation on Robert Frost," Atlantic Monthly, CLXXI (May 1943), 64-67.
An examination of "the many levels of implication beneath

H. ARTICLES

WHICHER, GEORGE F. (cont.)
the innocent-looking surfaces of Robert Frost's poems. . . ."
Defends Frost's use of poetry as a means of communication
and defends him against charges that he does not "take on the
class struggle."

1944

H149   BECK, WARREN. "Poetry's Chronic Disease," English Journal,
XXXIII (September 1944), 357-64 [363].
Urges teachers to recognize the distinctions among three
types of would-be poets: "those who want to be poets, because
poets are so spectacularly notable; those who want to write
'poetry,' because they just love poetry; and those who occasion-
ally want to write a poem, to best express this or that memorable experience or reflection."

H150   BENÉT, WILLIAM ROSE. "Poetry's Last Twenty Years,"
Saturday Review of Literature, XXVII (August 5, 1944), 100,
102, 104.
An overview of recent English and American poetry.

H151   CLAUSEN, BERNARD C. "A Portrait for Peacemakers," Friends
Intelligencer, CI (January 29, 1944), 71-72.
Gives brief biographical sketch and urges peacemakers
to take heart and strength from Frost.

H152   ADAMS, J. DONALD. "Speaking of Books," New York Times Book
Review, February 20, 1944, Sec. VII, p. 2.
Discussion of Frost's introduction, "The Figure a Poem
Makes," to his Collected Poems. Agrees with Frost's dictum
that "a poem may be worked over once it is in being, but it
may not be worried into being."

H153   COWLEY, MALCOLM. "Frost: A Dissenting Opinion," New Republic, CXI (September 11, 1944), 312-13.
Cowley takes issue with the more zealous admirers of
Frost who use him "as a sort of banner for their own moral or
political crusades." These admirers demand that "American
literature should be affirmative, optimistic, uncritical and
'truly of this nation,'" and in Frost they find a symbol of their
desires. He disagrees with those who say that Frost is "the

COWLEY, MALCOLM (cont.)

one great American poet of our time" and "the only living New Englander in the great tradition, fit to be placed beside Emerson, Hawthorne, and Thoreau." Such an analysis, according to Cowley, merely diminishes his stature. He says that faithfulness to the New England spirit was not something that Emerson, Hawthorne and Thoreau intentionally cultivated. They realized that a New England spirit, standing alone, would be narrow and that it needed cross-fertilization from alien philosophies.

H154 COWLEY, MALCOLM. "The Case Against Mr. Frost: II, " New Republic, CXI (September 18, 1944), 345-47.

Cowley presents "a case against Robert Frost as a social philosopher in verse and as a representative of the New England tradition." He argues, on the basis of sentiments expressed by characters in Frost's poems, that the poet is opposed to innovation, to new ideas and to Christian charity. He maintains that Frost sets before us the ideal of separateness rather than charity or brotherhood. Claims that Frost is outside the New England tradition because, unlike Thoreau, Emerson, and Hawthorne, he is concerned with only himself and his near neighbors. Frost does not compensate for what he lacks in breadth by greater depth; "he does not strike far inward into the wilderness of human nature."

H155 DE VOTO, BERNARD. "The Maturity of American Literature, " Saturday Review of Literature, XXVII (August 5, 1944), 14-18.

Brief mention of Frost.

H156 H., W. "Frost's 'The Death of the Hired Man', " Explicator, II (June 1944), Query 35.

Suggests that a resolution of the differing points of view expressed by Thompson in Fire and Ice and Coffin in American Literature might be achieved by an examination of lines 169-71.

H157 WALCUTT, CHARLES C. "Frost's 'The Death of the Hired Man', " Explicator, III (October 1944), Item 7.

An attempt to resolve the differing interpretations of Thompson and Coffin, in response to W.H.'s query (H156). The poem "is richer than either" Thompson and Coffin make it. All three persons in the poem "are fallible human beings.

H. ARTICLES

WALCUTT, CHARLES C. (cont.)
Robert Frost is too wise to sentimentalize an unreliable old
rascal; or to make Mary a saint and Warren hard-hearted and
irascible. His poem deals with the human region between such
extremes."

1945

H158 COOK, REGINALD L. "Robert Frost: A Time to Listen," College
English, VII (November 1945), 66-71.
On tone and style in Frost's conversation and poetry.
"Like Emerson, [Frost] speaks the thought that suggests itself
and, like Thoreau, he listens behind him for his wit, and thus
shows new proportions to the problem and sets the inquirer
thinking anew."

H159 HATFIELD, H. C. "Frost's The Masque of Reason," Explicator,
IV (November 1945), Item 9.
Answers query by Herzberg (H160). Traces source of the
quotation to Dante's Paradiso, I, 49-51.

H160 HERZBERG, MAX J. "Frost's The Masque of Reason," Explicator,
III (June 1945), Query 20.
Herzberg seeks the source of the phrase "the greatest
Western poem yet" referred to in Job's speech.

H161 MC GIFFERT, JOHN. "Something in Robert Frost," English Journal,
XXXIV (November 1945), 469-71.
On the deliberate philosophical uncertainty expressed in
Frost's poetry. "One of the poet's original gifts is ability to
endow a sharply specific experience with hints of man's doubt-
ful power to interpret it."

H162 "Robert Frost To Be Honored on His 70th Birthday," Publisher's
Weekly, CXLVII (March 10, 1945), 1120.
Cites events in honor of Frost's 70th birthday: publication
by Spiral Press of a limited edition (750 copies) of A Masque
of Reason; luncheon given by Holt at which Frost will dine with
J.W. Krutch, Archibald MacLeish, Louis Untermeyer and
Mark Van Doren and others; honorary dinner given by the PEN
Club; Jones Library at Amherst will present special exhibition
of Frost material.

H163 WHICHER, GEORGE F. "Frost at Seventy, " American Scholar,
XIV (Autumn 1945), 405-14.
Rebuttal to Cowley's case against Frost (H153-54). Sums
up the situation by saying: "But regardless of passing fashions
in criticism, the reading public has accepted Frost as the poet
of our time and country; and the ultimate test of a poet is not,
as Job whimsically remarks, how he treats the poor, but what
kind of artistic performance he is capable of giving. "

1946

H164 BARTLETT, DONALD. "A Friend's View of Robert Frost, " New
Hampshire Troubadour, XVI (November 1946), 22-25.
Bartlett writes that "good poets make good company just
as much as Good Fences Make Good Neighbors. It is the more
so if they are, like Frost, shrewd and solitary masters of
their craft who have the humor to know what they are about,
and when they mow, do not whack the timothy down, but take
time to whet their blade on a hard stone, and then cut it. "

H165 CLARK, SYLVIA. "Robert Frost: The Derry Years, " New Hampshire Troubadour, XVI (November 1946), 13-16.
Gives a brief history of Derry and Frost's connection with
the Pinkerton Academy.

H166 COX, SIDNEY. "Robert Frost at Plymouth, " New Hampshire
Troubadour, XVI (November 1946), 18-22.
Frost's year of teaching at the Plymouth Normal School
(1911-12).

H167 The Heritage of The English-Speaking Peoples and Their Responsi-
bility -- A Summary of The Conference held at Kenyon College,
Gambier, Ohio -- October 4, 5, and 6, 1946. [Gambier, Ohio]:
Kenyon College, 1946. [Unpaginated.]
Brief mention of Frost's prefatory remarks including some
short quotations.

H168 LAMBUTH, DAVID. "The Unforgettable Robert Frost, " New Hampshire Troubadour, XVI (November 1946), 25-29.
The "unforgettable" poetry flashes "into the mind in
moments of stress, moments of insight. "

H. ARTICLES

H169   MORSE, STEARNS. "Robert Frost and New Hampshire, " New
Hampshire Troubadour, XVI (November 1946), 6-8.
On Frost's reception in New Hampshire.

H170   POOLE, ERNEST. "When Frost Was Here, " New Hampshire
Troubadour, XVI (November 1946), 10-13.
On Frost's depiction of New Hampshire in his poetry.

H171   WAGGONER, H[YATT] H[OWE]. "Robert Frost's A Masque of
Reason, " Explicator, IV (March 1946), Item 32.
Suggests Emerson's "Uriel" as the source previously
sought by Herzberg (H160) and not Dante, as suggested by Hatfield (H159).

H172   WEST, HERBERT F. "Robert Frost--A Brief Biographical Sketch,"
New Hampshire Troubadour, XVI (November 1946), 5-6.
Introduces special Frost issue.

H173   WHICHER, GEORGE F. "Unit and Universe. . . ," Forum, CVI
(July 1946), 66-70.
Discusses some ambiguous lines in A Masque of Reason
and traces their source to Emerson.

H174   CAMPBELL, HARRY MODEAN. "Frost's 'Sitting by a Bush in
Broad Sunlight', " Explicator, V (December 1946), Item 18.
Disagrees with Thompson's interpretation in Fire and Ice.
Sees the poem as expressing "religious agnosticism. "

1947

H175   CHALMERS, GORDON KEITH. "Preface, " The Heritage of the English-Speaking Peoples and Their Responsibility-- Addresses at
the Conference October 1946--Kenyon College. [Gambier,
Ohio]: Kenyon College, 1947. [Unpaginated.]
Brief mention that Frost's remarks made prefatory to
reading were ex tempore and thus are not printed in this volume.

H176   COOK, REGINALD L. "Poet in the Mountains," Western Review,
        XI (Spring 1947), 175-81.
            Describes Frost's home in Vermont and his conversational
        ability. "His talk, like his poems, is not literary. It is an
        act of life. Part of the pleasure comes from its spontaneity.
        He doesn't spur an afflatus. The talk has not been worked up.
        It may waver or divagate but it does not break and grow dull."

H177   COOK, REGINALD L. "Robert Frost as Teacher," College Eng-
        lish, VII (February 1947), 251-55.
            On Frost's teaching methods and their power to make
        "human experience the end and art the means."

H178   FRANCIS, ROBERT. "Shared Solitude of Robert Frost," Forum,
        CVIII (October 1947), 193-97.
            Francis defines poetry as "shared solitude" in which the
        poet communicates part of his inner, solitary world. Frost is
        unlike many modern poets in that his is not a poetry of confes-
        sion masked in obscurity. Frost "does his best to communi-
        cate. . . all that he sees fit to confess."

H179   JARRELL, RANDALL. "The Other Robert Frost," The Nation,
        CLXV (November 29, 1947), 588, 590-92.
            Jarrell sets out to expose the "other Robert Frost"-- the
        one that is neglected and misunderstood because of the readers'
        "not knowing his poems well enough or from knowing the wrong
        poem too well." Lists his selection of Frost's best poems as
        follows: "The Witch of Coös," "Neither Out Far Nor In Deep,"
        "Design," "A Servant To Servants," "Directive," "Provide,
        Provide," "Home Burial," "Acquainted with the Night," "The
        Pauper Witch of Grafton," "An Old Man's Winter Night," "The
        Gift Outright," "Desert Places," "The Fear." Says that these
        poems are far from being optimistic and orthodox. "The limits
        which existence approaches and falls back from have seldom
        been stated with such bare exposure." Of Frost's new books
        (Steeple Bush, A Masque of Mercy and A Masque of Reason) he
        says they "have few of his virtues, most of his vices and all of
        his tricks; the heathen who would be converted to Frost by them
        is hard to construct."
            Reprinted in Poetry and the Age. New York: Knopf, 1953.
        Pp. 28-36.

H. ARTICLES

H180   MATHIAS, ROLAND. "Robert Frost: An Appreciation," Poetry
       Review, XXXVIII (March - April 1947), 102-06.
           On Frost's neglect in England and that he "belongs to an
       older English tradition, now all but extinct, a tradition which
       was always insufficiently represented among English poets --
       that of the craftsman-poet."

H181   "Portrait," Publisher's Weekly, CLI (June 7, 1947), Section One,
       2847.
           Poster portrait by Michael Gross to be used by Holt in
       promotion of all Frost titles.

H182   "Portrait," Time, XLIX (June 16, 1947), 102-03.
           ". . . what was once only granitic Yankee individualism in
       his work has hardened into bitter and often uninspired Tory
       social commentary."

H183   SPITZ, LEON, RABBI. "Robert Frost's Job Drama," American
       Hebrew, CLVII (September 12, 1947), 13, 89.
           On scriptural thought in A Masque of Reason. "Frost was
       . . . a groper for God."

H184   WARREN, ROBERT PENN. "The Themes of Robert Frost," Hop-
       wood Lecture. Michigan Alumnus Quarterly Review, LIV (De-
       cember 6, 1947), 1-11.
           Finds "After Apple-Picking" Frost's "masterpiece."
       "Man is set off from nature by the fact that he is capable
       of the dream, but he is also of nature, and his best dream is
       the dream of the fact, and the fact is his position of labor and
       fate in nature though not of her."

1948

H185   BROWN, WALLACE CABLE. " 'A Poem Should Not Mean But Be',"
       University of Kansas City Review, XV (Autumn 1948), 57-64
       [62-63].
           Contains a discussion of Frost's "Desert Places" in proof
       of the statement: "Much of the poetry of Robert Frost similarly
       involves the making of moral judgements, and the conceptual
       meaning is so dominant in some of his poems that they must be
       called didactic." Generally the article presents the view that
       one cannot take literally MacLeish's statement contained in the

BROWN, WALLACE CABLE (cont.)
title of the article, but rather one must be aware that "good poems can never be purely esthetic, if by definition the 'esthetic' is segregated from the other areas of human experience."

H186 COOK, REGINALD L. "Robert Frost's Asides on His Poetry," American Literature, XIX (January 1948), 351-59.
Frost on the process of writing poetry and the meaning of his own poems. "His method in the readings is invariably the same. The poem he quotes or reads stimulates brief, pungent reactions which show several tendencies. Either he identifies the poem with the experience in which it originates, or he indicates the way the poem impresses him in form or content."

H187 COX, SIDNEY. "Some Educational Beliefs and Practices of Robert Frost," Educational Record, XXIX (October 1948), 410-22.
Frost's teaching techniques and the means employed to encourage students to think, feel, and imagine independently.

H188 LONG, WILLIAM S. "Frost," CEA Critic, X (November 1948), 4.
Brief discussion of Frost as poet and person.

H189 MARDENBOROUGH, AIMEE. "Robert Frost: The Old and the New," Catholic World, CLXVIII (December 1948), 232-36.
On Frost's literary development and "a study in the ugly degeneration of great poetic genius." According to Mardenborough, Frost was "a butterfly before he became a cocoon, finally disguising his intellectual beauty behind a wall of bitterness, sarcasm and disillusionment." Accuses Frost of blasphemy in A Masque of Reason.

H190 O'DONNELL, W. G. "Frost and New England: A Revaluation," Yale Review, XXXVII (June 1948), 698-712.
Defends Frost against the notion that his popularity indicates a lack of depth in his poetry. Concludes that "in so far as Frost is a voice of New England, he is a minor figure in contemporary literature; to the extent that he makes his New England universal in meaning and implication, he is a significant writer."

H. ARTICLES

H191   S., C. M. "Frost's 'To Earthward'," Explicator, VII (November
        1948), Query 4. Reprinted in Explicator, XIII (May 1955),
        Query 3.
                Requests explanation of "To Earthward" which, it is felt,
        "functions on several levels."

H192   THOMPSON, LAWRANCE. "An Early Frost Broadside," New
        Colophon, I (January 1948), 5-12.
                On the discovery of a broadside copy of Frost's first
        separately printed poem, "The Later Minstrel," a tribute to
        Longfellow published in 1907.

H193   WINTERS, YVOR. "Robert Frost: or, The Spiritual Drifter as
        Poet," Sewanee Review, LVI (Autumn, 1948), 564-96.
                "Frost. . . may be described as a good poet in so far as
        he may be said to exist, but a dangerous influence in so far as
        his existence is incomplete. He is in no sense a great poet,
        but he is at times a distinguished and valuable poet."

1949

H194   COOK, REGINALD L. "Frost as a Parablist," Accent, X (Autumn
        1949), 33-41.
                On Frost's gift for "saying one thing and meaning another."
        "Frost's personal story-telling gift, which combines with an
        ability to perceive and join hidden relationships in metaphor, is
        a particular contribution to American literature."

H195   COOK, REGINALD L. "Frost Country," Vermont Life, III (Sum-
        mer 1949), 15-17.
                The importance of "locality," more specifically the land
        "north of Boston" in Frost's poetry. Illustrated by several
        photographs of Frost and his Vermont home.

H196   COX, SIDNEY. "Robert Frost and Poetic Fashion," American
        Scholar, XVIII (Winter 1948-49), 78-86.
                On A Masque of Mercy, A Masque of Reason, and Steeple
        Bush. Cox writes that these books have gone unnoticed because
        of their unfashionableness. Frost has never been in fashion
        because he will not adapt. Frost continues to write about the
        enduring human situation rather than about timely and ephemer-
        al problems.

H197   COX, SIDNEY. "Mischief in Robert Frost's Way of Teaching, "
        Educational Forum, XIII (January 1949), 171-77.
                Excerpted from Cox's A Swinger of Birches. Frost tried
        to resist the dull and the coercive and to stir the imaginations
        of his students.

H198   HORTON, ROD W. , AND LAWRANCE THOMPSON. "The Pasture, "
        CEA Critic, XI (February 1949), 4-5.
                An interpretation of the poem.

H199   HUTCHENS, JOHN K. "On an Author, " New York Herald Tribune
        Weekly Book Review, May 29, 1949, p. 2.
                Brief biographical sketch.

H200   O'DONNELL, WILLIAM G. "Parable in Poetry, " Virginia Quarter-
        ly Review, XXV (Spring 1949), 269-82.
                A discussion of Frost's religious poetry with special at-
        tention to A Masque of Mercy and "Directive" which is his
        "most successful religious poem because it conveys a major
        religious experience without sacrificing to the weight of the
        Christian tradition the author's wit and his highly distinctive
        diction, rhythm, and imagery. "

H201   PERRINE, LAURENCE. "Frost's 'Neither Out Far Nor In Deep,'"
        Explicator, VII (April 1949), Item 46.
                Disagrees with Corbin's explication (H143). Sees the poem
        as "an expression of Frost's humanism--his belief in human
        dignity, in creative effort and in 'man's unconquerable mind.'"

H202   "Robert Frost Awarded Limited Editions Club Medal, " Publisher's
        Weekly, CLVI (November 26, 1949), 2207-08.
                Citation on Frost's being awarded the Limited Editions
        Club Medal on November 16, 1949. Award for Complete Poems
        (1949).

H203   RYAN, ALVAN S. "Frost's A Witness Tree, " Explicator, VII
        (March 1949), Item 39.
                Meaning of "Beech" clarified by reference to recent article
        on Alfred D. Teare, New England woodsman and craftsman.

H204   VIERECK, PETER. "Parnassus Divided, " Atlantic Monthly,
        CLXXXIV (October 1949), 67-70.

H. ARTICLES

VIERECK, PETER (cont.)
Defends Frost against the misconception that popularity implies superficiality. Says of Frost's poetry: "Frost's stubborn conventionality of form makes many young poets and readers think his is also a conventionality of meaning. On the contrary, he is one of the most original writers of our time. It is the self-conscious avant-garde rebels who follow the really rigid and tiresome conventions."

1950

H205   HOLMES, JOHN. "Close Up of an American Poet at 75," New York Times Magazine, March 26, 1950, pp. 12, 72-73, 75-77.
"Robert Frost's lifelong loyalty to his own first principles makes him one of the really great radicals of this century."

H206   BOWRA, C. M. "Re-Assessments I: Robert Frost," Adelphi, XXVII (November 1950), 46-64.
"His poetry is concerned not merely with his own corner of New England but, strictly and accurately, with what he actually knows of it." Since the poetry deals with facts, it is realistic, but "this observation of real things is presented in a gentle and unobtrusive style."

H207   HOFFMAN, DAN G. "Frost's 'For Once, Then, Something'," Explicator, IX (November 1950), Item 17.
"Whatever that reality was he cannot know, but to have been made aware of another realm, though, is 'something'."

H208   HUFF, WILLIAM HOWARD. "Graphic Bio-Bibliographies," Wilson Library Bulletin, XXV (September 1950), 70.
A very brief sketch of Frost's life with a list of some of his works and their publishing dates.

H209   LARSON, MILDRED. "No False Curves: Robert Frost on Education," School and Society, LXXII (September 16, 1950), 177-80.
Frost believed a less formal schedule and method of teaching and less busy work are desirable developments. College should not mold or type people or leave a "group mark" on them. Our schools retard instead of foster artists. The aim of education is the development of the individual.

H210   LARSON, MILDRED. "Robert Frost as Teacher, " Journal of Education, CXXXIII (September 1950), 168-69.
        On the results of questionnaires sent to several of Frost's former students. Frost wanted to "teach a little and teach it hard" through informal but personal contacts.

H211   "Life Congratulates Hale, Hearty Old Folk Who Just Refuse to Quit, " Life, XXVIII (April 3, 1950), 44-45 [45].
        A salute to Frost, Arturo Toscanini, Connie Mack, and Winifred Robb, M.D. Frost's plans for his 90th year: "I'm going to bring out anthologies of other people's works. "

H212   MORGAN, CARLYLE. " 'Only More Sure. . .' --Back Over the Years with Robert Frost, " Christian Science Monitor Magazine, March 25, 1950, p. 3.
        Article with portrait calls Frost "even more than a great poet; he is virtually a way of life. " Discusses Frost's early years and decides Frost was right when he said his friends would not find him changed over the years .

They would not find me changed from him they knew--
Only more sure of all I thought was true.

H213   NASH, RAY. "The Poet and the Pirate, " New Colophon, II (February 1950), 311-21.
        On Frost's friendship with Thomas Bird Mosher, the bibliophile. With transcripts of Frost's letters. "The attraction of opposites must have governed that friendship. Offhand it would be hard to think of two personalities more integral and more unlike. "

H214   "The Senate Honors Frost on His 75th Birthday, " Publisher's Weekly, CLVII (May 20, 1950), 2175.
        On the resolution offered in the U.S. Senate by Taft of Ohio on March 24, 1950. The resolution was to pay tribute to Frost by extending "felicitations of the Nation which he has served so well. "

H215   STEGNER, WALLACE. "Fiction: A Lens on Life, " Saturday Review of Literature, XXXIII (April 22, 1950), 9-10, 32-34.
        Article supports Frost's statement that "A writer is entitled to anything the reader can find in him. " Also some discussion of Hemingway and Gertrude Stein.

H. ARTICLES

H216   "To Honor Robert Frost," Publisher's Weekly, CLVIII (October 14, 1950), 1784.
> On the various tributes the poet received on his 75th birthday: "an outpouring of respect and affection. . . from those who know and re-read the poems and who have known and loved the man who wrote them."

H217   "The Voice of New England," Coronet, XXVII (March 1950), 14.
> Calls Frost the dean of American poets. "His cracker-barrel wisdom. . ., his consistency has made him one of the world's most widely read writers and America's poet laureate."

H218   W., R., Jr. "Saturday Review Pulitzer Prize," Saturday Review of Literature, XXXIII (May 13, 1950), 18.
> Announces that Frost's Complete Poems is awarded the Saturday Review prize for poetry in 1949, though Gwendolyn Brooks' Annie Allen won the Pulitzer Prize.

H219   WEBSTER, H. T. "Frost's 'West Running Brook'," Explicator, VIII (February 1950), Item 32.
> "The poem seems to be a study in contraries constructed in a somewhat dialectical fashion." Also, "Perhaps somewhere in nature, the counterpull against change gives the cosmos some kind of stability."

H220   [WYLIE, JEFF.] "Pawky Poet," Time, LVI (October 9, 1950), 76-82.
> ". . . Frost is a poet with few disciples. Today's bright young men look to the intricate mannered, literary methods of T.S. Eliot and W.H. Auden for their models. They grudgingly admire Frost. . . and smart under the reproach: 'If Frost can make himself intelligible, why can't you?'" Frost's poetry is "a deceptively artless poetry of common speech. But behind the apparent artlessness, was a cracker-barrel Socrates with a sense of humor--a pawky humor, that was partly serious when it seemed most irreverent, gently mocking when it seemed most grave."
> Reprinted in condensed form in Reader's Digest, LVIII (January 1951), 91-94.

1951

H221   BARKER, ADDISON. "Good Fences Make Good Neighbors," Journal of American Folklore, LXIV (October - December 1951), 421.
> The proverb "Good Fences Make Good Neighbors" was printed in Blum's Farmer's and Planter's Almanac on page 13

BARKER, ADDISON (cont.)
of the 1850 issue, published in Winston-Salem, North Carolina.

H222   FOWLE, ROSEMARY. "The Indwelling Spider: An Aspect of the Poetry of Robert Frost," Papers of the Michigan Academy of Science, Arts, and Letters, XXXVII (June 1951), 437-44.
"He is popular and admired, but without imitators or influence." Frost's only greatness is in "his destruction, disorder, and brutality" themes. These lines from "Range Finding" illustrate "the characteristic way Frost's imagination fails to meet his problem."

The indwelling spider ran to greet the fly,
But finding nothing, sullenly withdrew.

H223   "Frost on Wax," Scholastic, LIX (November 7, 1951), 23T.
Article is a salute to Robert Frost on the appearance of the 1951 Robert Frost Recordings and his newest poetry collection, The Road Not Taken.

H224   HOFFMAN, DANIEL G. "Robert Frost's Paul Bunyan: A Frontier Hero in New England Exile," Midwest Folklore, I (April 1951) 13-18.
On Frost's interpretation of the Paul Bunyan myth in "Paul's Wife."

H225   LEWIS, ARTHUR O., Jr. "Frost's 'Departmental'," Explicator, X (October 1951), Item 7.
An attempt to answer D. W. M.'s query (H226). Frost wrote "many times his size," but editor Louis Untermeyer changed his to her.

H226   M., D. W. "Frost's 'Departmental, or, My Ant Jerry'," Explicator, IX (June 1951), Query 9.
Asks for reason for shift in pronoun in third and fourth lines of the poem.

H227   RANSOM, JOHN CROWE. "The Poetry of 1900-1950," Kenyon Review, XIII (January 1951), 445-54.
"There remain the five poets whom I think a common consent will rank as the major poets of our period." Frost is one of these, along with Hardy, Yeats, Robinson, and Eliot.

H. ARTICLES

H228   "Robert Frost, Cracker-Barrel Socrates, " Reader's Digest, LVIII
        (January 1951), 91-94.
             "In a literary age so preoccupied with self-expression that
        it sometimes seems intent on making the reader feel stupid,
        Robert Frost has won him by treating him as an equal. "
             Condensed from Time, LVI (October 9, 1950), 76-82
        (H220).

H229   VAN DOREN, MARK. "Robert Frost's America, " Atlantic Monthly,
        CLXXXVII (June 1951), 32-34.
             "The poet in Frost has never been different from the man,
        or the man from the poet; he has lived in his poetry at the
        same time he has lived outside of it, and neither life has inter-
        fered with the other. "

H230   "Vermont Talk, " Time, LVIII (September 24, 1951), 112.
             Frost is "a great, plain poet speaking in homely Vermont
        cadences. " After listening to recordings of Frost reading his
        poems "it becomes plain that, barring shyness, any Vermont
        hired hand would know how to read the poems right the first
        time. "

1952

H231   BROWN, MALCOLM. "The Sweet Crystalline Cry, " Western Re-
        view, XVI (Summer 1952), 259-74.
             On "the work of the climactic image. . . as it appears in
        Frost's 'Acquainted With the Night'. " In the poem "the con-
        cept . . . of indifference is first presented in a generalized
        figure, then it is restated in four variations of the same
        figure. "

H232   GIERASCH, WALTER. "Frost's 'Devotion', " Explicator, X (May
        1952), Item 50.
             "Not the mind but the heart thinks in a unity of feeling and
        thought demanded by devotion, of being the firm and dependable
        shore to the ever-moving ocean. "

H233   GIERASCH, WALTER. "Frost's 'The Last Mowing', " Explicator,
        X (February 1952), Item 25.
             "The combined meanings of the poem allow the poet to
        view himself as one of the tame and one of the wild at the same

GIERASCH, WALTER (cont.)
time, one of the destroyers as well as one of the lovers of the
tumultuous, colorful, and wasted beauty of the wild flowers."

H234　JARRELL, RANDALL. "To the Laodiceans," Kenyon Review,
XIV (Autumn 1952), 535-61.
Detailed explication of several Frost poems. "If some of
the poems come out of a cynical common sense that is only
wisdom's backward shadow, others come out of wisdom itself--
for it is, still, just possible for that most old-fashioned of old-
fashioned things, wisdom, to maintain a marginal existence in
our world."
Reprinted in his Poetry and the Age, New York: Knopf,
1953. Pp. 37-69.

H235　L., W. P. "Frost's 'Directive'," Explicator, X (March 1952),
Query 4. Reprinted in Explicator, XV (March 1957), Query 2.
Is the poem "really to be interpreted theologically as a
consideration of man's relation to the grace of God"?

H236　PEARCE, ROY HARVEY. "The Poet as Person," Yale Review, XLI
(Spring 1952), 421-40 [427-429].
On modern American poets. "Robert Frost is, in his own
way, a poet whose work is equally characterized by devotion to
culture. . . . Seeking to find a personality, yet turning away
from whatever there is of personality in his own time, he has
found for us his readers--only culture."

H237　POPKIN, HENRY. "Poets as Performers: The Revival of Poetry-
Reading," Theatre Arts, XXXVI (February 1952), 27, 74.
Frost is one of the best examples "of a poet who identifies
himself completely with the attitudes and avowals of his poetry." Frost in verse as in person "embodies the lonely, old-
fashioned recluse" who sometimes chats "with the city folk."

H238　"Robert Frost," Life, XXXIII (November 24, 1954), 106.
Brief note prefaces reprinting of Frost's "The Code."
"Frost was almost unknown in the U.S. until befriended by
Harriet Monroe" who defended "The Code" even though "it
sticks out in various directions like a fretful hedgehog."

H. ARTICLES

H239   SERGEANT, HOWARD. "The Poetry of Robert Frost," English
        Magazine, IX (Spring 1952), 13-16.
                Frost is the leading contemporary exponent of the colloqui-
        al style in the English language. "It is his regional outlook
        and feeling which makes him such a poet of the universe."
        Claims Frost's most striking characteristic is his use of
        speech rhythms. "Frost seldom moralizes, but his philosophy
        is implicit in all his work."

1953

H240   EDMAN, IRWIN. "Spoken Word," Saturday Review of Literature,
        XXXVI (April 25, 1953), 71.
                A review of a Library of Congress recording of Eliot and
        Frost reading their poetry. "Robert Frost's voice was made
        for the reading of Robert Frost's poetry. . . always genuine
        and never overwrought or faked or pretentious or rhetorical."

H241   FRANCIS, ROBERT. "Robert Frost From His Green Mountain,"
        Dalhousie Review, XXXIII (Summer 1953), 117-27.
                Frost "stands on a sort of Green Mountain and banters us
        about our inability to sit still for five minutes." The non-
        aggressive way to live "is beautifully shown in Frost's own
        life" and in his poetry which "is not an extreme laissez-faire.
        Effort is applied, but no unseemly effort."

H242   GAIGE, FRANKLIN. [Robert Frost Reading His Own Poems.]
        Arizona Quarterly, IX (Winter 1953), 377-78.
                A review of a recording. "To hear Mr. Frost read any
        line. . . is to know how that line must inevitably be spoken."

H243   GIERASCH, WALTER. "Frost's 'Brown's Descent'," Explicator,
        XI (June 1953), Item 60.
                On the two versions of the poem, a longer and a shorter
        one. Finds the longer version "inferior" because of Frost's
        "padding" of it with superfluous phrases and images.

H244   SERGEANT, ELIZABETH. "Roots of a Writer," Saturday Review
        of Literature, XXXVI (April 11, 1953), 50, 72.
                Describes one of Frost's birthday parties. ". . . that
        retiring faun, Robert Frost, who still tried for invisibility
        when he met the world."

THE CRITICAL RECEPTION OF ROBERT FROST

H245   WALCUTT, CHARLES. "Interpreting the Symbol," College English, XIV (May 1953), 446-54 [450].
　　　　A discussion of symbolism using "Stopping By Woods. . ."
as example. "If there is a symbol in Frost's poem, it is the
woods--'lovely, dark and deep'-- which are identified by the
clause that follows them as symbolizing the impulse to escape."

1954

H246   ANGOFF, ALLAN. "Robert Frost's Poems," Times Literary Supplement (London), September 17, 1954, lxxxviii-lxxxix.
　　　　"It is Frost's peculiar talent to give to his most delicate
utterance the air of a chance remark. . . ."

H247   ARCHIBALD, R. O. "The Year of Robert Frost's Birth," Notes
and Queries, CXCIX (Old series; I, New series), (January
1954), 40.
　　　　1874 is correct, not 1875.

H248   BEACH, JOSEPH WARREN. "Robert Frost," Yale Review, XLIII
(Winter 1954), 204-17.
　　　　A general survey of Frost's life and career including
Beach's memory of meeting Robert Frost in 1916 and a compari-
son of Emerson and Frost. "Self-Reliance" might have been
Frost's Bible, although he may not share the mysticism of the
"Oversoul." Like Emerson, Frost gives no hint of the natural
depravity of man.

H249   BREIT, HARVEY. "Birthday," New York Times Book Review,
April 11, 1954, p. 8.
　　　　On Frost's eightieth birthday party. Frost has "profound
innocence . . . thorough absence of guile."

H250   CANE, MELVILLE. "Are Poets Returning to Lyricism?," Saturday Review of Literature, XXXVII (January 16, 1954), 8-10,
40-41.
　　　　". . . in the adroit hands of a Robert Frost what was
nothing more than ordinary prose in its inception can be
transmuted and raised to the estate of verse."

H. ARTICLES

H251   COX, SIDNEY. "The Courage to be New: A Reappraisal of Robert
Frost," Vermont History, n. s., XXII (April 1954), 119-26.
      Frost realizes that outside of the Garden of Eden life is
"a diminished thing," but that man can achieve "form, meaningful, if often tragic."

H252   FARJEON, ELEANOR. "Edward Thomas and Robert Frost (from a
memoir)," London Magazine, I (May 1954), 50-61.
      On Frost's years in England and his relationship with
Thomas.

H253   GRIFFITH, BEN. "Frost's 'The Road Not Taken'," Explicator, XII
(June 1954), Item 55.
      "Frost is playing the role of everyman as he spoofs man's
tendency to make a whimsical choice between two equal impera-
tives and to praise his choice later as having made 'all the
difference.'"

H254   HOPKINS, BESS COOPER. "A Study of 'The Death of the Hired
Man'," English Journal, XLIII (April 1954), 175-76, 186.
      Praises Frost's "skill in putting the living speech of men
and women into poetry," and "his ability to take a simple oc-
curence in everyday life, transform its actuality into a thing
of beauty and universality, all the while creating the illusion
that real people are now talking."

H255   HUTCHENS, JOHN K. "On the Books--Eighty," New York Herald
Tribune Book Review, April 11, 1954, p. 2.
      On "the moving and memorable dinner" for Frost on the
eve of his eightieth birthday. Frost recited some poems and
explained the last line of "Stopping by Woods. . . ."
"All it means is that I wanted to go home."

H256   ISAACS, J. "Best Loved of American Poets," Listener, LI (April
1, 1954), 565.
      "At 80 Frost is the best known and the best loved of all
American poets."

H257   KAPLAN, CHARLES. "Frost's 'Two Tramps in Mud Time',"
Explicator, XII (June 1954), Item 51.
      "A narrative" with the "central idea of a delicately poised
equilibrium: the desire, means, and necessity of attaining

KAPLAN, CHARLES (cont.)
balance are the subject behind the incident. " The three stanzas dealing with nature consist of "details illustrating April's
delicate equilibrium between warmth and cold, spring and
winter. " Sees the poem as a symbolic act of "man's need to
achieve personal equilibrium. "

H258   SCHWARTZ, EDWARD. "Frost's 'The Lovely Shall Be Choosers',"
Explicator, XIII (October 1954), Item 3.
The "basic oppositions" in the poem are "between fate and
free will, love and pride, truth and self-delusion. "

H259   STYLITES, SIMEON. "I Wanted to Go Home, " Christian Century,
LXXI (August 4, 1954), 919.
"In these days of symbolism and hidden meanings, when a
host of literary critics are running around with Geiger counters
trying to detect esoteric, enigmatic meanings where there are
none, Mr. Frost's word comes like an acute attack of common
sense. "

H260   "Treasure Chest: Robert Frost, " New York Times Book Review,
March 21, 1954, p. 2.
J. Donald Adams on Frost's writing, especially the prose
piece, "The Figure a Poem Makes. "

H261   UNTERMEYER, LOUIS. "Poets Without Readers, The Sad State of
Poetry in the United States, " Americas, VI (September 1954),
3-5, 26.
Frost is a "self-contradiction. " The Frostian surface is
smooth, forthright and easygoing, but the simplicity is deceptive in Frost's nature as well as the nature of his works. ". . .
playfulness becomes mixed with profundity. "

H262   "What They Are Saying, " Look, XVIII (May 18, 1954), 20.
Frost defines freedom as "when you're easy in your harness. "

1955

H263   MULDER, WILLIAM. "Freedom and Form: Robert Frost's Double
Discipline, " South Atlantic Quarterly, LIV (July 1955), 386-93.
On Frost's ability to appear more usual and free within an

H. ARTICLES

MULDER, WILLIAM (cont.)
ordered form to "bring about successive momentary stays
against confusion."

H264   NITCHIE, ELIZABETH. "Frost's 'The Lovely Shall be Choosers',"
Explicator, XIII (April 1955), Item 39.
The woman is blameless "in the sight of the poet, who
finds the final irony in the circumstances that separated her
from the only 'one' who might have saved her." Disagrees
with Schwarz's interpretation (H258).

H265   "A Poet and a Plight," Life, XXXIX (November 28, 1955), 91-92.
At eighty Frost gave an hour-long recital at the Blackstone
Theatre to a paying audience. Thirty thousand dollars were
raised to pay printer's bills of Poetry: A Magazine of Verse.

H266   VERBILLION, JUNE. "A Poet Speaks," Today, II (December 1955),
8-9.
On one of Frost's readings. ". . . with only a book of his
collected poems and no visible notes, Mr. Frost advanced to
the lectern. . . . The audience soon realized that Mr. Frost
was not a man in a hurry."

H267   WATTS, HAROLD H. "Robert Frost and the Interrupted Dialogue,"
American Literature, XXVII (March 1955), 69-87.
Frost is "ethically curious." "The bulk of his poetry is a
dialogue in which the two speakers are Robert Frost himself
and the entity which we call nature or process." But in later
poems this dialogue is interrupted by a "dialogue with society."

H268   WATTS, HAROLD H. "Three Entities and Robert Frost," Bucknell
Review, V (December 1955), 19-38.
The "three entities" are man, nature, and the "solace" of
man. The conversation in Frost's poems is not for "us."
"Frost, in large part, converses with nature" with which he
has a true exchange. In Frost's poetry "nature is always kept
concrete" and has not "lost its power to be the vehicle of
moral instruction."

H269   WERNER, W. L. "Frost's 'The Lovely Shall Be Choosers',"
Explicator, XIII (April 1955), Item 39.
"The poem is about a lovely woman who refused the love

H. ARTICLES

WERNER, W. L. (cont.)
of a rich, honorable man and who married a poor man." Disagrees with Schwartz's interpretation (H258).

1956

H270   BRODERICK, JOHN C. "Frost's 'Mending Wall'," Explicator, XIV (January 1956), Item 24.
      The theme of the poem is "human separation," and concentrates on "varying ritual responses to nature," and concludes that there is some "supernatural responsibility for the gaps in the wall."

H271   BURGESS, O. N. "Hugh McCrae and Robert Frost," Southerly, XVII, (1956), 152-57.
      "In the two men [there is] the same sub-acidity and good humor." And the "same note of protest" in some of their poems. McCrae is the more oblique of the two. Frost is seldom, if ever, mandarinish. Contends that Frost "is addicted to developing the personal through sly touches of symbolism..."

H272   CHATMAN, SEYMOUR. "Robert Frost's 'Mowing': An Inquiry Into Prosodic Structure," Kenyon Review, XVIII (Summer 1956), 421-38.
      On the relationship of meter to linguistic structure. Analyzes "Mowing" using eight recordings, including one of Frost's. Sets the poem in Trager-Smith linguistic notation.

H273   COOK, REGINALD L. "Frost on Analytical Criticism," College English, XVII (May 1956), 434-38.
      Frost objects to the New Criticism because he is against "a deliberate analysis of the texture and structure of a specific poem. . . . What apparently most disturbs Frost is to see the idea of overthoroughness crowding out mental agility."

H274   COOK, REGINALD L. "Frost on Frost: The Making of Poems," American Literature, XXVIII (March 1956), 62-72.
      "Because his poetry means what it says, there is no reason to assume that it says all it means."

H275   COOK, REGINALD L. "Notes on Frost the Lecturer," Quarterly Journal of Speech, XLII (April 1956), 127-32.

H. ARTICLES

COOK, REGINALD L. (cont.)
Discussion of how Frost became a lecturer, what characterizes his pitch, and why he has been successful on the platform. Frost refers to public speaking as "a funny kind of fatality." Frost is "as responsible in lecturing as he is in his poetry. . . elusive, not evasive." He is "a dramatizer of ideas and an entertainer whose pitch happens to be poetry."

H276   GREENE, MARC T. "Robert Frost at Home," Poetry Review, XLVII (January - March 1956), 16-18.
Describes a visit with Frost at his "home of a simplicity that declares the character of the man himself." Frost answered the door like "a friend to man" and, looking less than "seventy-five by calendar reckoning, he is a convincing manifestation of the fact that 'age' is not to be measured by such standards." "He finds inspiration, even exaltation, in the eccentricities of northern New England weather. . . ."

H277   MCLAUGHLIN, CHARLES A. "Two Views of Poetic Unity," University of Kansas City Review, XXII (Summer 1956), 309-16.
Two methods of poetry interpretation are illustrated by "Stopping By Woods. . . ." "Thus while both interpretations take note that the speaker first sees the woods as property, the dialectical view takes this fact as the starting point for a series of broadening generalizations, and the Chicago view takes it as the sign of a mundane state of mind which is to undergo a psychological change during the course of the poem."

H278   PERRINE, LAURENCE. "Frost's 'Sand Dunes'," Explicator, XIV (March 1956), Item 38.
Takes issue with Yvor Winters' interpretation of the poem (H193). "Winters here uses a clear misinterpretation of the poem, buttressed by a misinterpretation of Emerson, in partial support of an adverse criticism of Frost. . . ." Perrine claims that "Sand Dunes" expresses "Frost's belief in the ability of the human mind to cope with the forces of nature and to emerge undefeated from natural catastrophe."

H279   PROCTOR, PERCY M. "A Tribute to Robert Frost," Sky and Telescope, XV (March 1956), 212.
"No other poet that I know of has matched Robert Frost in saying so many things so well about the stars."

H. ARTICLES

H280 RAGO, HENRY. "Why We're Still Here, " Poetry, LXXXVII (March 1956), 360-61.

 Thanks the poet for participating in Poetry Day (November 13, 1955) when Frost recited some of his poetry. Frost "snapped out the meter and rhyme with no nonsense about the pride he had in the way poems were made. . . . In between poems he talked some fine frolicsome talk, explained and admonished and joshed and maybe scolded, and he walked off at the end as briskly as he had come on. "

H281 THOMPSON, LAWRANCE. "Robert Frost's California Boyhood, " Princeton Alumni Weekly, LVII (November 9, 1956), 13-15.

 Frost lived the first eleven years of his life in California "with the result that California left an indelible mark on his life and works. "

1957

H282 BAKER, CARLOS. "Frost on the Pumpkin, " Georgia Review, XI (Summer 1957), 117-31.

 Title from James Whitcomb Riley's poem refers to Frost's way of conversing about anything and everything. The listener must "play at hint-and-seek with the poet behind his mask of words. . . . Frost on the pumpkin displays a remarkable skill in the art of making non-commitant commitments. " Baker recounts several meetings with Frost and also analyzes poems with these qualities in them.

H283 DOLBIER, MAURICE. "Star Figures in the Literary Spotlight - A Further Range, " New York Herald Tribune Book Review, April 28, 1957, p. 2.

 On Frost's plans for a trip to England. Frost "will give lectures and readings in London, Durham, and Edinburgh, and at Oxford and Cambridge where he will receive honorary degrees. "

H284 DUFAULT, PETER KANE. [Reminiscence.] Beloit Poetry Journal Chapbook Number Five. Summer 1957, pp. 16-17.

 Introduction to Dufault's poem, "The Edge, " criticized in its early stages by Frost.

H. ARTICLES

H285   EBERHART, RICHARD. [Reminiscence.] Beloit Poetry Journal
        Chapbook Number Five, Summer 1957, pp. 18-19.
            "Robert Frost was the first poet to encourage me in print.
        The year was 1925. I was twenty-one."

H286   GLAUBER, ROBERT H. "Introduction" to Beloit Poetry Journal
        Chapbook Number Five, Summer 1957, p. 4.
            "A Friendly Visit: Poems for Robert Frost."

H287   JARRELL, RANDALL. "In Pursuit of Beauty," New York Times
        Book Review, March 10, 1957, p. 5.
            Cox's A Swinger of Birches: A Portrait of Robert Frost
        reviewed very favorably.

H288   LORD, RICHARD D. "Frost and Cyclicism," Renascence, X
        (Autumn 1957), 19-25, 31.
            Examines "West-Running Brook" with respect to "cyclical
        imagery" and the "sense of time" to see "to what extent such a
        pagan influence has been felt in contemporary literature."
        Frost's meaning of life is that "man is part of the stream of
        being, but his individualism consists in 'sending up' a riffle
        towards the source. He is bound by fate, and yet he has free-
        dom."

H289   NAPIER, JOHN T. "A Momentary Stay Against Confusion," Virgin-
        ia Quarterly Review, XXXIII (Summer 1957), 378-94.
            On Frost's ideas on the poetic process as seen in three
        essays: "The Constant Symbol," "The Figure a Poem Makes,"
        and "Poetry and School." Finds Frost "at odds with the majori-
        ty of recent poets."

H290   ORNSTEIN, ROBERT. "Frost's 'Come In'," Explicator, XV (June
        1957), Item 61.
            The poem "develops a conflict between the sensuous appeal
        of nature and human commitments or responsibilities. But
        primarily it is a poem about poetic experience which makes a
        very tender and humorous comment on romantic sensibilities."
        The poet provides in "Come In" a clue to his own poetic temper,
        which is fundamentally romantic, "but which is chastened by an
        awareness of self-deception and by the saving grace of humor."

THE CRITICAL RECEPTION OF ROBERT FROST

H291   "Poet Robert Frost Finds Us the Freest People On Earth, " Saturday
Evening Post, CCXXIX (March 2, 1957), 10.
        Editorial on Frost's remark, "I don't feel that pressure
[to conform]; I think we're the freest people that ever were
free."

H292   "A Poet's Pilgrimage, " Life, XLIII (September 23, 1957), 109-12.
        On Frost's visit to England at 83 to "round off his life, "
by revisiting "the peaceful haunts where he had once lived."

H293   RESTON, JAMES. "A Personal Communique From Robert Frost, "
New York Times, October 27, 1957, p. 8E.
        "He is against everything and everybody that want people
to rely on somebody else."

H294   "A Review, " Time, LXX (December 9, 1957), 114, 116, 118.
        On Frost's recording ability. "Frost's cracked voice of-
ten sounds like that of the first progenitor of mankind, and his
lucid verse sings of subjects appropriate to that early time --
the whisper of a scythe in grass, the stumbling of a spindle-
legged calf, the rains of autumn."

H295   SPENDER, STEPHEN. "The Subtle Simplicity of Robert Frost, "
London Sunday Times, May 26, 1957, p. 6.
        Frost is not "obscure" or "terrifying"; his trade is "com-
mon simplicity, " but his art lies in subtlety.

H296   STALLMAN, R. W. "The Position of Poetry Today, " English Journal, XLVI (May 1957), 241-51 [246-49].
        A discussion of "Neither Out Far Nor in Deep." Frost
"ridicules the human mind for its absurd metaphysical quests,
for its intellectual probings into the unknown, for its blind
persistence in seeking beyond the horizon at the neglect of
present realities."

H297   STAUFFER, DONALD B. "Frost's 'The Subverted Flower', "
Explicator, XV (March 1957), Item 38.
        The poem is "essentially a dramatic narrative told almost
as a parable, in which a psychological change takes place in
both of the principal characters. . . . The title, with its
unusual word, 'subverted', points most explicitly at Frost's
intention of comparing the corrupted innocence of a young girl

H. ARTICLES

STAUFFER, DONALD B. (cont.)
to the crushing of a flower and to the final subversion of the girl into a dog-like creature in the last eight lines."

H298   "The Visitor," Time, LXIX (June 24, 1957), 62.
On Frost's receiving honorary degrees from Oxford, Cambridge, and Dublin. Quotes Frost as saying, "I would much rather. . . receive a degree from a university than an education."

H299   YATES, NORRIS. "An Instance of Parallel Imagery in Hawthorne, Melville, and Frost," Philological Quarterly, XXXVI (April 1957), 276-80.
On the image of the woodpile in all three writers.

1958

H300   "Ask the Man Who," Commonweal, LXIX (October 31, 1958), 118.
"We continue to admire the poetry of Robert Frost--in spite of everything," a reference to certain of Frost's more emphatic statements such as the one concerning Pound's Cantos. "I don't say I'm not up to them, I say they're not up to me. Nobody ought to like them, but some do, and I let them. That's my tolerance."
See also follow-up article "Twice Will Suffice" (H318).

H301   CHAPMAN, A. K. "Thomas Bird Mosher," Colby Library Quarterly, Series IV (February 1958), 229-44.
On Frost's friend the publisher and printer, with some references to Frost.

H302   CIARDI, JOHN. "Robert Frost: The Way to the Poem," Saturday Review of Literature, XLI (April 12, 1958), 13-15, 65.
Explication of "Stopping By Woods. . . ." The poem reveals duplicity at work, as artful double deception. It is "careful never to abandon its pretense to being simple narration," and its "movement from the specific to the general illustrates one of the basic formulas of all poetry." Ciardi suggests that the source of the poem lies in another poem, one that never developed.
Reprinted in Discussion, XLI (May 10, 1958), 19-20.

THE CRITICAL RECEPTION OF ROBERT FROST

H303   CIARDI, JOHN. "Letter to Letter Writers," <u>Saturday Review of Literature</u>, XLI (May 17, 1958), 15, 48.
      Ciardi responds to critics of his interpretation of "Stopping. . . ." "It may be that I analyzed badly, but the more general charge seems to be all analysis is inimical to poetry, and that general charge is certainly worth a closer look. . . . Certainly, whatever is said here, poetry will be talked about and must be talked about."

H304   COOK, REGINALD L. "Emerson and Frost: A Parallel of Seers," <u>New England Quarterly</u>, XXXI (June 1958), 200-17.
      Frost is more than an "Emersonian Romantic." There are temperamental and ideological differences between the two ("reserve vs. companionability," "moral absolutist vs. relationist," etc.). But both are individualistic and both cling to tradition. Also points out their "common addiction to metaphor." Whereas Emerson is interested in abstraction, Frost responds to "the fact in human experience."

H305   DOYLE, JOHN R., Jr. "Some Attitudes and Ideas of Robert Frost," <u>English Studies in Africa</u>, I (September 1958), 164-83.
      "Always a deep, clear, and broad love of earth, of the physical, has pervaded the poetry of Robert Frost" recorded "with a loving attention to detail that proves a human belief in individuality." Contains a discussion of "Death of the Hired Man." Frost believes that man's goal should be effort and accomplishment, not happiness.

H306   FINNEGAN, SISTER MARY JEREMY. "Frost's <u>Masque of Mercy</u>," <u>Catholic World</u>, CLXXXVI (February 1958), 357-61.
      " 'A Masque of Mercy' is on the whole profoundly serious, and moves to an impressive and solemn conclusion. . . . Job, centuries after his trial, [asks] God why he had to be so tested. The first answer is that the discipline man most needed was 'to learn his submission to unreason'."

H307   "Five Music Men of Words. . . Who They Are. . . As They Began and Today," <u>Newsweek</u>, LI (March 17, 1958), 110-111 [110].
      Very brief sketch of Frost's life. Frost "is a classic rural New England figure in personal tone and in the tone of his poetic voice. . . greatly admired by plain people and poetic specialists alike." Other sketches of Robert Penn Warren,

H. ARTICLES

"Five Music Men of Words. . ." (cont.)
Theodore Roethke, Randall Jarrell, and Archibald MacLeish.

H308   FRANKENBERG, LLOYD. "New Slants At Old Stars, " New York
Times Book Review, July 6, 1958, p. 4.
Review of Reginald Cook's Dimensions of Robert Frost.
"Mr. Cook succeeds, often brilliantly, in conveying the tone
and effect of a Frost poem. . . ."

H309   HARTSOCK, MILDRED. "Frost's 'Directive', " Explicator, XVI
(April 1958), Item 42.
Answer to W.P.L.'s query (H235). The poem is not to be
interpreted as a consideration of man's relation to the Grace of
God. The central meaning of the poem is that "man finds his
philosophic answer by recapturing the imaginativeness, the
make believe, the simple faith of a child who sees magic wonder in the smallest of things. . . . A specifically theological
interpretation of the poem would be pretentious. . . . The acceptance of life. . .is the theme of 'Directive'. "

H310   HOWARD, JANE. "A Superior Writing Talent, " Michigan Alumnus,
LXIV (June 7, 1958), 346-49.
Mentions Frost's influence on and encouragement of play-
wright Paul Osborn.

H311   "A Job For Robert Frost, " New York Times, May 25, 1958, Sec.
IV, p. 10E.
Editorial in approval of Frost's appointment as Poetry
Consultant.

H312   MILLER, LEWIS. "Frost, " in "Letters to the Editor, " New York
Times Book Review, September 7, 1958, p. 36.
On the interpretation of "Mending Wall" by Lloyd Franken-
berg in his review of Cook's Dimensions of Robert Frost
(H308). Miller suggests that the "I" of the poem is not Frost.

H313   MONTGOMERY, MARION. "Robert Frost and His Use of Barriers:
Man vs. Nature Toward God, " South Atlantic Quarterly, LVII
(Summer 1958), 339-53.
"His best poetry is concerned with the drama in nature
. . . ."Frost has written only two poems without a human being
in them. Discusses Frost's view of God and concludes that his

MONTGOMERY, MARION (cont.)
"hesitancy in speaking dogmatically on the subject of the supernatural is due more to his acceptance of mystery in existence
than to agnosticism." Discusses barriers as a theme in the
poetry.

H314   MOYNIHAN, WILLIAM T. "Fall and Winter in Frost, " Modern
Language Notes, LXXIII (May 1958), 348-50.
There are fall and winter metaphors throughout Frost's
poetry. Winter is usually associated with hardship and death
and fall with rebirth. Spring and summer are symbols of "the
transient, the unreal."

H315   "The Potato Brushed Clean, " Senior Scholastic, LXXIII (November
7, 1958), 13.
On Frost's appointment as Consultant in Poetry for 1958-
59 at the Library of Congress. Gives sketch of Frost's life
and says he does not think realism need be synonymous with
dirt or filth. Quotes Frost: "There are two types of realists
. . . . One offers a great deal of dirt with his potato to show
that it is a real potato, and the other is satisfied with the potato brushed clean. I'm inclined to be the second kind."

H316   RUSSELL, FRANCIS. "Frost in the Evening, " Horizon, I (November 1958), 34-35.
Frost is "unique in that for two generations now ordinary
people who do not read poetry have been reading his." Frost
always has "mock battle with his audience in which he always
loses." He always gives in and recites his old poems, "those
poems that half the people there could probably recite themselves."

H317   SCOTT, WILBUR S. "Frost's 'To Earthward', " Explicator, XVI
(January 1958), Item 23.
The speaker "has come to recognize that existence is
complex, and that he accepts this, even with joy." Therefore
experience "is characterized by the union of opposites, and
. . . one can accept and embrace it."

H318   "Twice Will Suffice, " Commonweal, LXIX (December 19, 1958),
305-06.
Reply to "proper Frostonians" upset by the appearance of

H. ARTICLES

"Twice Will Suffice." (cont.)
"Ask the Man Who," in October 31 issue (H300).

H319   BROWNING, J. P. " 'The Black Cottage'," Wingover, I (1958-59),
       11-12.
       Not verified.

H320   STEVENS, DONALD D. "For Once, Then, Something," Wingover,
       I (1958-59), 14-16.
       Not verified.

1959

H321   ADAMS, J. DONALD. "Speaking of Books" column, New York
       Times Book Review, March 22, 1959, p. 2.
             On Frost's 85th birthday; says Frost is overdue for the
       Nobel Prize. Reprints "Into My Own," "The Middleness of the
       Road," "To the Thawing Wind," and a paragraph from Eliza-
       beth Shepley Sergeant's Fire Under The Andes.

H322   ADAMS, J. DONALD. "Speaking of Books" column, New York
       Times Book Review, April 12, 1959, p. 2.
             Attacks the comments of Lionel Trilling at Frost's 85th
       birthday dinner. (See H342.) Accuses Trilling of "hasty
       symbol hunting" and concludes he is lost in the "Freudian
       Wood." Adams then gives the "final word." Frost is not as
       Trilling would have it--a terrifying poet; "he simply sees the
       universe as it is and accepts it."

H323   ADAMS, J. DONALD. "Speaking of Books" column, New York
       Times Book Review, November 1, 1959, p. 2.
             A comparison of Frost and Emerson. Frost is no "cloud
       treader" like Emerson, but their prose styles are similar in
       some respects. Frost says he owes to Emerson "his troubled
       thoughts about freedom . . . . Like Emerson, Frost has the
       country mind, one that has a close acquaintance with . . .
       natural laws, and is at home in the world" too much to be
       frightened by it.

H324   COOK, REGINALD L. "The Stand of Robert Frost, Early and
       Late," English Journal, XLVIII (May 1959), 233-41, 261.
             "What really means something to us is the way Frost,

COOK, REGINALD L. (cont.)
early and late, has practised the skills of a great tradition--
rhyming skilfully, metaphorizing adeptly, and striking off pas-
sages that stick in the mind. "

H325   COX, JAMES M. "Robert Frost and the Edge of the Clearing, "
Virginia Quarterly Review, XXXV (Winter 1959), 73-88.
"His New England is a microcosm which is also an extension of himself., Frost has created a magical world, a clearing between the wild and the tame, a clearing which represents
self-possession and self-denial, form, discipline, the ability
to rise above chaos while at the same time remaining close to
it. . . . To Frost, chaos is 'the spell of the dark woods, ' and
poetry is his way of breaking the spell. "

H326   DEEN, ROSEMARY. "The Voices of Robert Frost, " Commonweal,
LXIX (February 20, 1959), 542-44.
On the "many different images of Frost." Disputes the
idea that Frost is a lyric poet and says that his critical reputation has lagged because of this misconception. The better
view would be that he is "essentially a dramatic poet even in
his short poems. "

H327   DONOGHUE, DENIS. "The Limitations of Robert Frost, " Twentieth Century, CLXVI (July 1959), 13-22.
Frost is limited by "intellectual slackness" sometimes
disguised as disengagement, but he communicates through his
feeling for the human condition.

H328   E., C. D. "Frost's 'The Road Not Taken', " Explicator, XVII
(May 1959), Query 3.
Reader would "like to know how it is possible to take the
'less traveled by' road, which has been worn in passing the
same degree as the other. "

H329   HANLEY, PATRICIA. "A View of Robert Frost on the Hill, "
Tuftonian, XVI, (December 1959), 30-31.
A recollection of Frost's visit in 1915 --"his first public
appearance in the United States as a poet of established reputation"-- and frequent subsequent visits and readings.

H. ARTICLES

H330 HILL, ARCHIBALD A. "Principles Governing Semantic Parallels,"
      Texas Studies in Literature and Language, I (Autumn 1959), 356-65
           In an effort to discuss the laws of semantics and how those
      laws may be used in uncovering literary parallels in a given
      work, this article uses two couplets and two possible images
      from Frost's poem "Bereft."

H331 "How Terrifying a Poet?," Newsweek, LIV (July 27, 1959), 89.
           Article on the talk by Lionel Trilling at Frost's 85th
      birthday dinner where he described Frost as "a terrifying po-
      et." Admirers of Frost were enraged, but Frost was not
      bothered. The poet says of himself, "I'm not pessimistic, and
      I'm not optimistic. I never tell people what to say about my
      poems. But as far as Mr. Trilling is concerned, his was
      serious criticism and I couldn't be anything but pleased with
      serious criticism." (See H342.)

H332 JAMIESON, PAUL. "Robert Frost: Poet of Mountain Land," Appala-
      chia, XXXII (December 15, 1959), 471-79.
           "Mountain land north of Boston is geographical and spiritu-
      al home to Robert Frost. . . . Even where mountains are not
      specifically mentioned in his poems, we sense their presence
      in the crisp atmosphere. . . . Frost's love of earth is the
      impartial love of one who expects no return, no special favors
      or exemptions."

H333 LANGBAUM, ROBERT. "The New Nature Poetry," American
      Scholar, XXVIII (Summer 1959), 323-40.
           Frost's poetry does not reflect the religion of nature ex-
      pressed in 18th century nature poetry, but rather reflects "its
      nonhuman otherness." Analyzes "The Need of Being Versed in
      Country Things," "Stopping By Woods. . .," "An Old Man's
      Winter Night," "After Apple Picking," "Desert Places,"
      "Build Soil." Concludes: "In the sheer power to render nature,
      Frost may well be our best nature poet since Wordsworth.
      Yet his poetry is not likely to be the favorite poetry of the most
      serious readers just because Frost does not call into play all
      our faculties; he does not make poetry of our ideas." Also
      deals with Stevens, M. Moore, W.S. Merwin, and Richard
      Eberhart.

H334   LASSER, MICHAEL L. "The Loneliness of Robert Frost, " Liter-
          ary Review, III (Winter 1959-60), 287-97.
                "Frost advocates a retreat from society" and calls this
          his "lyric loneliness.... His retreat, in actuality, involves a
          damnation of society. . . coupled with a suffering, time utiliz-
          ing advance into a more agonizing self-knowledge. "

H335   MUNFORD, HOWARD. "Frost's 'The Subverted Flower', " Explica-
          tor, XVII (January 1959), Item 30.
                The poem has two points of view: the girl's and the poet's.
          The boy's feelings, like the flower "are a normal part of
          nature until subverted into abnormality by a meagre and un-
          natural response. " Claims Frost sympathizes with the boy.

H336   "Paean For a Poet By a Poet, " Life, XLVI (June 15, 1959), 65-66.
                A discussion of Paul Engle's poem, "To Praise a Man, "
          which honors Frost. (See J50.)

H337   OGILVIE, JOHN. "From Woods to Stars: A Pattern of Imagery in
          Robert Frost's Poetry, " South Atlantic Quarterly, LVIII (Sum-
          mer 1959), 64-76.
                On "the imagery of dark woods" in Frost's poems. Con-
          cludes that this imagery indicates "There must be periodic
          withdrawals from the world 'of considerations, ' but not a
          permanent withdrawal. "

H338   ROSENTHAL, M. L. "The Robert Frost Controversy, " The Nation,
          CLXXXVIII (June 20, 1959), 559-61.
                An answer to Adams' answer to Trilling. Frost is not the
          grey native nature poet Adams thinks. Also the description of
          Frost's reputation is of the rural and the natural. But "beyond
          the surface appeal of all this, there lurks the further implica-
          tion of the 'terrifying' which Trilling feels and every other
          perceptive reader must feel. " Frost has a powerful native
          voice, idiosyncratic and stubborn, but it is not yet really being
          listened to. (See H323.)

H339   RYAN, ALVAN S. "Frost and Emerson: Voice and Vision, "
          Massachusetts Review, I (October 1959), 5-23.
                ". . . Frost is, in the poems of the darker vision, like
          the Emerson recovered by such critics as Stephen Whicher,
          and, in the more serene lyrics, like Arvin's Emerson of 'the

H. ARTICLES

RYAN, ALVAN S. (cont.)
more-than-tragic emotion of thankfulness.' This constitutes
the poetic ground on which Frost and Emerson really meet."

H340   STUART, JESSE. "Meeting Mr. New England, America's Greatest
Poet," Educational Forum, XXIII (March 1959), 291-92.
"Robert Frost is not only the greatest poet in this country,
but he is the greatest poet in the world."

H341   THOMPSON, LAWRANCE. "A Native to the Grain of the American
Idiom," Saturday Review of Literature, XLII (March 21, 1959),
21, 55-56.
For Frost, man's most assertive act is to dare great
things. Therefore, "Frost has proved himself native to the
grain of the American idiom" and an eloquent advocate of individual courage.

H342   TRILLING, LIONEL. "A Speech on Robert Frost: A Cultural
Episode," Partisan Review, XXVI (Summer 1959), 445-52.
Trilling's controversial speech at a dinner in honor of
Frost's eighty-fifth birthday. Speech pays tribute to Frost as
a national symbol and calls him "a terrifying poet," in that he
truthfully portrays a terrifying universe. Concludes that
"Frost's devotees do not really understand his poetry."

1960

H343   BISHOP, FERMAN. "Frost's 'The Wood Pile'," Explicator, XVIII
(June 1960), Item 58.
Critics who "accept too easily the sentimental associations
in the mind of Frost's observer. . . miss entirely the main
idea of the poem." The main point is "the presentation of the
moment of insight, a presentation thoroughly convincing because it is made with the utmost objectivity."

H344   COOK, RAYMOND A. "Robert Frost: Poetic Astronomer," Emory
University Quarterly, XVI (Spring 1960), 32-39.
On Frost's frequent use of stars and planets in his poems.

H345   DRURY, MICHAEL. "Robert Frost: His Power and His Glory,"
McCall's, LXXXVII (April 1960), 81, 142, 144-46, 148-50.
This is a very general, very chatty article on Frost with

DRURY, MICHAEL (cont.)
>   amusing quotes to give the reader a sense of the man. It be-
>   gins with a description of Frost as "poet, philosopher, farmer,
>   teacher, humorist, classicist, thinker, neighbor to all mankind"
>   and discusses him in these terms, including a lengthy bio-
>   graphical section.

H346   DUVALL, S. P. C. "Robert Frost's 'Directive' Out of Walden, "
>   American Literature, XXXI (January 1960), 482-88.
>   Traces Frost's imagery and ultimate meaning to the in-
>   spiration of Walden. "When, then, Frost directs us back to
>   our sources, by utilizing image and metaphor from the peren-
>   nial spring of Walden he points us back at the same time to
>   one of the great watering places of American literature. "

H347   ELSBREE, LANGDON. "Frost and the Isolation of Man, " Clare-
>   mont Quarterly, VII (Summer 1960), 29-40.
>   "Because Frost's skepticism, his doubting of man's certain
>   destiny and extensive powers, is one of temperament, it is, I
>   think, best embodied in the dramatic narratives where he can
>   render human isolation immediately, where he can directly
>   show the reader the desolate woman or broken man. "

H348   FINNEGAN, SISTER MARY JEREMY. "Contrarieties of Robert
>   Frost, " Catholic World, CXCII (December 1960), 164-70.
>   "Viewed in its entirety, Frost's work discloses two con-
>   trasting attitudes: involvement in the human lot [and] the urge
>   to extrication from it. . . . "

H349   HOFFMAN, DANIEL G. "Thoreau's 'Old Settler' and Frost's
>   'Paul Bunyan', " Journal of American Folklore, LXXIII (July -
>   September 1960), 236-38.
>   Hoffman suggests that Frost may have found the idea for
>   "Paul's Wife" in Thoreau's chapter on "Solitude" in Walden.

H350   HOPKINS, VIVIAN C. "Robert Frost: Out Far and In Deep, "
>   Western Humanities Review, XIV (Summer 1960), 247-63.
>   "Because of the richness, the continued productivity, and
>   the breadth of Frost's poetic theory and practice, he is to
>   many Europeans and most Americans the representative living
>   American poet. "

H. ARTICLES

H351   IRWIN, W. R. "The Unity of Frost's Masques, " American Litera-
        ture, XXXII (November 1960), 302-12.
             The masques are complementary poems, one "an analysis
        and the other a synthesis. . . . " They treat of "problems
        which have plagued 'man thinking' ever since he became capa-
        ble of considering his own condition. "

H352   H., K. "By the Throat, " Christian Century, LXXVII (September
        14, 1960), 1060-61.
             Review of Sergeant's Trial By Existence. Frost: "Poetry
        is a way of taking life by the throat. " Provides outlines of
        Frost's early years as poet/farmer -- a favorable review of
        the biography.

H353   "Late Frost: Witty, Wise and Young, " Time, LXXVI (July 4, 1960),
        81.
             Snippets of Frost's conversation taken from Sergeant's
        Trial By Existence.

H354   MACDONALD, DWIGHT. "Masscult and Midcult [I], " Partisan
        Review, XXVII (Spring 1960), 203-33.
             An overview of American popular culture. Frost's ap-
        pointment as poetry consultant at the Library of Congress is
        discussed.

H355   PARKE, JOHN. "Frost, " in "Letters to the Editor, " New York
        Times Book Review, August 21, 1960, p. 16.
             Disagrees with Winfield T. Scott's review of Sergeant's
        book, in which he says that little has been added to the Frost
        canon since A Witness Tree.

H356   PETERS, ROBERT. "The Truth of Frost's 'Directive', " Modern
        Language Notes, LXXV (January 1960), 29-32.
             On the religious nature of the poem.

H357   PRITCHARD, WILLIAM H. "Diminished Nature, " Massachusetts
        Review, I (May 1960), 475-92.
             Frost sees diminution or deprivation in nature as educative,
        a clarification of life.

H358   SERGEANT, ELIZABETH. "England Discovers Robert Frost, "
        Atlantic Monthly, CCV (May 1960), 61-65.

SERGEANT, ELIZABETH (cont.)
>On how A Boy's Will came to be published in England and Frost's friendship with Ezra Pound.

H359   THOMPSON, LAWRANCE. "Nature's Bard Rediscovered, " Saturday Review, XLIII (July 2, 1960), 22-23.
>Review of Nitchie's Human Values in the Poetry of Robert Frost, Lynen's The Pastoral Art of Robert Frost, and Sergeant's Trial By Existence.

H360   UPDIKE, JOHN. "Why Robert Frost Should Receive the Nobel Prize, " Audience, VII (Summer 1960), 45-46.
>"I can think of no better way for the Nobel Prize Committee to make amends for the carnival of French Existentialists and Mississippi stream-of-consciousness purveyors who have recently degraded this award than to award it to him."

H361   "A Walk With Frost, " Reader's Digest, LXXVI (April 1960), 77-79.
>Quotations from Frost's conversation, lectures, and poems.

H362   WEEKS, EDWARD. "A Poet's Beginning, " Atlantic Monthly, CCVI (August 1960), 95-96.
>Review of Sergeant's Trial By Existence.

1961

H363   BLUM, MARGARET M. "Robert Frost's 'Directive': A Theological Reading, " Modern Language Notes, LXXVI (June 1961), 524-25.
>Rebuttal to Robert Peters (H356). Frost's poem is strictly theological, not humanistic.

H364   BROWER, REUBEN A. "Something For Frost, " New England Quarterly, XXXIV (June 1961), 243-52.
>Review of Nitchie's Human Values. . ., Lynen's Pastoral Art. . ., and Sergeant's Trial By Existence.

H365   COURSEN, HERBERT R., Jr. "A Dramatic Necessity: The Poetry of Robert Frost, " Bucknell Review, X (December 1961), 138-47.
>Filled with quotes from Frost poems, this essay examines Frost's language in an effort to uncover "the blending of opposing views [which] is for Frost a key to life" for "ultimately,

H. ARTICLES

COURSEN, HERBERT R., Jr. (cont.)
Frost's poetry neither accepts nor rejects the antithesis of involvement and withdrawal" but does both.

H366   FERGUSON, A. R. "Frost, Sill and 'A Wishing Well'," *American Literature*, XXXIII (November 1961), 370-73.
Frost's poem may be influenced by "Field Notes," a poem by Edward Rowland Sill.

H367   GIBSON, WALKER. "Three Books on Frost," *Carleton Miscellany*, II (Winter 1961), 105-09.
Review of Sergeant, Nitchie, and Lynen, finding some value in Lynen, none in the others.

H368   "Government and Poetry," *New York Times*, February 28, 1961, p. 32.
Editorial on the Frost-Kennedy relationship. ". . . we do need poets who without flattering us tell us how to face danger and how to conquer it."

H369   GREENBERG, ROBERT A. "Frost in England: A Publishing Incident," *New England Quarterly*, XXXIV (September 1961), 375-79.
Frost says that being first published in England was just an accident.

H370   HARRIS, MARK. "The Pride and Wisdom of Two Great Old Poets -- Sandburg. . . Frost -- A Novelist's Illuminating Visit," *Life*, LI (December 1, 1961), 101-22 [113-22].
Account of a visit with Frost at his Vermont cabin.

H371   IDEMA, JIM. "Prophet Honored in His Own Country," *Denver Post*, March 19, 1961, p. 1AA.
An appreciation by a *Post* staff writer. "He is the complete poet-patriarch, surely. His appearance, his sturdy bearing, most of all his voice, resonant with antiquity," make him our poet laureate.

H372   LYNEN, JOHN F. "Frost's Works and Days," *Journal of English and Germanic Philology*, LX (January 1961), 111-19.
Review of Sergeant's *Trial By Existence*. ". . .a sound, interesting, and, if not great, certainly intelligent, biography."

H373   MOST, STEVE. "Literary Find, " Saturday Review, XLIV (February 4, 1961), 25.
  A letter to the editor concerning Frost's second published poem, "The Traitor, " in the Mirror, the literary magazine of Phillips Academy, Andover, Massachusetts, in June 1892.

H374   "Next-door Neighbor to People of the World-- Robert Frost, " Modern Maturity, IV (October - November 1961), 11-13.
  A biographical sketch of "one of the towering figures of our time. "

H375   "Old Poet in a New Land, " Coronet, L (September 1961), 97-111.
  Quotations from Frost's remarks while in Israel as a guest of the Hebrew University.

H376   PEARCE, ROY HARVEY. "Frost's Momentary Stay, " Kenyon Review, XXIII (Spring 1961), 258-73.
  "The conditions which circumscribe Frost's poems are those of a world not yet dominated by urban, industrialized, bureaucratic culture -- the very world which, seeing its inevitable coming, Emerson and his kind strove to confront and save for man before it would be too late. Frost glances at this world, only to turn to one he knows better. "

H377   PERRINE, LAURENCE. "Frost's 'The Road Not Taken', " Explicator, XIX (February 1961), Item 28.
  Answer to C. D. E.'s query (E328). The difference between the roads is very slight and this slightness is vital to the meaning of the poem in that: (1) it shows that the choice represented by the two roads "is a choice between two goods, not a choice between good and evil"; and (2) it shows "the importance that a small difference may make to a man in later years. "

H378   PRESTON, STUART D. "Poems and Politics, " in "Letters to the Editor, " New York Times Magazine, January 29, 1961, p. 16.
  Letter, on January 15 article, quotes President Kennedy as having said the same thing in 1956. (See H380.)

H379   SAMUEL, RINNA. "Robert Frost in Israel, " New York Times Book Review, April 23, 1961, pp. 42-43.
  Frost's ten-day visit called a success.

H. ARTICLES

H380   SHAPIRO, HARVEY. "Story of the Poem, " New York Times Magazine, January 15, 1961, pp. 6, 86.
          On President John F. Kennedy's request that Frost deliver a poem at the presidential inaugural in 1960.

H381   SICKELS, ELEANOR M. "Frost's 'The Road Not Taken', " Explicator, XIX (February 1961), Item 28.
          Another answer to C.D.E. (H328). "The very closeness of the alternative claims -- nothing extreme in their difference or in either considered in itself-- is essentially Frostian. "

H382   STOCK, ELY. "A Masque of Reason and JB: Two Treatments of the Book of Job, " Modern Drama, III (February 1961), 378-86.
          Frost's Masque is not as dramatic as JB. "The considerable achievement of J.B.'s wife as opposed to the ironical womanly qualities which Job's wife displays in A Masque of Reason illustrates the different ways in which MacLeish and Frost treat the theme provided by the Book of Job. . . . Frost emphasizes the inadequacy of man's conception of the problem of evil when man thinks only in rational terms, while MacLeish asserts the ability of man to find a way of overcoming the terrors of the universe.

                        * * * *

          If [Frost's] play is not as meaningful or powerful as MacLeish's longer work, it is because Frost's final answer to the problems raised is deferred to A Masque of Mercy. "

H383   UDALL, STEWART L. "Frost's 'Unique Gift Outright', " New York Times Magazine, March 26, 1961, pp. 12-13, 98.
          On Frost's reading at the presidential inaugural of 1960. Reprints "Dedication: For John F. Kennedy His Inauguration, " the poem Frost wrote but was unable to read.

H384   WILLIGE, ECKHART. "Formal Devices in Robert Frost's Short Poems, " Georgia Review, XV (Fall 1961), 324-30.
          On Frost's rhyming techniques.

1962

H385   "Americans Abroad, " Time, LXXX (September 14, 1962), 31.
          Mentions Frost in Russia.

The Critical Reception of Robert Frost

H386   BURGESS, C. F. "Frost's 'The Oven Bird'," Explicator, XX
        (March 1962), Item 59.
                On the line "And comes that other fall we name the fall,"
        which may refer to the felling of the tree.

H387   CARLSON, ERIC W. "Robert Frost on 'Vocal Imagination: The
        Merger of Form and Content'," American Literature, XXXIII
        (January 1962), 519-22.
                A reconstructed account of Frost's lecture at Harvard, the
        second of six Charles Eliot Norton Lectures. "I care least
        for the merger of meaning to tone. . . . The tone is most
        important."

H388   CARNES, DEL. "On the Air" column, Denver Post, April 13, 1962,
        p. 26.
                ". . . there can be little doubt that television played a big
        part in the 'discovery' of Robert Frost."

H389   COURSEN, HERBERT J. "The Ghost of Christmas Past: 'Stopping
        by Woods on a Snowy Evening'," College English, XXIV (De-
        cember 1962), 236-38.
                The poem is about Santa Claus.

H390   "The Frost Bit," Newsweek, LIX (January 29, 1962), 81-82.
                On Shirley Clarke's feature-length documentary movie
        about Frost.

H391   GIBB, CARSON. "Frost's 'Mending Wall'," Explicator, XX (Febru-
        ary 1962), Item 48.
                The speaker is skeptical of walls, playful and tolerant of
        his neighbor, but he respects the wall. "In a way which the
        speaker may not be aware of and the neighbor could not under-
        stand, good fences do make good neighbors."

H392   "Happy 88 To An American Poet," New York Herald Tribune Books,
        March 25, 1962, p. 3.

H393   HEPBURN, JAMES G. "Robert Frost and His Critics," New Eng-
        land Quarterly, XXXV (September 1962), 367-76.
                "Being a poet rather than a critic, Frost perhaps under-
        values explication. . . . He is primarily a lyric poet; and, as

H. ARTICLES

HEPBURN, JAMES G. (cont.)
he says elsewhere, the aim in lyric poetry is not mainly implication: the aim is song."

H394   JEROME, JUDSON. "Six Senses of the Poet," Colorado Quarterly,
X (Winter 1962), 225-40.
The sixth sense is a sense of self. "When he writes and
we read successfully, we take hold of one another with all six
hands."

H395   KAHN, ROGER. "Roger Kahn Writes of His Lively Interest in
Robert Frost," New York Herald Tribune Books, March 25,
1962, pp. 3, 10.
A brief reminiscence.

H396   KANTAK, V. Y. "The Structure of a Frost Poem," Literary Criterion, V (Winter 1962), 115-27.
"If there is any doubt about the subtlety of Frost's manner,
one should read a poem like Directive and see whether it is
possible to read him as the simple good grey Nature poet of
the popular imagination."

H397   KHAN, SALAMATULLAH. "Levels of Meaning in Robert Frost's
Poetry," Literary Criterion, V (Winter 1962), pp. 110-14.
Discusses the levels of meaning in "Mending Wall" and
"For Once, Then, Something."

H398   LEYBURN, ELLEN D. "A Note on Frost's Masque of Reason,"
Modern Drama, IV (February 1962), 426-28.
Rebuttal to Ely Stock (H382). Finds the Masque "highly
symbolic."

H399   LOVE, KENNETH. "Poet of Love and Understanding," USA*I, I
(April 1962), 72-73.
A discussion of Frost's comments at a gathering in Wash-
ington, D.C., on Frost's eighty-eighth birthday. Compares
John F. Kennedy to Frost.

H400   " 'Mending Wall' In Moscow," New York Times Magazine, September 16, 1962, p. 34.
Photographs of Frost in Moscow, with Yevgeny Yevtushenko.

The Critical Reception of Robert Frost

H401   "Robert Frost Honored on 88th Birthday, " Publisher's Weekly,
        CLXXXI (April 9, 1962), 30-31.
            Frost in Washington, D. C., at the opening of an exhibit
        of Frostana at the Library of Congress. Meets with President
        John F. Kennedy.

H402   SCANNELL, VERNON. "Content With Discontent: A Note on Ed-
        ward Thomas, " London Magazine, n. s., I (January 1962), 44-
        51.
            Includes discussion of Frost.

H403   STEVENSON, ADLAI E. "The American People Find Their Poet, "
        New Republic, CXLVI (April 9, 1962), 20-23.
            "In Robert Frost, the American people have found their
        poet, their singer, their seer-- in short, their bard. "
            Reprints excerpts of Frost's remarks at 88th birthday
        dinner.

H404   SURKOV, A. "Robert Frost's Visit to the USSR, " Soviet Review,
        III (December 1962), 59-61.
            This is an account of Frost's trip to the Soviet Union in
        the fall of 1962. The article, translated from Pravda, stresses
        Frost's desire "to work for the good of friendship, mutual un-
        derstanding and trust" between the U. S. S. R. and the U. S., and
        talks of Frost's meeting with Khrushchev.

H405   " 'Too Liberal to Fight', " in "Letters to The Times, " New York
        Times, September 21, 1962, p. 28.
            Professors John P. Roche and Hans Blumenfeld letters on
        Khrushchev's statement to Frost that Americans are too liberal
        to fight and on a September 15 editorial.

H406   "Well Said, Mr. Frost, " Denver Post, March 27, 1962, p. 18.
            Editorial applauds Frost's birthday comments on Khrush-
        chev and Kennedy.

H407   WHITRIDGE, ARNOLD. "Robert Frost and Carl Sandburg: The
        Two Elder Statesmen of American Poetry, " Bulletin of New
        York Public Library, LXVI (March 1962), 164-77.
            A comparison and contrast of the two poets. Finds Frost
        "restrained, sceptical, critical of the world in which he finds
        himself. "

H. ARTICLES

1963

H408   "Acquainted With The Night," Times Literary Supplement (London),
February 1, 1963, p. 76.
      Enthusiastic review of John Robert Doyle, Jr., The Poetry
of Robert Frost.

H409   ANDERSON, CHARLES. "Robert Frost, 1874-1963," Saturday Review, XLVI (February 23, 1963), 16-20.
      Discussion of "Stopping By Woods. . .," "Acquainted With
the Night," "I Will Sing You One-O," "The Axe-Helve."
      "The greatest freedom Frost ever allowed himself was in
blank verse, without any of the shackles of stanza or rhyme.
Even in meter his departures from strict iambic pentameter
go as far as Shakespeare's latest experiments and anticipate
the relaxed verse-approximations of Eliot's plays.

H410   ANGOFF, CHARLES. "Three Towering Figures: Reflections Upon
the Passing of Robert Frost, Robinson Jeffers and William
Carlos Williams," Literary Review, VI (Summer 1963), 423-29.
      "These towering figures represent something large and
melodic and profound and joyous in American poetry. They
belonged to all time, but they were also deeply committed to
America."

H411   BAKER, ELLIOTT. "Tribute to Frost," London Sunday Times,
February 10, 1963, p. 28.
      Letter to the editor recalls Frost as saying that "The Road
Not Taken" is about Edward Thomas.

H412   BAUER, MALCOLM. "Fitzgerald, Frost Letters Lively, Revealing," Sunday Oregonian (Portland), October 20, 1963, p. 45.
      Favorable review.

H413   BONFILS, FREDERICK G. "The Open Forum" column, Denver
Post, May 8, 1963, p. 21.
      Annie R. Gray writes in to comment on Frost's sense of
solitude.

H414   BORT, BARRY. "Frost and the Deeper Vision, " Midwest Quarter-
        ly, V (October 1963), 59-67.
                Frost "is the only major poet who writes convincingly
        about nature, content with describing it in a matter of fact
        fashion."

H415   BRIGGS, PEARLANNA. "Frost's 'Directive', " Explicator, XXI
        (May 1963), Item 71.
                "Frost has given his 'directive' in veiled words, lest the
        insensitive should learn the way; he has carefully hidden his
        Grail under a spell, so that those unworthy of the high calling
        of poet cannot find it."

H416   BROWER, REUBEN. "Poetry, Puns and People, " New York Times
        Book Review, September 15, 1963, pp. 6, 42.
                Review of Untermeyer, Letters. . . An overview of the
        book, with frequent quotations.

H417   "Candid Poet Shied From Dubbing Self, " Denver Post, January 29,
        1963, p. 10.
                Associated Press article quotes Frost as saying: "I don't
        call myself a poet yet. It's for the world to say whether
        you're a poet or not."

H418   CARRUTH, HAYDEN. "Private Words and Public Art, " The Nation,
        CXCVII (December 14, 1963), 418-19.
                Review of Untermeyer, Letters. . . and others.

H419   CIARDI, JOHN. "Robert Frost: To Earthward, " Saturday Review,
        XLVI (February 23, 1963), 24.
                Frost has primal energy and wild ardent genius. He is
        our best but do not make it sentimental; he "is no lollipop."

H420   CLARKE, EDMUND PALMER. "I. M. Robert Frost." The First
        Parish of Watertown: Watertown, Mass., February 10, 1963,
        5 pp.
                Sermon following the death of Robert Frost. 1500 copies
        printed for private distribution. "When I think of the preten-
        tious pride with which most men display the academic hoods of
        honorary degrees, I remember that Frost cut his up to make
        patchwork comforters for his bed."

H. ARTICLES

H421   COLE, CHARLES W. "Metaphor and Syllogism, " Massachusetts
Review, IV (Winter 1963), 239-42.
> Reminiscence of Frost at Amherst in 1926-27. Describes
Frost's discussions of metaphor.

H422   COMBELLACK, C. R. B. "Frost's 'The Oven Bird', " Explicator,
XXII (November 1963), Item 17.
> Reply to Burgess (H386). "All the central lines of the po-
em appear to me to be the human being's summary of what the
bird seems to him to be saying."

H423   COOK, REGINALD L. "A Fine Old Eye/The Unconquered Flame, "
Massachusetts Review, IV (Winter 1963), 242-49.
> New England gives new impulse to American writing.
Discussion of Complete Poems and In the Clearing, which
"communicate the continuous freshness of self-surprise."

H424   COX, JAMES M. "The Stamp of a Heroic Life, " Saturday Review,
XLVI (October 5, 1963), 43-44.
> Review of Untermeyer, Letters. . . . "The letters. . .
reinforce the character of Robert Frost we have known almost
since the beginning. They are, after all, fatally in Frost's
style; and for Frost style is not so much the man as it is the
character."

H425   CRAIG, G. ARMOUR. "Robert Frost at Amherst, " Amherst Alumni News, XVI (Fall 1963), 9-13.
> Frost "was sturdily and bravely confident of what came to
him. He knew himself. He was never not working."

H426   DANZIG, ALLAN. "An Unexpected Echo of Beddoes in Frost, "
Notes and Queries, X (April 1963), 150-51.
> Parallels "Stopping by Woods. . ." and Beddoes' "Phantom
Wooer."

H427   DAVENPORT, GUY. "First National Poetry Festival: A Report, "
National Review, XIV (January 15, 1963), 25-26.
> A description of the first national poetry festival--"For
three days, the poets assembled fought the tired battles of the
twenties, then Robert Frost appeared and jolted the meeting
into focus."

H428   DICKEY, JOHN S. "Robert Frost: Teacher-at-Large," Saturday
        Review, XLVI (February 23, 1963), 21-22.
           "First as a student who gave up on two colleges, later as
both parent and teacher, [Frost] has never been able to put
much of a bet on salvation through classrooms, courses, a
curriculum, degree requirements, or most of the accounter-
ment of formal education."

H429   DONOGHUE, DENIS. "A Mode of Communication: Frost and the
        'Middle' Style," Yale Review, LII (Winter 1963), 205-19.
           "To propose Frost as a master of the 'middle' style is at
once to praise him, to point to his particular strength, and to
mark his limitations. For it is quite wrong to think of Frost
as a poet in command of all the poetic resources."

H430   DONOGHUE, DENIS. "The Sacred Rage: Three American Poets,"
        The Listener, LXIX (June 6, 1963), 965, 967 [967].
           On Frost, Wallace Stevens, and William Carlos Williams.
"The ideas of order which [Frost] implies are those of anthro-
pology; not Stevens' epistemology or Williams' grammar."

H431   EDEL, LEON. "Spirals of Reason and Fancy," Saturday Review,
        XLVII (September 5, 1964), 23-24.
           Review of Thompson's Selected Letters. "The volume suf-
fers from being a curious mixture of the transcendent and the
trivial; it has been planned in terms of a biography rather than
of epistolary art, but there is enough of that art to give us the
sense of Frost's qualities."

H432   "Ending in Wisdom," New York Times, January 31, 1963, p. 6.
           Editorial. "Not since Longfellow has an American poet
been so loved by his countrymen. He seemed one with them."

H433   "Ever Yours, Robert," Time, LXXXII (September 20, 1963), 102,
        104.
           Review of The Letters of Robert Frost to Louis Unter-
meyer. Hints of Frost's relentless self-preoccupation.

H434   FAULKNER, VIRGINIA. "More Frosting on the Woods," College
        English, XXIV (April 1963), 560-61.
           Rebuttal to Coursen (H389).

H. ARTICLES

H435   "The Fearless Wisdom of Robert Frost," Vogue, CXLI (March 15, 1963), 118-19.
        A series of quotes from Frost covering subjects from love to politics.

H436   FISCALINI, JANET. "Springtime Frost," Commonweal, LXXVIII (May 17, 1963), 228-29.
        Review of Squires, Major Themes; Brower, Poetry of Robert Frost; and Doyle, Poetry of Robert Frost.

H437   FRANCIS, ROBERT. "On Robert Frost: Two Pictures," Massachusetts Review, IV (Winter 1963), 237-39.
        On two interesting contrasting photographs of Frost, one made in 1915 or 1916, the other made in 1954.

H438   "Frost: 'Courage Is the Virtue that Counts Most'," Newsweek, LXI (February 11, 1963), 90-91.
        Obituary article on Frost's death. "People who had never thought of reading poetry took to Frost. His words were simple words; the images were of simple, most often country, things."

H439   FROST, LESLEY. "Our Family Christmas," Redbook, CXXII (December 1963), 45, 98.
        "Robert Frost's daughter recalls the joys of a holiday on which the most important gifts were those that could be read aloud."

H440   HOLMES, SUSAN P. "Robert Frost in Lawrence--A Remembrance of 60 Years," Lawrence Eagle-Tribune, May 9, 1963, p. 16.
        Not verified.

H441   HOWE, IRVING. "Robert Frost: A Momentary Stay," New Republic, CXLVIII (March 23, 1963), 23-28.
        "Despite a lamentable gift for public impersonations and for shrewdly consolidating his success in a country that cares little about poetry, Frost has remained faithful to what Yeats calls 'the modern mind in search of its own meanings.'"

THE CRITICAL RECEPTION OF ROBERT FROST

H442   HUNT, GEORGE P. "Editor's Note -- Our Own Remembrance of
      Robert Frost," Life, LIV (February 8, 1963), 3.
         Editorial appreciation on the occasion of Frost's death.

H443   HUNTING, ROBERT. "Who Needs Mending?" Western Humanities
      Review, XVII (Winter 1963), 88-89.
         The villain of the poem is the narrator, not the neighbor.

H444   "An 'Insight into the Human Soul,'" Senior Scholastic, LXXXII
      (February 13, 1963), 21.
         "The limit of his ambition. . . was 'to lodge a few pebbles
      where they will be hard to get rid of.'"

H445   IRVING, JEROME M. "A Parting Visit with Robert Frost," Hudson
      Review, XVI (Spring 1963), 54-60.
         Text of an interview with Frost in Detroit just before his
      death. Much of the article deals with Frost's recent visit to
      Russia.

H446   IRWIN, W. R. "Robert Frost and the Comic Spirit," American
      Literature, XXXV (November 1963), 299-310.
         "It would be idle to pretend that the comic muse is the
      only one which Frost has served. He has himself remarked,
      'The way of understanding is partly mirth.' The word 'partly'
      works in two directions. It indicates a limit; Meredith's
      'hypergelast' is an enemy alike to comedy and to good sense.
      But it indicates also that mirth participates integrally in total
      understanding."

H447   JACOBSEN, JOSEPHINE. "The Legacy of Three Poets," Common-
      weal, LXXVIII (May 10, 1963), 189-92.
         "The quintessence of Frost's vision of nature has under its
      measured serenity a shiver of the power of darkness which it
      has surmounted and controlled. Frost loves the verb 'to
      scare'." On Frost, Cummings, and W. C. Williams.

H448   JEROME, JUDSON. "Robert Frost," The Humanist, XXIII (March -
      April 1963), 67.
         Memorial remarks. "Robert Frost was the most modern
      and most difficult of modern poets."

H. ARTICLES

H449 JEROME, JUDSON. "A Tribute to Robert Frost," Writer's Digest, XLIII (April 1963), 15-18, 60.

"Now that the gravelly voice is stilled and the grey-browed eyes have ceased to sparkle, perhaps the world which insulted him by regarding him as everybody's grand-daddy will listen and look more closely. . . . There is wisdom for survival, searching wonder, wry satire and enlightening laughter, music and story, people and the world in" his poetry.

H450 JUDD, DOROTHY. "Reserve in the Art of Robert Frost," Texas Quarterly, VI (Summer 1963), 60-67.

Frost's reserve is "emotional, intellectual, and, in a sense, moral." Frost refuses to assert any definite beliefs. He is neither very positive nor completely negative.

H451 KAHN, ROGER. "Robert Frost: A Reminiscence," The Nation, CXCVI (February 9, 1963), 121-22.

Memories of coversations with Frost about writers and writing.

H452 KAHN, ROGER. "To Prayer I Go -- The Letters of Robert Frost to Louis Untermeyer," Saturday Evening Post, CCXXVI (September 14, 1963), 47.

Kahn prefaces selections from Frost letters to Untermeyer with a brief affectionate reminiscence of the poet.

H453 KENNEDY, JOHN F. "President's Convocation Address" and "The President's Remarks at the Library Ground Breaking," Amherst Alumni News, Fall 1963, Special Issue. 3 pp.

H454 "Kennedy Speaks at Frost Library Dedication," Wilson Library Bulletin, XXXVIII (December 1963), 317.

On President John F. Kennedy's remarks at the dedication of the Robert Frost Library at Amherst.

H455 KENNEY, HERBERT A. "Robert Frost, RIP," National Review, XIV (February 12, 1963), 100.

"Robert Frost not only worked hard to be a great man, he fought to be recognized as a great man, for there are forces at work in every society which would neglect and stunt the poet." It is these forces and Frost's fight which are emphasized in this obituary of "most likely America's greatest [poet] so far."

H456   LASK, THOMAS. "A Poet of Rural Spirit, " New York Times, Janu-
       ary 30, 1963, p. 5.
           "Frost's place in the history of American letters is as-
       sured, but like his verse, future readers are likely to find that
       he is less simple than he appears to be. "

H457   LERMAN, STEPHEN J. "Robert Frost on Ossipee Mountain, " Ap-
       palachia, n. s., XXIX (June 1963), 395-401.
           On Frost's brief residence there in order to be near Elinor
       White, soon to be his bride.

H458   LEWIS, C. DAY. "Robert Frost: 1874-1963, " The Listener, LXIX
       (February 7, 1963), 253.
           "Frost's personality could be quietly formidable, and was
       also an elusive one. He tended to slip away, in mind and some-
       times in body too, about his own business. "

H459   "A Lover's Quarrel With the World, " Time, LXXXI (February 8,
       1963), 84.
           "Robert Frost was no literary revolutionary, like Walt
       Whitman or T. S. Eliot. But he is more controlled and artful
       than Whitman, less narrowly contemporary than the early Eliot,
       wider-ranging than that fellow precisionist, Emily Dickinson. "

H460   MAC LEISH, ARCHIBALD. "Frost and Stone, " Amherst Alumni
       News, Fall 1963, Special Issue, [n. p.].
           A reprint of MacLeish's address at the groundbreaking
       ceremony for the Robert Frost Library. "Poems are not monu-
       ments. . . . Poems are speaking voices. "

H461   MARPLE, ALLEN. "Off the Cuff, " The Writer, LXXVI (May 1963),
       5-6, 38.
           Mainly a biographical obituary tribute.

H462   MEREDITH, WILLIAM. "Robert Frost and the Quintessence of
       Things, " Massachusetts Review, V (Autumn 1963), 177-80.
           Review of Brower, The Poetry of Robert Frost: Constella-
       tions of Intention.

H. ARTICLES

H463   NIMS, JOHN FREDERICK. "The Classicism of Robert Frost,"
        Saturday Review, XLVI (February 23, 1963), 22-23, 62.
           "Frost is not classical, surely, by virtue of adherence to
        any doctrine. Nor is he a classicist according to his own
        definition: 'one who knows all the Greek irregular verbs'."

H464   "Obituary Notes," Publisher's Weekly, CLXXXIII (February 11,
        1963), 96-97.
           Describes monetary value of first editions of Frost books.

H465   PARSONS, THORNTON H. "Thoreau, Frost, and the American
        Humanist Tradition," Emerson Society Quarterly, No. 33, Part
        One, Fourth Quarter (1963), pp. 33-43.
           Examines the work of Thoreau and Frost in terms of
        Irving Babbitt's view of nature and his humanistic beliefs.

H466   PLIMPTON, CALVIN H. "Reflections," Amherst Alumni News, XV
        (Spring 1963), 2-5.
           Memorial service at Amherst. "He was the poet who
        wanted 'to write a few lines that would be hard to get rid of'
        and he did."

H467   REEVE, F. D. "Robert Frost Confronts Khrushchev," Atlantic
        Monthly, CCXII (September 1963), 33-39.
           Frost "believed that the top thing a government could be-
        stow was character. This was the poet's role in government."

H468   "Robert Frost --1874-1963 ' His Last Poem," Life, LIV (February
        8, 1963), 46-47.
           Brief note precedes text of Frost's 1962 Christmas poem.

H469   "Robert Frost 1875 [sic] - 1963," The Reporter, XXVIII (February
        28, 1963), 20.
           This obituary begins "It was good to have Robert Frost
        around in a time like ours, to know that at least one serious
        poet spoke to a large audience." The article suggests that "He
        was a voice for our nostalgia, for the safety of the past" and
        this was a reason for his large following. But it also agrees
        with Trilling that he was a "terrifying" poet.

The Critical Reception of Robert Frost

H470   "Robert Frost Left a Monument to Life," Denver Post, January 30,
        1963, p. 18.
            Editorial appreciation of Frost and his work.

H471   ROSENBERRY, EDWARD H. "Toward Notes for 'Stopping By
        Woods' Some Classical Analogs," College English, XXIV
        (April 1963), 526-28.
            Compares the poem to the Twenty-third Discourse of the
        Second Book of Epictetus.

H472   S., R. D. "Synthesizing Opposing Elements," Saturday Review,
        XLVI (June 15, 1963), 27.
            Brief review of Squires, Major Themes of Robert Frost.

H473   SAMPLEY, ARTHUR M. "Quiet Voices, Unquiet Times," Midwest
        Quarterly, IV (April 1963), 247-56 [253-56].
            On Robinson, Eliot, Frost, and Yeats. Defends Frost's
        differentness from the others.

H474   SCOTT, WINFIELD TOWNLEY. "A Teacher and Friend," New
        York Times Book Review, November 3, 1963, p. 10.
            Review of Margaret Bartlett Anderson, Robert Frost and
        John Bartlett. ". . . this is an important contribution to the
        Frost story and one which for the moment the general reader
        will find of lively interest."

H475   THOMPSON, LAWRANCE. "The Verse of the Poet Reread," New
        York Times Book Review, June 23, 1963, p. 6.
            Review of Squires, The Major Themes of Robert Frost,
        and Brower, The Poetry of Robert Frost. Finds both books
        valuable, but each critic "has his own perversity."

H476   TODASCO, RUTH. "Dramatic Characterizations in Frost: A
        Masque of Reason," University of Kansas City Review, XXIX
        (Spring 1963), 227-30.
            Finds the masque structurally sound.

H477   TOWNSEND, R. C. "In Defense of Form: A Letter from Robert
        Frost to Sylvester Baxter," New England Quarterly, XXXVI
        (June 1963), 241-49.
            In this reprinted letter, written shortly after publication of
        "Stopping By Woods. . .," Frost defends form in poetry.

H. ARTICLES

H478   TYLER, DOROTHY. "Remembering Robert Frost," Among
Friends [Detroit Public Library], No. 29 (Winter 1962-63),
pp. 1-4.
        Recollections by a former student at Michigan.

H479   UNCLE DUDLEY [Pseud. for Herbert A. Kenney]. "The Secret
Sharer" [editorial], Boston Sunday Globe, September 8, 1963,
p. A2.
        Review of Untermeyer, Letters. . . . "In these letters
. . . Frost's rocky profile of individualism glints, his deter-
mination to stand or fall by himself. . . ."

H480   VAN DOREN, MARK. "Recollections of Robert Frost," Columbia
Library Columns, XII (May 1963), 3-6.
        Reminiscence finds Frost consistent throughout his work.

1964

H481   ADAMS, PHOEBE. "Reader's Choice," Atlantic Monthly, CCXIV
(September 1964), 118-20.
        Review of Thompson's Selected Letters.

H482   "Affectionately Rob," Newsweek, LXIV (August 31, 1964), 75-76.
        Review of Thompson's Selected Letters. ". . . the letters
will serve to provide a glimpse of the full range of Frost's
humanity, the dark and the light out of which the permanent poems came. He need never have feared. Some of them will
stick like burrs."

H483   ANDERSON, CHARLES R. "Frost's 'Nothing Gold Can Stay',"
Explicator, XXII (April 1964), Item 63.
        "The key to the poem lies in what he means by one line,
'So Eden sank to grief'."

H484   ANGOFF, CHARLES. "Robert Frost," Forum (Houston), IV (Fall
1964), 11-13.
        This article is for the most part an account of a conversa-
tion between Angoff and Frost in which Frost comments on the
beneficial relationship between story-telling and politics, poetry and poets (specifically John Ciardi), trees, H. L. Mencken
and other topics. The rest of the article contains other
reminiscences related to Frost.

THE CRITICAL RECEPTION OF ROBERT FROST

H485   ARMSTRONG, JAMES. "The 'Death Wish' in 'Stopping By Woods', " College English, XXV (March 1964), 440, 445.
     On the "death wish" in poetry in general.

H486   BENNETT, PAUL A. "Robert Frost: 'Best-Printed' U.S. Author, and His Printer, Spiral Press, " Publisher's Weekly, CLXXXV (March 2, 1964), 82-86.
     An account of Frost's relationship to Joseph Blumenthal of Spiral Press.

H487   CHILD, SARGENT B. "Robert Frost --The Honorary Member of '24, " Amherst Student, June 13, 1964, p. 2.
     On an examination given by Frost in 1924. His instructions were: "make up your own questions--good ones--and then answer them. "

H488   "Critic at Large" column, New York Times, September 11, 1964, p. 30.
     Review of Thompson, Selected Letters. Subtitle: "Letters of Robert Frost Reveal the Poet as a Determined, Self-Centered Man. "

H489   DAICHES, DAVID. "The Many Faces of a Poet, " New York Times Book Review, September 20, 1964, p. 5.
     Review of Thompson, Selected Letters, and Gould, The Aim Was Song. "Miss Gould is not the most penetrating observer of either men or poems. . . ."

H490   ENGLE, PAUL. "Pullets and Poetry, " New York Times Book Review, February 23, 1964, pp. 12, 14.
     Review of Lathem and Thompson, Robert Frost: Farm-Poultryman. Sees early signs of Frost's later poetic style in the articles on raising chickens.

H491   FERGUSON, JOE M., Jr. "Frost's 'After Apple-Picking', " Explicator, XXII (March 1964), Item 53.
     Rebuts Brooks and Warren, Understanding Poetry. ". . . Frost is suggesting that man is not superior to the woodchuck, or even that he is, in a sense, inferior. "

H. ARTICLES

H492   "Frost Books Donated to N.Y.U. Library," Publisher's Weekly, CLXXXV (January 20, 1964), 105-06.
       Poet's personal library of 3,000 books given by Lesley Ballantine.

H493   "Frost's Colder Notes," Times Literary Supplement (London), November 26, 1964, p. 1090.
       Review of Untermeyer, Letters. . . . "These letters, for all the occasional cantankerousness, make Frost the man in the end measure quite up to Frost the poet."

H494   "Frost's Personal Library Goes to NYU, Not to Library Named in His Honor," Library Journal, LXXXIX (February 1, 1964), 594.
       This article describes the controversy between Amherst and NYU concerning Frost's library which was given to the latter by Frost's daughter, Mrs. Lesley Frost Ballantine, wife of a NYU faculty member.

H495   FUCHS, DANIEL. "Images of Robert Frost," Chicago Review, XVI (1964), 193-200.
       Review of Brower's The Poetry of Robert Frost and Squires' The Major Themes. . . . On the "stances" Frost uses in the poems.

H496   GALBRAITH, J. KENNETH. "Robert Frost's Russian Junket," New Republic, CL (April 11, 1964), 30.
       Review of Reeves' Robert Frost in Russia.

H497   GWYNN, FREDERICK L. "Analysis and Synthesis of Frost's 'The Draft Horse'." College English, XXVI (December 1964), 223-25.
       On the formal devices in the poem.

H498   HARTSOCK, MILDRED E. "Robert Frost: Poet of Risk," The Personalist, XLV (Spring 1964), 157-75.
       One of Frost's beliefs is that man must take risks. "Man, using mind, trusting heart, accepting incompleteness and unreason, must take the posture of courage. It was a risk Frost had to take--and took."

THE CRITICAL RECEPTION OF ROBERT FROST

H499   IDEMA, JIM. "Frost's Letters Give Insight Into Poet's Personali-
        ty," Denver Post, August 30, 1964, p. 10.
            Review of Thompson's Selected Letters finds the book
        "fascinating" and "indispensable."

H500   JAMES, STUART B. "The Home's Tyranny: Robert Frost's 'A
        Servant to Servants' and Andrew Wyeth's 'Christina's World',"
        South Dakota Review, I (May 1964), 3-15.
            "It is doubtful that men know what meaning informs the
        universe, yet Wyeth and Frost, in effect, are saying, If it is
        meaninglessness that awaits us, my art transcends that mean-
        inglessness."

H501   JARRELL, RANDALL. "Good Fences Make Good Poets. Robert
        Frost's letters remind us that his life was as usual as his
        verse." New York Herald Tribune Book Week, August 30,
        1964, pp. 1, 10.
            Review of Thompson, Selected Letters. "For almost 40
        years [Frost] was poor enough to be able to say: 'I wrote about
        the poor because at the receptive and impressionable age I was
        poor myself and know none but the poor.'"

H502   JUHNKE, ANNA K. "Religion in Robert Frost's Poetry: The Play
        for Self-Possession," American Literature, XXXVI (May 1964),
        153-64.
            ". . . the Frost of the poems saves himself, though not in
        the Christian sense of being rescued by divine power for the
        divine power for the transforming of self and world. Rather,
        he preserves and possesses his old self and a part of his hand-
        me-down world through the power of imagination."

H503   KAZIN, ALFRED. "The Strength of Robert Frost," Commentary,
        XXXVIII (December 1964), 49-52.
            This is more a personal reminiscence about Frost than a
        review of Thompson's Selected Letters, which are mentioned
        only incidentally. Kazin writes: "I was fascinated by his sense
        of himself," his strength, his force, and his shrewd intelli-
        gence.

H. ARTICLES

H504 KENNEDY, JOHN F. "Poetry and Power," Atlantic Monthly, CCXIII (February 1964), 53-54.
"Our national strength matters; but the spirit which informs and controls our strength matters just as much. This was the special significance of Robert Frost."

H505 LEPORE, D. J. "Robert Frost--The Middle-Ground: An Analysis of 'Neither Out Far Nor In Deep'," English Journal, LIII (March 1964), 215-16.
How to teach the poem to students in grades nine through twelve.

H506 MAC LEISH, ARCHIBALD. "Gift Outright," Atlantic Monthly, CCXIII (February 1964), 50-52.
"Everything about him--the seeming simplicity of his poems, the silver beauty of his head, his age, his Yankee tongue, his love of talk, his ease upon a lecture platform--everything combined to put him within easy reach--which still could not quite reach him."

H507 MORSE, SAMUEL FRENCH. "A Beginning," Poetry, CIV (July 1964), 253-57.
Review of Untermeyer, Letters of Robert Frost to Louis Untermeyer; Margaret Bartlett Anderson, Robert Frost and John Bartlett; Lathem and Thompson, Robert Frost: Farm-Poultryman; Brower, Poetry of Robert Frost: Constellations of Intention; Squires, Major Themes of Robert Frost.

H508 MUNSON, GORHAM. "The Classicism of Robert Frost," Modern Age, VIII (Summer 1964), 291-305.
This essay discusses Frost as a classical poet of humanistic temper. Personal reminiscences of Frost are interspersed throughout the article. A good deal of space is devoted to an attack on Yvor Winters, who saw Frost as a romantic. An overview of Frost's critical reception and the phases of Frost's poetry concludes the essay.

H509 NIBLING, PHYLLIS. "Fond Memories of 'Rob' Frost," "Contemporary" magazine section, Denver Post, January 12, 1964, p. 2.
Margaret Anderson is interviewed; she describes her literary relationship with Frost and John Bartlett.

THE CRITICAL RECEPTION OF ROBERT FROST

H510   PENDLETON, CONRAD.   "The Classic Dimensions of Robert
       Frost," Prairie Schooner, XXXVIII (Spring 1964), 76-87.
          "While Yeats, Eliot, Pound, and others . . . invented
       elaborate mythic frames of reference," Frost stuck with ele-
       ments of Theocritus, Martial, Juvenal, Horace, and Aesop.

H511   "The Poet and the Public Man," Time, LXXXIV (December 11, 1964),
       127.
          Review of Thompson's Selected Letters. Frost's corre-
       spondence "was rarely tedious and frequently charming."

H512   POORE, CHARLES. "In 10 Summer Days Robert Frost Shook Rus-
       sia," in "Books of the Times" section, New York Times,
       March 24, 1964, p. 33.
          Review of Reeve, Robert Frost in Russia. Frost served
       as cultural ambassador with "cranky splendor."

H513   PRESCOTT, ORVILLE. "The Complexities of Robert Frost," in
       "Books of the Times" section, New York Times, August 31,
       1964, p. 23.
          Review of Thompson, Selected Letters. "Robert Frost
       was not a brilliant letter writer and some of these letters are
       dryly factual, but he managed to charge many of them with his
       own emotion and to enliven them with his mockery, his charm
       and his ideas on many subjects."

H514   "Robert Frost of San Francisco," in "Topics" column, New York
       Times, May 4, 1964, p. 28.
          Editorial comment on group stressing Frost's link to San
       Francisco, his birthplace. A bronze plaque will be placed at
       some "appropriate" place.

H515   SCHLUETER, PAUL. "Not Unlike Job," Christian Century, LXXXI
       (September 30, 1964), 1216-17.
          Review of Thompson's Selected Letters. A very favorable
       review which praises the introduction, organization, and index,
       and concentrates on finding consistency in Frost's religious
       beliefs.

H516   SHEFFEY, RUTHE T. "From Delight to Wisdom: Thematic Pro-
       gression in the Poetry of Robert Frost," College Language As-
       sociation Journal, VIII (September 1964), 51-59.

L. FOREIGN CRITICISM AND TRANSLATIONS

L62 _____ . "The Symbolism of Robert Frost," Bulletin (Tokyo
Gakugei University), XIII (1962), 1-10.
On Frost's use of woods and trees; in Japanese.

L63 SARADHI, K. P. "Frost and Browning: 'The Dramatic Mode',"
Kyushu American Literature (Fukuoka, Japan), X (1967), 11-27.

L64 Sekai Meishi-shu Taisei (Anthology of world poetry, volume 11:
America). Tokyo: Heibonsha, 1959. Pp. 157-178.
Japanese translation of poems selected from A Boy's Will
and A Witness Tree.

L65 TAKAGAKI, MATSUO. "Robert Frost as a Man," Eigo Kenkyu,
Kenkyusha, Tokyo (August 1928).

L66 TERAOKA, NORIKO. "A Study of Robert Frost's Early Poems in
A Boy's Will" (Bulletin of Kacho Junior College), 1966.

KOREAN

L67 SEONGMUNGAK. Frost Siseon. Seoul: Kim Dong Seong, 1958.
A translation of Selected Poems.

ROMANIAN

L68 DIANU, ROMULUS. "Robert Frost, sau dinastia poetillor patriarhali," Rômania Literară, II (October 1969), 19.

RUSSIAN

L69 KASHKIN, IVAN. Dva stikhotvoreniia Roberta Frosta. (K publikatsii.) [Two poems by Robert Frost. (On their publication)].
Ogonek, 1962, no. 38, p. 28.

L70 _____ . [Review of You Come Too.] New York, 1962. Sovremennaia khudozhestvennaia literatura za rubezhom, 1963, no.
1, pp. 78-80.

L71 _____ . "Robert Frost," Inostrannaya Literatura, X (October
1962), 195-201.

H524   BERGER, HARRY, Jr. "Cadmus Unchanged," Yale Review, LIV
(Winter 1965), 277-82.
      Review of Thompson's Selected Letters. "In the middle
of his great and many sufferings he knew that he had to resist
the urge to imagine himself placed safely in changed forms.
Making and saying poems was his alternative to this escape and
not its metamorphic masklike fulfillment."

H525   CARRUTH, HAYDEN. "On Yeats and Others," Poetry, CVII (December 1965), 192-95 [194].
      This is essentially a laudatory review of Lawrance Thomp-
son's Selected Letters with comments on the letters themselves. "They are a record of suffering and of a certain hardi-
hood, but also of immense vanity, cruelty, and emotional in-
capacity."

H526   CHAPIN, KATHERINE G. "The Prose He Did Not Write," New Republic, CLII (January 2, 1965), 16-17.
      Review of Thompson's Selected Letters.

H527   DE BELLIS, JACK. "Frost and Fitzgerald: Redeeming the Personal
Voice," Sewanee Review, LXXIII (Winter 1965), 166-70 [168-
70].
      Review of Untermeyer, Letters of Robert Frost to Louis
Untermeyer, and Andrew Turnbull, Letters of F. Scott Fitzgerald.

H528   DE FALCO, JOSEPH M. "Frost's 'Paul's Wife': The Death of an
Ideal," Southern Folklore Quarterly, XXIX (December 1965),
259-65.
      This essay argues that the character of Paul in "Paul's
Wife" suggests analogues to much greater figures than Paul
Bunyan, that he comes closer to being like St. Paul, a savior-
scapegoat, and that his wife is a composite of two ideals represented in her resemblance to Venus and Athena, beauty and
wisdom. Her "death" is the death of an ideal.

H529   ELLIS, JAMES. "Frost's 'Desert Places' and Hawthorne," English
Record, XV (April 1965), 15-17.
      The "idea" for Frost's poem is found in The Scarlet Letter.

L. FOREIGN CRITICISM AND TRANSLATIONS

L82   _____. "Otkrytoe pis'mo amerikanikomu poetu Robertu Frostu" [An open letter to the American poet Robert Frost], Inostrannaia literatura, 1962, no. 11, pp. 7-9.

L83   _____. "Velikii poet" [A great poet], Izvestiia, January 31, 1963, p.

L84   TUGUSHEVA, M. Literaturnaia Gazeta, September 1, 1962, p.

L85   ZENKEVICH, M. "Robert Frost i ego poeziia" [Robert Frost and his poetry]. In Frost, R. Iz deviati knig [From nine books]. Moscow, 1962. Pp. 5-10.

SOUTH AMERICAN

L86   Antología de Escritores Contemporáneos de Los Estados Unidos. Prosa y verso compilados por John Peale Bishop y Allen Tate. Santiago, Chile: Editorial Nascimento, 1944. Vol. I. Pp. 422-29.
     "Alto en el Bosque una Noche de Nieve" ("Stopping by Woods on a Snowy Evening") and "Pared a Refaccionar" ("Mending Wall").

L87   BROWN, PRADO OSWALDO. "Frost Y El Renaumiento De La Poesia Norteamericana, " IPNA, X (May - August 1954), 57-65.

L88   CASTILLEJAR, JORGE. "La Poesia de Robert Frost, " Bolivar, XLVI (November 1957), 39-43.

L89   DIÁZ-SOLÍS, GUSTAVO. Seis Poemas de Robert Frost. Caracas, Venezuela: Dirreción de Cultura de la Universidad Central de Venezuela, 1963.

L90   DIAZ SOSA, RAFAEL ANGEL. Robert Frost en los Bosques de Nueva Inglaterra [por Rafael Pineda (pseud.)]. Valencia: Universidad de Carabobo, 1960.

L91   "From Beyond the Andes, " O Estado de S. Paulo, August 18, 1954, pp. 17-18.
     Interview in South America when Frost was a delegate to the World Congress of Writers. Translation by Professor Joseph B. Folger of Dartmouth. Calls Frost "simple and

H537   LATHEM, EDWARD CONNERY. "Robert Frost: Assailant," New-England Galaxy, VI (Spring 1965), 27-29.
On Frost's quarrel with Herbert S. Parker in Lawrence in December 1896.

H538   MALBONE, R. G. "Frost's 'The Road Not Taken'," Explicator, XXIV (November 1965), Item 27.
Rebuts Sickels and Perrine (H381 and H377). On the importance of tense in the poem.

H539   MOORE, ROBERT P. "The Eminently Teachable Mr. Frost," English Journal, LIV (November 1965), 689-93, 703.
"[Frost] is not only a teachable poet because he, not unlike his definition of freedom, moves easy in harness --in this case the harness of the classroom, the textbook, the empty stomach, and the bureaucratic bell, he is also a teachable poet because he embodies the best of his art and craft in the most easily understood words --words, as we know, that are deceptive in their simplicity."

H540   O'CONNOR, WILLIAM VAN. "Frost, Robert Lee," World Book Encyclopedia. Chicago: Field Enterprises Educational Corporation, 1965. Vol. 7, p. 469.
"It is an error . . . to believe that Frost is essentially a simple poet, to be understood in a quick reading. And it is a mistake to believe that he is an unquestioning optimist. He is undoubtedly easier to read than many present-day poets and he is an optimist, but his optimism is that of a man who first accepts many hard facts and sees human life as difficult."

H541   OLIVAR, EDITH. "Will Geer As The Poet," New Yorker, XLI (October 23, 1965), 96, 98.
Review of An Evening's Frost.

H542   ROCKAS, LEO. "I Choose Frost," English Record, XV (February 1965), 2-13.
Chooses Frost over Eliot as the greatest poet of our time.

H543   SCOTT, WINFIELD TOWNLEY. "First-Hand Report," New York Times Book Review, September 12, 1965, p. 10.
Review of Mertins, Life and Talks-Walking. "A friendly, domestic, gossipy book. . . ."

H. ARTICLES

H544   SHEED, WILFRID. "Frost as Drama," Commonweal, LXXXIII
        (November 5, 1965), 147-48.
            Review of An Evening's Frost.

H545   STANLIS, PETER J. "Robert Frost: Individualistic Democrat,"
        Intercollegiate Review (University of Michigan), II (September
        1965), 27.
            "As an individualistic Democrat, Frost was against every-
        thing and everybody that made people rely upon somebody or
        something other than their own integrity, courage and re-
        sources."

H546   STONE, ALBERT E., Jr. "Robert Frost," Emory University Quar-
        terly, XXI (Spring 1965), 59-69.
            Mystery, myth, and meaning are the recurring qualities
        in Frost's poetry.

H547   SWEENEY, FRANCIS, S. J. "Francis Thompson," in "Letters to
        the Editor," New York Times Book Review, September 5, 1965,
        p. 22.
            On the influence of Thompson's "The Hound of Heaven" on
        Frost.

H548   TRASCHEN, ISADORE. "Robert Frost: Some Divisions in a Whole
        Man," Yale Review, LV (Autumn 1965), 57-70.
            Essay which tries to account for Frost's detractors in the
        limitation of his poetry that he "never risked his life, his
        whole being; he was never really lost, like the Eliot of The
        Waste Land. He remained in control, in possession of himself.
        He did this by keeping himself from the deepest experiences,
        the kind you stake your life on." This is reflected in various
        kinds of divisions in Frost's poetry--between "image and idea,
        matter and rhythm, the naturalist and the rationalist."

H549   VARGISH, ANDREA. "The Child and Robert Frost," Vermont
        History, XXXIII (October 1965), 469-75.
            Second prize essay in Edmunds Essays contest for high
        school students. Frost "seldom wrote poems about children"
        and "most of his child references are fleeting, yet arrestingly
        poignant. . . ."

1966

H550   AHLUWALIA, HARSHARAN SINGH. "The 'Conservatism' of Robert
       Frost," Bulletin of the New York Public Library, LXX (October
       1966), 485-94.
              Frost's "is a thinking kind of conservatism, qualified and
       never absolute."

H551   BARTLETT, DONALD. "Two Recollections of Frost," Southern
       Review, n. s., II (Autumn 1966), 842-46.
              Youthful reminiscence of Frost in the twenties.

H552   BLUM, MARGARET M. "Frost's 'The Draft Horse'," Explicator,
       XXIV (May 1966), Item 79.
              The poem "is an allegorical treatment of a religious ex-
       perience. . . ."

H553   CHICKERING, HOWELL D., Jr. "Robert Frost, Romantic Humor-
       ist," Literature and Psychology (University of Massachusetts),
       XVI (1966), 139-50.
              For Frost, communication is "both a selfish and an un-
       selfish act; the creation of the self in words is both a relentless
       re-possession and a gift. . . ."

H554   CRAIG, ARMOUR. "Views and Interviews," New York Times Book
       Review, July 24, 1966, pp. 4-5.
              Review of Lathem, Interviews. . ., and Cox and Lathem,
       Selected Prose. "Play-- the dramatic-- for Robert Frost was
       what his poetry was about."

H555   DE MOTT, BENJAMIN "Fire and Ice," New York Herald Tribune
       Book Week, November 13, 1966, p. 5.
              Review of Thompson, Robert Frost: The Early Years.
       What Thompson has found "is absolutely beyond price or valu-
       ing." Published simultaneously in Washington Post and Chicago
       Sun Times.

H556   DENDINGER, LLOYD N. "The Irrational Appeal of Frost's Dark
       Deep Woods," Southern Review, n. s., II (Autumn 1966), 822-29.
              "Like Sophocles, the most important thing he knew was
       that the dark, unfathomable core of human nature relates man
       most surely to his swirling, unmeasurable universe, to all its

235

H. ARTICLES

DENDINGER, LLOYD N. (cont.)
inhabitants, and to their common, most immediate environment, the lovely woods, dark and deep. "

H557 DICKEY, JAMES. "Robert Frost, Man and Myth, " Atlantic Monthly, CCXVIII (November 1966), 53-56.
  Essentially a review of Thompson's Robert Frost: The
Early Years. "What [Frost] accomplished, in the end, was
what he became. . . . He survives in what he made his own
invented being say. "

H558 DOUGHERTY, JAMES P. "Robert Frost's 'Directive' to the Wilderness, " American Quarterly, XVIII (Summer 1966), 208-19.
  "This poem is a step into time, for it is a conversion, a
surrender, that is irrevocable and unrepeatable. As its end
the initiate passes out of the tyrannies of time and the menace
of nature. But not by a geographical retreat, nor by a resort
to myth, nor by Titanism; these are well-established short
courses for the agonist American, but the guide observes that
those who follow them are 'wrong' and will never be delivered
from their agony. "

H559 EBERHART, RICHARD. "Robert Frost: His Personality, " Southern
Review, n.s., II (Autumn 1966), 762-88.
  "Robert Frost is large in scope. He teaches us courage
in the face of the enigmas of existence. We feel that he wears
no mask and speaks the truth directly and that his truth, if not
the whole truth, is worthy of our serious, steadfast, and con-
tinuing love. "

H560 FLINT, F. CUDWORTH. "A Few Touches of Frost, " Southern Review, n.s., II (Autumn 1966), 830-38.
  A reminiscence. "If Frost sometimes spoke maliciously
of literary rivals, he always, in my hearing at least, did so
with a flavor of wit. "

H561 GERBER, PHILIP L. " 'My Rising Contemptuaries' : Robert Frost
Amid His Peers, " Western Humanities Review, XX (Spring
1966), 135-41.
  On Frost's petty and sometimes vindictive attitudes toward
his rivals--Vachel Lindsay, Carl Sandburg, Edgar Lee
Masters, Amy Lowell, and others.

H562   HOWARTH, HERBERT. "Frost in a Period Setting," Southern Review, n.s., II (Autumn 1966), 789-99.
        "The subject of this essay is Frost as the secret sharer. It will briefly suggest what he had in common with three palpably unlike contemporaries and equals, Hueffer, Pound, and Eliot; and why; and why he is nevertheless unlike."

H563   JENSEN, ARTHUR E. "The Character of Frost," Southern Review, n.s., II (Autumn 1966), 860-61.
        On Frost's last visit to Dartmouth before his death.

H564   JONES, DONALD. "Kindred Entanglements in Frost's 'A Servant to Servants'," Papers on Language and Literature, II (Winter 1966), 150-61.
        The speaker in the poem is psychotic and cannot confide in anyone in her family.

H565   JOYCE, HEWETTE E. "A Few Personal Memories of Robert Frost," Southern Review, n.s., II (Autumn 1966), 847-49.
        Reminiscences of Frost by a member of the Bread Loaf School of English faculty.

H566   KNOX, GEORGE. "A Backward Motion Toward the Source," The Personalist, XLVII (Summer 1966), 365-81.
        "Throughout Frost's poetry one finds the theme of return, the backward step, the retreat to a source in Self. Accompanying this are recurring images; the broken drinking glass (goblet), the mountain stream and its source, the lost spring, the abandoned farm, and a quest-search."

H567   LAING, ALEXANDER. "Robert Frost and Great Issues," Southern Review, n.s., II (Autumn 1966), 855-59.
        On Frost's involvement in the "Great Issues Course," required of seniors at Dartmouth.

H568   LEPORE, D. J. "Setting and/or Statement," English Journal, LV (May 1966), 624-26.
        On teaching "Stopping By Woods. . ." to eighth-graders.

H569   LYNEN, JOHN F. "The Poet's Meaning and the Poem's World," Southern Review, n.s., II (Autumn 1966), 800-16.
        "Frost's finest poems seem to develop. . . as discoveries

H. ARTICLES

LYNEN, JOHN F. (cont.)
of the world he has known all along. This is a fiction which
the poet himself probably believed and which he has made so
credible that the simple truthfulness of his statements or their
eloquence often seem the only mysteries of his art. "

H570   M., S. "Yank From Yankville," Newsweek, LXVIII (October 31,
1966), 112, 114B, 116.
On the surprise of discivering Frost's "other" personality.
Review of Thompson's Robert Frost: The Early Years.

H571   MANSELL, DARREL, Jr. "Frost's 'Range-Finding'," Explicator,
XXIV (March 1966), Item 63.
"The rifleman in 'Range-Finding' has found his target by
what is called 'bracketing in', a compromise of the long and
short shots; and so has the poet. "

H572   MEIXNER, JOHN A. "Frost Four Years After, " Southern Review,
n. s., II (Autumn 1966), 862-77.
Review of Thompson, Selected Letters; Untermeyer, Let-
ters. . .; Margaret Bartlett Anderson, Robert Frost and John
Bartlett; Edward Connery Lathem, Interviews with Robert
Frost; and Jean Gould, The Aim Was Song.

H573   MORSE, STEARNS. "Something Like a Star, " Southern Review,
n. s., II (Autumn 1966), 839-41.
"I recorded in my journal that he and Thomas Hardy were
above all the two men of letters I had cared most to meet because with them it wasn't merely about books one would talk
but about the country and the country people. "

H574   NITCHIE, GEORGE W. "Frost as Underground Man, " Southern
Review, n. s., II (Autumn 1966), 817-21.
"Frost has a lover's quarrel with the world. He also had
a quarrel, and not always a lover's quarrel, with himself.
This too is to be human. If you have led the sort of catch-as-
catch-can life that the Frosts led, then it is good to believe
that planning is not really important, that you lose more by it
than you gain. "

H575   PERRINE, LAURENCE. "Frost's 'The Draft Horse'," Explicator,
　　　　XXIV (May 1966), Item 79.
　　　　　　　"The poem is patently allegorical, and has to do, I sug-
　　　　gest, with the decline of physical and sexual vigor in old age."

H576   POIRIER, RICHARD. "Tough Enough to Live," New York Times
　　　　Book Review, November 6, 1966, pp. 4, 36, 38, 40, 42, 44.
　　　　　　　Review of Thompson, Robert Frost: The Early Years.
　　　　Questions Thompson's handling of Frost's sexuality with a
　　　　lack of sympathy.

H577   PRIDEAUX, TOM. "A Warm Spell of Frost," Life, LX (March 4,
　　　　1966), 15.
　　　　　　　Review of Washington, D.C., production of An Evening's
　　　　Frost.

H578   QUINN, SISTER M. BERNETTA. "Symbolic Landscape in Frost's
　　　　'Nothing Gold Can Stay'," English Journal, LV (May 1966), 621-
　　　　24.
　　　　　　　"Frost's method in 'Nothing Gold Can Stay' is that of the
　　　　landscape artist, who does not merely 'photograph' but re-
　　　　creates a design in paint, a design which even though it looks
　　　　'realistic' to the naive eye is the product of rigid selectivity."

H579   ROBSON, W. W. "The Achievement of Robert Frost," Southern Re-
　　　　view, n.s., II (Autumn 1966), 735-61.
　　　　　　　"His principal weakness-- the one that makes for the most
　　　　doubt about his claim to high poetic rank-- is monotony. This
　　　　may be attributed in part to the very nature of his gift."

H580   SAMPLEY, ARTHUR M. "The Tensions of Robert Frost," South
　　　　Atlantic Quarterly, LXV (Autumn 1966), 431-37.
　　　　　　　Frost's "convictions are rarely absolutes: they are ten-
　　　　sions between opposites, and we discover Frost not by what he
　　　　pontificates but by the questions that disturb him. Again and
　　　　again we see him coming back to a few central problems, look-
　　　　ing nearly always at both sides, approaching but never quite
　　　　arriving, investigating rather than deciding." Among the ten-
　　　　sions examined are "the relation of self to God" and "the ten-
　　　　sion between the self and the world."

H. ARTICLES

H581   SAUL, GEORGE B. "A Frost Item," Bulletin of the New York Public Library, LXX (October 1966), 484.
      On a variant of "November."

H582   SHEA, F. X. " 'The Hill Wife': A Romance," English Record, XVI (February 1966), 36-37.
      On the sexual overtones.

H583   SINYAVSKY, ANDREI. "On Robert Frost's Poems," Massachusetts Review, VII (Summer 1966), 431-41. (Translated with an Introduction by Laszlo Tikos and Frederick C. Ellert from a review article in Novy Mir, January 1964.)
      On the very recent introduction of Frost's poetry into the Soviet Union.

H584   THOMPSON, LAWRANCE. "Robert Frost and Carl Burell," Dartmouth College Library Bulletin, n.s., VI (April 1966), 65-73.
      On their friendship, which began when Frost was a student at Dartmouth.

H585   TILLINGHAST, RICHARD. "Blueberries Sprinkled with Salt: Frost's Letters," Sewanee Review, LXXIV (Spring 1966), 554-65.
      Review of Thompson, Selected Letters; Margaret Bartlett Anderson, Robert Frost and John Bartlett; John Robert Doyle, The Poetry of Robert Frost; Elizabeth Isaacs, An Introduction to Robert Frost; Radcliffe Squires, The Major Themes of Robert Frost.
      "A myth of biography already surrounds the figure of Frost. How do these books of letters change that myth?"

H586   UNTERMEYER, LOUIS. "The Fates Defied the Muse," Saturday Review, XLIX (November 5, 1966), 32-33.
      "There may be more sharply delineated, closer-woven biographies of Robert Frost; there will be none more scrupulously detailed." Review of Thompson's Robert Frost: The Early Years.

H587   WALEN, HARRY L. "A Man Named Robert Frost," English Journal, LV (October 1966), 860-62.
      On Walen's acquaintanceship with Frost. "I felt that sometimes he posed, but that more often than not he spoke true."

1967

H588   ANDERSON, JAMES B. "Frost and Sandburg: A Theological Criticism," Renascence, XIX (Summer 1967), 171-83 [171-79].
Frost wants to understand life, Sandburg simply to be part of life.

H589   ANDERSON, QUENTIN. "Frost's Way: Making the Most of It," The Nation, CCIV (February 6, 1967), 182-84.
Review of Thompson's Robert Frost: The Early Years.

H590   BROWER, REUBEN A. "Americanness and Un-Americanness of Frost," 1967 Proceedings of the Conference of College Teachers of English of Texas (Texas Tech. College, Lubbock), XXXII (1967), 6-10.

H591   BROWER, REUBEN A. "Parallel Lives," Partisan Review, XXXIV (Winter 1967), 116-24.
A comparison of the careers of Frost and Bernard Berenson. Each in his own way illustrates "perfectly the two ways open to an American intellectual who reached maturity in the eighties and nineties. . . ."

H592   BURRELL, PAUL. "Frost's 'The Draft Horse'," Explicator, XXV (March 1967), Item 60.
Reply to Hoetker (H536). "I would read the poem as an illustration of the essential irrationality of the world, including also a stance which a man--the poet--may take in the face of it."

H593   CHILDS, KENNETH W. "Reality in Some of the Writings of Robert Frost and William James," Proceedings of the Utah Academy of Sciences, Arts, and Letters, XLIV (Part I, 1967), 150-58.
"Both Frost and James propose a conception of the world in which provision is made for defining reality not in terms of nature but in terms of human nature."

H594   COMPRONE, JOSEPH J. "Play and the 'Aesthetic State'," Massachusetts Studies in English, I (Spring 1967), 22-29.
Frost's poetry illustrates the ideas of Herbert Marcuse's Eros and Civilization and Johan Huizinga's Homo Ludens.

H. ARTICLES

H595   COOK, REGINALD L. "Frost the Diversionist," New England
        Quarterly, XL (September 1967), 323-38.
                "Robert Frost is a diversionist. First, in an historical
        sense, he makes a diversion by an imaginative play in individu-
        al variations within the demands of metrical verse. Secondly,
        he aims literally to divert us by the play of humor and wit.
        And thirdly, as a poetic strategist he practises a diversionary
        art, especially in the use of voice tones and paradoxes, irony
        and ambiguity."

H596   DRAGLAND, S. L. "Frost's 'Mending Wall'," Explicator, XXV
        (January 1967), Item 39.
                The "something there is that does not love a wall. . . is a
        blind primitive instinct to collectivity which wishes to tear
        down the fences of individuation."

H597   HOWES, BARBARA. "'Into Strained Relation'," Poetry, CX (Sep-
        tember 1967), 425-26.
                Review of Thompson's Robert Frost: The Early Years.
        Finds the book "both exhaustive and exhausting," but valuable
        nonetheless.

H598   LARSON, MILDRED R. "Frost out of Chaos," English Record,
        XVII (April 1967), 2-6.
                On Frost's metaphorical use of Chaos, drawn from Hesi-
        odic myth.

H599   MAXWELL, MARGARET. "Swinger of Birches," Senior Scholastic,
        XCI (October 19, 1967), Supplement, pp. 10-11.
                An interview with Lesley Frost Ballantine.

H600   MILLER, LEWIS H., Jr. "Two Poems of Winter," College English,
        XXVIII (January, 1967), 314-17.
                A comparison of "Desert Places" with the anonymous
        "Wynter Wakeneth Al My Care."

H601   MORRISON, THEODORE. "The Agitated Heart," Atlantic Monthly,
        CCXX (July 1967), 72-79.
                "After Mrs. Frost's death. . ., Frost wrote: 'Pretty near-
        ly every one of my poems will be found to be about her if
        rightly read.'"

THE CRITICAL RECEPTION OF ROBERT FROST

H602   PERRINE, LAURENCE. "Frost's 'Acquainted with the Night'," Explicator, XXV (February 1967), Item 50.
     "The clock against the sky, man made but 'at an unearthly height,' strikingly proclaims the absence of authoritative moral direction, human or superhuman, in an indifferent universe."

H603   ST. ARMAND, BARTON L. "The Power of Sympathy in the Poetry of Robinson and Frost: The 'Inside' vs. the 'Outside' Narrative," American Quarterly, XIX (Fall 1967), 564-74.
     Robinson gets inside the minds of the characters in his poems, but Frost's people are known "solely through their actions and not the workings of their minds, while many of them are totally uncommunicative."

H604   SPENCER, BENJAMIN. [Review of Thompson's Robert Frost: The Early Years.] American Literature, XXXIX (November 1967), 419-21.
     A penetrating and favorable review.

H605   THOMPSON, LAWRANCE. "First Love," Reader's Digest, XCI (August 1967), 55-58.
     A reminiscence of Frost's first love, Sabra Peabody, in Salem, N.H., when Frost was twelve years old.

H606   THORNTON, WELDON. "Frost's 'Out, Out'," Explicator, XXV (May 1967), Item 71.
     "The point of [the boy's] death. . . is not the inscrutability of fate and the tenuousness of human existence. Rather it is the waste of life brought on by the well-meaning but insensitive parents rushing the boy out of childhood into adulthood."

H607   "The Young Frost: A Yank from Yankville," Times Literary Supplement (London), December 14, 1967, pp. 1201-02.
     Longish biographical sketch. "He chose the crooked line of experience (in life), of revelation (in poetry). He chose to write in New England speech of mainly New England matters."

1968

H608   BERGER, HARRY, Jr. "Poetry as Revision: Interpreting Robert Frost," Criticism, X (Winter 1968), 1-22.
     The purpose of this essay is "the intensive exploration of

H. ARTICLES

BERGER, HARRY, Jr. (cont.)
a few poems within the perspective provided by the idea of revision," the characteristics of which "emerge from the interpretations and remain within the particular context of the poems
in which they are explored."

H609   BOWEN, JAMES K. "The Persona in Frost's 'Mending Wall':
Mended or Amended?" CEA Critic, XXXI (November 1968), 14.
The narrator is "a kind of everyman," not a villain.

H610   BOWEN, JAMES K. "Propositional and Emotional Knowledge in
Robert Frost's 'The Death of the Hired Man,' 'The Fear,' and
'Home Burial,'" CLA Journal, XII (December 1968), 155-60.
In these three poems, Frost places "a logically practical
approach to a particular problem in juxtaposition with an emo-
tionally intuitive approach to the same problem."

H611   BRODERICK, JOHN C. "Not Quite Poetry: Analysis of a Robert
Frost Manuscript," Manuscripts, XX (Spring 1968), 28-31.
On "Not Quite Social."

H612   COOK, REGINALD L. "Robert Frost's Constellated Sky," Western
Humanities Review, XXII (Summer 1968), 189-98.
"In the psychological struggle with experience Frost gradu-
ally discerns a clarification of order. In the clearing he finds
an association of one poem with another in variations on a
theme. It is indeed like the stars coming out; only in the dark
of life are the forms patent."

H613   DAVIS, CHARLES G. "Frost's 'An Old Man's Winter Night',"
Explicator, XXVII (November 1968), Item 19.
"The tension in the poem causes the reader to ask whether
the threats he fears are the real threats, whether his peace-
fulness is a sign of insensitivity, and whether he is isolated in
some way he may not realize."

H614   DOWELL, BOB. "Revealing Incident as Technique in the Poetry of
Robert Frost," CEA Critic, XXXI (December 1968), 12-13.
Frost's "revealing incident framework" takes one of two
general forms: "(1) a virtually effaced observer reports some
event and makes observations, or (2) a participant relates an
incident with or without commentary."

H615   DOYLE, JOHN R., Jr. "A Reading of Frost's 'Directive',"
Georgia Review, XXII (Winter 1968), 501-08.
        The poem is based on the Grail legend. ". . . Frost has
been true to his long established writing principle never to be
superficially obvious, and to the principle of all Grail quests
that the object sought must be concealed so that the unworthy
person cannot find it and be saved, as Saint Mark says he must
not."

H616   GOEDE, WILLIAM. "The 'Code-Hero' in Frost's 'Blueberries',"
Discourse, XI (Winter 1968), 33-41.
        "Should Frost by accident or design discover the sources
of the self ('honor', 'dignity'), he must convert his 'inner un-
certainties' into 'the deliberate self-containment of the tutor'
in the same way as Hemingway's 'code-hero'."

H617   GRADE, ARNOLD E. "A Chronicle of Robert Frost's Early Reading, 1874-1899," Bulletin of the New York Public Library,
LXXII (November 1968), 611-28.
        An annotated checklist, drawn from 22 different sources.

H618   GREINER, DONALD J. "Confusion and Form: Robert Frost as
Nature Poet," Discourse, XI (Summer 1968), 390-402.
        "The opposition of confusion and form. . . shapes both
[Frost's] thinking about the artistic process and his philosophy
of life, and it accounts for the organic unity we find in his
nature poetry."

H619   GREINER, DONALD J. " 'A Few Remarks and Acknowledgements':
An Unpublished Frost Note," Notes and Queries, n.s., XV
(August 1968), 294-95.
        This is a well-footnoted Frost note written in the spring of
1951 in which Frost has jotted down some of the highlights of
his career through his 1912-1915 sojourn in England.

H620   GRIFFITH, CLARK. "Frost and the American View of Nature,"
American Quarterly, XX (Spring 1968), 21-37.
        Frost's own view of nature is post-Emersonian. "There
are times in his poetry when the oppressiveness of the Natural
order seems to be too great to be anything other than a personal
and self-willed activity."

H. ARTICLES

H621   LOVE, GLEN A. "Frost's 'The Census-Taker' and de la Mare's 'The Listeners'," Papers on Language and Literature, IV (Spring 1968), 198-200.

         The de la Mare poem, which Frost often praised, has influenced Frost's poem.

H622   MARTIN, WALLACE. "Frost's 'Acquainted with the Night'," Explicator, XXVI (April 1968), Item 64.

         Contests Perrine's claim (H602) that "luminary clock" in line 12 is "a tower clock" rather than moon or star. As evidence that it could be the moon, Martin points to origins of word luminary and to possibility that phrase "the time is neither wrong nor right" may "refer to the time of month, or year, or any moment when chronological time is irrelevant to man's spiritual state."

H623   [MAYFIELD, JOHN S.] "Robert Frost in England," The Courier (Syracuse University Library Associates), No. 30 (Fall 1960), 5-6.

         Describes a work by the Reverend J. E. Gethyn-Jones, Dymock Down the Ages, which includes material on Frost's stay in Gloucestershire from April to September 1914.

H624   MONTEIRO, GEORGE. "Birches in Winter: Notes on Thoreau and Frost," CLA Journal, XII (December 1968), 129-33.

         Comparison of Thoreau's journal entries on winter birches and Frost's poem.

H625   MONTEIRO, GEORGE. "Redemption Through Nature: A Recurring Theme in Thoreau, Frost, and Richard Wilbur," American Quarterly, XX (Winter 1968), 795-809.

         All three writers deal with the theme of man in nature and nature's redemptive power.

H626   MORROW, PATRICK. "The Greek Nexus in Robert Frost's 'West-Running Brook'," The Personalist, XLIX (Winter 1968), 24-33.

         This is a detailed examination of "West-Running Brook" seen as a "Heraclitan universe couched within the tradition of Greek drama," for it is "the most classically oriented of his idea poems."

H627   MORSE, STEARNS. "The Phoenix and the Desert Places, " Massachusetts Review, IX (Autumn 1968), 773-84.
        A comparison and contrast of the poetry of Frost and D. H.
Lawrence.

H628   NARVESON, ROBERT. "On Frost's 'The Wood-Pile', " English
Journal, LVII (January 1968), 39-40.
        The poem is not about man's relation to nature but man's
relation to man.

H629   OSBORNE, WILLIAM R. "Frost's 'The Oven Bird', " Explicator,
XXVI (February 1968), Item 47.
        Rebuts Hyatt Waggoner's interpretation of the poem in his
The Heel of Elohim. "The lesson Frost learns from the bird
is precisely not the stoical shrug of the shoulders or the turn-
ing back to one's affairs, as suggested by Mr. Waggoner. "
(See G63.)

H630   PERRINE, LAURENCE. Letter to the Editor, New York Times
Book Review, May 5, 1968, p. 33.
        On Frost's antipathy toward free verse.

H631   PERRINE, LAURENCE. "Frost's 'The Rose Family', " Explicator,
XXVI (January 1968), Item 43.
        Rebuts interpretation of the poem by George W. Nitchie,
Human Values in the Poetry of Robert Frost. Attempts to show
that the poem is not "merely trivial. " (See F13.)

H632   POSS, STANLEY. "Frost, Freud, and Delmore Schwartz, " CEA
Critic, XXX (April 1968), 6-7.
        On the similarity, at least in Freudian terms, of
Schwartz's "A Dog Named Ego" to Frost's "Stopping By Woods."

H633   SNOW, WILBERT. "The Robert Frost I Knew, " Texas Quarterly,
XI (Autumn 1968), 6-48.
        A reminiscence of Frost's long friendship and correspon-
dence with Snow.

H634   WILCOX, EARL. "Frost's 'Stopping by Woods on a Snowy Evening,"
Explicator, XXVII (September 1968), Item 7.
        On the "solstitial allusion" in line eight.

H. ARTICLES

H635   YEVISH, IRVING A. "Robert Frost: Campus Rebel," Texas Quar-
        terly, XI (Autumn 1968), 49-55.
                "As a campus rebel. . . Frost gave the academic world a
        privileged glimpse into what goes on in the mind of one artist
        disillusioned with higher education. . . . More than that,
        Frost demonstrated both as poet and as teacher what, to his
        way of thinking, could be done to rekindle enthusiasm in the
        creative person."

                                 1969

H636   ALLEN, WARD. "Robert Frost's 'Iota Subscript'," English Lan-
        guage Notes, VI (June 1969), 285-87.
                The poem is about the commingling of lovers. ". . . the
        essence of the lover diminshes or even disappears into the es-
        sence of the beloved."

H637   BASLER, ROY P. "Yankee Vergil-- Robert Frost in Washington."
        Voyages, II (Spring 1969), 8-22.
                This is a personal reminiscence by one who knew well of
        Frost's activities on the Washington scene from 1958 through
        1962 as Consultant in Poetry at the Library of Congress.

H638   BORROFF, MARIE. "Robert Frost's 'The Most of It'," Ventures:
        Magazine of the Yale Graduate School, IX (Fall 1969), 76-82.
                On the reconciliation of opposites in the poems generally.

H639   CARPENTER, THOMAS P. "Robert Frost and Katherine Blunt: A
        Confrontation." American Notes and Queries, VIII (November
        1969), 35-37.
                A personal account of Frost's lecture at the Connecticut
        College for Women and of his confrontation with its President,
        Katherine Blunt, who reprimanded him for not "staying on the
        subject."

H640   CHAMBERLAIN, WILLIAM. "The Emersonianism of Robert
        Frost," Emerson Society Quarterly, No. 57, IV Quarter 1969,
        Part 2, pp. 61-66.
                ". . . Emersonianism is central to an understanding of
        the core of Frost's philosophy of poetry, the concept of a
        'momentary stay against confusion'."

The Critical Reception of Robert Frost

H641   DENDINGER, LLOYD N. "Robert Frost: The Popular and the Central Poetic Images," American Quarterly, XXI (Winter 1969),
792-804.
    On Frost as public and as private man. He is popular be-
cause he uses "the poetic mask of the traveler through the
natural world."

H642   DOWELL, PETER W. "Counter-Images and Their Function in the
Poetry of Robert Frost," Tennessee Studies in Literature,
XIV (1969), 15-30.
    There is a polarity in the images of Frost's poetry, thus
creating "counterimplications."

H643   GETHYN-JONES, REVEREND J. E. "Robert Frost-- 6th June
1957," The Courier (Syracuse University Library Associates),
No. 32 (Summer 1969), 1-8.
    Describes Frost's return visit to Gloucestershire.

H644   HANDS, CHARLES B. "The Hidden Terror of Robert Frost,"
English Journal, LVIII (November 1969), 1162-68.
    On "For Once, Then, Something," "Stopping By Woods,"
"The Runaway," and "Desert Places." Students ought "to be
encouraged to discover the terror that underlies much of
Frost's best work."

H645   HEFLIN, WILSON. "A Note on Frost's 'Love and a Question',"
Notes and Queries, XVI (July 1969), 262.
    This brief article links Frost's "Love and a Question" to
an earlier poem by him "In Equal Sacrifice," and both to a
Scottish ballad, "Jamie Douglas."

H646   HUSTON, J. DENNIS. " 'The Wonder of Unexpected Supply': Robert
Frost and a Poetry Beyond Confusion," Centennial Review,
XIII (Summer 1969), 317-29.
    This article begins with an interesting comparison of
Frost and Alfred Hitchcock based on the suddenness of events
in their works, the use of terror, and "their mutual fascination with the potential energy that can course. . . through the
inanimate objects of man's universe." The second part of the
article discusses the use of demonic elements in Frost, how
and why he uses them.

THE CRITICAL RECEPTION OF ROBERT FROST

H. ARTICLES

H647   KNAPP, EDGAR H. "Frost's 'Dust of Snow'," Explicator, XXVIII
        (September 1969), Item 9.
                ". . . on the level of wordless experience the poem
        speaks to us of life and death, as well as of mortal man's use
        of nature and his use of imagination."

H648   MONTEIRO, GEORGE. "Robert Frost and the Politics of Self,"
        Bulletin of the New York Public Library, LXXIII (May 1969),
        309-14.
                On "Two Tramps in Mud Time" and Frost's kinship with
        Thoreau.

H649   NARASIMHAIAH, C. D. "The Reputation of Robert Frost: A Point
        of View," Literary Criterion, IX (Winter 1969), 1-10.
                Finds Frost a minor poet.

H650   RAO, C. VIMALA. "The 'Other Mood': A Note on the Prose Works
        of Robert Frost," Literary Criterion, VIII (Summer 1969),
        63-69.
                An overview of Cox and Lathem, Selected Prose, and
        Lathem, Interviews.

H651   RUBINSTEIN, ANNETTE T. "A Stay Against Confusion," Science
        and Society, XXXIII (Winter 1969), 25-41.
                Frost is "the first serious poet of nature since Lucretius
        to write of her with an utterly matter-of-fact atheism which
        keeps him as far from seeking an immanent divinity in nature
        as he is from seeking a more conventional god in the church
        he has never attended."

H652   SASSO, LAURENCE J., Jr. "Robert Frost: Love's Question,"
        New England Quarterly, XLII (March 1969), 95-107.
                "Could a man demonstrate his love for a woman without
        yielding the fierce, individual pride which Frost associated
        with manhood? The quest for answers is apparent as Frost in
        poem after poem seeks to resolve this, love's question."

H653   SLIGHTS, CAMILLE AND WILLIAM. "Frost's 'The Witch of
        Coös'," Explicator, XXVII (February 1969), Item 40.
                "The narrator is convinced that the Mother's account of a
        walking skeleton is true."

H654   STEIN, WILLIAM BYSSHE. " 'After Apple-Picking': Echoic Parody,"
        University Review, XXXV (Summer 1969), 301-05.
        On Christian symbolism in the poem.

H655   TOOR, DAVID. "Frost's 'Spring Pools'," Explicator, XXVIII
        (November 1969), Item 28.
        "The poem is about the cycles of nature and how each sea-
        son must in its turn give way to the following one."

H656   WEINIG, SISTER MARY A. "A Note on Robert Frost's Tuft of
        Flowers," Concerning Poetry, II (Spring 1969), 79.
        The poem is obliquely about how art brings men together.

                              1970

H657   "A Poet Revealed," Time, XCVI (August 31, 1970), 70-71.
        Review of Thompson's Robert Frost: The Years of Tri-
        umph.

H658   ALDRIDGE, JOHN W. "Frost Removed from Olympus," Saturday
        Review, LIII (August 15, 1970), 21-23, 29-30.
        Review of Thompson's Robert Frost: The Years of Tri-
        umph.

H659   BACHE, WILLIAM B. "Rationalization in Two Frost Poems," Ball
        State University Forum, XI (Winter 1970), 33-35.
        On "The Road Not Taken" and "Two Tramps in Mud Time."
        The speakers offer rational statements, "not just a rendered
        situation with a tacked-on moral."

H660   BALLANTINE, LESLEY FROST. "Somewhat Atavistic," Ball
        State University Forum, XI (Winter 1970), 3-6.
        A reminiscence of her father and her grandparents.

H661   BOSMAJIAN, HAMIDA. "Robert Frost's 'The Gift Outright': Wish
        and Reality in History and Poetry," American Quarterly, XXII
        (Spring 1970), 95-105.
        This is a discussion of Frost's "The Gift Outright" written
        especially for John F. Kennedy's Inauguration. The poem is
        viewed as far less optimistic and much more qualified in its
        hope and belief in the future of America than has hitherto been
        noted. The article is extremely well thought out, shedding
        light on the many nuances and subtleties of this complex poem.

H. ARTICLES

H662   CANE, MELVILLE. "Robert Frost: An Intermittent Intimacy,"
American Scholar, XL (Winter 1970-71), 158, 160, 162, 164, 166.
A reminiscence.

H663   COHEN, EDWARD H. "Robert Frost in England: An Unpublished
Letter," New England Quarterly, XLIII (June 1970), 285-87.
Prints a 1938 letter from Frost to Jessie Rittenhouse concerning A Boy's Will having been published there. Frost did
not go to England solely to publish his books there.

H664   COX, KEITH. "A Syntactic Comparison of Robert Frost's '. . .
Snowy Evening' and 'Desert Places'," Ball State University
Forum, XI (Winter 1970), 25-28.
There are two sets of comparisons: "(1) a class of similari-
ties--compact syntax, parallel syntactic and prosodic struc-
tures, bipartite lines--which mark the poems as Frost's; (2)
a class of differences--predication, use of affixes-- which
distinguish tone and mood."

H665   DUBE, GUNAKAR. "Autumn in Frost and Keats," Literary Criterion, IX (Winter 1970), 84-88.
A brief comparison and contrast of the two poets.

H666   FLEISSNER, ROBERT F. "Frost's Response to Keats' Risibility,"
Ball State University Forum, XI (Winter 1970), 40-43.
A comparison of Frost's "Demiurge's Laugh" with Keats'
"Why Did I Laugh Tonight?"

H667   FRENCH, R. W. "The 'Success' of Robert Frost," The Nation,
CCXI (September 7, 1970), 185-86.
Review of Thompson's Robert Frost: The Years of Tri-
umph.

H668   HALL, DOROTHY J. "Painterly Qualities in Frost's Lyric Poetry,"
Ball State University Forum, XI (Winter 1970), 9-13.
"The painterly quality of Frost's lyrics is not adventitious;
it is a direct outgrowth of aesthetic principle --of the conviction that 'sight and insight are the whole business of poetry'."

H669   HERNDON, JERRY A. "Frost's 'The Oven Bird'," Explicator,
XXVIII (April 1970), Item 64.
"Knowledge of the actual bird's song greatly enriches the

HERNDON, JERRY A. (cont.)
  meaning of this poem by suggesting more clearly the function
  of the bird as teacher, even as 'a voice crying in the wilderness' concerning the greatest of all diminished things: fallen
  man."

H670 HIATT, DAVID. "Frost's 'In White' and 'Design', " Explicator,
  XXVIII (January 1970), Item 41.
    On the revision of "In White" into "Design. "

H671 KERN, ALEXANDER C. "Frost's 'The Wood-Pile', " Explicator,
  XXVIII (February 1970), Item 49.
    "Frost projects his grim and powerful perception in a
  metaphorical relationship: the first person narrator is to the
  little bird as an unknown x is to the absent wood-cutter. "

H672 KYLE, CAROL A. "Emerson's 'Uriel' as a Source for Frost, "
  Emerson Society Quarterly, No. 58, Part Three, First Quar-
  ter 1970, p. 111.
    On Frost's well-known reference in A Masque of Reason
  to Emerson's "Uriel. "

H673 LASK, THOMAS. "The Man and the Masks, " in "Books of The
  Times" column, New York Times, August 11, 1970, p. 31.
    Review of Thompson, The Years of Triumph. "It is Mr.
  Thompson's triumph that he isolates the three sides of the man
  and yet keeps the human being whole. "

H674 LERNER, LAURENCE. "An Essay on Pastoral, " Essays in Criticism, XX (July 1970), 275-97 [275-77].
    Discusses works by Frost, R. S. Thomas, Sidney, Shake-
  speare, Marvell, Sannazaro, Shelley, Guarini.

H675 LIGHT, J. F. " 'I Shan't be Gone Long', " The Nation, CCX (January 12, 1970), 26-28.
    Review of Lathem, The Poetry of Robert Frost.

H676 LOGAN, H. M. "Some Applications of Linguistic Theory to Poetry, " Humanities Association Bulletin (Canada), XXI, (Spring
  1970), 40-47 [43-47].
    Analyzes "The Span of Life. "

H. ARTICLES

H677   MARTIN, R. GLENN. "Two Versions of a Poem by Robert Frost, "
Ball State University Forum, XI (Winter 1970), 65-68.
On revisions in "Our Hold on the Planet." "Perhaps none
of these changes really strengthened the species' hold on the
planet, but collectively the tightening effect is unmistakable. "

H678   MORRISON, THEODORE. "Frost: Country Poet and Cosmopolitan
Poet, " Yale Review, LIX (Winter 1970), 179-96.
Frost is not limited to the countryside but is a citizen of
the world.

H679   PARSONS, D. S. J. "Night of Dark Intent, " Papers on Language
and Literature, VI (Spring 1970), 205-10.
An interpretation of the possible significance of the
phrase, "Put out the light. . ., " in "Once by the Pacific."

H680   PRITCHARD, W. H. "Frost Revised, " Atlantic Monthly, CCXXVI
(October 1970), 130, 132-33.
Review of Lathem, The Poetry of Robert Frost.

H681   "Robert Frost -- The Years of Triumph 1915-1938, " Harper's Ba-
zaar, CIII (July 1970), 70-73.
Excerpts from Thompson's Robert Frost: The Years of
Triumph.

H682   SUDERMAN, ELMER F. "The Frozen Lake in Frost's 'Stopping by
Woods on a Snowy Evening', " Ball State University Forum, XI
(Winter 1970), 22.
"If the narrator. . . is half in love with easeful death, he
is also aware of hate as a way to death. With the woods on one
side and the frozen lake on the other, he is surrounded by
malignant forces, and his decision to go on and keep his promise is more complex and more difficult to fulfill than has often been realized. "

H683   SUTTON, WILLIAM A. "A Frost-Sandburg Rivalry?" Ball State
University Forum, XI (Winter 1970), 58-61.
"Because it appears that Frost had less inner tranquility
than Sandburg, it may be more of a sense of jealousy and
rivalry existed within him. "

H684 SWENNES, ROBERT H. "Man and Wife: The Dialogue of Contraries in Robert Frost's Poetry," American Literature, XLII (November 1970), 363-72.

"The marriage dialogue poems do not show man and woman merging into a single identity, rather the joy of love is in the mutual recognition of each other's virtues--the reconciliation of the sexes, not their erasure."

H685 THERESA, SISTER CATHERINE. "New Testament Interpretations of Robert Frost's Poems," Ball State University Forum, XI (Winter 1970), 50-54.

On biblical echoes in Frost's poetry. Frost's "amazing knowledge of the Bible and the ingenious absorption of its verses into his poetry cannot be refuted."

H686 THORNBURG, THOMAS R. "Mother's Private Ghost: A Note on Frost's 'The Witch of Coös'," Ball State University Forum, XI (Winter 1970), 16-20.

"The mother in this poem assumes that she can rid herself of her fears by admitting the reality of her part in the murder and the reason for the murder, but she is wrong, for she has lived too long with her own state of reality, a reality which does exist for her."

H687 VAN DORE, WADE. "Robert Frost and Wilderness," Living Wilderness, XXXIV (Summer 1970), 47-49.

Frost "was so truly universal and unpretentious in a local manner, some future president will do well to name a national park for him."

H688 VINSON, ROBERT S. "The Roads of Robert Frost," Connecticut Review, III (April 1970), 102-07.

On the symbolic use of roads in the poems.

H689 WOLFF, GEOFFREY. "Mask of a Poet," Newsweek, LXXVI (August 24, 1970), 66-67.

Review of Thompson's Robert Frost: The Years of Triumph.

H. ARTICLES

1971

H690 DOXEY, W. S. "Frost's 'Out, Out'," Explicator, XXIX (April 1971), Item 70.
"Unconsciously -- or perhaps consciously -- [the boy] 'gives' his hand to the saw as a manifestation of his desire to escape his inescapable predicament."

H691 FREEDMAN, WILLIAM. "Frost's 'The Pasture'," Explicator, XXIX (May 1971), Item 80.
"The 'spring' he is 'going out to clean' is not merely nature at its life giving source, but nature as the source of the poet's art."

H692 GRIEDER, JOSEPHINE. "Robert Frost on Ezra Pound, 1913: Manuscript Corrections of 'Portrait D'une Femme'," New England Quarterly, XLIV (June 1971), 301-05.
On Frost's suggestions for revision.

H693 HIERS, JOHN T. "Robert Frost's Quarrel with Science and Technology," Georgia Review, XXV (Summer 1971), 182-205.
Frost found that science was not a "complete guide to understanding man." But he did admire "intellectual audacity when it is properly limited."

H694 JACOBSON, DAN. "Vurry Amurk'n," The Review (London), No. 25 (Spring 1971), 3-10.
A review of Thompson, Years of Triumph, and Lathem, Poetry of Robert Frost. Concentrates on Thompson's work -- with many quibbles.

H695 JEROME, JUDSON. "The Triumph of Lawrance Thompson" in "Poetry: How and Why" column, Writer's Digest, LI (February 1971), 43-47.
Review of Thompson's The Years of Triumph. ". . . Thompson has taken the facts tendered to his care and transformed them into data. He has created a monster. May it haunt his dreams."

H696 MONTEIRO, GEORGE. "Robert Frost's Solitary Singer," New England Quarterly, XLIV (March 1971), 134-40.
On "The Oven Bird." "In seasons of human displacement,

MONTEIRO, GEORGE (cont.)
the muse will continue to spite. . . by disdaining silence. Transposed to a different key, it will speak, but only to that poet whose lyric voice has been stripped of all traditional lyricism."

H697   SAMPLEY, ARTHUR M. "The Myth and the Quest: The Stature of Robert Frost," South Atlantic Quarterly, LXX (Summer 1971), 287-98.

"The critics of Frost are right in saying that he has a tendency to oversimplify, that he is sometimes anti-intellectual, and that he did not sufficiently comprehend the necessity for social planning, especially to take care of the needy. But Frost is right, too, in asserting the priority of an independent spirit, the importance of pride, and the dignity of the lowly."

H698   SPENCER, BENJAMIN. [Review of Thompson's Robert Frost: The Years of Triumph.] American Literature, XLIII (March 1971), 139-42.

A thorough and favorable review.

H699   UNTERMEYER, LOUIS. "The Law of Order, The Promise of Poetry," Saturday Review, LIV (March 20, 1971), 18-20, 60.

On order and design in modern poetry. The question of design in nature "bothered Robert Frost. Time and again in our conversations he referred to the mystery; he posed it as a query in one of his not so well known poems [Design]."

H700   WATSON, CHARLES N., Jr. "Frost's Wall: The View From the Other Side," New England Quarterly, XLIV (December 1971), 653-56.

"We have only the speaker's word for it that the neighbor fails to understand him. But surely the central failure of understanding belongs to the speaker himself."

H701   "A Writer of Poems: The Life and Work of Robert Frost," Times Literary Supplement (London), April 16, 1971, pp. 433-34.

Review of Thompson, Years of Triumph, and Lathem, The Poetry of Robert Frost. Compares Frost with other nature poets, including Wordsworth.

H. ARTICLES

1972

H702   LENTRICCHIA, FRANK. "Experience as Meaning: Robert Frost's 'Mending Wall'," CEA Critic, XXXIV (May 1972), 8-12.
    " 'Mending Wall' dramatizes the playfully imaginative man who has his world under full control, who in his inner serenity is riding his realities, not being shocked by them into traumatic response."

H703   EDELSON, ARLENE. "On Frost, fences and neighbors," in Letter to the editor, New York Times Magazine, October 22, 1972, pp. 10, 78.

H704   UDALL, STEWART L. " '. . . and miles to go before I sleep': Robert Frost's Last Adventure," New York Times Magazine, June 11, 1972, pp. 18-19, 22, 26, 28, 30, 33.
    Another view of Frost and his trip to Russia, by a close friend.

1973

H705   "John F. Kennedy: Poetry and Power," Washington Post, November 22, 1973, p. A18.
    Editorial on the tenth anniversary of President Kennedy's assassination recounts the friendship of President and poet. Also reprints an adaptation of Kennedy's remarks at the dedication of the Robert Frost Library at Amherst.

H706   MORSE, STEARNS. "Lament for a Maker: Reminiscences of Robert Frost," Southern Review, n.s., IX (January 1973), 53-68.
    A thoughtful and intelligent appraisal of a friendship with Frost for forty years.

I. ANTHOLOGIES

I1   BRAITHWAITE, WILLIAM STANLEY, ed. Anthology of Magazine Verse for 1915 And Year Book of American Poetry. New York: Gomme and Marshall, 1915. Pp. 54-55, 61, 163-69.
         Includes "Birches," "The Road Not Taken," "The Death of the Hired Man."

I2   BRAITHWAITE, WILLIAM STANLEY, ed. Anthology of Magazine Verse for 1916 And Year Book of American Poetry. New York: Laurence J. Gomme, 1916. Pp. 81-82, 90-97.
         "The Oft-Repeated Dream" and "The Impulse" from "The Hill Wife," "In the Home Stretch."

I3   BRAITHWAITE, WILLIAM STANLEY, ed. Anthology of Magazine Verse for 1917 and Year Book of American Poetry. Boston: Small, Maynard, 1917. Pp. 133-36, 163.
         Includes "The Bonfire," "Not To Keep." Brief biographical note on p. 396.

I4   COOK, HOWARD WILLARD. "Robert Frost" in his Our Poets of Today. New York: Moffat, Yard, 1918. Pp. 30-34.
         Brief biographical sketch. Reprints excerpts from "The Wood-Pile" and from "Birches."

I5   WILKINSON, MARGUERITE, ed. New Voices: An Introduction To Contemporary Poetry. New York: Macmillan, 1919. Pp. 3, 7-8, 11, 63-64, 127-28, 139-41, 179, 195, 207, 321, 337, 352, 354, 364-65, 386, 391-93.
         "It is probable that critics who have called Mr. Frost's work lumpy and uneven have simply failed to understand his idea of what poetry ought to be."

I. ANTHOLOGIES

I6   BRAITHWAITE, WILLIAM STANLEY, ed. Anthology of Magazine
     Verse for 1920 And Year Book of American Poetry. Boston:
     Small, Maynard, 1920. P. 98.
         Includes "To E.T."

I7   [No editor.] A Miscellany of American Poetry 1920. New York:
     Harcourt, Brace and Howe, 1920. Pp. 21-30.
         Includes "Plowmen," "Good-bye and Keep Cold," "The
     Runaway," "The Parlor Joke," "Fragmentary Blue," "The Lock-
     less Door."

I8   WILKINSON, MARGUERITE. New Voices: An Introduction To Con-
     temporary Poetry. Revised and enlarged. New York: Macmil-
     lan, 1921.
         Only minor changes since 1919 edition.

I9   UNTERMEYER, LOUIS, ed. Modern American and Modern British
     Poetry. New York: Harcourt, Brace, 1922. Pp. 109-17.
         Contains a biographical headnote. "The fanciful by-play,
     the sly banter, so characteristic of this poet, has made his
     grimness less 'gray' than some of his critics are willing to ad-
     mit." Includes "Mending Wall," "The Tuft of Flowers," "Blue-
     Butterfly Day," "Birches," "The Onset."

I10   COOK, HOWARD W., ed. Our Poets of To-day. New York: Moffat,
     Ward, 1923. Pp. 50-53, 151, 275, 372.
         Only slightly revised from 1918 edition. Includes "Bond
     and Free."

I11   UNTERMEYER, LOUIS, ed. This Singing World: An Anthology of
     Modern Poetry For Young People. New York: Harcourt, Brace,
     1923. Pp. 61, 86-87, 137, 199-200, 383-84.
         Includes "The Pasture," "Stopping by Woods. . .," "A
     Brook in the City," "The Runaway," "A Hillside Thaw," "The
     Tuft of Flowers."

I12   MOULT, THOMAS, comp. The Best Poems of 1923. Decorated by
     Philip Hagreen. London: Jonathan Cape, 1924. Pp. 36, 101-04.
         Includes "Stopping by Woods. . ." and "The Star-Splitter."

I. ANTHOLOGIES

I13   BENÉT, WILLIAM ROSE, ed. "Robert Frost (1875-[sic]), " in <u>Poems</u>
<u>for Youth, An American Anthology</u>. New York: E. P. Dutton,
1925. Pp. 333-39.
      Includes a brief biographical sketch describing Frost as
". . . a shrewd philosopher, both a dreamer and a man of his
hands, both a man of soil and a spirit absorbed in the true
reasons for and inwardness of material phenomena."
      Includes "Mending Wall, " "Birches, " "The Sound of the
Trees."

I14   SCHAUFFLER, ROBERT HAVEN, ed. <u>The Poetry Cure, A Pocket</u>
<u>Medicine Chest of Verse</u>. New York: Dodd, Mead, 1925. Pp.
242-44.
      Includes "The Tuft of Flowers."

I15   STEVENSON, BURTON EGBERT, ed. <u>The Home Book of Modern</u>
<u>Verse</u>. New York: Henry Holt, 1925. Pp. 60-61, 272, 309-10,
313, 314-15, 330, 519-20, 560.
      Includes "Birches, " "Fire and Ice, " "Going for Water, "
"Mowing, " "My November Guest, " "An Old Man's Winter
Night, " "Stopping by Woods on a Snowy Evening, " "To Earthward."

I16   THOMPSON, BLANCHE JENNINGS, ed. <u>Silver Pennies: A Collec-</u>
<u>tion of Modern Poems for Boys and Girls</u>. New York: Macmil-
lan, 1925. P. 33.
      Includes "The Pasture."

I17   UNTERMEYER, LOUIS, ed. <u>Modern American Poetry</u>. Third
Edition, Harcourt, Brace, 1925. Pp. 215-37.
      A four-page biographical sketch and brief discussion of
<u>A Boy's Will</u>, <u>North of Boston</u>, and <u>New Hampshire</u>. Says of
Frost ". . . what his emotion or his poetry may lack in windy
range, is trebly compensated for by its untroubled depths."
      Includes "The Pasture, " "The Tuft of Flowers, " "Reluc-
tance, " "Mending Wall, " "The Death of the Hired Man, "
"Birches, " "The Runaway, " "Good-Bye and Keep Cold, " "To
Earthward, " "Two Look at Two, " "Fire and Ice, " "A Sky
Pair, " "Stopping by Woods. . . ."

THE CRITICAL RECEPTION OF ROBERT FROST

I. ANTHOLOGIES

118   WILKINSON, MARGUERITE, ed. Yule Fire. New York: Macmillan, 1925. Pp. 176-78.
     Includes "Christmas Trees."

119   CARHART, GEORGE S., AND PAUL A. MC GHEE, eds. Magic Casements. New York: Macmillan, 1926. Pp. 363-67.
     Includes "Birches," "The Runaway," "New Hampshire," "Mending Wall."

120   SHURTER, EDWIN DUBOIS, AND DWIGHT EVERETT WATKINS, eds. Masterpieces of Modern Verse. New York: Noble and Noble, 1926. Pp. 21-23.
     Includes "Birches."

121   UNTERMEYER, LOUIS, ed. Yesterday and Today, A Comparative Anthology. New York: Harcourt, Brace, 1926. Pp. 142-47, 159, 255-56, 290.
     Includes "The Code," "Mowing," "A Prayer in Spring," "Wing and Window Flower," "The Woodpile."

122   ZEITLIN, JACOB, AND CLARISSA RINAKER, eds. Types of Poetry. New York: Macmillan, 1926. Pp. 428-31, 610-11.
     Includes "Mending Wall," "Birches," "The Death of the Hired Man." An anthology of English and American poetry illustrating several poetic forms.

123   AIKEN, CONRAD, ed. Modern American Poets. New York: Modern Library, 1927. Pp. 107-27.
     Includes "The Road Not Taken," "Home Burial," "The Woodpile," "The Fear," "Birches," "The Sound of the Trees," "Hyla Brook," "The Oven Bird."

124   AUSLANDER, JOSEPH, AND FRANK ERNEST HILL, eds. The Winged Horse, The Story of Poets and Their Poetry. Garden City: Doubleday, Page, 1927. Pp. 407-08.
     Two paragraphs comparing Frost's use of language and subject matter with E. A. Robinson's. Robinson brought the homely speech of everyday into poetry; Frost made a more careful marriage of the lilt of common talk and the beauty of poetic truth. Includes "Nothing Gold Can Stay."

125   BRAITHWAITE, WILLIAM STANLEY, ed. Anthology of Magazine
Verse for 1927 and Yearbook of American Poetry. Boston:
B.J. Brimmer, 1927. Pp. 119-22.
        Includes "The Cocoon, " "The Times Table, " "Tree at My
Window, " "The Minor Bird, " "The Common Fate. "

126   CARMAN, BLISS, ed. The Oxford Book of American Verse. Brief
Preface. New York: Oxford University Press, 1927. Pp. 590-
95.
        Includes "Storm Fear, " "The Telephone, " "The Road Not
Taken, " "Good-Bye and Keep Cold, " "The Onset, " "My November Guest. "

127   GAY, ROBERT M. , ed. The College Book of Verse, 1250-1925.
Boston: Houghton Mifflin, 1927. Pp. 586-94.
        Includes "The Death of the Hired Man, " "Mending Wall, "
"Stopping by Woods on a Snowy Evening. "

128   HALL, HOWARD JUDSON, ed. Types of Poetry: Exclusive of the
Drama. With Introduction. Boston: Ginn, 1927. Pp. 119-20,
165, 645-47.
        Includes "Birches, " "The Code, " "The Death of the Hired
Man. " Frost included briefly in "Biographical Index, " p. 663.

129   MIKELS, ROSA M. R. , AND GRACE SHOUP, eds. Poetry of To-
Day, An Anthology. With Introduction. New York: Charles
Scribner's Sons, 1927. Pp. 6-8, 18-19, 189-90.
        Includes "Birches, " "The Sound of the Trees, " "Mending
Wall. " In fifteen-to-twenty-line headnotes to each poem, the
editors attempt to tell what the poem is about.

130   RITTENHOUSE, J. B. , ed. The Third Book of Modern Verse.
Boston: Houghton Mifflin, 1927. Pp. 4-5, 264, 272, 275-76.
        Includes "To Earthward, " "Misgiving, " "Stopping by
Woods. . .," "The Onset. "

131   BRAITHWAITE, WILLIAM STANLEY, ed. Anthology of Magazine
Verse for 1928 And Year Book of American Poetry. New York:
Harold Vinal, 1928. Pp. 137-39.
        Includes "The Armful, " "Blood, " "The Bear. "

263

I. ANTHOLOGIES

132   DE LA MARE, WALTER, ed. Come Hither: A Collection of Rhymes and Poems for the Young of All Ages. Embellished by Alec Buckels. New York: Alfred A. Knopf, 1928. Pp. 26-27, 560-61, 642-43.
        Includes "The Runaway, " "A Minor Bird, " "Stopping By Woods. . ." [Mistitled "The Wild Woods".]

133   UNTERMEYER, LOUIS, ed. Modern American and British Poetry. Revised and enlarged. New York: Harcourt, Brace, 1928. Pp. 139-49.
        A brief discussion of Frost's poetry. Surveys Frost's career up to his "idle professorship" at Amherst College.
        Includes "The Pasture, " "Mending Wall, " "The Tuft of Flowers, " "Blue Butterfly Day, " "Birches, " "The Onset, " "An Old Man's Winter Night, " "Sand Dunes, " "The Passing Glimpse. "

134   WILKINSON, MARGUERITE, ed. New Voices: An Introduction to Contemporary Poetry. New York: Macmillan, 1928. Pp. 139-40, 141, 337, 364-65, 391-93, 482-83.
        Frost ". . . is for the nation and for the world simply because he knows one section, with all its intimate particularities, perfectly. "
        Includes "The Gum Gatherer, " "The Cow in Apple Time, " "The Sound of the Trees, " "An Old Man's Winter Night, " "Brown's Descent, " "The Runaway. "

135   AIKEN, CONRAD, ed. American Poetry, 1671-1928. New York: Modern Library, 1929. Pp. 267-76.
        Includes "The Telephone, " "The Road Not Taken, " "To Earthward, " "The Sound of the Trees, " "Stopping by Woods . . ., " "My November Guest, " "Home Burial, " "Hyla Brook, " "Mowing, " "Fire and Ice. "

136   AUSLANDER, JOSEPH, AND FRANK ERNEST HILL, eds. The Winged Horse Anthology. Garden City: Doubleday, Doran, 1929. Pp. 607-09.
        Includes "Stopping By Woods. . ., " "Nothing Gold Can Stay, " "Fire and Ice, " "Mending Wall. "

137   BATES, HERBERT, ed. Modern Lyric Poetry. Evanston, Ill.:
       Row, Peterson, 1929. Pp. 105-09.
           Includes "After Apple-Picking," "The Tuft of Flowers,"
       "Mowing," "Stopping by Woods...."

138   BRAITHWAITE, WILLIAM STANLEY, ed. Anthology of Magazine
       Verse for 1929 and Yearbook of American Poetry. New York:
       George Sully, 1929. Pp. 113-17.
           Includes "Acquainted With the Night," "The Middletown
       Murder."

139   DRINKWATER, JOHN, HENRY SEIDEL CANBY, AND WILLIAM
       ROSE BENÉT, eds. Twentieth-Century Poetry. Cambridge,
       Mass.: Houghton Mifflin, 1929. Pp. 326-38.
           Brief biographical sketch. Describes Frost's style as
       "quiet, unstressed." Includes "The Death of the Hired Man,"
       "Mending Wall," "Birches," " 'Out, Out-- '," "To Earthward."

140   NEWCOMER, ALPHONSO GERALD, ALICE E. ANDREWS, AND
       HOWARD JUDSON HALL, eds. Three Centuries of American
       Poetry and Prose. Revised edition, Chicago: Scott, Foresman,
       1929. Pp. 820-22.
           Contains a brief biography and description of Frost's poet-
       ry. "It is the comedy or more often the tragedy of the hill
       country and the remote valleys that is notable in his books...."
           Includes "Mending Wall," "The Death of the Hired Man,"
       "Storm Fear."

141   VAN DOREN, MARK, AND GARIBALDI M. LAPOLLA, eds. A
       Junior Anthology of World Poetry. New York: Albert and
       Charles Boni, 1929. Pp. 659-62.
           Includes "The Runaway," "An Old Man's Winter Night,"
       "The Oven Bird," "The Tuft of Flowers."

142   BURNS, VINCENT GODFREY, ed. The Red Harvest: A Cry for
       Peace. With Introduction. New York: Macmillan, 1930. Pp.
       40-43, 153, 405.
           Includes "Not to Keep," "The Bonfire," "To Edward
       Thomas."

I. ANTHOLOGIES

I43   FARMA, WILLIAM JOSEPH, ed. Prose, Poetry and Drama for
        Oral Interpretation, First Series. New York: Harper, 1930.
        Pp. 272-74.
            Includes "Birches" in "Lyric Poetry" section.

I44   GORDON, MARGERY, AND MARIE B. KING, eds. A Magic World:
        An Anthology of Poetry with Lessons in Poetry. New York:
        D. Appleton, 1930. Pp. 135-36.
            Includes "Stopping by Woods. . . ." "Lesson" on page
        312 instructs reader to observe the sensual images.

I45   HARRINGTON, MILDRED P., ed. Ring-a-Round: A Collection of
        Verse for Boys and Girls. New York: Macmillan, 1930. Pp.
        119.
            Includes "The Pasture."

I46   KREYMBORG, ALFRED, ed. An Anthology of American Poetry
        Lyric America (1630-1930). Including Supplement 1930-1935.
        Revised edition. New York: Coward-McCann, 1930. Pp. 278-
        88.
            Includes "Our Singing Strength, " "An Old Man's Winter
        Night, " "After Apple-Picking, " "Not to Keep, " "Two Look at
        Two, " "Paul's Wife."

I47   SCOLLARD, CLINTON, AND JESSIE B. RITTENHOUSE, eds. The
        Bird-Lovers' Anthology. Boston: Houghton Mifflin, 1930. Pp.
        5, 93.
            Includes "A Minor Bird, " "The Oven Bird."

I48   SMITH, WILLIAM PALMER, ed. Prose and Verse for Speaking and
        Reading. New York: Harcourt, Brace, 1930. Pp. 283-84.
            Includes "Birches" in "Three-Minute Selections" category.

I49   GORDON, MARGERY, AND MARIE B. KING, eds. Verse of Our
        Day: An Anthology of Modern American and British Poetry.
        New York: D. Appleton, 1931. Pp. 53-54.
            One-paragraph biographical sketch on page 331. Includes
        "The Sound of [the] Trees."

I. ANTHOLOGIES

I50   HALL, HOWARD JUDSON, ed. Types of Poetry: Exclusive of the
Drama. Revised and abridged by John Robert Moore. Boston:
Ginn, 1931. Pp. 156-61, 408-10.
   Includes "The Death of the Hired Man," "Birches."

I51   LIEBERMAN, ELIAS, ed. Poems for Enjoyment. New York:
Harper, 1931. Pp. 96, 189-95, 381-83.
   Includes "The Freedom of the Moon," "The Death of the
Hired Man," "Mending Wall."
   Includes a biographical synopsis, pages 432-33.

I52   MENDEL, VERA, AND FRANCIS MEYNELL, eds. The Week-end
Book. Bloomsbury, Eng.: Nonesuch, 1931. Pp. 143-44.
   Includes "Mending Wall."

I53   BRADDY, NELLA, comp. The Standard Book of British and Ameri-
can Verse. Preface by Christopher Morley. New York:
Doubleday, 1932. Pp. 700-01.
   Includes "Mending Wall," "Stopping by Woods. . . ."

I54   GRIFFITH, WILLIAM, AND MRS. JOHN WALTON PARIS, eds.
The Garden Book of Verse. New York: William Morrow, 1932.
Pp. 64-65.
   Includes "Lodges."

I55   MONROE, HARRIET, AND ALICE CORBIN HENDERSON, eds.
The New Poetry, An Anthology of Twentieth-Century Verse in
English. New York: Macmillan, 1932. Pp. 197-212.
   Includes "Mending Wall," "After Apple-Picking," "My
November Guest," "Mowing," "Storm Fear," "Going for Wa-
ter," "The Code," "A Hillside Thaw," "An Old Man's Winter
Night," "Fire and Ice," "The Aim Was Song," "The Hill Wife,"
"On Looking Up by Chance at the Constellations," "Once by
the Pacific," "Acquainted with the Night," "Stopping by Woods
on a Snowy Evening."

I56   MORTON, DAVID, ed. Shorter Modern Poems 1900-1931. New
York: Harper, 1932. Pp. 21-23.
   Includes "The Runaway," "Spring Pools," "Stopping by
Woods. . . ."

I. ANTHOLOGIES

I57   PRESCOTT, FREDERICK C., AND GERALD D. SANDERS, eds.
       An Introduction to American Poetry. New York: F. S. Crofts,
       1932. Pp. 783-801.
           A two-paragraph biographical introduction. ". . . it is
       humanity that interests him most."
           Includes "The Tuft of Flowers, " "Mending Wall, "
       "Birches, " "The Hill Wife, " "Snow, " "Fire and Ice, " "Stopping
       by Woods. . .," " "For Once Then, Something, " "The Onset, "
       "A Hillside Thaw."

I58   SCOLLARD, CLINTON, AND JESSIE B. RITTENHOUSE, eds.
       Patrician Rhymes: A Résumé of American Society Verse From
       Philip Freneau to the Present Day. With Introduction. Boston:
       Houghton Mifflin, 1932. P. 226.
           Includes "The Rose Family."

I59   UNTERMEYER, LOUIS, ed. The Book of Living Verse: Limited
       to the Chief Poets. New York: Harcourt, Brace, 1932. Pp.
       542-47.
           Includes "My November Guest, " "An Old Man's Winter
       Night, " "Home Burial, " "Tree at my Window, " "To Earthward,"
       "Stopping by Woods. . .," " "Nothing Gold Can Stay, " "Two
       Tramps in Mud Time."

I60   BENÉT, WILLIAM ROSE, ed. "Robert Frost, " Fifty Poets, An
       American Auto-Anthology. New York: Duffield and Green,
       1933. Pp. 30-32.
           Includes a one-paragraph introduction and "Birches, "
       which Frost selected for inclusion. He said in a letter: "My
       reasons might be forced and unreal. But if I must defend my
       choice, I will say I took it for its vocality and its ulteriority."

I61   DEL PLAINE, FRANCES KELLY, AND ADAH GEORGINA GRANDY,
       eds. College Readings in Poetry, English and American. New
       York: Macmillan, 1933. Pp. 486-88.
           Includes "To the Thawing Wind, " "The Pasture, " "Mend-
       ing Wall."

I62   HERZBERG, MAX J., ed. Off to Arcady: Adventures in Poetry.
       New York: American Book, 1933. Pp. 296-98.
           Includes "Birches."

I. ANTHOLOGIES

163   ROSS, DAVID, ed. <u>Poet's Gold: An Anthology of Poems to Be Read
       Aloud</u>. New York: Macarday, 1933. Pp. 195-97.
              Includes "The Road Not Taken, " "The Oft Repeated
       Dream, " "The Sound of the Trees. "

164   HUFFARD, GRACE THOMPSON, AND LAURA MAE CARLISLE,
       eds. <u>My Poetry Book: An Anthology of Modern Verse for Boys
       and Girls</u>. Introduction by Booth Tarkington. Illustrated by
       Willy Pogány. Chicago: John C. Winston, 1934. P. 196.
              Includes "The Runaway. "

165   MARKHAM, EDWIN, ed. <u>The Book of American Poetry</u>. With In-
       troduction. New York: William H. Wise, 1934. Pp. 484-88.
              One-paragraph discussion of Frost's style precedes po-
       ems anthologized. "Frost is endowed with the reserve and
       balance of the New England character. "
              Includes "Lodged, " "Loneliness, " "House Fear, " "Snow
       Dust, " "The Road Not Taken, " "Mending Wall, " "Blue-Butter-
       fly Day. "

166   MOULT, THOMAS, ed. <u>The Best Poems of 1934</u>. London: Jonathan
       Cape, 1934. Pp. 118-19.
              Includes "On the Heart's Beginning to Cloud the Mind. "

167   PHELPS, WILLIAM LYON. <u>What I Like in Poetry</u>. New York:
       Charles Scribner's Sons, 1934. Pp. 219-21, 270-72, 308-09.
              Phelps likes "Birches, " "After Apple-Picking, " "Mending
       Wall, " "Good Hours. " Includes chatty, one-or-two line head-
       notes before each poem.

168   UNTERMEYER, LOUIS, AND CARTER DAVIDSON, eds. <u>Poetry,
       Its Appreciation and Enjoyment</u>. New York: Harcourt, Brace,
       1934. Pp. 35-36, 115-17, 211-12, 241.
              Frequent mention of Frost throughout the book, particular-
       ly in regard to realism. His poetry is compared to Robinson's
       and contrasted with Eliot's.
              Includes "Birches, " "A Brook in the City, " "The Death of
       the Hired Man, " "The Runaway. "

I. ANTHOLOGIES

I69   FROST, LESLEY, ed. <u>Come Christmas: A Selection of Christmas Poetry</u>. New York: Coward-McCann, 1935. Pp. 4-5.
       Includes reproduced holograph of "Good Relief" as epigraph to the book, and printed version in the text.

I70   LE GALLIENNE, RICHARD, ed. <u>The LeGallienne Book of English and American Poetry</u>. Two volumes in one. With Introduction. Garden City, N.Y.: Garden City, 1935. Pp. 297-300.
       Includes "After Apple-Picking," "The Road Not Taken," "Birches."

I71   UNTERMEYER, LOUIS. <u>Modern American Poetry: A Critical Anthology</u>. Fifth Revised edition. New York: Harcourt, Brace, 1936. Pp. 208-33.
       30 Frost poems, with a five-page overview of Frost's life and career.

I72   LEGALLIENNE, RICHARD, ed. <u>The Modern Book of American Verse</u>. With Introduction. New York: Sun Dial Press, 1939. [Reissue of Boni & Liveright edition of 1925.] Pp. 297-300.
       Includes "After Apple-Picking," "The Road Not Taken," "Birches."

I73   SPEARE, M.E., ed. <u>The Pocket Book of Verse: Great English and American Poems</u>. New York: Washington Square Press, 1940. Pp. 339-42.
       Incorrectly gives Frost's birthdate as 1875.
       Includes "Mending Wall," "Stopping by Woods. . .," "Birches."

I74   BENÉT, WILLIAM ROSE, AND CONRAD AIKEN, eds. <u>An Anthology of Famous English and American Poetry</u>. With Introductions. New York: Random House, 1945. Pp. 745-56.
       Includes fourteen poems.

I75   MATTHIESSEN, F. O., ed. <u>The Oxford Book of American Verse</u>. With Introduction. New York: Oxford University Press, 1950. Pp. 538-84.
       Includes 40 poems.

THE CRITICAL RECEPTION OF ROBERT FROST

176   DUFFEY, BERNARD I., ed. Modern American Literature. With
       Introduction. New York: Holt, Rinehart and Winston, 1951.
       Pp. 215-26.
           Includes "Home Burial, " "After Apple-Picking," "The
       Witch of Coös, " "Stopping by Woods. . .," "Fire and Ice, "
       "The Oven Bird. "
           Biographical note pp. 359-60.

177   PALGRAVE, F. T., ed. The Golden Treasury of the Best Songs
       and Lyrical Poems. Revised, enlarged and brought up to date
       by Oscar Williams. New York: New American Library of
       World Literature, 1953. Pp. 429, 481, 487-88, 493-94, 499,
       504.
           Includes "Fire and Ice, " "Once by the Pacific, " "The Road
       Not Taken," "Mending Wall," "Stopping by Woods. . .,"
       "Come In. "

178   STALLMAN, R. W., AND R. E. WATTERS, eds. Creative Read-
       er: An Anthology of Fiction, Drama, and Poetry. New York:
       Ronald Press, 1954. Pp. 771-77.
           Quotes excerpts from "The Figure a Poem Makes." Re-
       prints Reginald L. Cook's "Robert Frost: A Time to Listen. "

179   FADIMAN, CLIFTON, ed. The American Treasury: 1455-1955.
       New York: Harper and Brothers, 1955. Pp. 589-95, 847-48.
           Reprints quotable fragments from both the poems and the
       prose.

180   MAC VEAGH, LINCOLN, ed. The Week-end Book. New York:
       Dial Press, 1955. Pp. 101-02.
           Includes "Mending Wall. "

181   UNTERMEYER, LOUIS, ed. In consultation with Karl Shapiro and
       Richard Wilbur. Modern American and Modern British Poetry.
       Revised, shorter edition. New York: Harcourt, Brace and
       World, 1955. Pp. 45-82.
           Includes 38 poems.

182   WILLIAMS, OSCAR, ed. The New Pocket Anthology of American
       Verse From Colonial Days to the Present. A variant edition,
       slightly abridged. New York: Washington Square Press, 1955.
       Pp. 191-215.
           Includes twenty poems.

I. ANTHOLOGIES

183 AUDEN, W. H., ed. The Criterion Book of Modern American
Verse. With Introduction. New York: Criterion Books, 1956.
Pp. vii, 43-52.
"The Gift Outright" serves as epigraph to the book. In-
cludes "The Oven Bird," "The Pauper Witch of Grafton," "Two
Look at Two," "Neither Out Far Nor in Deep," "Design," "The
Most of It," "Never Again Would Birds' Song Be the Same,"
"The Middleness of the Road," "Directive."

184 FOERSTER, NORMAN, ed. American Poetry and Prose. Fourth
Edition. Cambridge, Mass.: Riverside Press, 1957. Pp.
1304-23.
". . . in its main aspect the poetry of Frost is personal
and universal. While rooted in his region, it flowers into
fruit" for the entire nation.
Includes 26 poems.

185 CECIL, DAVID, AND ALLEN TATE, eds. Modern Verse in Eng-
lish, 1900-1950. With Introduction to American Poetry by Tate.
New York: Macmillan, 1958. Pp. 187-95.
Contains a brief biographical sketch (pp. 652-53). In-
cludes "My November Guest," "Mending Wall," "After Apple-
Picking," "An Old Man's Winter Night," "Birches," "Fire and
Ice," "Stopping by Woods. . .," "To Earthward," "Tree at
My Window," "Desert Places," "Moon Compasses."

186 LEGGETT, GLENN, ed. Twelve Poets. New York: Rinehart,
1958. Pp. 250-67.
Shakespeare, Donne, Pope, Wordsworth, Keats, Browning,
Dickinson, Housman, Yeats, E. A. Robinson, and T. S. Eliot.
Includes a brief biographical sketch and 22 poems.

187 WILLIAMS, OSCAR, ed. The Pocket Book of Modern Verse: Eng-
lish and American Poetry of the Last Hundred Years From
Walt Whitman to Dylan Thomas. Revised edition. New York:
Washington Square Press, 1958. Pp. 232-46.
Includes fourteen poems.

188 BRAITHWAITE, WILLIAM STANLEY, ed. Anthology of Magazine
Verse for 1958, and Margaret H. Carpenter, ed., Anthology of
Poems From the Previously Published Braithwaite Anthologies.
New York: Schulte Publishing, 1959. Pp. 69, 285-90.

I. ANTHOLOGIES

BRAITHWAITE, WILLIAM STANLEY (cont.)
Braithwaite includes "Kitty Hawk, " and Carpenter "Acquainted with the Night, " "The Need of Being Versed in Country Things, " "The Road Not Taken, " "To Earthward, " "Stopping by Woods. . . ."

189 CIARDI, JOHN, ed. How Does A Poem Mean? Part Three of An Introduction to Literature. Boston: Houghton Mifflin, 1959. Pp. 670, 753-57, 812, 875-76, 994.
College anthology with much explanatory matter includes "Stopping by Woods. . ., " "The Death of the Hired Man, " "Mowing, " "Departmental, " "The Span of Life. "

190 KENNER, HUGH. The Art of Poetry. New York: Rinehart, 1959. Pp. 41-42 and 208-12.
College anthology includes "Nothing Gold Can Stay" and "The Witch of Coös. " With discussion questions.

191 MILES, JOSEPHINE, ed. The Poem: A Critical Anthology. Englewood Cliffs, N.J.: Prentice Hall, 1959. Pp. 3, 126-27.
Includes discussions of "Design, " "The Oven Bird, " "The Pasture, " "Reluctance. "

192 VAN NOSTRAND, ALBERT D., AND CHARLES H. WATTS, Jr., eds. The Conscious Voice, An Anthology of American Poetry from the Seventeenth Century to the Present. With Introduction. New York: Liberal Arts Press, 1959. Pp. 251-89.
Contains introductory headnote describing Frost's concern for the "shape" of a poem. Includes 25 poems, early and through 1947.

193 COFFIN, CHARLES M., ed. The Major Poets: English and American. Second edition. Revised and edited by Gerrit Hubbard Roelofs. New York: Harcourt, Brace & World, 1961. Pp. 480-90.
Includes 19, mostly short, poems.

194 COLE, WILLIAM, ed. Poems for Seasons and Celebrations. Cleveland: World Publishing, 1961. Pp. 160-61.
Includes "Stopping by Woods. . . ."

I. ANTHOLOGIES

I95 FRIEDMAN, NORMAN, AND CHARLES A. MC LAUGHLIN, eds.
Poetry: An Introduction to Its Form and Art. With Introduction.
New York: Harper and Brothers, 1961. Pp. 16-18, 29-32, 51-
53, 61, 69-74, 77-78, 81, 93-94, 100-02, 118-20, 129, 143-48,
162-64, 167, 179-81.
        Includes "Come In," "Desert Places" (with discussion),
"Design," "Provide, Provide," "Revelation," "Stopping by
Woods. . ." (with discussion), "To Earthward."

I96 MAIN, C. F., AND PETER J. SENG, eds. Poems: Wadsworth
Handbook and Anthology. San Francisco: Wadsworth Publishing,
1961. Pp. 6, 35, 139, 291-92, 303, 311.
        Introductory college anthology with explanatory matter and
discussion questions. Includes " 'Out, Out--'," "The Road
Not Taken," "Neither Out Far Nor In Deep," "Dust of Snow,"
"Stopping by Woods. . .," "Desert Places."

I97 BOGAN, LOUISE, ed. "Robert Frost," in Perry Miller (General
Editor), Major Writers of America. Volume Two. New York:
Harcourt, Brace and World, 1962. Pp. 643-69.
        Contains an overview of Frost's career, themes, and
techniques. Includes 26 poems, "The Waterspout," "An Introduction to King Jasper," and "The Figure a Poem Makes."

I98 GIBSON, WILLIAM M., AND GEORGE ARMS, eds. Twelve American Writers. New York: Macmillan, 1962. Pp. 651-77.
        Brief biographical sketch and overview of Frost's career,
describing his use of synecdoche, metaphor, and language in
the poems. Includes 25 poems, "The Constant Symbol," "On
Emerson," and reprints short critical pieces by Ezra Pound
and Randall Jarrell.

I99 SANDERS, GERALD D., JOHN H. NELSON, AND M. L. ROSEN-
THAL, eds. Chief Modern Poets of England and America.
Fourth edition. Volume Two --The American Poets. With
Introduction. New York: Macmillan, 1962. Pp. 71-112.
        Includes 38 poems.

I100 UNTERMEYER, LOUIS, ed. Modern American Poetry and Modern
British Poetry. New and enlarged edition. With Foreword.
New York: Harcourt, Brace & World, 1962. Pp. 163-96.
        Pages 163-67 contain a biographical sketch and overview of
Frost's work by a longtime friend. Includes 41 poems.

I. ANTHOLOGIES

I101 WILLIAMS, OSCAR, AND EDWIN HONIG, eds. The Mentor Book
of Major American Poets. With Introduction. New York: New
American Library, 1962. Pp. 235-54.
Includes "Mending Wall," "After Apple-Picking," "The
Oven Bird," "Birches," "The Subverted Flower," "The Gift
Outright," "To Earthward," "Tree at My Window," "Two
Tramps in Mud Time," "The Witch of Coös," "Once by the
Pacific," "Acquainted With the Night," "On Looking Up by
Chance at the Constellations," "Stopping by Woods. . .,"
"The Road Not Taken," "Neither Out Far Nor in Deep," "The
Vantage Point," "The Tuft of Flowers," "Directive."

I102 ALTENBERND, LYNN, AND LESLIE L. LEWIS, eds. Introduction
to Literature: Poems. New York: Macmillan, 1963. Pp. 428-
32.
Includes "Mending Wall," "The Road Not Taken,"
"Birches," " 'Out, Out-- ," "Fire and Ice," "Nothing Gold Can
Stay," "Stopping by Woods. . .," "Once by the Pacific," "A
Soldier," "Design."

I103 BRINNIN, JOHN MALCOLM, AND BILL READ, eds. The Modern
Poets: An American-British Anthology. New York: McGraw-
Hill, 1963. Pp. 133-39.
Contains a brief biographical headnote, full-page photo-
graph, "Acquainted With the Night," "Stopping by Woods. . .,"
"The Road Not Taken," "The Runaway," "Provide, Provide,"
"The Silken Tent."

I104 KEYES, FRANCES PARKINSON, ed. A Treasury of Favorite Poems. New York: Hawthorn Books, 1963. Pp. 420-21.
Includes "Stopping by Woods. . .," "A Boundless Moment."

I105 COLLINS, ROWLAND L., ed. Fourteen British and American Poets. New York: Macmillan, 1964. Pp. 268-88.
Includes a one-page biographical sketch and twenty poems.

I106 DRIVER, TOM F., AND ROBERT PACK, eds. Poems of Doubt and
Belief: An Anthology of Modern Religious Poetry. With Intro-
duction by Tom F. Driver. New York: Macmillan, 1964. Pp.
75-76.
Includes "The Strong Are Saying Nothing," "Fire and Ice,"
"Bereft."

I. ANTHOLOGIES

I107   ALLEN, GAY WILSON, WALTER B. RIDEOUT, AND JAMES K.
ROBINSON, eds. American Poetry. New York: Harper and
Row, 1965. Pp. [660-86].
        Contains a brief biographical headnote. Includes twenty
poems, mostly the early ones.

I108   STAFFORD, WILLIAM T., ed. Twentieth Century American
Writing. New York: Odyssey Press, 1965. Pp. 42-74.
        Contains a chronology and short bibliography, 22 poems,
"An Introduction to King Jasper, " and "The Figure a Poem
Makes. "

I109   WALLACE, ROBERT, AND JAMES G. TAFFE. eds. Poems On Poetry: The Mirror's Garland. New York: E.P. Dutton, 1965.
Pp. 5, 200.
        Includes "The Aim Was Song" and "In a Poem. "

I110   BLAIR, WALTER, THEODORE HORNBERGER, RANDALL STEW-
ART, AND JAMES E. MILLER, Jr., eds. The Literature of
the United States. Third edition. Volume Two. Chicago:
Scott, Foresman, 1966. Pp. 915-40.
        Contains a two-page Introduction to Frost and his poetry,
with headnotes to most of the twenty poems included.

I111   BOGAN, LOUISE, ed. "Robert Frost, " in Perry Miller (General
Editor), Major Writers of America. Shorter edition. New
York: Harcourt, Brace and World, 1966. Pp. 925-46.
        Essentially the same as the regular edition, though ex-
cluding "An Introduction to King Jasper, " "The Wind and the
Rain, " and "The Ingenuities of Debt. "

I112   BROWER, REUBEN A., D. FERRY, AND DAVID KALSTONE, eds.
Beginning With Poems: An Anthology. New York: W.W. Norton,
1966. Pp. 320-31.
        Includes "Mowing, " "A Servant to Servants, " "After Apple-
Picking, " "The Oven Bird, " "For Once, Then, Something, "
"Spring Pools, " "Once by the Pacific, " "Acquainted With the
Night, " "Investment, " "Design, " "The Silken Tent, " "All
Revelation, " "Come In, " "Directive. "

I113   MARTZ, WILLIAM J., ed. The Distinctive Voice: Twentieth-Century American Poetry. With Introduction. Glenview, Ill. :

MARTZ, WILLIAM J. (cont.)
Scott, Foresman, 1966. Pp. 39-48.
In the Introduction, Martz describes Frost's voice as
"personal" and "regional." However, "Frost's regional voice
wastes no time in becoming universal, as does Williams'
voice, but the difference is that Frost is creating a consistent
fictional character, a persona." Includes "The Pasture,"
"Mowing," "A Line-Storm Song," "Birches," "Putting in the
Seed," "For Once, Then, Something," "The Rose Family,"
"Two Tramps in Mud-Time," "The Strong Are Saying Nothing,"
"Design," "But God's Own Descent" from "Kitty Hawk," "Gift
Outright of 'The Gift Outright'," "The Gift Outright."

I114 WATKINS, FLOYD C., AND KARL F. KNIGHT, eds. Writer to
Writer: Readings on the Craft of Writing. Boston: Houghton
Mifflin, 1966. Pp. 155-66.
Reprints "Education by Poetry: A Meditative Monologue."

I115 BRADLEY, SCULLEY, RICHMOND C. BEATTY, AND E. HUDSON
LONG, eds. The American Tradition in Literature. Third
edition. Volume Two. New York: W. W. Norton, 1967. Pp.
1063-98.
Contains a brief biographical sketch describing Frost, in
spite of his realism, as "a poet of meditative sobriety." Includes 23 poems, several of them the longer ones, e.g. "The
Death of the Hired Man" and "Paul's Wife."

I116 MURPHY, FRANCIS, ed. Major American Poets to 1914. Boston:
D.C. Heath, 1967. Pp. 419-22.
Includes "Stars," "Rose Pogonias," "The Vantage Point,"
"October," "Mowing," "The Wood-Pile."
Two-paragraph biographical note, page 430.

I117 BROWN, HARRY, AND JOHN MILSTEAD, eds. Patterns in Poetry.
Glenview, Ill.: Scott, Foresman, 1968. Pp. 14, 43, 81-82,
380, 381-82.
Includes "Acquainted With the Night," "Design," "A Soldier," "The Road Not Taken," "The Most of It," "The Onset."

I118 CHATMAN, SEYMOUR, ed. An Introduction to the Language of Po-
etry. Boston: Houghton Mifflin, 1968. Pp. 314-16.
Includes "Mending Wall," "Fire and Ice," "The Onset,"
"Design," "A Semi-Revolution," and discussion passim.

I. ANTHOLOGIES

I119   HALL, DONALD, ed. The Modern Stylists: Writers on the Art of Writing. New York: Free Press, 1968. P. 57.
Two brief excerpts from The Preface to "A Way Out" and "An Introduction to King Jasper."

I120   STEWART, VINCENT, ed. Three Dimensions of Poetry: An Introduction. New York: Charles Scribner's Sons, 1969. Pp. 70-71, 75-76, 193-98.
An instructional anthology for college use. Includes "Mending Wall," "Acquainted with the Night," "After Apple-Picking," " 'Out, Out -- ," "Fire and Ice," "Stopping by Woods. . .," "Provide, Provide," "In Divés Dive," "A Cabin in the Clearing," "Questioning Faces."

I121   EASTMAN, ARTHUR M., ALEXANDER W. ALLISON, HERBERT BARROWS, CAESAR R. BLAKE, ARTHUR J. CARR, AND HUBERT M. ENGLISH, Jr., eds. The Norton Anthology of Poetry. New York: W. W. Norton, 1970. Pp. 939-52.
Includes "The Tuft of Flowers," "Mending Wall," "The Wood-Pile," "The Oven Bird," "Birches," "The Hill Wife," "The Aim Was Song," "Stopping by Woods. . .," "To Earthward," "Spring Pools," "West-Running Brook," "A Lone Striker," "The White-Tailed Hornet," "The Strong Are Saying Nothing," "Neither Out Far Nor in Deep," "Design," "Never Again Would Birds' Song Be the Same," "The Gift Outright," "In Winter in the Woods Alone."

I122   HOGAN, HOMER, ed. Poetry of Relevance: I. Toronto: Methuen, 1970. P. 137.
Includes "Acquainted With the Night."

I123   WILLIAMS, OSCAR, ed. A Little Treasury of Modern Poetry: English and American. Third edition. With Introduction. New York: Charles Scribner's Sons, 1970. Pp. 164-88.
Includes nineteen poems, early and late.

I124   ABCARIAN, RICHARD, ed. Words in Flight: An Introduction to Poetry. Belmont, Calif.: Wadsworth, 1972. Pp. 46-47, 55, 75-76, 96, 115-16, 246.
Includes "The Silken Tent," "Design," " 'Out, Out-- '," "A Semi-Revolution," "Departmental," "In White" (early version of "Design").

I125   BACH, BERT C., WILLIAM A. SESSIONS, AND WILLIAM WAL-
LING, eds. The Liberating Form: A Handbook-Anthology of
English and American Poetry. New York: Dodd, Mead, 1972.
Pp. 32-33, 63, 129, 158-59, 205-07, 356, 369-70.
     Includes "The Road Not Taken," "Desert Places," "Mow-
ing," "The Tuft of Flowers," "Birches," "Stopping by Woods
. . .," "Mending Wall."

I126   BARNES, R. G., ed. Episodes in Five Poetic Traditions: The Sonnet, The Pastoral Elegy, The Ballad, The Ode, Masks and
Voices. San Francisco: Chandler, 1972. Pp. 413-18.
     Includes "A Servant to Servants," "After Apple-Picking"
in "Masks and Voices" section.

I127   CLARK, ADMONT G., ed. An Introduction to Poetry: The Real
Imagination. Chicago: Science Research Associates, 1972.
Pp. 21, 118-19, and discussion passim.
     Includes " 'Out, Out--'," "Stopping by Woods. . . ."

I128   HIEATT, A. KENT, AND WILLIAM PARK, eds. The College
Anthology of British and American Poetry. Second edition.
Boston: Allyn and Bacon, 1972. Pp. 525-36.
     Includes "The Wood-Pile," "The Cow in Apple Time,"
"Range-Finding," "Out, Out--'," "Fire and Ice," "Stopping
by Woods. . .," "To Earthward," "The Egg and the Machine,"
"Desert Places," "Neither Out Far Nor In Deep," "Design,"
"Provide, Provide," "The Silken Tent," "All Revelation," "The
Most of It," "Directive."

I129   MONTAGUE, GENE, ed. Poetry and a Principle. Philadelphia:
J.B. Lippincott, 1972. Pp. 61, 72.
     An instructional anthology for college use. Includes
"Stopping by Woods. . ." and "Nothing Gold Can Stay."

J. POEMS TO OR ABOUT

J1 UNTERMEYER, LOUIS. "Robert Frost Relates 'The Death of the Tired Man'," in his And Other Voices. New York: Henry Holt, 1916. Pp. 22-24.

J2 THOMAS, EDWARD. "The Sun Used to Shine," in his Poems. New York: Henry Holt, 1917. Pp. 47-48.

J3 GIBSON, WILFRED. "The Golden Room," Atlantic Monthly, CXXXVII (February 1926), 204-05.
    Poem about Frost and other poets, including Rupert Brooke, Edward Thomas, and Lascelles Abercrombie. Collected in his Golden Room: Poems, 1925-27. London: Macmillan, 1928.

J4 GUITERMAN, ARTHUR. "The Poet's Housekeeping," Saturday Review of Literature, II (July 3, 1926), 904.

J5 UNTERMEYER, LOUIS. "Robert Frost Takes It up to New Hampshire," in his Collected Parodies. New York: Harcourt, Brace, 1926. Pp. 110-11.

J6 UNTERMEYER, LOUIS. "The Sagging Bough By Rob-rt Fr-st," in his Collected Parodies. New York: Harcourt, Brace, 1926. P. 304.

J7 HOUSH, SNOW LONGLEY. "Bookshelf," University of California Chronicle, XXXI (April 1929), 196-201.
    A long poem on various poets, with one stanza on Robert Frost.

J8 HAINES, JOHN W. "Reunion: To Robert Frost," Hazards. London: Macmillan, 1930. Pp. 48-49.

J9 HILLYER, ROBERT. A Letter to Robert Frost and Others. New York: Alfred Knopf, 1937.

J. POEMS TO OR ABOUT

HILLYER, ROBERT (cont.)
A 234-line poem first delivered before the chapter of Phi
Beta Kappa at Columbia University in June 1936 and first pub-
lished in Atlantic Monthly, CLVIII (August 1936), 158-63.

J10   LESLIE, KENNETH. "Cobweb College: An Antinomian Fable, "
New York Times, April 3, 1938, p. 8E.

J11   ULRICH, DOROTHY LIVINGSTON. "A New Englander to Robert
Frost, " Mark Twain Quarterly, III (Spring 1940), 2.

J12   HALL, JAMES NORMAN. "Reading and Meditating: Robert
Frost's Poems, " Atlantic Monthly, CLXXIV (September 1944),
59.

J13   BAUMAN, DORIS. "New Poet to Old (on reading Robert Frost), "
New Masses, LVI (July 31, 1945), 8.

J14   KEITH, JOSEPH JOEL. "Robert Frost, " Saturday Review of Literature, XXXI (August 21, 1948), 13.

J15   BULKELY, MORGAN. "Chores with Robert Frost, " Saturday Review of Literature, XXXIX (March 24, 1956), 27.

J16   ROSENBAUM, NATHAN. "To Robert Frost (On his seventy-eighth
birthday, March 26, 1954), " Create the World. [New York]:
Whittier Books, 1956. P. 35.

J17   ATKINS, RUSSELL. "A Wood Stopped By, " Beloit Poetry Chapbook
Number Five (Summer 1957), 5.

J18   BELVIN, WILLIAM. "Nature's Man, " Beloit Poetry Chapbook Number Five (Summer 1957), 6.

J19   BROOKS, GWENDOLYN. "Of Robert Frost, " Beloit Poetry Chapbook Number Five (Summer 1957), 7.

J20   BYNNER, WITTER. "The Road Home, " Beloit Poetry Chapbook
Number Five (Summer 1957), 8.

J21   DEUTSCH, BABETTE. "Heard in Old Age, " Beloit Poetry Chapbook Number Five (Summer 1957), 9.

J. POEMS TO OR ABOUT

J22   DICKEY, JAMES. "To Be Edward Thomas," Beloit Poetry Chapbook Number Five (Summer 1957), 10-15.

J23   DUFAULT, PETER KANE. "The Edge," Beloit Poetry Journal Chapbook Number Five (Summer 1957), 17.

J24   HAY, JOHN. "The Circle," Beloit Poetry Journal Chapbook Number Five (Summer 1957), 20-21.

J25   HOLMES, JOHN. "The Folding Key," Beloit Poetry Chapbook Number Five (Summer 1957), 22.

J26   HONIG, EDWIN. "Pleas," Beloit Poetry Chapbook Number Five (Summer 1957), 23.

J27   HUGHES, LANGSTON. "Acceptance," Beloit Poetry Journal Chapbook Number Five (Summer 1957), 24.

J28   HUNT, JOHN DIXON. "Robert Frost at Cambridge, England," Michigan Alumnus Quarterly Review, LXVII (Spring 1961), 219.

J29   INGALLS, JEREMY. "Epilogue to a Reasonable Masque," Beloit Poetry Journal Chapbook Number Five (Summer 1957), 25.

J30   KINNELL, GALWAY. "Indian Bread," Beloit Poetry Journal Chapbook Number Five (Summer 1957), 27.

J31   KREYMBORG, ALFRED. "The Past is Present," Beloit Poetry Journal Chapbook Number Five (Summer 1957), 28-29.

J32   KROLL, ERNEST. "Lines for Robert Frost," Beloit Poetry Chapbook Number Five (Summer 1957), 30.

J33   LOGAN, JOHN. "Two Trees," Beloit Poetry Journal Chapbook Number Five (Summer 1957), 31.

J34   MAC DONALD, LACHLAN. "The Small Boy," Beloit Poetry Journal Chapbook Number Five (Summer 1957), 32-33.

J35   MILES, JOSEPHINE. "Universe," Beloit Poetry Journal Chapbook Number Five (Summer 1957), 34.

J. POEMS TO OR ABOUT

J36   MOORE, ROSALIE. "The Uncomfortable Tic," Beloit Poetry Journal Chapbook Number Five (Summer 1957), 35.

J37   MORSE, SAMUEL FRENCH. "Place and Time," Beloit Poetry Journal Chapbook Number Five (Summer 1957), 36-37.

J38   NEMEROV, HOWARD. "Trees," Beloit Poetry Journal Chapbook Number Five (Summer 1957), 38.

J39   OSTROFF, ANTHONY. "Unmended Wall," Beloit Poetry Journal Chapbook Number Five (Summer 1957), 39.

J40   RICH, ADRIENNE. "Much As I Own I Owe," Beloit Poetry Journal Chapbook Number Five (Summer 1957), 40.

J41   SANDBURG, CARL. "New Hampshire Again," Beloit Poetry Chapbook Number Five (Summer 1957), 41-42.
        Reprinted from Good Morning America. New York: Harcourt, Brace, 1928, 1955.

J42   SCOTT, WINFIELD TOWNLEY. "An Old Boy's Will," Beloit Poetry Chapbook Number Five (Summer 1957), 43.

J43   SMITH, WILLIAM JAY. "Robert Frost: The Road Taken," Beloit Poetry Chapbook Number Five (Summer 1957), 44.

J44   SWENSON, MAY. "R.F. at Breadloaf --His Hand Against a Tree," Beloit Poetry Chapbook Number Five (Summer 1957), 45-46.
        Reprinted in her A Cage of Spines. New York: Rinehart, 1958. Pp. 55-56.

J45   WEISS, THOMAS. "Frost in Peru," Beloit Poetry Chapbook Number Five (Summer 1957), 47.

J46   WILLIAMS, WILLIAM CARLOS. "This is Pioneer Weather," Beloit Poetry Journal Chapbook Number Five (Summer 1957), 48.

J47   HOLMES, JOHN. "Photograph of Robert Frost," College English, XLX (March 1958), 237-38.

J48   CIARDI, JOHN. "Sonnet for Robert Frost But Not About Him," Saturday Review of Literature, XLII (March 21, 1959), 20.

The Critical Reception of Robert Frost

J. POEMS TO OR ABOUT

J49   ENGLE, PAUL. "Robert Frost," Broadside issued by The State
       University of Iowa Library, Ames, April 13, 1959.

J50   ENGLE, PAUL. "To Praise a Man," Life, XLVI (June 15, 1959),
       65-66.

J51   HURLEY, JAMES F. "For Robert Frost," The Spokesman (Loras
       College, Dubuque, Iowa), LVI (Summer 1959), 24.

J52   West of Boston. Poems from the State University of Iowa Poetry
       Workshop in Honor of the Visit of Robert Frost. Iowa City:
       Qara Press, 1959. [15 pp. unnumbered.]
           Only Paul Engle's "A Man" actually to or about Frost.

J53   WYLIE, PHILIP. "Memo to Mr. Frost. On 'A-Wishing Well',"
       Atlantic Monthly, CCVI (July 1960), 84.

J54   FARNHAM, JESSIE. "For An Eighty-Seventh Birthday," McCall's,
       LXXXVIII (April 1961), 198.

J55   BEZNER, HENRY. "In Remembrance," "Open Forum" column,
       Denver Post, January 31, 1963, p. 21.

J56   TENNEY, DENNIS. "Robert Frost," "Open Forum" column,
       Denver Post, February 3, 1963, p. 3.

J57   FOSBROKE, KATHERINE M. "Robert Frost--In Memoriam."
       Appalachia, n.s., Vol. XXIX, No. 7 (June 1963), p. 394.

J58   ROSELIEP, RAYMOND. "Family: On the Night Robert Frost Died,"
       Commonweal, LXXVII (February 22, 1963), 559.

J59   HOLDEN, RAYMOND. "Interval between Felled Trees," The Re-
       minding Salt. Second edition. New York: Dodd, Mead, 1964.
       Pp. 108-10.

J60   KINNELL, GALWAY. "For Robert Frost," Flower Herding on Mt.
       Monadnock. New York: Houghton Mifflin, 1964. Pp. 22-25.

J61   ROSELIEP, RAYMOND. "That Robert Frost," The Lamp, LXII
       (April 1964), 31.

J. POEMS TO OR ABOUT

J62   FRANCIS, ROBERT. "In Memoriam: Four Poets, " Come Out Into
         The Sun. Amherst: University of Massachusetts Press, 1965.
         P. 41.

J63   BOULGER, JAMES D. "Great-Grandfather's Farm, " Holy Cross
         Quarterly, III (Summer 1970), 27.

J64   BOULGER, JAMES D. "Robert Frost: Thanksgiving Day, 1968, "
         Holy Cross Quarterly, III (Summer 1970), 25.

J65   MC DOWELL, E. A. "To Robert Frost: I, " Ball State University
         Forum, XI (Winter 1970), 14-15.

J66   MC DOWELL, E. A. "To Robert Frost: II, " Ball State University
         Forum, XI (Winter 1970), 80.

J67   MEREDITH, WILLIAM. "In Memory of Robert Frost, " Shenandoah,
         XXI (Spring 1970), 105-06.

J68   ORTON, VREST. Vermont Afternoons with Robert Frost. Rutland,
         Vt. and Tokyo: Charles E. Tuttle, 1971. 63 pp.
              A collection of eighteen poems written as dialogues be-
         tween Frost and a long-time friend, Vrest Orton.

J69   PETERS, FRANK. "To Robert Frost, " in Charles Angoff, Gustav
         Davidson, Hyacinthe Hill, and A.M. Sullivan, eds. The Dia-
         mond Anthology. New York: A.S. Barnes, 1971. (For the
         Poetry Society of America.)

J70   VAN EGMOND, PETER. "To Robert Frost: The Great Old Guy, "
         CEA Critic, XXXIII (January 1971), 27.

J71   BERRYMAN, JOHN. "Lines to Mr. Frost, " Delusions. New York:
         Farrar, Straus & Giroux, 1972. P. 39.

J72   BOWEN, JAMES K. "Frost, " CEA Critic, XXXIV (May 1972), 12.

K. DOCTORAL DISSERTATIONS

K1   LARSON, MILDRED R. "Robert Frost As A Teacher. " New York University. [Abstract in New York University School of Education: Abstracts of Theses, Oct. 1948 - June 1949, pp. 89-95.]
    Study seeks to organize data on Frost as teacher and philosopher, and analyze him as a teacher. Attempts to explore Frost's philosophy of education, of life, and his teaching techniques and forces behind it. Source materials include interviews with Frost, questionnaires sent to his students and reference works.

K2   SMITH, MARY E. "The Function of Natural Phenomena in the Poetry of Robert Frost. " Iowa University. [Abstract in State University of Iowa Doctoral Dissertations Abstracts and References, 1951, IX, p. 415.]
    Examination insists on difference between "symbol" and "metaphor" before providing close reading of Frost's poetry. This study serves: (1) to determine the metaphorical importance of phenomena selected and, (2) to study operation of above theory in practice. The investigation ends with a study of unifying themes in Frost's poetry.

K3   MC COY, DONALD E. "Robert Frost: The Reception and Development of his Poetry, " University of Illinois. [Abstract in Dissertation Abstracts, 1953, XIII, p. 97.]
    An examination of what critics have written about Frost and thereby an attempt to show the shifts in reason for Frost's esteem as a poet. Study provides a Frost checklist of approximately 700 items, including reviews, scholarly research and biographical commentary.

K4   COOK, CHARLES H. "Robert Frost, American Symbolist: An Interpretative Study. " Boston University. [Abstract in Dissertation Abstracts, 1957, XVII, p. 1552.]
    Applies a symbolic approach to interpretation of Frost's poems to demonstrate the dominant symbolic themes and their

K. DOCTORAL DISSERTATIONS

COOK, CHARLES H. (cont.)
changes throughout the poetry. These symbolic themes under-
line Frost's broadly Christian view of man's relationship to
God and other men.

K5   ISAACS, EMILY E. "Robert Frost: The Man And His Art."
Washington University. [Abstract in Dissertation Abstracts,
1957, XVII, p. 2267.]
    The study links the poet's life, views on the art of poetry
and his poetic practice and demonstrates their interaction.
Analysis includes the relationship of content, form and tone,
as well as detailed explication of twelve poems which under-
line Frost's poetic principles.

K6   SMYTHE, DANIEL W. "Robert Frost's Poetry as Self-Clarifica-
tion." University of Pennsylvania. [Abstract in Dissertation
Abstracts, 1957, XVII, p. 2273.]
    Exploration of thought of Frost as it reveals his individual
poetic style. The writer had at his disposal records of conversations, stenographic notes--from personal friendship with
the poet--otherwise not available. Provides a biographical
survey, a study of Frost's individuality, his writing as self-
clarification and an analysis of the growth of his ideas. Two
appendices provided of journals and lectures--accounts here-
tofore unrecorded.

K7   NITCHIE, GEORGE W. "Human Values in the Poetry of Robert
Frost: A Study in a Poet's Convictions." Columbia University.
[Listed in Columbia University Libraries: Masters' Essays and
Doctoral Dissertations, 1957-58, p. 22.]

K8   DODGE, CHARLES. "The Use of Evolutionary Theory by American
Poets." University of Illinois. [Abstract in Dissertation Abstracts, 1959, XIX, p. 1077.]
    Examination of the work of seven major American poets of
first half of 20th century demonstrates their point of view and
their approaches to evolution. Asserts the influence of evolutionary theory and science on the writers' works.

K9   PARSONS, THORNTON H. "The Humanism of Robert Frost: A
Study in Parallels," University of Michigan. [Abstract in Dissertation Abstracts, 1959, XX, p. 1366.]

288

K. DOCTORAL DISSERTATIONS

PARSONS, THORNTON H. (cont.)
Presents five lines of modern humanism from Babbitt and Thoreau and parallels Frost's poetry to them. Compares Babbitt's and Frost's attitudes towards sensibility and ascertains Frost's spirit of independent humanism.

K10   DENDINGER, LLOYD N. "Robert Frost: Popular Image of a Poet." Louisiana State University. [Abstract in Dissertation Abstracts, 1967, XXVII, 2527A-28A.]
Investigates the two basic attitudes towards Frost's popularity and their relationship to the "Americanness" of Frost. Delves into Frost's poetic vision to relate his writings both to the mainstream of American literature and to his popularity.

K11   HIEBEL, WILLIAM R. "The Skepticism of Robert Frost." Northwestern University. [Abstract in Dissertation Abstracts, 1967, XXVII, 3457A.]
Studies Frost's philosophical skepticism based on three epistemological ranges: the finite human mind, time and motion, and the problem of idealism. Points out possible influences on Frost and claims that skepticism is at the very core of Frost's poetic theory and practice.

K12   KOPERSKI, RONALD J. "An Analysis of Selected Dramatic Poems Robert Frost." University of Missouri. [Abstract in Dissertation Abstracts, 1967, XXVII, 3159A-60A.]
Critical comment on poetic theory as it relates to nine dramatic poems by Frost. The study explores Frost's use of dialogue, characters, and narration, and their function in universalizing Frost's characters.

K13   LANE, MILLICENT T. "Agnosticism as Technique: Frost's Poetic Style." Cornell University. [Abstract in Dissertation Abstracts, 1967, XXVIII, 2252A.]
At the heart of Frost's poetic technique lies his belief that knowledge only momentarily clarifies the universal truths. This study reports what close examination of Frost's poetry reveals about his use of metrics, language, structure and use of poetic "metaphor."

K14   DE JONG, MARY C. "Structure in the Poetry of Ralph Waldo Emerson, Emily Dickinson and Robert Frost." University of

289

K. DOCTORAL DISSERTATIONS

DEJONG, MARY C. (cont.)
Michigan. [Abstract in Dissertation Abstracts, 1968, XXIX, 867A.]
Outlines a structural approach to analysis of lyric poetry and applies this approach to the poetry of Emerson, Dickinson and Frost. Explication of poems and examination of respective poetic canons disclose structural outlines that shape the poems.

K15 EIKEL, ELIZABETH M. "Robert Frost and the Colloquial Tradition in American Poetry." University of Maryland. [Abstract in Dissertation Abstracts, 1968, XXVIII, 4626A.]
Explores the colloquial style that underlines the writings of Frost and other American poets. It also analyzes the influence of other writers on Frost and its reflection in his use of words.

K16 GANZ, ROBERT N., Jr. "The Pattern of Meaning in Robert Frost's Poetry." Harvard University. [Listed in James L. Woodress, Dissertations in American Literature, 1891-1966 (North Carolina: Duke University Press, 1968), Item 1013.]

K17 GEYER, CHARLES W. "Whose Woods? Postures and Tradition in the Prose and Poetry of Robert Frost." Auburn University. [Abstract in Dissertation Abstracts, 1968, XXVIII, 4126A.]
This study explores the importance of dramatic tones of voices in poetry, Frost's native humor and "oral lore," and the exposition of motives and defenses in his poetry. These three aspects of Frost's poetry make it relevant to the modern urban man.

K18 GREINER, DONALD J. "Robert Frost's Theory and Practice of Poetry." University of Virginia. [Abstract in Dissertation Abstracts, 1968, XXVIII, 2684A.]
Study attempts a comprehensive statement of Frost's poetics through analysis of poems, letters, manuscripts and conversations. It focuses on Frost's originality, his form, his theory of sentence sounds and use of metaphor to assert Frost's significance as a poet.

K19 LYNEN, JOHN F. "Pastoralism in the Poetry of Robert Frost." Yale University. [Listed in James L. Woodress, Dissertations in American Literature, 1891-1966 (North Carolina, 1968), Item 1018.]

K. DOCTORAL DISSERTATIONS

K20   PRITCHARD, WILLIAM H. "The Uses of Nature: A Study of Robert
Frost's Poetry." Harvard University. [Listed in James
Woodress, Dissertations in American Literature, 1891-1966
(North Carolina: Duke University Press, 1968), Item 1022.]

K21   ROBERTS, ESTHER L. "The Thought of Robert Frost's Poetry."
Boston University. [Listed in James L. Woodress, Disserta-
tions in American Literature, 1891-1966 (North Carolina: Duke
University Press, 1968), Item 1023.]

K22   VANDER VEN, TOM R. "Inner and Other Voices of Robert Frost:
Dramatic Theory and Practice." University of Colorado.
[Abstract in Dissertation Abstracts, 1968, XXIX, 918A.]
     Voices in Frost's poetry that create conflict and movement
and provide meaning, are intrinsically related to the poet's
words, style and tone. The inner voices--lyrics, philosophical and dramatic--interact with other voices--monologues,
dialogues, one-act plays and the masques to enhance Frost's
position as dramatic artist in intent and execution.

K23   CAMP, DENNIS D. "Wordsworth and Frost: A Study in Poetic
Tone." University of Wisconsin. [Abstract in Dissertation
Abstracts International, 1969, XXX, 1129A-30A.]
     Explores the different views of Nature in Wordsworth and
Frost and its effect on the tone and ultimate goal of their
poetry.

K24   DOMINA, LYLE D. "Frost and Thoreau: A Study in Affinities."
University of Missouri. [Abstract in Dissertation Abstracts,
1969, XXIX, 2705A-06A.]
     Study discusses the "New England mind," Frost's and
Thoreau's creation of mythical country and mythical hero and
their similar view of life as a process. Examines how these
similarities achieve expression in their artistic attitudes and
work.

K25   KYLE, CAROL A. "Epistemological Dualism in the Poetry of
Robert Frost." University of Pennsylvania. [Abstract in Dissertation Abstracts, 1969, XXIX, 2267A-68A.]
     The tension in Frost's poetry arises from his dual source
of knowledge--intuition and the "rational empirical." Duality
outlined by critical analysis in poems categorized into five

K. DOCTORAL DISSERTATIONS

KYLE, CAROL A. (cont.)
  major areas: psychology, education, myth, science, and religion.

K26 LYFORD, ROLAND H. "Grammatical Categories in Robert Frost's
  Blank Verse: A Quantitative Analysis." University of California, Davis. [Abstract in Dissertation Abstracts, 1969, XXIX,
  4475A.]

  Presents the most accurate and thorough description and
  study of Frost's blank verse style to date. Grammatical elements employed by Frost categorized in structural linguistic
  techniques. Findings of study presented in lists, charts, and
  tables.

K27 MERSCH, ARNOLD, R. G., F. S. C. "Themes of Loneliness and
  Isolation in the Poetry of Robert Frost." St. Louis University.
  [Abstract in Dissertation Abstracts International, 1969, XXX,
  3470A.]

  Examines the development of themes of isolation and loneliness in Frost's works as underlined by biographical material
  and symbolic landscape. Furthermore, it demonstrates how
  these themes form an integral part of his subject matter and
  contain negative and positive implications.

K28 STONE, VIRGINIA S. "Robert Frost: The Breathless Swing Between Content and Form." East Texas State University.
  [Abstract in Dissertation Abstracts International, 1969, XXX,
  2501A.]

  Through an analysis of framework and meaning in
  Frost's poems, this study attempts to better understand
  Frost's method. Divides frameworks of poems into four
  categories and shows the relationship of meaning to these
  frameworks.

K29 WALZ, SISTER VINCENT, D. C. "The Doubleness of Nature in
  Robert Frost's Poetry of Paradox." St. Louis University.
  [Abstract in Dissertation Abstracts, 1969, XXIX, 2727A.]

  Frost's use of paradox is based on the dichotomy between
  the personal and non-personal, on the tension between spiritual
  and material, all of which affect his concept of nature. This
  study attempts to show how well Frost weaves his thought into
  the fabric of his art. Doubleness is the basis of Frost's artistic ideal and is achieved partly through paradoxical metaphors
  and symbols.

K. DOCTORAL DISSERTATIONS

K30   CHAMBERLAIN, WILLIAM F. "Robert Frost, Pragmatic Emer-
       sonian." University of Indiana. [Abstract in Dissertation Ab-
       stracts International, 1970, XXX, 5440-41A.]
           Examines Frost's search for transcendence through poet-
       ry as based on "pragmatic Emersonianism." Investigation in-
       cludes a comparison of Emerson and Frost's theory of creation
       and subject matter, and the role of William James as inter-
       mediate influence.

K31   HAYNES, DONALD T. "The Evolution of Form in the Early Poetry
       of Robert Frost: The Emergence of a Poetic Self." University
       of Notre Dame. [Abstract in Dissertation Abstracts Interna-
       tional, 1970, XXX, 4453A.]
           Analyzes the change in form of four early volumes of
       Frost's poetry (1913-1923). Examines the evolution of the way
       Frost sought to unify his volumes and concludes that shift in
       form is indicative of Frost's search and emergence of poetic
       identity.

L. FOREIGN CRITICISM AND TRANSLATIONS

CZECH

L1   Na Sever od Bostonu. Zanglického originálu přel. a předml. napsala Hana Žantovská. Praha: Státni naki krásné literatury a umění, 1964.
Translation of North of Boston.

ESTONIAN

L2   LEHTEDEL SAMMUJA. Tolkinud M. Nurme. Tallinn, Kirjastus "Eesti Raamat," 1965.
Translation of Complete Poems (1961).

FINNISH

L3   Tuhat Laulujen Vuotta. Valikoima Länsimaista Lyrikkaa. Osakeyhtiö: Werner Söderström, 1957. Pp. 694-99.
"Mending Wall" (Muuria Korjaamassa), "After Apple-Picking" (Omenainkorjum Jälkeen).
English and Finnish on opposite pages.

FRENCH

L4   ASSELINEAU, ROGER. "Robert Frost, poète et paysan," Informations et Documents, No. 177 (March 1, 1963), pp. 18-22.

L5   ASSELINEAU, ROGER, ed. Robert Frost, Présentation par Roger Asselineau; choix de textes, bibliographie, portraits, facsimilés. Paris: Editions Pierre Seghers, 1964.

L6   BARRE, MICHAEL. "Robert Frost en France," Le Bayou, XXIV (Spring 1959), 289-97.

L. FOREIGN CRITICISM AND TRANSLATIONS

L7 BOSQUET, ALAIN. "Robert Frost est Mort, " Le Monde, January 30, 1963, p. 11.

L8 BOSQUET, ALAIN. "Robert Frost, " Nouvelle Revue Française, XI, No. 123 (March 1963), 536-37.

L9 CATEL, JEAN. "La Poésie américaine d'aujourd'hui, " Mercure de France, (March 15, 1920).

L10 CHAMAILLARD, PIERRE. Revue Anglo-Américaine, X (June 1933), 452-53.

L11 FEUILLERAT, ALBERT. "Poètes américains d'aujourd'hui, " Revue des Deux Mondes, XVII (September 1, 1923), 185-210.

L12 "La Femme de Paul, " Henri Thomas, tr. La Nouvelle Nouvelle Revue Française, No. 47 (1er novembre 1956), 952-60. "Paul's Wife" printed in English with a French translation.

L13 LE BRETON, MAURICE. "Robert Frost, Poète Lyrique, " Etudes Anglaises, V (May 1952), 136-42.

L14 LE VOT, ANDRÉ. "La voix de Frost, " Les Langues Modernes, LIX (May - June 1965), 349-56.

L15 Mercure de France, (April 1918). Review of A Boy's Will, North of Boston, and Mountain Interval.

L16 MICHAUD, RÉGIS. Panorama de la littérature américaine contemporaine, Paris: Kra, 1928, pp. 7-274.

L17 MOHRT, MICHEL. "Robert Frost: Un Barde américain, " Nouvelles littéraires, February 7, 1963, p. 3.

L18 PREVOST, JEAN. "Robert Frost, le poète et le sage, " Nouvelle Revue Française, LII (May 1939) 818-40. Includes some translated excerpts of poems.

L19 "Robert Frost. " In C. Cestre and B. Gagnot, eds. Anthologie de la Littérature Américaine. Paris: Librairie Delagrave, 1926. Pp. 361-68.

L. FOREIGN CRITICISM AND TRANSLATIONS

"Robert Frost. " (cont.)
　　　Includes translations by Edmée Hitzel of "An Old Man's
Winter Night" and "A Servant to Servants. " Pp. 362-68; and
introductory note on Frost pp. 361-62.

L20　TREDANT, PAUL. "New York: Les poètes meurent aussi, "
　　　Nouvelles littéraires, March 14, 1963, p. 6.

GERMAN AND AUSTRIAN

L21　BERNUS, ALEXANDER VON. Gesämmelte Gedichte. Mannheim:
　　　Kessler, 1952.
　　　　　Translation of Collected Poems.

L22　BRUNS, FRIEDRICH. Die amerikanische Dichtung der gegenwart.
　　　Leipzig and Berlin: B. G. Teubner, 1930. Pp. 81-86.
　　　　　Brief discussion of Frost as a lyric poet. In German.

L23　BUCHLOH, PAUL G. "Das Verhältnis des amerikanischen Dichters
　　　zum Staat, dargestellt an Robert Frosts 'The Gift Outright'
　　　und Randall Jarrells 'The Death of the Ball Turret Gunner', "
　　　Jahrbuch für Amerikastudien, XIII (1968), 205-14.

L24　COMBECHER, HANS. "Versuch Einer Interpretation von Vica
　　　Gedichten des Neuenglanders Robert Lee Frost, " Die Neueren
　　　Sprachen, XI (June 1957), 281-88.

L25　Englisch Horn. Anthologie Angelsächsicher Lyrik von den Anfängen
　　　bis zur Gegenwart. Phaidon, 1953. Pp. 192-95.
　　　　　"Unser Teil Gold" ("A Peck of Gold"), "Beim Laubsamm-
　　　eln" ("Gathering Leaves"), "Versprengtes Blau" ("Fragmentary
　　　Blue"), "Die Wiese" ("The Pasture").

L26　FISCHER, WALTER. Die englische Literatur der Vereinigten
　　　Staaten von Nordamerika. Wildpark-Potsdam, 1929.

L27　Gedichte aus der Neuen Welt. Amerikanische Lyrik seit 1910.
　　　München: R. Piper Verlag, 1956. Pp. 16-18.
　　　　　"Birken" ("Birches").

L. FOREIGN CRITICISM AND TRANSLATIONS

L28   JÄGER, DIETRICH. "Das Verhältnis zwischen Wirklichkeit und menschlicher Ordnung als Thema der Lyrik: Robert Frost und Wallace Stevens im Vergleich mit europäischen Dichtern, " Die Neueren Sprachen, XVII (1968), 65-83.

L29   _____. "Robert Frost und die Traditionen der Naturdichtung: Die aussermenschliche Welt als Thema deutscher amerikanischer Lyriker des 20. Jahrhunderts, " Literatur in Wissenschaft und Unterricht (Kiel), I (1968), 2-26.

L30   KELLNER, LEON. Geschichte der nordamerikanischen Literatur (Lüpzig, 1927), Vol. II, p. 98.

L31   Lyrik der Welt: Lyrik und Weisheit des Auslandes. Berlin: Safari-Verlag, 1953. Pp. 370-74.
        "Rast in Winterwald" ("Stopping by Woods. . ."), "Schneestaub" ("A Dust of Snow"), "Es Ward Gesang" ("The Aim Was Song"), "Verspregtes Blau" ("Fragmentary Blue"), and "Wüste Stätten" ("Desert Places").

L32   PAPAJEWSKI, HELMUT. "Grundzuge und Substrat in der Lyrik Robert Frost, " Archiv, CXCIII (June 1956), 113-28.

L33   RONNINGER, LISBETH. "Die Kunstform der Dichtung Robert Frost's" (Vienna, 1939).
        Dissertation.

L34   RYAN, ALVAN S. "Symbolic Action in the Poetry of Robert Frost." In Hammond, Lewis, Dieter Sattler, and Emil Lehnartz, eds. Geist einer freien Gesellschaft: Festschrift zu Ehren von Senator James William Fulbright aus Anlass des zehnjährigen Bestehens des deutschen Fulbright-Programms. Heidelberg: Quelle und Meyer, 1962.

L35   SCHÖNEMANN, FRIEDRICH. Die Vereinigten Staaten von Amerika (Stuttgart and Berlin, 1932): Deutsche Verlags-Gestalt, 2 vols. No pp.

L36   SCHULZ, FRANZ. " 'A Momentary Stay Against Confusion': A Discussion of Robert Frost's Poetry as Seen By Four of His Critics. " In Hans Helmcke, Klaus Lubbers, and Renate Schmidt, eds. Literatur und Sprache der Vereinigten Staaten:

L. FOREIGN CRITICISM AND TRANSLATIONS

SCHULZ, FRANZ (cont.)
Aufsätze zu Ehren von Hans Galinsky. Heidelberg: Winter, 1969. Pp. 124-34.
"The purpose of this article is to compare and evaluate different statements made by four American literary critics (Louis Untermeyer, Lawrance Thompson, Randall Jarrell and Yvor Winters) in their attempts at interpreting Robert Frost's poetic work."

L37   SCHWARTZ, KARL. "Robert Frost --Ein Dichter New Englands," Hochschule und Ausland, XIII (March 1935).

L38   Sonette der Völker. Siebenhundert Sonette aus sieben Jahrhundert-en. Heidelberg: Drei Brücken Verlag, 1954. P. 280.
"Vor einem über den Weg Gestürzten Baum" ("On a Tree Fallen Across the Road").

GREEK

L39   [Anthology of American Poetry.] Edited by Steph. Tsatsoulas. Athens, 1958. Pp. 85-88.
In Greek.

ICELANDIC

L40   WARD, HERMAN M. "Skaldskapur Roberts Frost." Andvari (Reykjavik), V (1963), 97-107.

INDIAN

L41   GANGAPATHY, R. "Browning in Three Poems of Robert Frost," Newsletter Number 11, American Studies Research Centre, Hyderabad, India, 1967 [1968].

IRANIAN

L42   [Selected From the Best American Poetry. Edited and translated by Skojaeddin Shefa. Teheran: Ibncina, 1956. Pp. 67-69.]
"The Road Not Taken," "Mending Wall," "Fire and Ice," in Persian translation.

L. FOREIGN CRITICISM AND TRANSLATIONS

ITALIAN

L43 CAMILLUCCI, MARCELLO. "Il Virgilio della Nuova Inghilterra [Robert Frost]." Persona, IV (1963), 18-19.

L44 CELLI, ALDO. "Il momento simbolico nella poesia di Robert Frost," In Mario Praz, et al. Il Simbolismo nella letteratura Nord-Americana: Atti del Symposium tenuto a Firenze 27-29 novembre 1964. Firenze: La Nuova Italia, 1965. Pp. 207-57.

L45 Epoca, IL (Ottobre 7, 1962), 94.
"Ottobre" ("October") and "Fuoco e ghiaccio" ("Fire and Ice"). Printed with an article by Bonaventura Caloro, entitled "Chi E Frost."

L46 GARLAND, H. B. "Robert Frost," Nostro tempo (Napoli), XII (1963), 16-17.

L47 GORLIER, CLAUDIO. "E.A. Robinson e Robert Frost," Paragone, n. s., XII (February 1966), 126-32.

L48 MAURIN, MARIO. "Visite A Robert Frost," Figaro Littéraire, DLXXXII (May 1957), 9.

L49 PISANTI, TOMMASO. "La natura nella poesia di Robert Frost," Ausonia, XVIII (1963), v-vi, 48-50.

L50 Poeti del Novecento. Italiani e Stranieri. Antologia a cura di Elena Croce. Torino: Giulio Einaudi, 1960. Pp. 534-39.
"La tenda di seta" ("The Silken Tent"), "Sosta Presso i boschi una sera di neve" ("Stopping by Woods. . ."), "Entra" ("Come In").

L51 Poeti Stranieri del '900. Tradotti da Poeti Italiani a cura di Vanni Scheiwiller. Milano: All 'Insegna del Pesce d'Oro, 1956. P. 107.
"Albero alla finestra" ("Tree At My Window").

L52 SANESI, ROBERTO, ed. Poeti Americani, da E.A. Robinson a W.S. Merwin (1900-1956). Milano: Feltrinelli, [1958]. Pp. 92-123.
"Sostando presso dei boschi in una sera di neve" ("Stopping by Woods. . ."), "La tenda di seta" ("The Silken Tent"),

L. FOREIGN CRITICISM AND TRANSLATIONS

SANESI, ROBERTO, ed. (cont.)
"Disegno" ("Design"), "Polvere di neve" ("Dust of Snow"), "Il Pascolo" ("The Pasture"), "Né lontano né in profondità" ("Neither Out Far Nor In Deep"), "La strega di coos" ("The Witch of Coös"), "Luoghi deserti" ("Desert Places"), "Dopo la raccolta delle mele" ("After Apple-Picking"), "Amica della notte" ("Acquainted With the Night"). English and Italian on opposite pages.

L53   SERPICI, ALESSANDRO. "Robert Frost, " Il Ponte, XIX (1963), 162-64.

JAPANESE

L54   ANDERSON, CHARLES R. "On Robert Frost's Stopping by Woods on a Snowy Evening, " Kyushu American Literature (Fukuoka, Japan), X (1967), 1-10.

L55   ANDO, ICHIRO. "On Robert Frost, " Area and Culture Studies (Tokyo University of Foreign Studies), I (November 1951), 13-29.

L56   _____. Robert Frost. Tokyo: Kenkyusha, 1958.
A critical appraisal of Frost, with some poems printed in English and in Japanese.

L57   CHUJO, AIKO. "Robert Frost and His New England, " Kasui Review (1964).

L58   HASHIGUCHI, YASUO. "The Poetry of Robert Frost, " American Literary Review (1956).

L59   MAEDA, CANA. "Robert Frost: A Stay Against Confusion, " Review of Liberal Arts (Otaru University of Commerce), No. 8 (July 1954), 73-96.
An intelligent overview.

L60   NAKANISHI, MASAO. "A Study of Robert Frost, " English Language and Literature Society (Chuo University), 1966.

L61   OKA, JUKICHI. "Animals in Robert Frost's Poems, " Bulletin (Tokyo Gakugei University), XIV (March 1963), 1-5.
In Japanese.

L. FOREIGN CRITICISM AND TRANSLATIONS

L62   _____. "The Symbolism of Robert Frost," Bulletin (Tokyo Gakugei University), XIII (1962), 1-10.
On Frost's use of woods and trees; in Japanese.

L63   SARADHI, K. P. "Frost and Browning: 'The Dramatic Mode'," Kyushu American Literature (Fukuoka, Japan), X (1967), 11-27.

L64   Sekai Meishi-shu Taisei (Anthology of world poetry, volume 11: America). Tokyo: Heibonsha, 1959. Pp. 157-178.
Japanese translation of poems selected from A Boy's Will and A Witness Tree.

L65   TAKAGAKI, MATSUO. "Robert Frost as a Man," Eigo Kenkyu, Kenkyusha, Tokyo (August 1928).

L66   TERAOKA, NORIKO. "A Study of Robert Frost's Early Poems in A Boy's Will" (Bulletin of Kacho Junior College), 1966.

KOREAN

L67   SEONGMUNGAK. Frost Siseon. Seoul: Kim Dong Seong, 1958.
A translation of Selected Poems.

ROMANIAN

L68   DIANU, ROMULUS. "Robert Frost, sau dinastia poetillor patriarhali," Rômania Literară, II (October 1969), 19.

RUSSIAN

L69   KASHKIN, IVAN. Dva stikhotvoreniia Roberta Frosta. (K publikatsii.) [Two poems by Robert Frost. (On their publication)]. Ogonek, 1962, no. 38, p. 28.

L70   _____. [Review of You Come Too.] New York, 1962. Sovremennaia khudozhestvennaia literatura za rubezhom, 1963, no. 1, pp. 78-80.

L71   _____. "Robert Frost," Inostrannaya Literatura, X (October 1962), 195-201.

The Critical Reception of Robert Frost

L. FOREIGN CRITICISM AND TRANSLATIONS

L72　KHITROV, M. Izvestiia, September 3, 1962, p. 1.

L73　KHRUSHCHEV, N. S. "Vydaiuschchiisia poet i grazhdanin SShA. Sem'e Roberta L. Frosta. 29 ianvaria 1963 goda". [An outstanding poet and citizen of the U.S. To the family of Robert L. Frost. January 29, 1963.] In N.S. Khrushchev, prizvanie literatury i iskusstva [The high calling of literature and art]. Moscow, 1963. P. 245.

L74　LEVONEVSKII, D. "Robert Frost v Pushkinskom Dome" [Robert Frost in the Pushkinskii Dom (of the Academy of Sciences)], Literatura i zhizn', September 7, 1962.

L75　Novji mir. [New World]. Literaturno-politicheskii i nauchnyi zhurnal. Moscow, August 1962, pp. 167-71.
　　　"Two Tramps in Mud-Time," "Two Look at Two," and "The Star-Splitter."

L76　Robert Frost. "Sobstvennyi golos". [Robert Frost. His Own Voice.] Za rubezhom, 1963, no. 5, p. 24.

L77　SERGEEV, A. "Pamiati Robert Frosta" [In memory of Robert Frost], Literaturnaia Rossiia, February 1, 1963.

L78　SIMONOV, K. "Pamiati Roberta Frosta" [In memory of Robert Frost], Literaturnaia gazeta, January 31, 1963.

L79　Slyshu. Poet Amerika. (Poets of the U.S.A.). Collected and translated by Ivan Kashkin. Moscow: Publisher of Foreign Literature, 1960. Pp. 42-44.
　　　"The Pasture," "Dust of Snow," "My November Guest," "Stopping by Woods. . . ."

L80　"Stikhi Roberta Frosta," (Predislovie k perevodam) [The poems of Robert Frost. (Foreword to translations)], Literaturnaia gazeta, March 3, 1960.

L81　SURKOV, A. "Molodoe serdtse poeta" [The young heart of a poet], Pravda, September 10, 1962, p. 4.

L. FOREIGN CRITICISM AND TRANSLATIONS

L82   _____. "Otkrytoe pis'mo amerikanikomu poetu Robertu Frostu" [An open letter to the American poet Robert Frost], Inostrannaia literatura, 1962, no. 11, pp. 7-9.

L83   _____. "Velikii poet" [A great poet], Izvestiia, January 31, 1963, p.

L84   TUGUSHEVA, M. Literaturnaia Gazeta, September 1, 1962, p.

L85   ZENKEVICH, M. "Robert Frost i ego poeziia" [Robert Frost and his poetry]. In Frost, R. Iz deviati knig [From nine books]. Moscow, 1962. Pp. 5-10.

SOUTH AMERICAN

L86   Antología de Escritores Contemporáneos de Los Estados Unidos. Prosa y verso compilados por John Peale Bishop y Allen Tate. Santiago, Chile: Editorial Nascimento, 1944. Vol. I. Pp. 422-29.
        "Alto en el Bosque una Noche de Nieve" ("Stopping by Woods on a Snowy Evening") and "Pared a Refaccionar" ("Mending Wall").

L87   BROWN, PRADO OSWALDO. "Frost Y El Renaumiento De La Poesia Norteamericana," IPNA, X (May - August 1954), 57-65.

L88   CASTILLEJAR, JORGE. "La Poesia de Robert Frost," Bolivar, XLVI (November 1957), 39-43.

L89   DIÁZ-SOLÍS, GUSTAVO. Seis Poemas de Robert Frost. Caracas, Venezuela: Dirreción de Cultura de la Universidad Central de Venezuela, 1963.

L90   DIAZ SOSA, RAFAEL ANGEL. Robert Frost en los Bosques de Nueva Inglaterra [por Rafael Pineda (pseud.)]. Valencia: Universidad de Carabobo, 1960.

L91   "From Beyond the Andes," O Estado de S. Paulo, August 18, 1954, pp. 17-18.
        Interview in South America when Frost was a delegate to the World Congress of Writers. Translation by Professor Joseph B. Folger of Dartmouth. Calls Frost "simple and

L. FOREIGN CRITICISM AND TRANSLATIONS

"From Beyond the Andes . . ." (cont.)
cordial" with a "complex personality." Praises Frost's
"youthful spirit." Quotes Frost as saying "Tell your readers
that without poetry it is impossible to live. . . . Counter to
all that there is ugly and unpleasant on the earth, there still
remains for us this hope and this incentive: that poetry is un-
avoidable in the contemporary world."

L92   NABUCO, CAROLINA. "Frost, Poeta da Terra," Inter-American
        Review of Bibliography, I (1961), 12-16.

L93   ORTIZ-VARGAS, A. "Perfiles Angloamericanos," R. Iberoameri-
        cano, IV (November 1941), 163-69. Translated.
                Reprinted as "Robert Frost," New Mexico Quarterly, XIV
        (Winter 1944), 403-08.
                "An interesting example of a Latin American's approach to
        a North American poet."

L94   TEDESCHINI LALLI, BIANCAMARIA. "Il 'regionalismo' di Robert
        Frost," Studi Americani, IV (1958), 317-42.

L95   Tres escritores norteamericanos: Ernest Hemingway, William
        Faulkner, Robert Frost. Madrid: Editorial Gredos Traduccion
        Angela Figuera, 1961. 153 pp.

INDEX OF CRITICS

Abbot, Waldo, B29, D60
Abcarian, Richard, I124
Abercrombie, Lascelles, A7
Adams, Franklin Pierce, A8
Adams, Frederick B., Jr., F20, H83
Adams, J. Donald, A176, D127, D128, D180, H152, H321, H322, H323
Adams, Phoebe, H481
Adams, Walter Wood, A219
Agard, Walter R., H99
Agnew, J. Kenner, G83
Ahluwalia, Harsharan Singh, H550
Aiken, Conrad, A177, I23, I35, I74
Akins, Zoë, A9
Aldridge, John W., H658
Allen, Don Cameron, G115
Allen, Gay Wilson, I107
Allen, Ward, H636
Allison, Alexander W., I121
Altenbernd, Lynn, I102
Anderson, Charles R., H409, H483, L54
Anderson, James B., H588
Anderson, Margaret Bartlett, F20
Anderson, Quentin, H589
Ando, Ichiro, L55, L56
Andrews, Alice E., I40
Angoff, Allan, H246
Angoff, Charles, H410, H484
Anthony, Joseph, B6
Archibald, R. O., H247

Arms, George, I98
Armstrong, James, H485
Arvin, Newton, A85
Asselineau, Roger, L4, L5
Atkins, Russell, J17
Auden, W. H., G113, I83
Auslander, Joseph, I24, I36
Austin, Mary, G25
Aykroyd, George O., H43

Bach, Bert C., I125
Bache, William B., H659
Bacon, Leonard, A178, A204
Baker, Carlos, H282
Baker, Elliott, H411
Baker, Russell, B134
Ball, Markham, B85
Ballantine, Lesley Frost, See Frost, Lesley
Barber, Carter, B99
Barc, Helen, B41
Barker, Addison, H221
Barnes, R. G., I126
Barre, Michael, L6
Barrett, Alfred, A130
Barron, John, B100
Barrows, Herbert, I121
Barry, Elaine, F51
Barry, Mary Ruth, B47
Bartlett, Donald, H164, H551
Bartlett, John T., D1
Bascom, Elva L., A62
Basler, Roy P., F10, H637
Batal, James A., B21

Bates, Esther Willard, A205
Bates, Herbert, I37
Bauer, Malcolm, H412
Bauman, Doris, J13
Baxter, Sylvester, H1
Baym, Nina, F48, H523
Beach, Joseph Warren, G36, H248
Beatty, Richmond C., I115
Beaty, John O., G22
Beck, Warren, H149
Belvin, William, J18
Benét, Laura, G58, G121
Benét, Stephen Vincent, A143
Benét, William Rose, A86, H84,
    H118, H150, I13, I39, I60, I74
Benjamin, Philip, B146, D285, H13
Bennett, Paul A., H486
Berger, Harry, Jr., H524, H608
Berkelman, Robert G., H136
Bernus, Alexander von, L21
Berryman, John, J71
Bezner, Henry, J55
Bishop, F. J., A162
Bishop, Ferman, H343
Blackmur, R. P., A87
Blair, Walter, I110
Blake, Caesar R., I121
Blankenship, Russell, G23
Blum, Margaret M., H363, H552
Blumenthal, Hans, H405
Blumenthal, Joseph, F22
Bogan, Louise, A131, A179, A239,
    G64, I97, I111
Bolté, Charles G., H140
Bonfils, Frederick G., H413
Booth, Philip, A242
Borroff, Marie, H638
Bort, Barry, H414
Bosmajian, Hamida, H661
Bosquet, Alain, L7, L8
Boulger, James D., J63, J64
Boutell, H. S., E1
Bowen, James K., H609, J72
Bowen, Stirling, B11
Bowles, Ella Shannon, H28

Bowra, C. M., H206
Boyle, Frances Alter, A182
Boynton, Percy Holmes, G4, H18
Brace, Gerald, H100
Bracker, Milton, B102, B131, D144
Braddy, Nella, I53
Bradford, Gamaliel, G26
Bradley, Sculley, I115
Bradley, W. A., A24
Bragdon, Elspeth, A89
Braithwaite, William Stanley, A1, A10,
    A25, A58, B2, G14, I1, I2, I3, I6,
    I25, I31, I38, I88
Brégy, Katherine, A133, A146, A183,
    A207, H141
Breit, Harvey, B72, B82, B154, G94,
    H249
Brenner, Rica, G21
Brickell, Herschel, A39, A90, A91
Briggs, Pearlanna, H415
Brinkley, David, B94
Brinnin, John Malcolm, I103
Broderick, John C., H270, H611
Brooks, Cleanth, G44, G59, G73
Brooks, Gwendolyn, J19
Brooks, Philip, A92
Brower, Reuben A., F23, G65, H364,
    H416, H590, H591, I112
Brown, Harry, I117
Brown, Malcolm, H231
Brown, Prado Oswaldo, L87
Brown, Terence, G134
Brown, Wallace Cable, H185
Browne, George H., H5
Browning, J. P., H319
Bruns, Friedrich, L22
Bryer, Jackson R., E4
Buchloh, Paul G., L23
Bulkely, Morgan, J15
Burgess, C. F., H386
Burgess, O. N., H271
Burns, Vincent Godfrey, I42
Burnshaw, Stanley A., G15
Burrell, Paul, H592
Byers, Edna Hanley, E2

INDEX OF CRITICS

Bynner, Witter, J20

Cady, Edwin Harrison, G95
Callahan, John P., D192
Caloro, Bonaventura, L45
Camillucci, Marcello, L43
Camp, Dennis D., K23
Campbell, Gladys, A209
Campbell, Harry Modean, H174
Canby, Henry Seidel, G37, G38, I39
Cane, Melville, H250, H662
Carey, Francis E., B64
Carhart, George S., I19
Carlisle, Laura Mae, I64
Carlson, Eric W., H387
Carman, Bliss, I26
Carnes, Del, H386
Carpenter, Frederic I., A63
Carpenter, Thomas P., H639
Carr, Arthur J., I121
Carroll, Gladys Hasty, H62
Carruth, Hayden, H418, H525
Carter, Everett, G84
Castillejar, Jorge, L87
Catel, Jean, L9
Cecil, David, I85
Celli, Aldo, L44
Cestre, Charles, H35, L19
Chalmers, Gordon Keith, H101, H175
Chamaillard, Pierre, L10
Chamberlain, John, D118
Chamberlain, William F., H640, K30
Chapin, Darlene, D272
Chapin, Katherine G., H526
Chapin, L. A., B48
Chapman, A. K., H301
Chatman, Seymour, H272, I118
Chickering, Howell D., Jr., H553
Child, Sargent B., H487
Childs, Francis Lane, H6
Childs, Kenneth W., H593
Chujo, Aiko, L57

Church, Richard, A64, H119
Ciardi, John, A243, B107, H302, H303, H419, I89, J48
Clark, Admont G., I127
Clark, Delbert, B8
Clark, Sylvia, H165
Clarke, Edmund Palmer, H420
Clausen, Bernard C., H151
Cleghorn, Sarah N., A40, D32
Clemens, Cyril, A134, B65, G45
Clymer, W. B. Shubrick, E3, H63
Cockayne, C. A., G15
Coffin, Charles M., I93
Coffin, Robert P. Tristram, F5, G85, H142
Coffman, Stanley K., Jr., G66
Cohen, Edward H., H663
Cohen, Helen Louise, G16
Cole, Charles W., H421
Cole, William, I94
Collamore, H. B., H94
Collins, Rowland L., I105
Collins, Thomas Lyle, A165
Colum, Mary M., A147
Colum, Padraic, A26, H69, H120
Combecher, Hans, L24
Combellack, C. R. B., H422
Comprone, Joseph J., H594
Cook, Charles H., K4
Cook, Howard Willard, I4, I10
Cook, Luella B., G100
Cook, Raymond A., H344
Cook, Reginald L., B84, B87, E4, F9, G122, H158, H176, H177, H186, H194, H195, H273, H274, H275, H304, H324, H423, H595, H612
Coon, Henry, B78
Cooper, Charles W., G52
Corbin, Harold H., Jr., H143
Cosgrave, John O'Hara, G50
Coursen, Herbert R., Jr., H365
Cowie, Alexander, G96
Cowles, Jason, B17
Cowley, Malcolm, H153, H154
Cox, Hyde, G105

Cox, James M., F16, F48, H325, H424
Cox, Keith, H664
Cox, Sidney Hayes, A27, A220, F2, H59, H166, H187, H196, H197, H251
Craig, Donald W., D91
Craig, G. Armour, H425, H554
Crawford, John, A41
Croce, Elena, L50

Dabbs, James McBride, A93, H60, H70
Dabney, Lewis M., G135
Daiches, David, A227, H489
Dame, Lawrence C., D101
Damon, Damuel Foster, G126
Danzig, Allan, H426
Davenport, Guy, H427
Davidson, Carter, I68
Davidson, John F., D124
Davis, Charles G., H613
Davison, Peter, A244
De Bellis, Jack, H527
Deen, Rosemary F., A245, H326
De Falco, Joseph M., H528
De Jong, Mary C., K14
De La Mare, Walter, I32
Del Plaine, Frances Kelly, I61
De Mott, Benjamin, H555
Dendinger, Lloyd N., F48, H556, H641, K10
De Selincourt, Basil, A94
Deutsch, Babette, A42, A43, G33, G74, J21
De Voto, Bernard, H85, H95, H155
Dianu, Romulus, L67
Díaz-Solís, Gustavo, L89
Diaz Sosa, Rafael Angel, L90
Dickey, James, H557, J22
Dickinson, Porter, H102
Dodd, Loring H., G106
Dodge, Charles, K8
Dolbier, Maurice, B110, B121, H283
Dole, Nathan Haskell, D2

Domina, Lyle D., K24
Donaghy, William A., A148, A166
Donoghue, Denis, H327, H429, H430
Dougherty, James P., H558
Doughty, Legarde S., A95
Douglas, Lois Smith, G67
Douglas, Norman, A2
Dowell, Bob, H614
Dowell, Peter W., H642
Doxey, W. S., H690
Doyle, John Robert, Jr., F17, H305, H615
Dragland, S. L., H596
Drew, Elizabeth, G108
Drew, Fraser B., B152
Drinkwater, John, I39
Driver, Tom F., I106
Drury, Michael, H345
Dube, Gunakar, H665
Du Bois, Arthur E., H125
Dufault, Peter Kane, H284, J23
Duffey, Bernard I., I76
Dunbar, Olivia Howard, G54
Dupee, F. W., A184
Duvall, S. P. C., H346
Dyer, Walter A., D86

Eastman, Arthur M., I121
Eastman, Max, G68
Eaton, Walter P., A59
Eberhart, Richard, H285, H559
Eckert, Robert P., Jr., H126
Edel, Leon, H431
Edelson, Arlene, H703
Edman, Irwin, H240
Edson, Arthur, D169
Eikel, Elizabeth M., K15
Eisenhard, John, H61
Elliot, George R., H12, H29
Ellis, James, H529
Elmen, Paul, G123
Elsbree, Langdon, H347
Emerson, Dorothy, A96
Engle, Paul, H103, H490, J49, J50
English, Hubert M., Jr., I121
Enright, D. J., A246

Erskine, John, H7

Faber, Doris, F28
Fadiman, Clifton, H530, I79
Fair, Jessie Frances, H49
Fairchild, Hoxie Neale, G114
Farjeon, Eleanor, G101, H252
Farma, William Joseph, I43
Farnham, Jessie, J54
Farrar, John, A30, G5, H40
Faulkner, Virginia, H434
Feeney, Leonard, A97
Feld, Rose C., B18
Ferguson, A. R., H366
Ferguson, Joe M., Jr., H491
Ferry, D., I112
Feuillerat, Albert, L11
Finnegan, Sister Mary Jeremy,
    H306, H348
Fiscalini, Janet, H436
Fischer, C. M., D115
Fischer, Walter, L26
Fisher, Dorothy Canfield, D120,
    G79, H36
Fitts, Dudley, A98
Fitzgerald, Robert, A228
Fleissner, Robert F., H531, H666
Fletcher, John Gould, A3, G42,
    H127
Flint, F. Cudworth, H560
Flint, F. S., A4
Foerster, Norman, I84
Ford, Caroline, F3
Forgotson, E. S., A185
Fosbroke, Katherine M., J57
Foster, Charles H., H104
Fowle, Rosemary, H222
Francis, Robert, F49, H178,
    H241, H437, J62
Frankenberg, Lloyd, H308
Freedman, William, H691
Freeman, Ira Henry, B79
Freeman, John, G18, H31
Fremantle, Anne, A186
French, R. W., H667

Friedman, Norman, I95
Frost, Lesley, D34, F41, F50, H439,
    H660, I69
Fuchs, Daniel, H495
Furman, Bess, B101, D170

Gaige, Franklin, H242
Galbraith, J. Kenneth, H496
Gangapathy, R., L41
Gannett, Lewis, A101
Ganz, Robert N., Jr., K16
Garland, H. B., L46
Garland, Hamlin, H128
Garnett, Edward, A12
Gay, Robert M., I27
Gelb, Arthur, D234
Gelb, Barbara, D234
Gerber, Philip L., F37, H561
Gethyn-Jones, J. E., H643
Geyer, Charles W., K17
Gibb, Carson, H391
Gibson, Walker, H367
Gibson, Wilfred, J3
Gibson, Wilfrid Wilson, A13
Gibson, William M., I98
Gierasch, Walter, H232, H233, H243
Gilchrist, Halley Phillips, D30
Gillis, Adolph, G39
Gilroy, Harry, D291, D298, D303
Glauber, Robert H., H286
Goede, William, H616
Gordon, Jan B., G136
Gordon, Margery, I44, I49
Gorlier, Claudio, L47
Gottlieb, Dan, B133
Gould, Jack, D132, D217
Gould, Jean, F29
Grade, Arnold, C4, F41, F50, H617
Grandy, Adah Georgina, I61
Grant, Douglas, F35
Graves, Robert, B149, G118
Green, Charles R., E3
Green, Elizabeth Lay, G7
Green, Paul, G7
Greenberg, Robert A., F15, H369

Greene, Marc T., H276
Gregory, Horace, A102, G53
Greiner, Donald J., E8, F42, H618, H619, K18
Grieder, Josephine, H692
Griffith, Ben, H253
Griffith, Clark, H620
Griffith, William, I54
Grigson, Geoffrey, A67
Gross, Leonard, B91
Grover, Edwin Osgood, G26
Guiterman, Arthur, J4
Gussow, Alan, B76
Gwynn, Frederick L., H497, H533

Haight, Gordon S., H534
Haines, John W., J8
Halberstam, David, D224, D225
Hall, Donald, I119
Hall, Dorothy J., H668
Hall, Edward B., A46
Hall, Howard Judson, I28, I40, I50
Hall, James Norman, A103, H56, J12
Halleck, Reuben Post, G31
Hamburger, Philip, B77
Hands, Charles B., H644
Handy, Mary, B88
Hanley, Patricia, H327
Harcourt, Alfred, G69
Hard, Margaret, G129
Harding, Walter, A248, G122
Harrington, Mildred P., I45
Harris, Mark, B127, H370
Hartsock, Mildred E., H309, H498
Hashiguchi, Yasuo, L58
Hatfield, H. C., H159
Havighurst, Walter, G102
Hay, John, J24
Haycraft, Howard, G86
Haynes, Donald T., K31
Hedges, M. H., H8
Heflin, Wilson, H645
Henderson, Alice Corbin, A14, I55
Hendricks, Cecilia Hennel, H144

Hepburn, James G., F15, H393
Herndon, Jerry A., H669
Herrick, Daphne, H129
Herzberg, Max J., H160, I62
Hewes, Henry, H535
Heywood, Terence, H121
Hiatt, David, H670
Hicks, Granville, A68, G29, G34, G40, H87
Hieatt, A. Kent, I128
Hiebel, William R., K11
Hiers, John T., H693
Hill, Archibald A., H330
Hill, Frank Ernest, I24, I36
Hillyer, Robert, A149, H53, J9
Hoetker, James, H536
Hoffman, Daniel G., H207, H224, H349
Hoffman, Frederick J., G95
Hogan, Homer, I122
Holden, Raymond, J59
Holliday, Robert Cortes, G8
Holmes, John, A83, A104, A105, A229, A249, D98, D103, D123, G52, H72, H205, J25, J47
Holmes, Susan P., H440
Honig, Edwin, I101
Hopkins, Bess Cooper, H254
Hopkins, Vivian C., H350
Hornaday, Mary, B80
Hornberger, Theodore, I110
Horton, Rod W., H198
Housh, Snow Longley, J7
Howard, Jane, H310
Howarth, Herbert, H562
Howe, Irving, G119, H441
Howe, M. A. DeWolfe, H122
Howells, William Dean, A15
Howes, Barbara, H597
Howes, Martin K., E5
Hudson, Arthur Palmer, B157
Huff, William Howard, H208
Huffard, Grace Thompson, I64
Hughes, Langston, J27
Humphries, Rolfe, A106, A230
Hunt, George P., H442

INDEX OF CRITICS

Hunt, John Dixon, J28
Hunting, Robert, H443
Hurd, John, Jr., D56
Hurley, James F., J51
Huston, J. Dennis, H646
Hutchens, John K., B69, B73,
    H199, H255
Hutchison, Percy, A47, A60

Idema, Jim, H371, H499
Ingalls, Jeremy, J29
Irving, Jerome M., B150, H445
Irwin, W. R., H351, H446
Isaacs, Emily Elizabeth, F18, K5
Isaacs, J., H256

Jackson, Gardner, B20
Jacobsen, Josephine, H447
Jacobson, Dan, H694
Jäger, Dietrich, L28, L29
Jakeman, Adelbert M., A167
James, Stuart B., H500
Jamieson, Paul, H332
Jarrell, Randall, A211, G115,
    H179, H234, H287, H501
Jennings, Elizabeth, F30
Jensen, Arthur E., H563
Jepson, Edgar, H9
Jerome, Judson, H394, H448,
    H449, H695
Johnston, J. H., A232
Jones, Donald, H564
Jones, Llewellyn, G9, H25
Jordan, Alice M., A168
Joyce, Hewette E., H565
Judd, Dorothy, H450
Juhnke, Anna K., H502
Junkins, Donald, B117

Kahn, Roger, B118, H395, H451,
    H452
Kalstone, David, I112
Kantak, V. Y., H396
Kaplan, Charles, H257
Karsh, Yousuf, G109

Kashkin, Ivan, L69, L70, L71, L79
Kazin, Alfred, F48, H503
Keith, Joseph Joel, J14
Kell, Richard, A250
Kellner, Leon, L30
Kennedy, John Fitzgerald, F24, F31,
    H453, H454, H504
Kennedy, Leo, A188, A233
Kenner, Hugh, I90
Kenney, Herbert A., H455, H479
Kern, Alexander C., H671
Kerr, David, D93
Ketchum, Roland, G39
Keyes, Frances Parkinson, I104
Khan, Salamatullah, H397
Khitrov, M., L72
Khrushchev, Nikita S., L73
Kilmer, Kenton, A189
Kimbrough, Richard, A251
King, Marie B., I44, I49
Kinnell, Galway, J30, J60
Kjørven, Johannes, G131
Knapp, Edgar H., H647
Knight, Karl F., I114
Knowlton, Edgar C., A107
Knox, George, H566
Koperski, Ronald J., K12
Kreymborg, Alfred, G10, G20, H57,
    H58, I46, J31
Kroll, Ernest, J32
Kunitz, Stanley Jasspon, A252, G24,
    G86
Kyle, Carol A., H672, K25

Ladd, Henry A., H107
Laing, Alexander, H567
Laing, Dilys, B155
Lamar, Mary, G22
Lambuth, David, E3, H168
Landis, Benson Y., B45
Lane, Millicent T., K13
Langbaum, Robert, H333
Lapolla, Garibaldi M., I41
Larson, Mildred R., H209, H210,
    H598, K1

Lask, Thomas, H456, H673
Lasser, Michael L., H334
Lathem, Edward Connery, B106,
    B151, B156, F25, F47, H537
Leach, Henry G., A136
Leaning, John, D307
LeBreton, Maurice, L13
Lee, Henry, B66
La Gallienne, Richard, I70, I72
Leggett, Glenn, I86,
Leisy, Ernest E., G22
Lentricchia, Frank, H702
Lepore, D. J., H505, H568
Lerman, Stephen J., H457
Lerner, Laurence, H674
Leslie, Kenneth, J10
Levonevskii, D., L74
LeVot, André, L14
Lewis, Arthur O., Jr., H225
Lewis, C. Day, B98, H458
Lewis, Leslie L., I102
Lewisohn, Ludwig, G27
Leyburn, Ellen D., H398
Lieberman, Elias, I51
Light, J. F., H675
Littell, Robert, A31
Logan, H. M., H676
Logan, John, J33
Loggins, Vernon, G43
Long, E. Hudson, I115
Long, William S., H188
Lord, Richard D., H288
Lorenz, Charles J., B111, B112
Love, Glen A., H621
Love, Kenneth, H399
Loveman, Amy, H64
Lowden, Samuel Marion, G17
Lowe, Orton, H42
Lowell, Amy, A16, G1
Ludwig, Richard M., G117
Lyford, Roland H., K26
Lynen, John Fairbanks, F12, H372,
    H522, H569, K19
Lyons, Louis Martin, F26

Mabie, Janet, B30
Mabie, Murchison, B19
Mac Carthy, Desmond, A84
Mac Donald, Dwight, H354
Mac Donald, Lachlan, J34
Mac Leish, Archibald, H460, H506
Mac Veagh, Lincoln, H132, I80
Maddry, Lawrence, D304, D305
Madison, Charles A., G127
Maeda, Cana, L59
Magill, Frank, G104
Main, C. F., I96
Malbone, R. G., H538
Mansell, Darrel, Jr., H571
Mardenborough, Aimee, H189
Margoshes, Adams, A151
Marple, Allen, H461
Martin, R. Glenn, H677
Martin, Wallace, G128, H622
Martz, William J., I113
Mathias, Roland, H180
Matthiessen, Francis O., G70, I75
Maurin, Mario, L48
Maxwell, Margaret, H599
May, Stacy, H108
Mayfield, John S., H623
Maynard, Theodore, A169, G2
Mc Carthy, Agnes L., G83
Mc Cord, David, H26
Mc Coy, Donald E., K3
Mc Donald, Gerald, A212, A234
Mc Dowell, E. A., J65, J66
Mc Ghee, Paul A., I19
Mc Giffert, John, H161
Mc Grory, Mary, B104
Mc Kenna, Patsy, B76
Mc Laughlin, Charles A., H277, I95
Mc Millin, Lawrence, A221
Mc Neill, Louise, H109
Mears, Louise W., G87
Medina, Harold R., G88
Meiss, Edwin R., D24
Meixner, John A., H572
Melcher, Daniel, B35
Melcher, Frederic, E9

Mendell, Vera, I52
Meredith, William, A253, H462, J67
Mersch, Arnold, R. G., F.S.C., K27
Mertins, Esther, E10
Mertins, Louis, A152, E10, F36
Meynell, Francis, I52
Michaud, Régis, L16
Mikels, Rosa M. R., I29
Miles, Josephine, G71, I91, J35
Miller, David, B144
Miller, James E., Jr., I110
Miller, Lewis, H312
Miller, Lewis H., Jr., H600
Miller, Perry, I111
Miller, Vincent, A254
Milstead, John, I117
Mohrt, Michel, L17
Monroe, Harriet, A28, A54, G12, H27, I55
Montague, Gene, I129
Monteiro, George, H624, H625, H648, H696
Montgomery, Marion, H313
Moore, Harry T., G116
Moore, John, G46
Moore, Merrill, A110
Moore, Robert P., H539
Moore, Rosalie, J36
Moore, Virginia, A69
Morgan, Carlyle, H212
Morley, Christopher, A111
Morris, Richard B., G80
Morrison, Chester, B109
Morrison, Theodore, H601, H678
Morrow, Patrick, H626
Morse, Samuel French, H507, J37
Morse, Stearns, H146, H169, H573, H627, H706, J38
Morton, David, A32, I56
Most, Steve, H373
Moult, Thomas, I12, I66
Moynihan, William T., H314
Mulder, William, H263

Munford, Howard, H335
Munson, Gorham B., B49, F1, F19, G13, H30, H47, H508
Murphy, Francis, I116

Nabuco, Carolina, L92
Nakanishi, Masao, L60
Napier, John T., H289
Narasimhaiah, C. D., H649
Narveson, Robert, H628
Nash, Ray, E11, H137, H213
Nelson, James, B97
Nelson, John H., I99
Nemerov, Howard, J38
Nethercot, Arthur H., A112
Newcomer, Alphonso Gerald, I40
Newdick, Robert S., A82, A113, A114, A115, D105, E6, E7, H66, H67, H73, H74, H75, H76, H88, H89, H90, H91, H92, H111, H123, H124
Nibling, Phyllis, H509
Nicholl, Louise Townsend, A70
Nichols, Lewis, D181, D278
Nims, John Frederick, H463
Nitchie, Elizabeth, H264
Nitchie, George W., F13, H574, K7
Nordell, Rod, B135

O'Connor, William Van., G81, G116, H540
O'Donnell, William G., A255, H190, H200
Ogilvie, John, H337
O'Hagan, Thomas, H54
Oka, Jukichi, L61, L62
Olivar, Edith, H541
Olson, Lawrence, A222
Opie, Thomas, A192
Ornstein, Robert, H290
Ortiz-Vargas, A., L93
Orton, Vrest, A138, J68
Osborne, William R., H629
Ostroff, Anthony, J39

Pack, Robert, I106
Palgrave, F. T., I77
Papajewski, Helmut, L32
Parameswaran, Uma, E12, E13
Paris, Mrs. John Walton, I54
Park, William, I128
Parke, John, H355
Parsons, D. S. J., H679
Parsons, Thornton H., H465, K9
Payne, L. W., Jr., A116
Pearce, Roy Harvey, G95, G112,
    H236, H376
Pendleton, Conrad, H510
Perrine, Laurence, H201, H278,
    H377, H575, H602, H630, H631
Peters, Frank, J69
Peters, Robert, H356
Petersen, Anna, B108
Phelps, Robert H., G110
Phelps, William Lyon, H10, I67
Phillips, Mc Candlish, D218, D286
Pierce, Frederick E., A48
Pisanti, Tommaso, L49
Plimpton, Calvin H., H466
Poirier, Richard, B113, H576
Poole, Ernest, H170
Poore, Charles, A236, A256,
    D136, H512
Popkin, Henry, H237
Poss, Stanley, H632
Potter, John Mason, B75
Pound, Ezra, A5, A17
Pound, Louise, H68, H78
Praz, Mario, L43
Prescott, Frederick C., I57
Prescott, Orville, A193, H513
Preston, Stuart D., H378
Prevost, Jean, L18
Prideaux, Tom, H577
Pritchard, William H., F48, G137,
    H357, H680, K20
Proctor, Percy M., H279
Purcell, W. H., D125

Quinan, Dorothy C., B158
Quinn, Arthur Hobson, G73
Quinn, Sister M. Bernetta, H578

Rago, Henry, H280
Raiziss, Sona, G75
Ransom, John Crowe, H227
Rao, C. Vimala, H650
Rascoe, Burton, B16
Read, Bill, I103
Redlich, Rosemarie, G76, G97
Reed, Meredith, G120
Reely, Mary Katherine, A49, A72,
    A119, A157, A170, A194
Reeve, F. D., F32, H467
Reichert, Victor Emanuel, F43
Renick, Dorothy, D41
Reston, James, D214, H293
Rich, Adrienne, J40
Richards, E. A., H112
Richards, Norman, F40
Richards, Robert F., G90
Rideout, Walter B., I107
Ridge, Lola, H15
Rinaker, Clarissa, I22
Ritchey, John, A139, D108
Rittenhouse, Jessie B., A18, G14, I30,
    I47, I58
Robbins, J. Albert, G124
Roberts, Esther L., K21
Robinson, James K., I107
Robson, W. W., H579
Roche, John P., H405
Rockas, Leo, H542
Rodman, Tom, H113
Rogers, W. G., B114
Ronninger, Lisbeth, L33
Root, Edward Tallmadge, H79
Root, E. Merrill, A51, A120, H114
Roseliep, Raymond, J58, J61
Rosenbaum, Nathan, J16
Rosenberry, Edward H., H471
Rosenthal, M. L., G111, H338, I99
Ross, David, I63
Ross, Malcolm, A213

Roy, Ruth, B70
Rubinstein, Annette T., H651
Rukeyser, Muriel, A140
Russell, Francis, H316
Ryan, Alvan S., F48, H203, H339, L34

St. Armand, Barton L., H603
Salzman, Eric, D177
Sampley, Arthur M., H473, H580, H697
Sampson, Paul, D167
Samuel, Rinna, H379
Sandburg, Carl, J41
Sanders, Gerald D., I57, I99
Sanesi, Roberto, L52
Saradhi, K. P., L63
Sasso, Laurence J., Jr., H652
Saul, George Brandon, H138, H581
Sayler, Oliver M., H16
Scannell, Vernon, H402
Schauffler, Robert Haven, I14
Scheiwiller, Vanni, L51
Scherer, Ruth Von Back, H32
Scherman, David E., G76, G97
Schlauch, Margaret, G98
Schlueter, Paul, H515
Schneider, Isdor, A75
Schoenfield, Allen, B28
Schönemann, Friedrich, L35
Schorer, Mark, A195
Schott, Fred, B71
Schreiber, Georges, G41
Schultz, Franz, L36
Schwartz, Delmore, G103
Schwartz, Edward, H258
Schwartz, Karl, L37
Scollard, Clinton, I47, I58
Scott, Nathan A., Jr., A123
Scott, Wilbur S., H317
Scott, Winfield Townley, A158, H474, H543, J42
Seng, Peter J., I96
Sergeant, Elizabeth Shepley, F14, H33, H244, H358

Sergeant, Howard, H239
Sergeev, A., L77
Serpici, Alessandro, L53
Sessions, Ina B., G30
Sessions, William A., I125
Shabad, Theodore, D252
Shapiro, Harvey, H380, I81
Shea, F. X., H582
Sheed, Wilfrid, H544
Shefa, Skojaeddin, L42
Sheffey, Ruthe T., H516
Sherrill, John, B86
Shippey, Lee, B50
Shoup, Grace, I29
Shurter, Edwin Dubois, I20
Sickels, Eleanor M., H381
Simonov, K., L78
Simpson, Claude, G117
Simpson, Lewis P., F48
Sinyavsky, Andrei, H583
Skogstad, Katherine, B105
Slights, Camille, H653
Slights, William, H653
Sloan, Florence Bethune, A171
Smith, Chard Powers, G125
Smith, Fred, H55
Smith, Katherine G., B14
Smith, Lewis, G13, H30
Smith, Mary E., K2
Smith, Mary Gilbert, B56
Smith, William Jay, J43
Smith, William Palmer, I48
Smythe, Daniel W., F33, K6
Snell, George, A214
Snow, C. P., G131
Snow, Wilbert, A121, A159, H633
Sohn, David A., F44
Southworth, James G., G60
Speare, M. E., I73
Spencer, Benjamin, H604, H698
Spencer, Stephen, H295
Spencer, Theodore, A55
Spiegel, Irving, D219
Spiller, Robert E., G56, G91
Spitz, Leon, Rabbi, H183

Spivak, Lawrence, B94
Squire, J. C., G18
Squires, Radcliffe, F27
Stafford, William T., I108
Stallman, R. W., H296, I78
Stanlis, Peter J., H545
Stauffer, Donald A., A215, H297
Stegner, Wallace, H215
Stein, William Bysshe, H654
Stephens, James, A122
Stevens, Donald D., H320
Stevenson, Adlai E., H403
Stevenson, Burton Egbert, I15
Stewart, Bernice, B13, D22
Stewart, Randall, I110
Stewart, Vincent, I120
Stock, Ely, H382
Stone, Albert E., Jr., H546
Stone, Edward, B122
Stone, Virginia S., K28
Strachan, Pearl, A172
Strobel, Marion, A123
Strong, L. A. G., A76
Stroup, J. Martin, D195
Stuart, Jesse, H340
Stylites, Simeon, H259
Suderman, Elmer F., H682
Sullivan, Mark, G35
Surkov, A., H404, L81, L82, L83
Sutton, William A., H683
Swain, Frances, H34
Swallow, Alan, A173
Sweeney, Francis, S. J., H547
Swennes, Robert H., H684
Swenson, May, J44

Taffe, James G., I109
Taggard, Genevieve, A77
Takagaki, Matsuo, L65
Talese, Gay, B140
Tate, Allen, G89, I85
Tatham, David, F45, H517
Taylor, Walter Fuller, G99
Tedeschini Lalli, Biancamaria,
    L94

Templeton, Richard H., E15
Tenney, Dennis, J56
Teraoka, Noriko, L66
Terte, Robert H., D233
Thal, Norman R., H39
Theresa, Sister Catherine, H685
Thomas, Edward, A20, J2
Thomas, Henri, L12
Thompson, Blanche Jennings, I16
Thompson, Lawrance, A198, C3, E16,
    F6, F7, F11, F25, F38, F41, F46,
    G104, H192, H198, H281, H341,
    H359, H475, H518, H519, H584
Thompson, Ralph, A124
Thornburg, Thomas R., H686
Thornton, Richard, F4
Thornton, Weldon, H606
Thorp, Willard, G56
Tilley, M. P., B5
Tillinghast, Richard, H585
Tinker, Edward L., A141
Todasco, Ruth, H476
Toor, David, H655
Topping, Seymour, B143
Townsend, R. C., H477
Traschen, Isadore, F48, H548
Tredant, Paul, L20
Trilling, Lionel, D191, H342
Tsatsoulas, Steph., L39
Tugusheva, M., L84
Tyler, Dorothy, H478
Tyre, Richard H., F44

Ubell, Earl, B120
Udall, Stewart L., H383, H704
Ulmann, Doris, H45
Ulrich, Dorothy Livingston, J11
Unger, Leonard, G81
Untermeyer, Louis, A22, A34, A52,
    A78, A125, A200, A217, C2, F34,
    G3, G22, G47, G50, G61, G92, G111,
    H46, H98, H261, H586, H699, I9,
    I11, I17, I21, I33, I59, I68, I71, I81,
    I100, J1
Updike, John, H360

INDEX OF CRITICS

Vander Ven, Tom R., K22
Van Dore, Wade, H115, H687
Van Doren, Carl, G6, H23
Van Doren, Mark, A56, A201,
    A237, G48, H80, H229, H480,
    I41
Van Egmond, Peter, J70
van Gelder, Robert, B67
Van Nostrand, Albert D., I92
Vargish, Andrea, H549
Verbillion, June, H266
Viereck, Peter, A238, H204
Vinson, Robert S., H688
Virtue, Maxine B., G88

Waggoner, Hyatt Howe, G62,
    G132, H135, H171
Waitt, Paul, B7
Walcutt, Charles C., H157, H245
Walen, Harry L., H587
Wallace, Robert, I109
Walling, William, I125
Walpole, Hugh, A48
Walton, Eda Lou, A126
Walz, Sister Vincent, K29
Ward, A. C., G28
Ward, Herman, M., L40
Warren, Austin, G49
Warren, C. Henry, A79, A80
Warren, Robert Penn, F48, G59,
    H184
Watkins, Dwight Everett, I20
Watkins, Floyd, I114
Watson, Charles N., Jr., H700
Watters, R. E., I78
Watts, Charles H., Jr., I92
Watts, Harold H., H267, H268
Wayne, Francis, B51
Webster, H. T., H219
Wecter, Dixon, D42
Weeks, Edward, H362
Weinig, Sister Mary A., H656
Weiss, Thomas, J45
Wellek, Rene, G49
Wells, Henry W., G51, G57

Werner, W. L., H269
West, Herbert Faulkner, G55, G77,
    H172
Weygandt, Cornelius, G32
Whalley, George, G82
Wheeler, Edmund J., A23
Wheelwright, John, H81
Whicher, George F., A161, A175,
    A203, A218, G63, G72, G93, H86,
    H148, H163, H173
Whicher, Harriett F., A127
Whipple, Leon, A53
Whipple, T. K., G19
White, Jean, D236
White, Owen S., H116
Whited, Charles, B130
Whitridge, Arnold, H407
Wickenden, L. D., D89, D90
Wilcox, Earl, H634
Wilkinson, Marguerite, H11, I5, I8,
    I18, I34
Williams, Oscar, I82, I87, I101, I123
Williams, William Carlos, A223, J46
Willige, Eckhart, H384
Wilmore, Carl, B3
Wilson, Edmund, G78
Wilson, Ellen, F39
Wilson, James Southall, A81, A142, H51
Winterich, John T., H82, H93
Winters, Yvor, H193
Wolfe, Carmie S., H134
Wolfe, Thomas, B123
Wolff, Geoffrey, H689
Wood, Clement, G11
Wylie, Jeff, H220
Wylie, Philip, J53

Yates, Norris, H299
Yevish, Irving A., H635
Young, Stark, H117

Zabel, Morton D., A129
Zaturenska, Marya, G53
Zeitlin, Jacob, I22
Zenkevich, M., L85